YANKEE CITY SERIES

VOLUME
I

PUBLISHED ON THE
Richard Teller Crane, Jr., Memorial Fund

The Yankee City Series is Dedicated to
CORNELIUS CRANE

THE
SOCIAL LIFE
OF A
MODERN COMMUNITY

BY
W. LLOYD WARNER
AND
PAUL S. LUNT

NEW HAVEN
YALE UNIVERSITY PRESS
LONDON · GEOFFREY CUMBERLEGE · OXFORD UNIVERSITY PRESS

COPYRIGHT, 1941, BY YALE UNIVERSITY PRESS

Printed in the United States of America

First published, December, 1941
Second printing, July, 1944
Third printing, November, 1945
Fourth printing, December, 1946

All rights reserved. This book may not be reproduced, in whole or in part, in any form (except by reviewers for the public press), without written permission from the publishers.

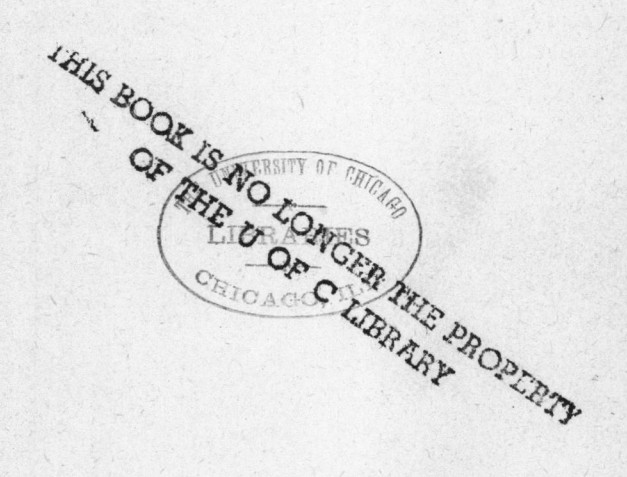

THIS VOLUME IS DEDICATED TO

Wallace Donham and *Elton Mayo*

YANKEE CITY RESEARCH STAFF

Writer W		Analyst A	Field Worker F	
W. Lloyd Warner	W	A F	Sylva Beyer	A
Leo Srole	W	A F	Fay Abrams	A
Paul S. Lunt	W	A F	Eve Goddard	A
J. O. Low	W	A F	Dorothy Jones	A
Eliot Chapple		A F	Rosamond Brown	A
Buford Junker		A F	Margaret Mack	A
Solon Kimball		A F	Viola Vanderhorck	A
Marion Lee		A F	Grace Senders	A
Conrad Arensberg		A F	Mildred Warner	A
Robert G. Snider		A F	Joseph Weckler	A
Allison Davis		A F	J. O. Brew	F
Elizabeth Davis		A F	Dorothea Mayo	F
Burleigh Gardner		A F	O. S. Lovekin	F
Dorothy Moulton		A	Gwenneth Harrington	F
Alice Williams		A	Hess Haughton	F

ACKNOWLEDGMENTS

The research staff of the Yankee City Series are indebted to many people for aid in the inception, course of research, and publication of this work. We cannot thank all of them here.

Above all we wish to express our appreciation to the citizens of Yankee City who generously gave their knowledge of the community and maintained a coöperating interest in our work. We are grateful to the Committee of Industrial Physiology of Harvard University for sponsoring and financing the field research. Professor Elton Mayo and Dean Wallace Donham of the Graduate School of Business Administration of Harvard University have contributed incalculably to the study by their wise guidance, insight, and understanding. In simple expression of our gratitude we have dedicated to them this first volume of the series.

The entire series is dedicated to our generous benefactor, friend, and colleague in social anthropology, Cornelius Crane, as an inadequate recognition of his deep and sympathetic interest in our work and of his consuming concern for the problem, the nature of man.

We are very grateful to the Social Science Research Committee of the University of Chicago, the Emergency Relief Administration, the National Youth Administration, and the Works Progress Administration, all of which have contributed aid in the laborious and expensive analysis of the data of these six volumes.

The authors are particularly indebted to Professors E. B. Wilson, Carl Doering, and Earnest Hooton, all of Harvard University, and Professor Samuel Stouffer of the University of Chicago, for advice and assistance on statistical problems.

We wish to thank Professor George Peter Murdock of Yale University for his interest in the publication of these volumes and for his unerring aid in the editing of the manuscripts.

Dr. Stephen Reed and Dr. Allan Holmberg of Yale University, Dr. Joseph Weckler of the Smithsonian Institution, and Mildred Hall Warner have contributed their skill in the preparation of the manuscripts for publication. It is evident to all of the research staff that without their aid we would have been heavily handicapped in completing our task.

We wish to thank our friend and colleague, Dr. Mark May, and his staff of the Institute of Human Relations at Yale University, for the encouragement they gave us by their critical and sympathetic interest.

To John Dollard of the Institute of Human Relations we owe a very special debt of gratitude for his recognition of the significance of the scientific problems we attacked and for his help in the solution of many of them. The searching questions he asked us and the generous acclaim he gave our research have been deep sources of scientific and spiritual strength to all of us.

CONTENTS

List of Tables		xv
List of Charts		xvii
Preface		xix
I.	The Genesis of the Research	1
II.	The Conceptual Framework	8
III.	The Field Techniques Used and the Materials Gathered	38
IV.	General Description of Yankee City	76
V.	How the Several Classes Were Discovered	81
VI.	Class and Social Structure	92
VII.	Profiles from Yankee City	127
VIII.	Biological Composition of the Six Classes	202
IX.	The Ethnic Minorities of Yankee City	211
X.	Ecological Areas of Yankee City	227
XI.	The Houses of Yankee City	239
XII.	Marriage and the Family in Yankee City	252
XIII.	Economic Life of the Community	256
XIV.	The Control of Property	280
XV.	How the Six Classes Spent Their Money	287
XVI.	The Formal and Informal Associations of Yankee City	301
XVII.	The Church and School in Yankee City	356
XVIII.	The Political Structure in the Class System	366
XIX.	Reading and Other Symbolic Behavior of the Six Classes	378
XX.	The Social Characteristics of the People of the Two Upper Classes	422
XXI.	The Social Characteristics of the People of the Two Middle Classes	435
XXII.	The Social Characteristics of the People of the Two Lower Classes	444
Index		451

TABLES

1.	A Measurement of Interconnectedness of the Several Classes in their Associational Relations	125
2.	Distribution of Population by Class	203
3.	Birthplace of People of Different Ages	208
4.	Birthplace of the People of the Six Classes	209
5.	Distribution of Ethnic Groups by Age	219
6.	The Birthplace of Ethnic Groups	221
7.	Class and Ethnic Group	225
8.	Population of the Twelve Areas	229
9.	Weekly and Monthly Rentals by Area	230
10.	Median Monthly Rentals for Each Area	231
11.	Ethnic Distribution in the Twelve Areas	233
12.	Areas Preferred by the Six Classes	235
13.	House Type According to Ecological Area	241
14.	Distribution of Houses among the Six Classes	246
15.	Ethnic Group and House Type	247
16.	The Ethnic Groups in the Various Industries	258
17.	Occupation and Class	261
18.	Employment in the Various Industries	265
19.	Amount of Ethnic Unemployment	269
20.	Ethnic Unemployment in the Various Industries	274
21.	Median Value of Individual Ownership by Age and Sex	280
22.	Median Value All Real Estate by Ethnic Group	281
23.	Real Estate and Class	283
24.	The Comparative Rank Order of the Proportion of the Budget of Each Class Which Was Spent for Each Item	293
25.	Per Cent of the Budget of Each Class Spent on Each Item	295
26.	Amount Spent by Each Class on Each Category	296
27.	The Structural Types of Associations	322
28.	Membership Types of Satellites	323
29.	The Number of Associations to Which the Members of Each Class Belonged	332
30.	Sex and Age Composition of Associations	338
31.	Religious Faith and Associations	346
32.	Membership in Associations by Sex in Each Class Type	352
33.	Class Composition of Church Membership	360
34.	Crime and Ethnic Group	375
35.	Class and Crime	376
36.	Book Reading of the Six Classes	384

37.	Magazine Preferences of the Six Classes	388
38.	The Distribution of the Purchasers of Each Magazine in the Six Classes	390
39.	Newspaper Reading of the Ethnic Groups	407
40.	Newspaper Readers in the Six Classes	409

CHARTS

I.	Types of Social Adaptation	22
II.	The Place of the Individual in Society	27
III.	Typology of Age and Sex Divisions	30
IV.	The Class Hierarchy of Yankee City	88
V.	Marriage Levels	93
VI.	Marriage, Family Descent, and the Maintenance of Class Position	94
VII.	The Clique Vertical Axis	112
VIII.	The Clique Quadrants	113
IX.	The Function of Associations	115
X.	The Divisions of Age and Sex and Associational Types	123
XI.	Certain Groupings Discussed in Chapter XVII	199
XII.	Percentage of Each Sex in the Six Classes	204
XIII.	The Age of the Members of the Six Classes	206
XIV.	The Percentage of Ethnic Groups in the Total Population	214
XV.	The Birthplace of the Native and Combined Ethnic Groups	220
XVI.	The Ethnic Composition of the Six Classes	222
XVII.	What Classes Get What Houses	245
XVIII.	Marital Status of the Members of the Total Community	252
XIX.	Marital Status of the Ethnic Groups	253
XX.	Age at Marriage of Men and Women	254
XXI.	Marital Status of the Six Classes	255
XXII.	The Percentage of Workers Employed in the Several Industries	256
XXIII.	The Occupations of the Six Classes	262
XXIV.	Duration of Unemployment	264
XXV.	Employment among the Ethnic Groups	270
XXVI.	Duration of Ethnic Unemployment	271
XXVII.	The Amount of Employment in the Six Classes	278
XXVIII.	Structural Types of Associations	310
XXIX.	The Associational Structure	324
XXX.	Class and Number of Associations	331
XXXI.	Number of Men in Each Class Who Belonged to One or More Associations	335
XXXII.	Number of Women in Each Class Who Belonged to One or More Associations	336

XXXIII.	Cliques in the Class System	354
XXXIV.	The Courses Selected by High School Students from the Six Classes	364
XXXV.	The Class Composition of the Officeholders and Voters	370
XXXVI.	The Types of Library Books Selected by the Six Classes	383
XXXVII.	Class Composition of a Magazine's Readers	405
XXXVIII.	Newspaper Purchases of the Ethnic Groups	408
XXXIX.	The Newspaper Purchases by Members of the Six Classes	410

Map of the Ecological Areas of Yankee City 228

PREFACE

THE "Yankee City Series," which is inaugurated by the present work, will be complete in six volumes. Each will deal with a significant aspect of the life of a modern community as it has been recorded and analyzed by the combined and co-operative labors of a group of social anthropologists. The same techniques and viewpoints applied by them to the study of societies of simpler peoples are here subjected to empirical testing in a concrete case study in modern American society. The town chosen (for reasons given below) was an old New England community.

The present volume, *The Social Life of a Modern Community*, describes in detail the cultural life of the community, emphasizing particularly the way in which these people have been divided into superior and inferior classes. It also presents the reader with an interpretation of the systematic analysis of the techniques, methods, and conceptual framework used in the research, a summary of the findings, and a general orientation.

The second volume, *The Status System of a Modern Community*, by W. Lloyd Warner and P. S. Lunt, gives a detailed description and careful analysis of the social institutions of this community. It shows how our New England subjects live a well-ordered existence according to a status system maintained by these several social institutions.

The third volume, *The Social Systems of American Ethnic Groups*, by W. Lloyd Warner and Leo Srole, is a detailed study of the social life of a number of ethnic groups, including the Irish, French Canadians, Jews, Armenians, and Poles; it explains how they maintain their old cultural traditions but at the same time undergo social changes which make them more and more like the larger American community.

The fourth volume, *The Social System of the Modern Factory*, by W. Lloyd Warner and J. O. Low, is specifically concerned with the study of the social organization of the modern factory. It shows not only how industrial workers co-operate in producing manufactured goods, but also how they fit into the larger community.

The fifth volume, *American Symbol Systems*, by W. Lloyd Warner, deals with the conceptual processes which Americans use when they think about themselves and their own behavior. It analyzes the myth and ritual as well as the secular behavior of the members of Yankee City.

The concluding volume, *Data Book for the Yankee City Series*, by W. Lloyd Warner, supplies additional data for those who wish to examine the more detailed aspects of the subjects treated in the other volumes.

I

THE GENESIS OF THE RESEARCH

A STATEMENT BY THE DIRECTOR

1. *Reasons for the Yankee City Research*

THE Yankee City research was one of several scientific investigations conducted by the Committee of Industrial Physiology at Harvard University for the general purpose of acquiring a better understanding of human behavior. In his *Human Problems of an Industrial Civilization*,[1] Dr. Elton Mayo of the Department of Industrial Research of the Harvard Graduate School of Business Administration wrote an introductory summary of the many research activities of the various members of the larger group. In this summary he included such diverse investigations of human life as the changing chemistry of the blood and its relation to fatigue (under observation in Dr. L. J. Henderson's laboratories) and the examination of the social behavior of factory workers in a large industrial organization.

The study of the employees of a great factory in Chicago by means of the techniques developed by the disciplines of psychology and social anthropology has made it increasingly clear to those of us who are attempting to understand human relations in action that a large number of the relationships of a worker in the plant, his activities, and his attitudes can be better understood by knowing the place the worker occupies within the immediate or larger context of the factory. Although his relations with fellow workers and with management are of very great importance, they are but part of the total number of interrelations which make up the worker's behavior and tie him not only to the factory but to the total community. The many thousands of interviews gathered from workers in the Chicago factory all clearly demonstrated that the worker brought his outside life with him into the factory; and when

---

1. Elton Mayo, *The Human Problems of an Industrial Civilization* (New York, The Macmillan Co., 1933).

he returned home at night to his family and friends, he took part of his factory life with him. We in the Industrial Research, therefore, set for ourselves the general problem implicit in the following statement:

> . . . the effect of life in a modern industrial centre upon individual capacity and attitude. Janet, for all his descriptive excellence with respect to any present situation, nowhere concerns himself with the origin in different individuals of the tendency to irrational thinking or mild melancholy. The research division had accordingly given some attention to Freudian theories of the importance of personal history; it had also given even more attention to recent developments in social anthropology. A representative of the Harvard Department of Anthropology had called attention to the logical insufficiency of a merely psychological study of the individuals in a department. Laboratory and clinical psychological studies are interested in the individual—his vocational capacity or incapacity, his social "adjustment" or "maladjustment." These studies are, and always will be, exceedingly important; but they do no more than touch the fringe of human inquiry. The individuals who make up a working department are not merely individuals; they constitute a group within which individuals have developed routines of relationship to each other, to their superiors, to their work, and to the policies of the Company. A high incidence of so-called "social maladjustment" in a given group may refer itself to something in these routine relationships to the work and to each other rather than to some primary irrationality in the individual. Interviewers had noticed that an individual who is not very capable, or not very well adjusted socially, may behave capably and normally when he works in a human surrounding that suits and sustains him. And, on the contrary, an exceedingly capable and normal human being will behave as if he were neither when he works in inappropriate surroundings.[2]

Dr. Mayo concludes:

Human collaboration in work, in primitive and developed societies, has always depended for its perpetuation upon the evolution of a non-logical social code which regulates the relations between persons and their attitudes to one another. Insistence upon a merely

---

2. *Ibid.,* pp. 115 ff.

economic logic of production—especially if the logic is frequently changed—interferes with the development of such a code and consequently gives rise in the group to a sense of human defeat. This human defeat results in the formation of a social code at a lower level and in opposition to the economic logic.[3]

Thus it was found that an investigation of the social relations of the workers needed to be extended to the whole of their lives rather than to only one part. It was for this purpose that the social anthropologists were invited to join the larger group of investigators.

I had returned only recently from a three-year study of the community life of a Stone Age people in Australia.[4] The techniques I had used there to understand the social organization and mental life of the Australian blacks were those of social anthropology. Although I had been deeply interested in the life of these particular people, my objective in studying them was not simply to understand how they organized their own social relations, but also to obtain a better understanding of how men in all groups, regardless of place or time, solve the problems which confront them. The more simple types of communities—with their smaller populations, less numerous social institutions, less complex ideational and technical systems—provide the social anthropologist with the equivalent of a laboratory wherein to test his ideas and research techniques. By investigations of these simple societies he is able to equip himself better for the analysis of more complex forms of human society. An obvious analogy here suggests itself between the social anthropologist and the biologist who examines the physiology of more simply constructed organisms to arm himself for his scientific attack on the problems of the human organism.

When I went to Australia, I told my friends, Professor Robert H. Lowie and Professor Alfred Radcliffe-Brown, that my fundamental purpose in studying primitive man was to get to know modern man better; that some day I proposed to investigate (just how I did not then know) the social life of a modern man with the hope of ultimately placing the researches in a larger framework of comparison which would include the

3. *Ibid.*, pp. 120–121.
4. W. Lloyd Warner, *A Black Civilization—A Social Study of an Australian Tribe* (New York, Harper & Bros., 1937).

other societies of the world. On my return from Australia I went to Harvard and had already begun teaching in the Department of Anthropology when I met Professor Elton Mayo. In our many discussions he told me of the several researches in which he was interested, and I told him of the one I had just done and of my desire to study a modern community using the same techniques I had employed among the Australian aborigines. At that time Dr. Mayo spoke particularly of the problem of relating the Chicago factory, which he and his associates had been studying, to the larger community.

The excellent researches of Dr. Robert Park, Dr. Ernest W. Burgess, and their many students in the social life of Chicago were of very great value and contributed much to the general knowledge we had of the Chicago factory workers. However, their work did not tell us specifically what we needed to know about the individual and group existences of the men and women whose lives in the factory the Harvard researches had studied in such intimate detail. We wanted not only to know what these people were like as "total personalities" in the larger society, but also to understand in the same detail what the larger community itself, with its multiple activities and complex relations, was like. To know this about the whole city of Chicago was an impossible task for one or several researchers in the period of time available. Rather it was the work of several "generations" of researchers and their students. We were faced with the alternatives of abandoning the whole project, of taking only a small part of Chicago for our study, or of selecting a small community elsewhere in which the problems of the factory workers within a whole social context and the total community itself could be examined in all their interrelations.

Our reasons for choosing Yankee City for our research on the modern community, once we were no longer limited to the environs of the Chicago factory, are presented in Chapter III. It seems wise, however, to say here that one of the reasons we abandoned any idea of investigating Cicero and Hawthorne (where the Western Electric factory which we had been studying was located) and other industrial subcommunities in the area of Chicago was that these districts seemed to be disorganized; they had a social organization which was highly disfunctional, if not in partial disintegration. If we were to compare easily the other societies of the world with one of our own civilization, and if we were readily to accommodate our techniques, developed by the study of primitive society, to modern groups, it seemed wise to choose a community with a social organization which had developed over a long period of time under the domination of a single group with a coherent tradition. In the United States only two large sections, New England and the deep South, we believed, were likely to possess such a community. Despite the many ethnic migrations to its shores, New England still contains many towns and cities whose Puritan tradition remains unshattered, communities which are still capable of meeting the crises of modern life without revolutionary adaptations in their social structure. The deep South, too, changes in terms of an old and well-defined tradition, as can be seen when one looks into the lives of those who live in a great number of its communities.

The community in New England, for reasons stated in Chapter III, was first selected. Nevertheless, it became increasingly clear as our research progressed that forms of social behavior characteristic of New England were variations within a type, and that we could, to great advantage, broaden our field of investigation and include a community in the deep South. We did this later.

2. Reasons for a Report on Research Operations

RESEARCH reports of social scientists usually present no more than brief summaries of their methods and even less of the theoretical assumptions and postulates which governed (1) the selection of their specific field of investigation, (2) the choice of facts collected, and (3) the ordering and classification of data during analysis and synthesis. Most reports tend to emphasize what are called results which, on the whole, are made up of facts, ordered and classified with no mention of how they were gathered. These "facts" and their classifications are but the momentary end result of a long sequence of activity. That is to say, they are but expressions of what the researcher was doing, thinking, and observing when he constructed his report. Thus had he presented it earlier, the "results" would have been what he was observing, thinking, and doing at that moment in time; or had he postponed it until later and continued his labors, they would have been, in general terms, much the same, except for his knowing that implicit within his last report was the state of his knowledge at a previous date.

The research which presents "facts" and "results" alone is too frequently based on the assumption that what is being said is *only* an explicit statement of the more exact movements of the world outside the operator. Actually, such an account is also an implicit statement of the changes taking place in the thinking and other activities of the researcher. Results ideally not only give a more exact measurement of a piece of reality under examination (and sometimes a firmer conviction that we know more about what we are looking at) but also tell how all or part of the conceptual framework, which was a fundamental part of the original research apparatus, has undergone modification during subsequent activities.

Many scientific social researches are notoriously guilty of beginning as if no other work had been done in the field. Other weaknesses in the methods of the social researcher are due to his not stating (1) what fundamental assumptions he started with, (2) what techniques he used, and (3) what changes his ideas and methods underwent as he learned more about his subject. Research is fundamentally a learning process for the scientist who does it; if what he learns is to be successfully transmitted to others, he must be able to communicate how and why he did it. Those who understand are then able to test his methods and conclusions by repeating what he did.

Criticisms of the conclusions arrived at by different techniques and methods have often resulted in confusion rather than in clarifying our knowledge of society. Results are meaningful only when operations are known, and to know the operations the critic must be acquainted with not only what was being done at the end of a research but also what took place from the beginning to the end. Hence our report will not only embody what we found out about Yankee City, but also attempt to describe what we were thinking and doing during various stages of our work.

To perform the task before us, we will briefly present the outlines of the community investigated, give the general theoretical point of view which guided the field operations, present the field and later analytical operations, and, finally, state the ideas and methods which were used when we began writing and closed the present research. Although the other volumes will present our results and conclusions, it will at times be necessary to review here certain of our findings in order that we may trace for the reader the development of our ideas.

W. LLOYD WARNER.

II

THE CONCEPTUAL FRAMEWORK

1. Science, the Social Sciences, and Social Facts

"THE ancients," says Confucius, "who wished to exemplify illustrious virtue throughout the Empire first ordered well their own states. Wishing to order well their own states, they first regulated their families. Wishing to regulate their families, they first regulated their persons. Wishing to cultivate their persons, they first regulated their hearts. Wishing to rectify their hearts, they first sought to be sincere in their thoughts. Wishing to be sincere in their thoughts, they first extended to the utmost their knowledge. *Such an extension of knowledge lay in the investigation of things.* Things being investigated, knowledge became complete. Their knowledge being complete, their thoughts were sincere. Their thoughts cultivated, their families were regulated. Their families being regulated, their states were rightly governed. Their states being rightly governed, the whole Empire was made tranquil and happy. *It cannot be when the root is neglected that what should spring from it will be well ordered.*"

Modern man, too, has sought to extend his knowledge by "the investigation of things" and to cultivate the roots by examining the natural world around him. By applying the knowledge resulting from his inquiries into the nature of things, he has attempted at times to cultivate a well-ordered life for himself, his contemporaries, and those who are to follow him. If the methods used have a certain exactness and are capable of satisfying certain tests or proofs, these investigations are ranked as sciences. Modern science may have a more explicit view of itself but it is much less sure of its ultimate rightness, perhaps, than were the "ancients" of Confucius. Its theorists have answered the question of "what is a natural science?" by describing the working behavior of those who are said to be scientists. In general, the three characteristic activities of modern science are the observation of "relevant" phenomena, the arrangement of the facts collected by such observation into classes and orders, and the explanation of the ordering and classification of the collected data by means of so-called laws or principles. These several operations, ideally speaking, tend to take place in the described sequence. For example, our scientific knowledge of the heavenly bodies began with the observation of the different positions of the planets and their relative position to each other. Later classification showed the planets moved around the sun and, still later, the "law of gravitation" grouped the observed phenomena and their classification into one formula.

Laws or principles obviously are not observable in nature but are the formulations of modern man as one way of relating himself to the world around him, very much as his primitive contemporaries and his and their forebears use mythological formulae for this purpose. The difference between myth and scientific law is largely one of degree and emphasis. Both science and mythology depend on observed "facts"; but of course greater emphasis is placed by modern scientists on facts and methods of testing them. The laws of the modern sciences must explain all the known facts and be capable of "proof" by the constant testing of new observations.

Since in our research into the social behavior of a modern American community we have applied the methods of modern anthropology, the question arises whether or not this discipline is sufficiently developed to satisfy the demands of the above criteria. If we are to judge it by its present results, the answer is negative. If, however, we are to evaluate it by the points of view of its several present-day practitioners, there is not one answer but several, and the answers we receive are confused and conflicting. "Culture," usually used as a synonym for society, the subject matter of the ethnologist or social anthropologist, has often been called by American anthropologists "an amorphous product," "a chaotic jumble," and "an unorganized hodgepodge." Obviously, if the facts to be studied exist in "chaos," it is impossible to apply scientific methods to them; but even were they capable of systematic treatment, such a viewpoint as this would make it impossible to perform more than the first operations of observing their chaos. This viewpoint in anthropology, largely historical in its approach to social facts, represents only a part, although a very important part, of one school of anthropological thought. The exact opposite of this position is held by another group of social anthropologists, one of whom has said:

> The social realm is a natural realm which differs from the others only by a greater complexity. Now it is impossible that nature should differ radically from itself in the one case and the other in regard to that which is most essential. The fundamental relations that exist between things . . . cannot be essentially dissimilar in the different realms.[1]

The emphasis here is on the coherent relations that exist between things and the establishment of the thesis that social facts are capable of the same scientific treatment as the other facts of nature.

Durkheim further points out that the investigation of social facts

> . . . raises other problems than history or ethnography. It does not seek to know the passed forms of civilization with the sole end of knowing them and reconstructing them. But rather, like every positive science, it has as its object the explanation of some actual reality which is near to us, and which consequently is capable of affecting our ideas and our acts: this reality is man, and more precisely, the man of to-day. . . . [We study various aspects of man's social behavior] to show an essential and permanent aspect of humanity.[2]

To Durkheim and to those social scientists who have utilized a similar approach to the facts of social behavior, "the essential and the permanent aspects of humanity" are those generalizations which can be made by the inductive method after an examination of various kinds of social phenomena such as law, religion, social organization, or technology.)

Although we admit that few, if any, generalizations of this kind have been made or possibly can be made at the present time, it has been the general hypothesis of this research from its beginning that social facts are capable of scientific treat-

---

1. Émile Durkheim, *The Elementary Forms of the Religious Life* (New York, The Macmillan Co., 1926), p. 18.
2. *Ibid.*, pp. 1–2.

ment, and that the purpose of the social scientists must be to formulate these generalizations. While there are other and equally valuable objectives of social anthropology, e.g., the reconstruction of the past sequence of unique events which constitute the life of an individual or the history of a people, such investigations constitute only one of the more important branches of modern social research. The problem of human social behavior in long sequences of past time, while an important one, is not the sole aim of the anthropologist interested in social behavior, as many, if not most, of the American and European anthropologists have insisted.

Our results and the methods we used (which are described in the many pages that follow) are expressions of the partly tested hypothesis that social phenomena are capable of the same general treatment by all the scientific operations used on other natural phenomena.[3] The scientific techniques used may or may not be different, but in general the way of looking at the facts under observation must be the same as those of the other sciences.

2. *The Individual and the Society*

WHEN one examines the methods and findings of modern social scientists, a fundamental dichotomy can be seen in almost all their thinking. Those who hold one point of view examine all human behavior with the individual as the ultimate to which all collected facts are related for meaning. Those who hold the other viewpoint regard human social behavior as a group phenomenon and the emphasis is placed on the interaction of individuals within a set of relations. The continuous interaction of a number of individuals within a relational framework, placed in a separate and particular space, has been called a community or society.

As Durkheim has pointed out, a society or individual can be observed for the purpose of reconstructing its history or of explaining the nature of its present existence. On the whole, anthropological students of social behavior have emphasized the ethnological or temporal aspects of social behavior and

---

[3]. "Scientific operations" is here used in the same sense as it is used by Bridgman. Cf. P. W. Bridgman, *The Logic of Modern Physics* (New York, The Macmillan Co., 1927).

have tended to neglect the scientific problems of explanation of the facts by classification and their interpretation by the formulation of laws and principles.

The Yankee City research, on the whole, has been inspired by the belief in a scientific collection of facts not for their own sake, but for the purpose of later scientific generalization in an effort to understand their nature. Although our emphasis has been on the group aspects of social behavior, we have attempted to avoid the conventional dichotomy of the individual and the society by a restatement of the problem of individuals in interaction.

A well-stated hypothesis of the general nature of society was advanced by Georg Simmel, who said, "Society exists whenever a number of individuals enter into reciprocal relations." He maintained that society "is an objective unity, judged by the one valid criterion of unity, namely, the reciprocal activity of parts." He further clarified this statement: "The group is a unity because of . . . processes of reciprocal *influencing* between the individuals." [4]

Throughout our research we have employed the concepts of interaction between two or more individuals and the social interrelationships within which these interactions take place. The explicit, overt behavior of individuals, verbal or bodily, as well as "mental attitudes or psychological occurrences within the minds of the individuals" studied, have been understood by us "as a product of mutual determinations and reciprocal influences." Although our interest has centered on the aspect of the individual's behavior in a group, it must be obvious that there has been no attempt to view such phenomena, including collective representations, as beyond the individual or as manifestations of the so-called group mind. The larger systems of interrelations which compose the extremely complex and highly elaborate society of Yankee City were studied in specific detail, as were the interactions, direct and indirect, of the individuals who constituted the biological units of the group.

It must be admitted that the analogy of the organism was in our thinking when we looked at the total community of Yankee City and the various parts of its internal structure.

4. Nicholas J. Spykman, *Social Theory of Georg Simmel* (Chicago, University of Chicago Press, 1925), p. 27.

The organism, seen as Simmel saw it, is "a unity because its organs are in a more intimate interchange of energies with one another than any outside agent."[5]

The simplest unit of social interaction we studied was that of two individuals in one or more relations. Such a relationship, we hypothecated, has the elements of both an inward and an outward pull, which is to say that there are attitudes of both cohesion and opposition within any dyadic relationship of "mutual influencing." The introduction of a third individual into this dyadic relation not only adds to the *numerical* complexity of social behavior but greatly increases the *social* complexity of the relationships involved. The one direct relation between two individuals (A-B) has two more direct relations added to it (B-C and A-C) by the introduction of a third person in a triadic relationship and several indirect (or once removed) relations, which multiply the complexity of the social phenomena being studied. Every addition of one individual greatly increases the complexity of the society and the difficulty of its examination by students. When it is remembered that there are many thousands of individuals in Yankee City, the problem of scientific observation seems unsolvable.

Society is a group of mutually interacting individuals. Hence, if any relationship of a given social configuration is stimulated, it will influence all other parts and in turn will be influenced by them.

It is impossible, once the structure is in action (as are all social configurations), to determine which is cause and which effect, since the several relations mutually determine the activities which take place at any given time in one or all of the relations. We therefore attacked the problem of understanding an event or a number of events, in sequence or not, by attempting (1) to place the events or activities under observation in an immediate social relational context, (2) to articulate the immediate relational situation with a larger one, and (3) to place this larger configuration in the total situation of interrelations which compose the whole community of Yankee City. A given set of social relations, such as a family system, can be studied in interaction with the different social bonds within it seen in mutual dependence. The direct relationship of mother

---

5. *Ibid.*, p. 27.

and son, for example, is influenced by that of father and son, as is the direct husband-wife relation, since it is part of the system of interacting persons who form the immediate family in our society.

The research on Yankee City was not directed toward collecting a mass of separate, atomic social items (or traits) which had only a quantitative relationship with each other. Rather, the investigation viewed the total community as a complex configuration of relations, each relation being a part of the total community and mutually dependent upon all other parts. Yankee City, we assumed, was a "working whole" in which each part had definite functions which had to be performed, or substitutes acquired, if the whole society were to maintain itself. The problem faced by the research was a structural one. Each institution had to be studied from the point of view of its direct and primary internal relations; how it was articulated externally to the rest of the total community; and how it was affected by the remainder of the society.

We have spoken of social structure without explicitly stating what we mean by the term. A social structure is a system of formal and informal groupings by which the social behavior of individuals is regulated. To describe a social structure (e.g., the family), the variations and norms of given types of relationships, such as those of father and son and of husband and wife, must be collected and described. For purposes of immediate analysis, it is necessary to separate out the different relations. Later, they can be examined in their context as interacting parts of the total social structure.

3. *Comparative Sociology, Social Anthropology, and Social Evolution*

SOCIAL anthropologists are essentially comparative sociologists. They attempt to discover the nature of society and to understand better any one type of society by a comparative study of the several types found throughout the world. The research in Yankee City has been a practical attempt to use the techniques and ideas which have been developed by social anthropologists in primitive society in order to obtain a more accurate understanding of an American community. Heretofore, social anthropology has confined itself largely to studies of more simple societies and has left the investigations of our own society to representatives of other disciplines. This, on the whole, has had deleterious effects on understanding our own and the other "high" cultures. It seems likely that once we place the study of civilization in the framework of an inductive systematic, comparative sociology, we can increase our knowledge of our own social behavior with the same rapidity that the biologists did when they placed knowledge of our physical structure in the framework of comparative biological science. Simpler societies have been more carefully and exactly studied since they are easier to observe not only because the number of individuals and of relations is smaller, but also because, being outside our own social world, they can be examined by us with more objectivity.

When we say our own society is complex, we mean that there are more numerous internal groupings, a larger number of social relations, and greater social differentiation within the total number of relations composing the entire society. Social evolution consists in a change from the simple to the complex with an increase in the social relations within a society. This means a greater complexity of social structure, an increasing extension of the social relations, and a greater development of the social personalities of the individuals who are members of the society. Individuality, as we define the term, increases, since the greater differentiation of social relations is accompanied by a greater differentiation of individual behavior. Among the contemporary primitive societies, moreover, the greater part of social behavior is subsumed under kinship organization and only a bare minimum under economic and political organization. In our society, on the other hand, organized kinship behavior is but one of the several types of social organization controlling behavior.

Social evolution may be viewed as a progressive growth in complexity and in the coalescence of smaller units into larger ones . . . each step an advance in the direction of wider integration and complexity and heterogeneity. But greater organization brings with it increasing specialization and inevitably this process must foster the development of individualism. *Pro tanto* the difficulties of maintaining integration increase and they can only be overcome by an increase in the efficiency of organization. When organization and efficiency fail to keep pace with the process of evolution, disintegration sets in and we witness the decay of culture. This, broadly speaking, has been the rise and fall of civilization.[6]

As a corollary of the increasing complexity of the social organization of our society and the vast increment of population, the difficulties of maintaining order in the relations of the members of the group greatly increase. Many specific problems recognized under other names in our own society are part of the larger problem of maintaining group unity under the overwhelming burden of the number and complexity of social relations and the physical bulk of population.

4. The Biological Group of the Social Community

THE life of all human beings is a social one; which is to say that all human beings live in groups or in communities. Although the term "community" has been used largely to refer to modern life, any general definition which takes into account the variety of local groups of modern men will also necessarily describe social units of similar kind among primitive men. The community, as defined by the sociologists, is found everywhere. It has been called a "body of people having a common organization or common interests and living in the same place under the same laws and regulations."

The word community denotes a number of people sharing certain interests, sentiments, behavior, and objects in common by virtue of belonging to a social group. The researcher among the simpler people terms their communities "tribes," "bands," "villages," or "clans"; the social scientist who studies modern life designates certain of the local groups as "metropolitan areas," "cities," "towns," "neighborhoods," "villages," and "rural areas." Nevertheless, the several varieties of modern and primitive groups, although varying widely among themselves, are essentially the same in kind. All are located in a given territory which they partly transform for the purpose

---

6. G. H. Pitt-Rivers, *Clash of Culture and the Contact of Races* (London, George Routledge & Sons, 1927).

of maintaining the physical and social life of the group, and all the individual members of these groups have social relations directly or indirectly with each other. The social relations are ordered and their totality forms the social structure of the group. With an amount of change that is proportionately small, the structure of a group continues through the changing generations of individuals born into it. There may or may not be great variation in the autonomy exercised by any one group and in its differentiation from other communities, yet all local groups differ sufficiently everywhere for the individuals in them to be aware of belonging to one group and not to another, even though the other may be but little different from their own.

The minimum essentials for the maintenance of an autonomous community, or tribe of individuals, are fundamentally biological: the first problems to be solved are those which will insure the biological continuity of the group. Biological continuity depends on the maintenance of a regular and dependable supply of organic necessities, and either directly or indirectly demands the possession or control of the land, water, and other resources found there. All social groups have provided themselves with an apparatus for getting physical necessities from their environment and for protecting the source of supply from the ravages of other groups, of other species, and of drastic natural change.

This apparatus is their technological system. It consists of a variety of tools and weapons with a system of skills for the construction of the tools and for their use in adjusting the outside environment to man's needs. The skills consist of (1) the operative mechanisms necessary for the making and handling of the tools and weapons, and (2) the knowledge necessary for the use of the tools and the use of the physical environment in which they operate. The whole constitutes the technical system of a given group. If the protection of the creature necessities is designed to prevent attacks from outside marauders of other species, or if it is designed to protect the group from the changes in nature, it is part of the ordinary technical adaptive system and directly relates man to his natural environment. If, however, the members of a group protect their natural necessities from other men, the form of behavior changes and becomes part of a different system which can be understood only in the general context of the group's social organization.

In addition to the maintenance of an adequate supply of creature necessities, an autonomous group, to maintain its biological continuity, must provide a sufficiently favorable environment to allow the older individuals to reach maturity, reproduce, and bring their immature offspring to an age when they can survive without the aid of their parents or other older members of the biological group. The physical necessities for the maintenance of the life cycles of the individuals and the continuation of the group (through the processes of the dying of certain individuals and the birth and growth of others) involve the following sets of relations: (a) sexual intercourse and the attendant interaction of the two sexes; (b) the later caring for and protection of the young; (c) the protection of a sufficient number of organisms from any harmful aggression which might mean the destruction of the physical group.

Such aggression may come from within the society and, in a biological group, may align older members against the less mature, or the mature against the biologically old, or one sex against the other, etc. The whole problem of physical dominance arises here. Among animals it appears, though evidence is inconclusive, that certain individuals dominate other individuals physically and are in turn dominated by still others. Among chickens, a "peck-order" has been observed. S. Zuckerman found a hierarchy of dominance among the primates he studied.

Social relationships based upon dominance occur throughout the animal world. Rutting seals secure that piece of territory in the breeding ground allowed them by their order of dominance within the group. The dominance of a stag determines the number of females he includes in his harem during a mating season. Monkeys and apes are therefore not peculiar in this respect. Their dominant relationships, however, are conspicuous because they characterize every field of behavior. If a group of monkeys finds itself in a feeding ground in which there is an abundance of food, every animal will be able to eat. If, on the other hand, food is passed into a cage containing two or more monkeys, the strongest animals will secure all.[7]

Every ape or monkey enjoys a position within a social group that is determined by the inter-relation of its own dominant characteristics and those of its fellows. The degree of its dominance determines how far its bodily appetites will be satisfied. Dominance determines the number of females that a male may possess, and except on occasions when there is a superfluity of food, it also determines the amount a monkey eats.[8]

(Social relationships based upon dominance [among primates] may be regarded as a series of adapted responses conditioned through pain and fear. The scope of an animal's activities within a group will be limited by the possibility of danger arising from its desires overlapping those of a more dominant animal. The only equality within a social group is an equality of dominant characteristics. A state of balance is only temporary, and at any moment may be disturbed to a greater or lesser extent, the members of the group readjusting their mutual relationships. The group then settles down in a new equilibrium. Within a group each animal seems to live in potential fear lest another animal stronger than itself will inhibit its activities. A dominant monkey will take all the food passed into the cage, but will start in a momentarily terrified way when one of its weaker fellows, in moving some object, makes an unusual noise. An inferior animal will move towards some food that is proffered, stop suddenly, turn to look at its dominant companion, and then retreat, making those noises that are associated with situations of fear and submission.[9]

Yerkes, in speaking of the great apes, says:

Dominance and subordination are evident in every group of primates. Apparently there is no such thing as equality of status and opportunity. Leadership, mastery, control are manifest. So in their relations with persons, the monkeys and apes merely exhibit their natural aptitudes and types of social behavior. Ordinarily there is aggressive leadership in cage, colony, or family group. Domination may be by either sex, but dominance there must be, and instead of a single leader associated with individuals of rela-

7. S. Zuckerman, *The Social Life of Monkeys and Apes* (New York, Harcourt, Brace, 1932), p. 234.
8. *Ibid.*, p. 233.
9. *Ibid.*, p. 237.

tive equality, there is likely to be serial subordination. So that each individual secures in its social group the degree of opportunity for control and self-expression to which its characteristics and stage of development entitle it. Sometimes one wonders whether this type of social organization might not be valuable for man.[10]

Despite Yerkes' implication that no order of physical dominance exists among men, it seems highly likely that such is the case. Certainly it cannot be overlooked when we study the problems of superordination and subordination in Yankee City, with all their attendant social phenomena.

Although change lies implicit in what we have said about the natural environment and man's physical interaction with it, we have not sufficiently emphasized certain kinds of physical rhythms found in the environment and in man. The changes in the natural environment to which the technical system must adjust itself for the biological group to survive are: (a) the seasonal cycles, and (b) the more fundamental and permanent changes which radically alter the environment but which are noncyclical for man (that is to say, which are climatically cyclical but of such long duration that they are nonrhythmical for man). The physical changes in man are the various phases of his life cycle. This biological change can be categorized (and this is done by the social order of most societies) as (1) changes occurring around the event of birth of the organism; (2) changes occurring around the maturation (immaturity into maturity) of the organism; (3) the "lack" of observable changes during maturity; and (4) changes occurring in old age and death. The changing phases which constitute the cycle of nature and the changing physical structure of man are nonsocial phenomena to which the biological group must adjust in order to maintain its biological continuity.

When the various natural environments of man and the various types of physical man are studied ecologically, an important fact for the understanding of any community's behavior in a comparative system becomes clear. The natural environments inhabited by groups of men vary greatly, while the men who occupy them vary physically but little. Among

---

10. R. M. and A. W. Yerkes, *Almost Human* (The Century Co., 1925), p. 155.

the natural environmental systems to which a group must adjust, many offer a maximum or minimum of creature necessities, and the adjustments necessary for the maintenance of the essential biological continuity are accordingly great or small. However, the physical equipment of the group of individuals occupying such environments will show no essential variations which change the type of physical interactions necessary for biological continuation.

Let us now examine the forms of social behavior which any given group uses to organize these physical interactions (at a given moment in time or through several generations) into socially communicable systems which may be transmitted from one generation to another or from one autonomous social group to another with whom it may be in social interaction.

5. *General Types of Social Control and Adaptation*

THREE fundamental types of social behavior may be conveniently distinguished and isolated in every society, be it the Australian aborigines living in Stone Age simplicity by hunting and gathering or the modern industrial community of Yankee City. These three types of behavior are designed to adapt man to his natural environment, to other individuals, and to the unknown supernatural world around him. Such adaptations give him a partial control over the things to which he is adjusting and place those things in a social relation with him and with the other members of his group. It must be remembered that, by placing all things socially in a system of relations, any given member of a community is *himself* socially placed.

The type of behavior by which a group of individuals adjusts itself to, and partially controls, the natural environment is, as we have said, its technical system; the system of adjustments and controls of the interactions of individuals with each other is the social organization; and the system of adjustments made by the group to the unknown or the supernatural is the religious system which consists of beliefs and sanctions relating man to the gods and the gods to man. Thus a fundamental organization of behavior, with several systems of ordered regulations of human conduct, is found everywhere. There is wide variation among peoples in any one of the several types of behavior. Consequently, to understand the general forms of human conduct, it is necessary to examine the individual societies in all their variations. *Yankee City is but one of the thousands which must be studied.*

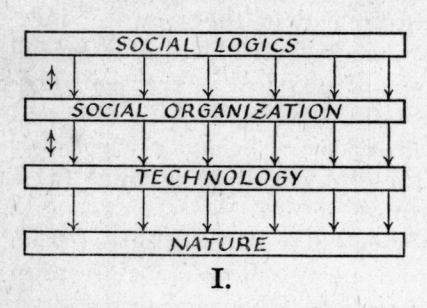

Several types of adjustment found in Yankee City and in all other societies which have been studied may be examined by the aid of Chart I. The social organization or secondary organization used by all groups includes the forms of interrelationship which constitute the organizational system, the conceptual recognition of these forms (secular logics), and the sanctions which individuals in the system use to regulate the ordinary behavior of the members. Implicit or explicit within the rules recognized by members of a society as controlling the interactions of individuals and their various relations are obligations, duties, rights, and privileges. Individuals interacting within a social organization are socially placed at any given moment of time and throughout their lives by participating in their sphere of the social framework.

The individual's social behavior consists of a continuing series of interactions with other individuals within a set of relations. The relations are part of a social system continuing in time, while the interacting individuals who make up the continuity of generations change by the entrance of new units and the departure of old ones. The application of sanctions to an individual who breaks the rules recognized by the group tends to preserve a clear definition of the rules and to maintain their force in the lives of the members of the group.

The system of absolute logics and its sanctions constitute an ideology or ideologies which conceptualize the supernatural world. Ordinarily associated with such ideologies is a set of ritual relations which organize the sacred relations of men with each other and with supernatural beings. In many, if not all, groups studied, including our own, the symbolic system is explicitly stated by using dramatic symbols of sacred ritual.

Absolute ideologies and sanctions ordinarily, if not always, are sacred in character. They usually serve to integrate the total group and assist in maintaining its unity since, even though they are changing, they provide a framework beyond which individual knowledge does not extend. All societies possess such symbolic systems which differ according to the kind of social organization they have. That is to say, there is an interactive relationship between the symbolic system and social organization.

The several types of social adaptation and control limit individual variation and make for unification of the group. Some individual variation is, of course, permitted in every group; but this must be confined to certain limits or the group itself will disintegrate. It is impossible, for example, for differentiation to proceed to a point where individuals may have private symbolic or social systems. Only the insane and certain unaccepted artists and inventors, and then only after our society has exercised extreme sanctions, are allowed these privileges.

Symbolic systems are on various levels of abstraction. As social scientists we can, for example, observe the physical expression of social interaction between two people if they talk with each other, making certain gestures and sounds. At only a slightly more general level of abstraction, the relationship of the two individuals may be seen as that of husband and wife. The larger group to which these two belong is the limited family. Abstracting even more generally, we reach a point where the family is conceptualized not only as a symbol of human social life but as a religious symbol. It becomes the Holy Family of Scripture and is fitted into a still larger symbolic system of the Cross, Christianity, and the whole apparatus of our religious ideology. Consequently we must know with what levels of abstraction we are dealing if we are to understand the verbalizations of an informant.

A detailed examination of Chart I, which represents these adaptations, will give us a better understanding of how the various parts of a society are integrated. The downward-pointing single-headed arrows on the topmost rectangle of the chart represent the ultimate influence of the absolute logics over the social organization, while the double-headed arrows between the two uppermost rectangles show the interrelations between two parts of a society. The downward-pointing arrows from the rectangle representing social organization indicate that it is the function of the social organization not only to regulate the behavior of interactive individuals in the group but also to regulate and organize socially the use of the technological system.

The social, as contrasted with the technical, regulation of the behavior of man consists fundamentally of (1) a division of labor necessary for manipulating tools in acquiring a living from nature, and (2) a distribution of the newly formed desirable goods. The type of social organization possessed by a group will determine the allocation of pleasant and unpleasant tasks among its members as well as the sharing of spoils. If a society is, in all parts of its structure, democratic (as are most simple societies), the division of labor and of goods will tend to be equal; but if it is stratified, the rules which govern the division of work and goods will make for inequalities.

The control of the manipulation of tools together with the sharing of the results of technical activities means that the products of the labor are socially placed. If these products are not immediately consumable, their social placement must continue through time. In the case of less perishable objects, they must be given place through several generations. The social organization, then, places the members of the group and also the objects created by them when they manipulate their technical system.

(Skills are utilitarian in their nature.) They are techniques which transform matter from nonusable into socially usable forms. One of the fundamental differences between (skill and ritual acts is that the former is directly valuable and utilitarian in its nature and is so recognized, while the latter (express secondarily (that is, symbolically) the social value of some part of social behavior.) The two, however, can be combined into one activity so that a technical act may be highly ritualized. Modern etiquette and the table manners surrounding eating, e.g., the proper use of a knife or fork, are examples of the ritualization of technical behavior, for putting food into one's mouth with a tool is something more than a skillful act. The technical system serves to satisfy certain biological needs which have been socialized. Another example shows this. The

The Conceptual Framework

hungry European, like his primitive contemporaries, satisfies his hunger by selecting his food from a diet which is highly restricted socially. Certain foods highly prized among many peoples, such as grasshoppers, caterpillars, ants, and grubs, he believes to be unsuitable for human consumption. Although his hunger is physical, his recognition of how he will satisfy it is cultural.

6. The Comparative Sociology of the Social Types of Adaptation and Control

TECHNICAL systems of the world range from very simple ones of hunting and gathering societies to highly complex ones of the modern community. This has been demonstrated with some degree of success by Hobhouse[11] and his associates who have classified them on the basis of two major criteria: (1) the way in which various groups extract their food from nature and (2) the comparative complexity of the forms of adaptation they make. According to these criteria Hobhouse has constructed the following types: (1) hunting and gathering, (2) pastoral, and (3) agricultural, the latter being further subdivided into three grades depending upon the complexity within the system. Yankee City clearly falls at one extreme in this scale of measurement, that of the most complex of the agricultural groups.

The above-mentioned technical systems tend to be relatively stable or unstable; that is to say, like that of the Australian aborigines, for instance, they are subject to but little, or no, observable change or, like our own, to extremely rapid change. With respect to this latter point a significant problem emerges. If a society can be described as a system whose parts are all mutually interdependent, then any changes in its technology and general adjustments to the natural environment should presumably result in an effect on the social organization which should react on the system of absolute logics; these in their turn should react with each other and back again on the technology. Our observations in Yankee City tend to confirm this point. Ideas of progress, of freedom, of democracy, and

---

11. L. T. Hobhouse, G. C. Wheeler, and M. Ginsberg, *The Material Culture and Social Institutions of the Simpler Peoples* (London, Chapman & Hall, 1915).

other values which are highly cherished in Yankee City as well as elsewhere in the United States all sanction certain kinds of change, particularly technological, but they facilitate to a lesser degree changes in social organization and absolute ideologies. However, as long as a technical system continues to undergo change, a corollary of our general research hypotheses must be that the social organization must also change or be sufficiently flexible in its existing form, at least, to regulate the newer technical forms that develop.

A further corollary to be added to our original theoretical apparatus is that if change does take place, it need not necessarily be in the direction of "progress"; that is to say, it need not be satisfactory change. Many associated manifestations of social change may be evaluated by the group as harmful. Consequently Durkheim's analysis of suicide, in which he proposed the hypothesis that a certain kind of suicide is due to *anomia*, or a breakup of social relations in our industrial world, was enlarged by us to include other "asocial" behavior. This does not mean that we assumed all such behavior to be connected with social breakdown, but that part of it, at least, might be better understood by using such a concept to guide our investigations.

7. Social Personality, Individuality, Adjustment, and Maladjustment

THROUGHOUT the Yankee City research we distinguished "social personality" from "individuality." We were not concerned with individuality but with the study of social personality which we defined as the total participation of an organic item in its particular part of the society. It was found possible to diagram the social area of the society and the individual's place in it. Because a given individual occupies a particular place in the social space of a given society, out of the multitude of places it would be possible for him to be in, and participates in this one place, he has a social personality different from that of anyone else.

Oversimplifying for the sake of exposition, we may assume that the social space of our society has but two dimensions, vertical and horizontal. The vertical dimension is a hierarchical order in which people occupy higher and lower positions, and the horizontal represents a social differentiation of behavior at any given vertical level. In Chart II, the rectangle represents the whole society: lines A_1, A_2, A_3, etc., represent the vertical dimensions, and lines B_1, B_2, B_3, etc., the horizontal. The shaded portion represents the social place (or social personality) of an individual. Other individuals may resemble him because they participate in approximately the same place in the society. One can say, for example, that they are upper-lower-class persons who are of a certain family and who belong to certain occupational groups.

The operations just described make use of both the individual and societal points of view. They use the techniques and results of each general science of human behavior and yet do not discard the leading ideas of either. Such a procedure does not produce two kinds of findings—the one psychological, the other sociological. On the contrary, the same individual can be studied with the techniques of the psychologist and then examined within his social place, and his social place related to the larger society. Individuals with similar social personalities and similar problems can thus be compared with greater exactitude, while individuals who occupy quite different parts of the social structure and who possess different social personalities can be studied separately within their respective social contexts.

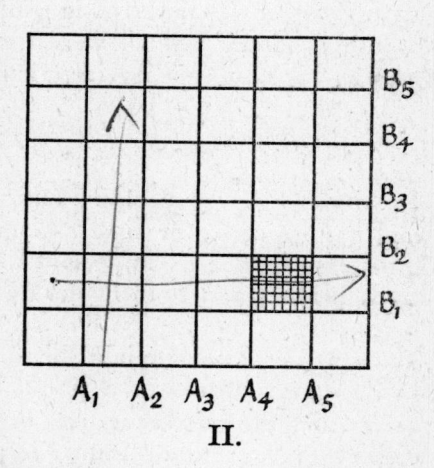

The degree of complexity of an individual's social personality will be determined by the simplicity or complexity of the society in which he lives, and particularly of that part of the society in which he participates. Moreover, since certain parts are by social function involved in greater conflict than others, individuals who have their social place in those parts will be in greater conflict than those who are in other areas of the society.

The symbolic system of an individual will differ according to the part of the society he occupies. In studying the social system of western Ireland, my colleagues and I found several class groups, among them the Ascendancy or Protestant Irish, the Catholic Irish who make up the vast middle class, and the so-called Tinkers, a small group at the bottom, Catholic in name, who must marry within their own group but who are scorned by the others. The Tinker group, though nominally Catholic, shares only in part the symbols of the Catholics. The religious symbols of the Protestant Ascendancy are different from those of either Catholic group. Corresponding differences in the symbolic system were also observed for the different groups in Yankee City, particularly in interview situations.

8. *The Several Types of Social Structure*

IN EVERY society certain subunities tend to be established and maintained over time as characteristic structures, distinguishable by the arrangement of their members with relation to each other and to members of the larger community. Structures of the same type will differ from society to society, and a given type may sometimes be lacking altogether. The several kinds of structures in a particular society differ more from each other than do structures of the same type in different societies. The immediate family in modern America, for example, resembles more closely the immediate family in many African tribes than it does, let us say, the contemporary American economic or political organizations. The similarity in kind of structures in different societies facilitates scientific comparison, while the differences in kind of the several institutions in one society facilitate the analysis of human behavior in complex modern communities like Yankee City. Among the various subgroupings of individuals in the larger community, the family, the association, the clique, the political organization or government, the church (as a social structure), economic institutions (e.g., the company, the factory, and the store, or in a primitive group the horde or hunting band), castes and classes, and age or sex groupings have been differentiated. These several structures, according to the theoretical orientation with which we began the study and prosecuted it during its later stages, were conceived as constituting the social organization of the Yankee City community.

The family in Yankee City, as elsewhere throughout the world, may be viewed as an interactive system of relationships involving the social personalities of husband, wife, father, mother, son, daughter, brother, and sister. Its primary functions are the socialization of sexual behavior and the social orientation of newly born and immature organisms within the general society. Along with age-grading institutions, it helps in solving the problem of maintaining the unity of the group despite the disruptive changes recurrently wrought by death and birth. If a whole generation died at one time and a newly born one attempted to succeed it, society could not maintain itself. Since, however, the members of an older generation pass on and new organisms take their places one by one, the amount of change and the consequent shock to social relations at any one time are comparatively slight.

In all societies all individuals are socially differentiated, either formally or informally, according to their age or degree of physical maturity. The social factors defining the several categories may be few or complex, but there are usually at least the major divisions of the immature, the mature, and the old. Where age arrangements are formal, definite rules prescribe the appropriate behavior for each age grade and for the relations between them.

The passage from one age grade to the next is commonly ritualized. The *rites de passage* attending such change within the life of an individual are the ceremonies attending birth, puberty, the attainment of maturity, marriage, the first child, "becoming an elder," and death. Birth and death ceremonies express changes in the social status of an individual in regard to his relationships with the ordinary world and with the supernatural society. The rituals attending birth symbolize the severance of the ties of the soul of the newly born individual with the other world and identify him with the society of the living by assigning him a social place and defining his status. Funerary rites redefine the relations of the departed with the living and with the supernatural society of the dead and the gods. Between these two terminal rites, the rituals in the life of an individual express the changes.

The assignment of individuals to age categories is generally associated with a social recognition of the differences between the two sexes. For certain purposes males are placed in one group and females in another. In other situations the same community may disregard this sex dichotomy and treat the two sexes as undifferentiated members of the society with no formal differences in status. This social-sexual dichotomy—or trichotomy, if instances of lack of differentiation be included—enters into various combinations with age divisions in the different societies of the world. Of the various possibilities we shall consider only one, namely, the combination of a sexual trichotomy with three age divisions, as illustrated in Chart III.

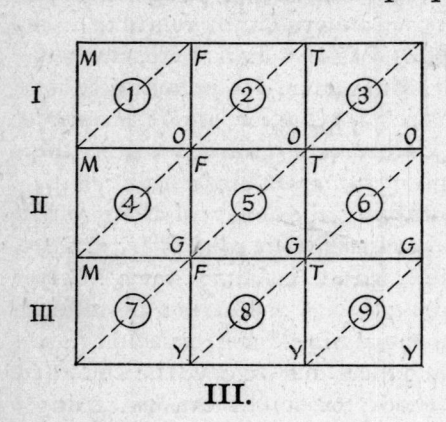

CHART III

TYPOLOGY OF AGE AND SEX DIVISIONS

The upper level (I) includes:
1. Old males (O = old; M = males)
2. Old females (F = females)
3. Old males and females (T = together or undifferentiated)

The intermediate level (II) includes:
4. Grown or mature males (G = grown)
5. Grown females
6. Grown males and females

The lower level (III) includes:
7. Young or immature males (Y = young)
8. Immature females
9. Immature males and females

The articulation of sex and age divisions is commonly associated with phenomena of subordination and superordination.

The immature age group is always subordinate to the older mature groups and the mature are usually, but not always, subordinate to the old. This subordination of the younger to the older generations permits the mature to indoctrinate the young with the social behavior of the group. The young are dependent upon the old for learning the social tradition and for acquiring their social status. This domination of the young by the old insures social stability over successive generations and thus maintains the continuity of a social system.

The subordination of one sex by the other is likewise found in most societies. Males usually constitute the dominant sex group, but in a few cases the evidence indicates female dominance. The relation of social to physical dominance is an open question, but the fact of the former is well established. In some societies both male and female groups are age-graded, and the several age levels of each equated. In others one sex may be arranged into age groups, while the other—ordinarily the women—remains undifferentiated. In this case females are classed with the lowest male age grade and excluded from initiations which would raise their status.

In a society which is but little differentiated, the age and sex arrangements tend to be simple, but when there is a high social differentiation, e.g., a complex variety of occupations or associations or the presence of several social strata, the age arrangements conform to this complexity. In such a situation the age divisions, instead of crosscutting the entire society and grouping all persons of a certain age and sex together, apply only to particular segments of the community. One association, like the Y.M.C.A., may be stratified with respect to age and sex whereas another is not, or the rules of such a structure as the church or state may forbid the participation of one sex or certain age divisions. This shattering of the age and sex arrangements in complex societies tends to make the social age or sex of a person dependent upon the various positions he occupies in different aspects of his life. A man or a woman may belong to some associations which are bisexual and to others which are sex-limited, practice an occupation restricted to one sex or open to both, and live in a state where only males can vote and hold offices. Similarly a man may belong to an association which rules that he is "old enough" to join when he is sixteen, whereas the state in which he lives may not allow him to vote until he is twenty-one. Social relations may thus be greatly complicated by differing social evaluations of an individual's age.

The *association*, a type of grouping highly favored by our own society, arranges individuals in a structure which does not crosscut the whole society but characteristically includes some and excludes others. The presence of associations in a society segments the members of the group into subunities. The association differs from kinship institutions in that a person joins it instead of being born into it. The behavior it regulates may include every kind of activity to be found in the whole society. The association may be formally organized with rules of entrance and exit, with additional regulations controlling the behavior of its members. All such rules are usually explicitly stated and, if the community is literate, they are commonly recorded in writing.

Certain associations may be informal; that is to say, the rules of entrance, departure, and membership are customary rather than explicitly stated. Nevertheless there is a feeling that the group is "ours," that a member should do and not do certain things lest he offend those who belong to his association. There is ordinarily a close identity among the various members and usually a feeling of intimacy among them. The *clique* in our society is an example of an informal association.

Economic organizations are found everywhere. The simple horde of Australia and the hunting bands of the more lowly Indian societies are examples of clearly defined economic groups among primitive communities. The horde organizes the food gathering or productive activities of a hunting and gathering people in a set of relations as does a modern factory in Yankee City. The control of property is frequently the chief function of one variety of economic structure; this type may arrange people into a set of relations different from that organized by the productive group. Economic structures control the technology by (1) organizing its use in production and (2) dividing the goods at the time they are produced, or, if the goods are durable, determining their use and place in the social system. If the economic structure has a large number of individuals and a multiple division of tasks to be performed, the arrangement of its separate members tends to assume the form of a hierarchy with certain groups superordinate to other groups.

In most societies the *church*, as a set of social relations which organizes people into a structural unity, is all-pervading. It ordinarily organizes the members of the whole society into arrangements which relate the separate members with each other; and it further relates them in a group which organizes the relations of the everyday world to those of the supernatural. The inhabitants of the supernatural society (including any or all of such personae as the souls of the dead, the souls of the unborn, and the gods) are related systematically to each other and to the members of the church by a system of ritual and myth.

The church ordinarily, but not always, produces offices which have to be filled by a professional staff. In the more complex communities of the world, this official group frequently becomes highly superordinate. The same kind of hierarchy is found here as is found in the economic structures of complex societies. The functions of the official group, i.e., relating the dangerous other world to the needs of the ordinary world of men, provide a ready means of dominance which can be exercised by any individual occupying the office. Although in the simpler societies the church includes the whole group, in the more complex societies it tends to segment into different groups with separate memberships. Even though the explicit and more general social functions of the church do not change, the organizational functions do alter when the one church is superseded by many. With this change in organization, the church, in its normal behavior, approximates certain types of associations. The Masons in modern society and some secret societies of the South Seas and West Africa are, for example, very like the modern church in the arrangement of their members in relation to each other, to the community, and to the supernatural society of the dead and the gods.

In almost all societies there are found formal or informal groups whose members are recognized by the whole society as occupying a social place which is ranked as superior or inferior, or equated with another social position which is evaluated as low or high. The very simplest societies have no arrangement of people in higher or lower classes, but the principles of superordination and subordination operate in their kinship, sex, and age segments. The highly complex societies ordinarily possess an elaborate permanent status system, usually a *class or caste structure*. A detailed analysis of the arrangement of people into hierarchical groups will be presented in a later chapter.

The *school*, as a separate institution, is a very recent phenomenon in the history of society. Considered as part of the age-grading divisions of the non-European societies, however, it is extremely old and in all societies forms a part of the larger system for orienting the young to the social tradition.

The *governmental structures* of the diverse societies of the world range from groups where there is no organized government to certain modern states where the political structure dominates the rest of the behavior of the group. Hobhouse and his associates[12] demonstrate clearly that there is a steady rise in the frequency of organized government and political institutions as one passes from the lower hunters to the higher agriculturists. Furthermore, there is a constant tendency for the governmental structure to become more complex, to create hierarchies of control, and to extend its dominion over a larger number of activities. Associational structures are often closely interrelated with governmental institutions, and when this happens the association may occupy a position of dominance. The political party is an association whose domination of the political structure may be socially sanctioned. A secret society, in modern America as well as in primitive West Africa, may exert control over a political structure without the full approval of the larger society. The governmental organization of a community arranges its members in a controlled and controlling set of relations. The officers of the controlling group function to relate the members of the whole community to other communities and to organize ultimately the internal relations of the members and apply sanctions when the rules are broken. The relations formally organized by the government, as well as the type and severity of the sanctions applied, vary greatly throughout the societies of the world.

12. *Ibid.*

9. The Fundamental or Integrative Structure

THESE several internal structures or arrangements of the members of a society may or may not be present in any given group which is under observation, as for example Yankee City. The simpler societies, on the whole, organize their members into kinship groupings which are ordinarily supplemented by age-sex divisions. All societies seem to place emphasis on one structure which gives form to the total society and integrates the other structures into a social unity in much the same way that the skeleton provides a framework or scaffolding on which the flesh parts of the body are placed. The Murngin aborigines of Australia, for example, depend upon an elaborate kinship system for their fundamental structure, and the other internal relations are organized around it. In certain parts of Africa many of the Negro societies accent their age-grade divisions, as do some of the New Guinea groups. In other cases the fundamental structure may consist of a combination of two structures.

The fundamental structure determines the basic outlook of an individual and the larger context to which he ultimately refers his definitions of social usage. Thus the decisions of a Murngin native are determined finally by the position he occupies at any given time in the kinship structure. Such a society as India, for example, organizes the activities of the total community around a caste hierarchy, as did the Natchez and other Indian groups who once occupied part of the territory now belonging to our southern states. The fundamental structure of certain modern communities seems to be economic, while other communities depend upon their political institutions to give form and cohesion to their multiple parts. This concept of a fundamental structure was basic throughout the earlier stages of our research.

10. Conclusion

THE rather simple formulations stated above served as our leading ideas and basic theoretical apperceptions when we entered the field to study Yankee City. The concept of interrelation or interconnectedness of the multiple relations of the individual members, all in mutual dependence, and the concept of types of fundamental controls and adaptation guided our detailed investigations. The idea of structure and variety of structures—i.e., the family, the extended kin, the association, and age grading—was taken from social anthropology and the other social sciences. The observation that most, if not all, societies have a fundamental structure or structures which integrate and give characteristic form to the rest of the society was a leading idea in our theoretical equipment.

This explicit examination of our theory and the later examination of our methods and techniques are presented because the results of our efforts can only be understood and their validity appraised if the reader is thoroughly acquainted with our operations. As Bridgman says:

The new attitude toward a concept is entirely different. We may illustrate by considering the concept of length: what do we mean by the length of an object? We evidently know what we mean by length if we can tell what the length of any and every object is, and for the physicist nothing more is required. To find the length of an object, we have to perform certain physical operations. The concept of length is therefore fixed when the operations by which length is measured are fixed: that is, the concept of length involves as much as and nothing more than the set of operations by which length is determined. In general, we mean by any concept nothing more than a set of operations; *the concept is synonymous with the corresponding set of operations.*[13]

A reigning idea among most anthropologists has been that the researcher should enter the field with no preconceived ideas, and be proud of having no theoretical position. The writings of many social anthropologists have been criticized because they admitted the assumptions and hypotheses they used and tested in their work. The usual criticism takes the form of accusing the investigator of bias. This obviously must be admitted, for no one is free from bias. However, it seems to us there is far less likelihood of the work's being skewed by the writer or misunderstood by the reader if the former's theoretical position, methods, and techniques are explicitly presented. Too frequently the protested lack of a theoretical

13. P. W. Bridgman, *op. cit.,* p. 5.

position when field work is presented merely masks a set of unconscious or partly conscious assumptions which, though neither the researcher nor the reader may be aware of it, biases the results of the research and prevents an adequate treatment of the social reality being studied, either in the collection of the facts, in later analysis and synthesis, or in both.

III

THE FIELD TECHNIQUES USED AND THE MATERIALS GATHERED

1. *Criteria Used in Selecting the Community*

WHEN it was decided not to select a community in direct social relation with the Chicago industrial plant already studied, and when it was decided to place our emphasis on understanding the social system of the community itself, we had, it might seem, all the communities in the United States among which to choose. Certain fundamental criteria, however, limited our choice.[1] We shall briefly mention these criteria and why we used them.

We sought above all a well-integrated community, where the various parts of the society were functioning with comparative ease. We did not want a city where the ordinary daily relations of the inhabitants were in confusion or in conflict. We desired a town whose population was predominantly old American, since our interest was in seeing how the stock which is usually thought of as the core of modern America—the group which ordinarily assimilates the newer ethnic groups—organizes its behavior when not suffering from an overpowering impact of other ethnic groups. A community was sought which had a long tradition, that is, where the social organization had become firmly organized and the relations of the various members of the society exactly placed and known by the individuals who made up the group. We wanted a group which had not undergone such rapid social change that the disruptive factors would be more important than those which maintained a balanced grouping of the members of the society. We did not want a society in which several ethnic traditions were equally dominant since, obviously, total-community integration would tend to be low, subcommunity integration high, and ethnic conflict probable.

Although we desired an old New England community with

1. See an earlier discussion of this problem in chap. i, pp. 4–5.

Field Techniques Used and Materials Gathered 39

an uninterrupted tradition back of it (after we had eliminated the deep South as the other section of the United States with a firmly planted tradition for our first study), we did not select one at random in the New England area. We wanted to make sure that the community we picked would have a large number of the characteristics of its own kind. We specified that it should have a few industries and several factories, because (1) we wished to see how the factory and the workers were geared into the life of the larger community, and (2) we wanted to be sure our community was not an aberrant one.

Our search was for a community sufficiently autonomous to have a separate life of its own, not a mere satellite in the metropolitan area of a large city. Hence we hoped to find a place with a farming area around it, since this could be taken to imply that the community possessed a certain separation from other urban areas and a unity of its own.

A number of ethnic groups, we believed, should be a part of the life of the city studied, since they are typical factors in the life of the greater number of American communities. Furthermore, many of the problems of socially organizing the relations of the larger community are of a different kind from those found where alien stocks are not present. The presence both of old ethnic groups like the Irish and Jews and of newer ones like the Greeks and Italians was considered desirable.

These criteria necessarily tended to limit the size, in area and population, of the city to be studied. A further limitation in size was necessary since, if the community were too large, our detailed methods of observation could not be applied because of the factors of time, the smallness of our research staff, and financing. We therefore wanted a city under 20,000 and preferably one nearer 10,000. The community we chose had a population of about 17,000 people. Such a community, we believed, would manifest much of the complexity of modern life but would not be beyond the possibilities of detailed examination. A final consideration was that the city be near enough to Cambridge so that the research men could go back and forth without difficulty or loss of time.

Most cities were quickly eliminated by a brief examination of census data. The few which remained were visited and quickly surveyed by observation of the town and interviewing the townsmen or other informed people. When our preliminary survey of the several communities was completed, the community we have called Yankee City appeared the most likely to meet the test of all our criteria. A further survey then became necessary to be sure we were not mistaken in our estimate that it met the standards we had set.

2. Testing Our Selection

TO BE sure that we were not ethnocentrically biased in our judgment, we decided to use no previous summaries of data collected by anyone else (maps, handbooks, histories, etc.) until we had formed our own opinion of the city. In part this was a mistake since it greatly lengthened our field work; in compensation, once we had arrived at our conclusions, we were certain of the facts and operations on which our opinions were founded.

The several researchers at first surveyed the whole community, street by street and house by house, in order to work out the distribution of dwelling areas, the open spaces, the schools, the parks and other public places, the business and industrial areas, as well as other spatial aspects of the community and the natural environment. The different kinds of businesses, office buildings, and factories were all described and classified in our field notes. Railways and interstate highways were plotted as were the names and locations of all the city streets.

From these data a map of the city and its natural environs was constructed and all the collected information spotted upon it. We now had a physical index of the general kind of activity to be expected in the various parts of the city as well as an ordered set of information about the city on the basis of which we could start our interviewing program. At this time we still were not certain that Yankee City was to be chosen for our study and we had yet to inform any one of its citizens of our intentions.

The interviews gathered during our preliminary survey had satisfied us that Yankee City seemed to possess all the requirements we had asked of it except ethnic communities. We had been told that there were no ethnic concentrations of population in the city. Our ecological survey had indicated otherwise, but to make sure another reconnaissance was made of a more specialized kind. From the city directory we took the addresses of all those whose names indicated they might have an ethnic background other than that of the older American stocks. We realized that this method was not sufficiently exact for our later purposes, but it served to tell us roughly what stocks were to be found in the community and whether they were concentrated in any particular areas. The names taken from the city directory were placed on spot maps which, when completed, demonstrated that there were a number of fairly large ethnic groups in the community and that at least some of them were ecologically organized.

The last doubt being eliminated, Yankee City was selected and we faced the not altogether easy task of telling its people we proposed to study them and of our hope for their sympathy and active co-operation. We knew we could accomplish little without their wholehearted support in an enterprise which demanded investigation of such private matters as the amount of money a Yankee had in the bank and the details of his or her sexual behavior. Thus our introduction to the city had to be carefully and expertly handled or we would be defeated before we started.

There was, of course, the choice of attempting to keep our investigation secret. It seemed likely, however, that this would prevent a good part of our work from being done, and, as it later developed, it would have been impossible. We decided upon announcing our intentions.

3. *How We Were Introduced*

AFTER the first two surveys had been made, we were ready to begin an intensive interviewing program. To do this, it seemed highly advisable to secure the consent and co-operation of the more important men in the community lest we later find it impossible to obtain certain vital information. We finally selected one prominent and, it later developed, much-trusted individual who, we knew, was important in the town and who, we believed, might be interested in the work we proposed doing. We obtained introductions to him, told him in general what we wanted to do, and asked his co-operation. After asking us a number of questions and showing a decided interest in our work, he agreed to help us in any way he could. We then asked him to introduce us to some of his friends who were leaders in the city's activities. This he did, and from his friends we received other introductions which shortly spread our sources of information from the top to the bottom of the city.

The men of high status in the community were approached first because it was felt that with their approval of our project we could more easily gain the confidence of the smaller businessmen and of the town generally. It was easy to use the stereotyped introduction, "Mr. So-and-so has expressed great interest in our work and has sent me to talk to you about it." This remark always gave us an immediate entrance and a willing co-operation from the prospective informant.

The field research started with four people including the director of the work, increased to five, then six, and eventually employed between ten and fifteen investigators. The various tasks were allotted to members of this group according to their several aptitudes and also according to our various avenues of approach. For example, we very early made contacts with the superintendent of schools and the school departments, and since one of the researchers was of old New England stock and had an excellent knowledge of the New England educational mores, he was put in charge of this work. The school system was divided into two parts for our purposes: the high school was studied by one researcher, and the rest of the school system by another. An investigator who had a special aptitude for languages and was interested in the ethnic situation in the town was given this field. An economist was assigned to work with the banks and stores, in which he was particularly interested. One man studied the French Canadians, Greeks, Poles, and Russians; another studied the Italian community; a third, the Jewish population; and a fourth surveyed the Negroes of the town.

One man was placed in the assessor's office because he had made excellent contacts there at the very beginning of our work. He collected the following items of information from the assessor's records: the names and addresses of persons owning property, the location of property, the description and value of chattels, the amount of land owned and its assessed valuation, and the aggregate value of all assessed property. Actually the presence of this man in the assessor's office had a still better justification: the place was a clearinghouse for political gossip, and this gave us an excellent opportunity to keep in close touch with the various political movements in the city. This was of very great importance since many of the city's underlying antagonisms were centered around the incumbent mayor, a nationally known figure at that time whose term of office was marked by innumerable conflicts.

The researchers always tried to adopt a positive attitude toward their own problems as well as the larger research. We assumed that everyone would have the good sense to know that what we were doing was important and deserving of confidence. The use of the name of the Harvard Graduate School of Business Administration greatly aided our acceptance because it identified us as responsible and respectable. We made no attempt to explain all our aims to any one person. Since our interests were most varied, all information offered to us was grist for our mill. Most of the older inhabitants were "historically minded" and thought of any social research as historical. To them we were social historians. To the industrialists and some of the businessmen we were social economists, and to many of the older ladies we were students interested in genealogical history. To the members of the various ethnic groups we were fair-minded gentlemen interested in seeing that their groups received their rightful place in the economic and historical study we were making. To those who saw us at entertainments and parties, I fear, we were young men having a good time, not too intent upon our work. Nevertheless, in such gatherings we were able to obtain some of our most valuable information.

After the research had been in progress for some little time, fieldmen were put into factories to observe the behavior and relationships there. Others were placed among the workers, especially when strikes occurred. Still others interviewed and collected budgets. Certain men were put to work on the study of associations, and others investigated the churches. Eventually in this way we made an intensive examination of the total society.

4. *The Several Techniques Used in the Field*

ONCE we were favorably received and had placed our investigators in strategic positions to gather the information we wanted, the question arose: what should we do and how should we go about it? In other words, what techniques and observations were we to use and how, when, where, and why were we to use them? Given the theoretical framework described in an earlier chapter, and given the social reality briefly summarized in the next chapter, how should a social researcher look at the concrete reality of human behavior?

The researcher must constantly keep in mind his own position as an observer; the objective scientist is aware of his own prejudices. With this in mind, human behavior can be observed in four ways: (1) the observer can watch the behavior of an individual or individuals; (2) he can record verbalizations; (3) he can observe the concrete products of social behavior (technological objects); and (4) he can see any two or all three combined at once. There is little else that he can do by way of collecting concrete facts to be used later as a basis for his inductions and his scientific generalizations about human behavior.

The fundamental and most important technique we used to gather material in the field was the interview; evidence documented from this source was our basic raw material. In addition to the interview, various types of sustained observations were made; a great variety and number of printed documents were collected; case histories, biographies, autobiographies, and other intimate histories were gathered from our informants; photographs were made of houses and other objects of significance; and an aerial survey was made. Many other surveys were also pursued, and the newspapers were systematically used. The distribution of various kinds of phenomena was mapped. Each of these separate techniques will be described in detail, and the use of some of them in the Yankee City research will be evaluated according to the tests of (1) reliability; (2) time required; (3) area of social relations covered; (4) insight into the social behavior which use of the technique gives to the investigator; (5) comparative depth or superficiality; (6) value at various periods in the research and not at others; (7) special uses, such as quantification of behavior already defined and isolated and prepared for measurement; (8) availability for the isolation and definition of social behavior at that time unknown or not yet sufficiently understood to define; and (9) special uses associated with particular techniques.

A. THE INTERVIEW

The task of the interviewer is to isolate and define all the social relations which constitute the social group and to record all the variable events which take place in these relationships. If social research is to be done extensively and intensively, the size and complexity of the interviewer's labors are seemingly limitless, for the study of even a comparatively small population and of all the simple relations of a town or tribe seems beyond human effort.

The complete study of the social life of a community by the use of the interview method would demand that every individual in the interactive group be interviewed many times until the interviewer, by hearing the informant verbalize about his total past and present participation with the other individuals with whom he was and is in relation, would have a complete history of the individual himself and a full account of how he saw the lives of the others with whom he directly or indirectly interacted. The accumulated information would also include the observations of the informant's behavior as well as the statements he made.

The information collected in Yankee City included personal data on almost 17,000 men, women, and children. Obviously, if we had had a hundred interviewers and twenty years of field work, we could not have studied all these individuals intensively and completely. Our interviewing methods had to conform to the exigencies of time, the size of the area of investigation, and the criteria of adequacy of the quality and quantity of the data collected.

In working with a modern community, the social anthropologist is forced to modify and also to elaborate on the older ethnographic techniques. The field techniques we used in the study of Yankee City were those of the ethnographer and the psychoanalyst.

Interviewing and observing are two parts of the one process of investigation. Although they are too closely interrelated to be readily isolated for description, we have nevertheless attempted to give them separate discussion. The basis for differentiation is as follows. The activity of the investigator has been classed as observation when the emphasis fell on the observer's seeing behavior of an individual; as interviewing, when emphasis fell on listening to what was said. If the researcher is largely outside the interactive behavior being studied, his estimates are those of an observer; if, however, he is skillfully relating himself to an informant or informants, the behavior has been called interviewing even though in the course of his listening he has made certain observations in regard to the overt physical behavior of the informant.

The combination of the techniques of observation and interviewing may be illustrated by an ethnographical example. Certain members of an Australian tribe paint themselves, then dance and sing a song (which is a secret ritual) under the direction of a ceremonial leader.[2] The fieldworker, if he knows what is going to occur, (1) interviews the participants before the rite takes place in order to ascertain what they think is about to happen, what the participants themselves ideally expect, what their physical actions are, the words of their song, and the interrelations of the words and actions; (2) becomes, during the ritual event, an observer and records what he sees of the ceremony; and (3) reviews, with participants and others after the performance is over what has taken place. Thus the interviewer accumulates a knowledge of what the participants say the relations should be, what he observes them to be at a given moment in a rite, and what the several individuals say of them after the event has occurred. A comparison of the several accounts and an analysis, combined with later interviewing for discrepancies, are always most illuminating and rewarding.

Substitution of the leader of an American Legion Memorial Day parade for the Australian ritual leader and his totem dancers does not essentially alter the situation as far as the interview technique is concerned. Similar sequences of research technique can be applied wherever the behavior itself is open to observation. This alternation of interviewing for what is

2. See Warner, *op. cit.*

thought should happen and for what is believed has happened, coupled with observation of the informants participating in social activities with each other, gives the social researcher the best check on all aspects of the event or situation under investigation.

a. The Interview as a Social Relation. In a society such as ours, where great emphasis is placed on protecting certain behavior from outside knowledge by calling it private and intimate, why should the ordinary person in a community, without coercion, inform an investigator about certain experiences of his life? When this "protection of privacy" is seen to function as a method of maintaining an individual's feeling of security and social position, the question of why an individual talks intimately to someone outside the circle of his confidants becomes even more complex. Added to this is a further difficulty. Frequently when people wish to exchange intimate information, they cannot because of the arduousness of meaningfully verbalizing their thoughts and actions. How, then, does the interview yield data of an intimate nature? The answer to these questions involves an examination of the general context in which the interview takes place and an analysis of the techniques used by the interviewer within this context.

The communication that occurs between an informant and his interviewer is a social one; it is part of a social relation in which there is reciprocal activity. Each influences the other. This is true even in the most tenuous kind of contact between the two, such as that in a questionnaire. The questions and the words used in a questionnaire are selected by the interviewer and are partly controlled by what he thinks the informant is like as a person. This bias undoubtedly influences the informant, who can never be exactly what the researcher has thought him, and it causes the informant to change his behavior, perhaps ever so slightly, but nevertheless to change it, when he reacts to the stimuli presented to him by the researcher.

In evaluating the social relation between the interviewer and his informant and the demands made on the informant by the researcher, we find at one extreme the ideal interview, with a complete statement of the present and past participation of the individual in his society, and, at the other, the informant who refuses to talk or who lies systematically and thereby communicates no valid information. If the former ideal is to be approximated and the latter impasse avoided, the definition of the relation between informant and interviewer must be clearly understood, and the kind of behavior demands likely to arise known and carefully organized by the interviewer. It must be clearly understood that information is always gathered in the context of a relation of reciprocal interaction and that all facts gathered are necessarily contingent on this condition. The interviewer, consequently, should have a thorough understanding of himself and of the kinds of influence he exerts on various types of people, and he should develop techniques for discounting the resulting bias in the interview situation.

b. The Objectives of the Interview. Since the general objective of our research was to determine the complete set of social relations which constituted the Yankee City society, the general objective of a series of interviews with a particular informant was to learn his total participation in those social relations. The interviewer, therefore, wanted to know the time, place, frequency, and duration of the relations of his informants with other individuals, the kinds of physical and verbal behavior which occurred under such circumstances, and what was thought and said about it. The various contexts of social interaction in which each informant participated were ultimately related with those of other informants until the whole fabric of interrelationships which is the society was known.

The first objective of an interview with a particular individual was to discover his approximate place in the society. Any researcher looking at our own society knows in advance that the individual being studied is a member of a family, that he probably has an occupation, that he is likely to be a Protestant, Catholic, or Jew, that he will have a certain income status, and that he may belong to some kind of association. By his appearance, the interviewer can determine his sex and, within limits, his age. Common knowledge provides a rough general framework within which a given individual must be placed; the task of the interviewer is to ascertain the specific social position occupied by the informant. Beginning with general information about family and church membership, participation in associations, income, occupation, residence, and the like—information verifiable by the testimony of other individuals, by the use of documents, and by other techniques —the interviewer proceeds to examine more and more specifically the exact social relations of his informant until he is able to define adequately the entire social context in which the individual interacts. Then he can turn his attention to the events in this context of relationships.

c. *The Role of the Interviewer and the Rules Governing His Behavior in the Interviewer-Informant Relationship.* The informant brings to his dyadic relation with the interviewer a set of present and past relations about which the interviewer attempts to learn; the interviewer also brings a somewhat similar set of past and present relations which he must not allow to bias or interfere with the talk of the informant. Psychoanalysis early pointed out that there are two important factors which interfere with the informant's talking about himself. The first is a conscious and unconscious "resistance" to describing his own private life, the second is a tendency, with the establishment of continuing social relations, for one or both of the people involved to allow their sentiments to operate directly in their relationship and so bias the informant's account. The student of society has neither the time nor the immediate interest in his informants to attempt to enter into the realm of the unconscious explored by so-called "depth psychology." His objective is achieved when his informant is talking easily and freely about all the present and past behavior of which he is conscious.

The techniques to be used in the immediate context of the informant-interviewer relationship have been best stated by F. J. Roethlisberger and W. J. Dickson.[3] Although their emphasis tends to be more on the individual and less on the individual's social relations, the same operations for obtaining information hold in either context. Roethlisberger and Dickson cite five rules for the control of the immediate relations of the interviewer to his informant:

1. The interviewer should listen to the speaker [informant] in a patient and friendly, but intelligently critical, manner.

3. F. J. Roethlisberger and William J. Dickson, *Management and the Worker* (Cambridge, Harvard University Press, 1939), p. 287.

2. The interviewer should not display any kind of authority.

3. The interviewer should not give advice or moral admonition.

4. The interviewer should not argue with the speaker [informant].

5. The interviewer should talk or ask questions only under certain conditions:

    a. To help the person talk.

    b. To relieve any fears or anxieties on the part of the speaker [informant] which may be affecting his relation to the interviewer.

    c. To praise the interviewee for reporting his thoughts and feelings accurately.

    d. To veer the discussion to some topic which has been omitted or neglected.

    e. To discuss implicit assumptions, if this is advisable.

A skilled interviewer, Roethlisberger and Dickson add, ". . . [should] guard against having fixed and preconceived ideas which would prevent him from catching anything new; on the other hand, he [should] guard against allowing the interview to become incoherent because of no guiding hypothesis." [4] In other words, "free association" should be allowed within the area of general interest. While the interviewer listens to what is being said, he should follow certain simple rules of interpretation:

I. The interviewer should keep what is said in an interview as an item in a context.

    A. The interviewer should not pay exclusive attention to the manifest content of the intercourse.

    B. The interviewer should not treat everything that is said as either fact or error.

    C. The interviewer should not treat everything that is said as being at the same psychological level.

II. The interviewer should listen not only to what a person wants to say but also to what he does not want to say or cannot say without help.

III. The interviewer should treat the mental contexts described in the preceding rule as indices and seek through them the personal reference that is being revealed.

4. *Ibid.*, p. 271.

IV. The interviewer should keep personal reference in its social context.[5]

The interviewing attitude is a pleasant, friendly one which is always affirmative. When questions are asked, they should not betray any emotion but that of interest. The questions should point the informant's attention to what is important to the research, but they should be phrased to appear as remarks rather than questions in order to minimize their chance of biasing the reply.

When interviewing in a community, the role of the interviewer must change according to the context in which he finds himself. This demands extreme flexibility in the personality of the researcher, and but few men or women are "all-around" interviewers. Some may succeed in bringing excellent interviews from the parishioners of a church or from the social elite but fail miserably when trying to find out what a worker or a hard-boiled politician is thinking about. The surrounding social and physical situations differ enormously in a sociological program of interviewing. There may be one or twenty people present and the interview may take place in the cell of a jail or at a Sunday School picnic. The interviewer may either let his informant know he is consciously interviewing or disguise the fact. Many of our best interviews took place when the subject of the analysis was unaware of being studied.

Most discussions of interviewing methods center upon the informant rather than upon the interviewer, but from what has just been said it is apparent that the latter should receive careful scrutiny. The researcher must acquire the art and discipline to control himself in the interview relation. In the present study, training in the theory and methods of social anthropology was held to satisfy this prerequisite, and all the interviewers were so trained by the director of the research.

Ordinarily it is not difficult to get people to talk on almost any subject. (For many people in Yankee City the most difficult subject was not sex or religion, as we had anticipated, but the way they spent their money. One lady "went to bed for several days because of nervous exhaustion" after a long interview in which she divulged the amount she spent and the sepa-

---

5. *Ibid.*, pp. 272–273.

rate items of her budget.) The question is: Why do many people, even when unaided, talk so freely? One reason is that their lives are often a series of minor and major crises to which they must constantly make adjustment. Most of the topics which are of deep interest to them are the commonplaces of life in which the ordinary person has little interest. The interviewer never shows boredom, he always listens, and he rarely talks. This attitude invites what is known as conversation by the informant. When a man talks about his troubles and the things which worry him in order to "get them off his chest," it is the task of the researcher to help but not influence him while he does this.

The problem of adequate sampling in the study of Yankee City was a twofold one: we had to have an assurance that we had covered extensively all the social situations found in this modern community and that at the same time we had studied intensively the several types of situations found. This demanded that we interview systematically with the purpose of surveying the variety of situations and, having discovered them, that we put interviewers in strategic places and with properly equipped informants in order to obtain the requisite detailed analysis that was finally necessary. Thus we combined extensive with intensive interviewing in addition to the use of other techniques.

The problem of verification has been briefly alluded to. The researcher does not always know whether he is being lied to or whether he is being told the "truth." However, the information gathered about social relations is always social fact if the informant believes it, and it is always fact of another kind if he tells it and does not believe it. If the informant does not believe it, the lie he tells is frequently more valuable as a lead to understanding his behavior or that of others than the truth. The danger of being misled by deliberate lying is greatly reduced by the repetition of interviews with a single informant and by corroborative interviews with many individuals in each relational context.

Indirect verification by the means just noted is not always necessary. Certain statements can be objectively checked completely and by direct means. Thus the income a man says he has may be checked against the pay roll lists of the factory which employs him. Other statements made during an interview are partly verifiable by similar means. The rules of evidence in the social sciences will become more secure as we further analyze our operations into explicitly known behavior, and as we do this, it seems likely that more of our information will be directly verifiable and that we shall develop better criteria of indirect verification.

B. Observation

While interviewing, the researcher is observing the voluntary and involuntary behavior associated with the verbalizations of the informant. Of this variety of observation we have spoken, and we have separated it from the type which will now be described. We can discriminate between a research situation in which the interviewer is actively engaged in establishing relations with the subject of his interest and directing the relationships so established, and one in which the researcher is an onlooker and cannot be said to be an active factor in the situation under observation except in a most secondary and minor way. Two varieties of inactive observation may be distinguished: one in which the researcher is still in part a minor participant in the situation he is examining, and the other in which he is completely on the outside.

Observations of this latter variety conducted by the Yankee City group of researchers included the study of certain factories, retail stores, and banks, of the mass activities of a strike, of the meetings associated with loss of income and unemployment, of sacred and secular rituals such as those on Memorial Day, and of the ceremonies of the churches and associations. The *rites de passage* surrounding marriage, birth, and death were observed. The police desk, with its flow of arrests, convictions, and discharges, was kept under long-term observation and the behavior of such officials as the truant officer and the policeman on the beat was studied. The mayor's office, the poor-relief, the health office, the office of the superintendent of schools, with their several systems of behavior were each observed by one or more fieldworkers. In the schoolhouses and the schoolyards the relations of teachers, of pupils, and of each to the other and to the principal were recorded over periods of time by field workers.

When the factories were studied, the plant as a physical object and as an arrangement of concrete objects in spatial relations was first examined and its several functions noted. The workers' behavior was studied in relation to the tools and machines, then to each other, and finally to the foremen and managers. When the employees went out on strike, their parading and picketing behavior was recorded. The complex relations of the union officials, the workers, and the owners were observed in detail, as were the meetings of the workers and those of the managers when the representatives of the larger community entered into the conflict.

The Memorial Day ceremonies, organized as a tribute of respect by the whole community to those who had served it in the crises of war, provided opportunities of participation to churches and other social groups. Interviewing was carried on before, during, and after the several events, while the words and actions of the participants were recorded by a score of observers stationed at cemeteries, monuments, and churches, and along the route of the parade which gave communal unity to the entire ceremony. This same general procedure was followed at marriages and funerals as well as at the church and lodge ceremonies we were allowed to attend. The role of the observer here changes according to whether it is expedient for him to admit that he is an observer or merely to act as an interested participant or spectator.

Observers were also placed at the moving-picture house to see who attended the pictures and with whom they came. The ticket seller and the cashier aided us in identifying most of the individuals who were not known to the field workers. The one large magazine and newsstand in the community also had an observer to compile a list of those who bought magazines and papers and to find out what journals were purchased.

The virtues of a combination of interview and observation are manifold. When these two techniques are used to check each other, they unquestionably yield the most valuable insight into the life of the community. No other technique proves so helpful to the fieldworker in uncovering new varieties of phenomena, in forcing him to test his guiding hypotheses in the light of new facts, and in taxing his ingenuity to formulate new practical methods. The interview is the most flexible of field techniques and can be expanded and contracted in its scope to meet the general needs of a study in its opening phases and to answer the more detailed investigations of particular problems incident to the later period of research.

Despite all these virtues, when the research must study a whole society, interview and observation techniques have certain definite limitations. They are time-consuming and consequently greatly limit the extent and variety of social relations which can be studied in the field. It is impossible to quantify all the relations and phenomena under investigation by the interview technique alone if the society being studied exceeds a few thousand in population. The number of investigators required would be too large to make it financially possible, and if a smaller force were used over a longer period of time, too many changes would take place in the social relations. Other techniques, such as the schedule, the questionnaire, and the collection of written documents, can be used when the object of study has been carefully defined by observation and interview.

C. The Questionnaire and the Schedule

The questionnaire and schedule are research tools which provide the quickest and easiest method of gathering selected data. Their entries can be readily analyzed because they ordinarily are designed for immediate transfer to statistical punch cards. The research in Yankee City did not use questionnaires except under very special circumstances when it was believed that the ordinary errors of measurement to which this method is liable had been eliminated or reduced to unimportance.

Though easy, the questionnaire lends itself to statistical manipulation; the data obtained can be arranged in tables to prove almost anything the researcher's original bias or predisposition dictates. Consequently it does not usually reach the underlying realities of the social situation being examined. Items of behavior are too frequently taken out of their social context and placed in direct relation with other items which have been taken out of other contexts, and the conclusions are then drawn after the statistical operations have been carried out. The results are anything but adequate. Discriminations not made when the data are gathered cannot, with rare exceptions, be made at a later stage. The statistical method itself is not to be blamed, as is sometimes done, since the results can be no better than the facts collected.

The use of the questionnaire at the beginning of a research implies that the researcher knows the general nature of the area under investigation and that his questions are designed to find out certain specific relationships. This assumption is partly justified since the questionnaire can be used properly only for limited objectives and is not to be thought of as a technique for a research when the hypotheses are constantly undergoing change in the light of new data. The bias of the researcher is implicit within the framework and the detail of a questionnaire or schedule. The answers to the questionnaire are not answers to the questions asked but to what the subject thinks is being asked, and there is little or no opportunity for the fieldworker using such a technique to discover the difference. The same question or set of questions can elicit consistent misunderstandings which may indicate fictitious uniformities or differences.

In the Yankee City field work we inquired very carefully into the general and specific situation by means of interviews before we asked ourselves whether or not a schedule was necessary and could be used. If a particular situation seemed to call for it, we sometimes used a schedule or questionnaire, but always with extreme caution and only when we felt that we could anticipate fairly accurately the replies from different classes of informants.

If the general limits of the area under investigation are clearly defined, if the specific relations within the social context have been isolated and also defined, if the several behavioral modes within the relationship have been observed and defined, the problem of quantification may then be attacked. It becomes important to know how many times a relation occurs within a given context and how many times one kind of behavior as compared with another takes place in the situation under observation. At this point the schedule or questionnaire was sometimes used. For example, when the general ethnic organization and the various internal relations of the several ethnic groups had been studied and their several types of interrelation with the larger community had been investigated, it became important to know how many social relations of the various types there were and how many individuals were acting within the several relations. To gain an adequate understanding of how the ethnics were or were not maintaining their social unity, we examined their behavior in the city schools. The social organization of the school and of the ethnics had been studied. Since we knew the relations we wanted quantified and had determined what questions and what answers pertained to this situation, it was with a minimum of difficulty and error that we ascertained just how many ethnics were involved in these relations.

Schedules and questionnaires were used to study the income and expenditures of a selected number of families in Yankee City. The budget study was a very detailed analysis of the income and outgo of money in the various kinds of families within the social structure of Yankee City. The schedule itself consisted of forty-one mimeographed sheets, each of which required a detailed set of answers. The larger divisions of the schedule called for a description of the family, a description of the residence, a statement of the income of the several members, and information on the following: rent or shelter, food, clothing, house operation, automobile, amusement, charity, education, gifts given, medical expense, mortuary expense, taxes, travel and vacation, surplus, savings and investments, payment on debts, and many other smaller items.

A similar method was used in our ethnic survey. A schedule called "Historical and Genealogical Census of the Schools of New England," with two pages of detailed questions, was prepared for use in the schools. It was designed to secure the following information: name and address of student, age, school and grade, country, province, or city of birth, languages spoken, churches and church schools attended, nationality or racial descent of each parent, place of birth of each parent, year and age when each parent arrived in America, country in which the four grandparents were born, their present residence, occupation of each, names and places of residence of siblings, time of arrival of the mother's and father's families in Yankee City, places they had lived before coming to the community, names and ages of brothers and sisters in school or out, clubs and the friends of the father, and the names of the English and foreign-language magazines and newspapers which were read in the home.

The teachers were told what was wanted and they, in turn, instructed the children. In addition to this, the students were told that the information was confidential, impersonal, and scientific, and that the questionnaire had the backing of the mayor, the superintendent of schools, the pastors of the two Catholic churches and the Jewish synagogue, and other important people in the community. They were informed that the co-operation of the parents was also essential, since we wanted to write not only about the Yankees of the community but also about other important ethnic groups.

Through automobile traffic, the relations of transients with the natives of Yankee City were studied. Where the main artery of traffic traverses one of the better residential areas, the houses are of poor quality and the people in them are of lower-income status. At the entrance and exit of the through highway stand the usual gasoline stations, quick-lunch stands, and other small enterprises which serve the traveler and are related to the traffic rather than to the citizens of the town. Some of the phenomena of social "breakdown" as studied by Park, Burgess, and their group seemed to be present.[6] After interviewing and observing, a questionnaire designed to find out the number of automobiles and passengers that entered, left, or passed through Yankee City, was prepared to study the social composition of the traffic. The several questions included: where the car came from; where it was going; where the purchases of gas, oil, meals, and other goods were made in Yankee City; how many people were in the car; what their sex, age, and occupations were; what type of car or truck was being used; and whether the trip was for business or pleasure. We sampled the kinds of individuals who went through the town and the nature of their contacts with Yankee City. State surveys had given us the totals per hour for the different days of the week. Our sampling made it possible to work out a classification of the total traffic flow and the percentages of transients and natives involved in it.

This study helped us to understand better one of the most

6. See such references as: Robert E. Park, Ernest W. Burgess, and Roderick D. McKenzie, *The City* (Chicago, University of Chicago Press, 1925); and Clifford R. Shaw, *Natural History of a Delinquent Career* (Chicago, University of Chicago Press, 1931).

obvious effects of the automobile, namely, the tremendous increase in lateral mobility which it facilitates. The automobile is said to have wrought as fundamental a change in the life of the American people as did the introduction of the horse in the Plains Indian culture. It has generally been assumed that the change is largely in the direction of disorganization, but not all indications point in this direction. There has been, for example, an extension of the individual's contacts with people outside the community; he may visit people in other towns and thus maintain reciprocal relations with them. At the same time this extension of the spatial range of social interaction tends to weaken the primary contacts of the immediate community.

When the size of the community is considered and the multiplicity of relations noted, it will be seen why the schedule and questionnaire were used only to a limited extent and for special purposes.

D. Case Histories, Biographies, Life Histories, and Autobiographies

The case history was not employed as a field technique in the Yankee City research itself. However, a large number were collected from various social agencies which had made them, including child-placement bureaus, social service agencies, public and private mental hospitals, and the public-welfare agency.

Biographies and autobiographies of former members of the society were also collected. The lives of several successful shoe manufacturers and bankers were documented in this manner, giving us the detailed story of the rise of a man and his family from poverty and obscurity to prominence and wealth. The lives of several political personalities were available in biographies and autobiographies, as were the personal histories of certain artists. The variant behavior of the eccentric, either as personally recorded or as it was observed and treated with scorn and ridicule in the writings of fellow townsmen, furnished excellent material for the analysis of approved and disapproved behavior.

The interview technique merges into that of the life history when interviews are multiplied and the individuals are encouraged to talk about their own public and private life. However, the life history as such was not used as an important part of the Yankee City research. It is best used to reach levels of human mentality in which we were not directly interested, and it has, in an exaggerated form, the chief weakness of the interview since it consumes time and confines the attention of the research to a very circumscribed field.

Partial diaries and scrapbooks containing details of the intimate life of the possessor were also collected. These yielded a mass of highly useful and valuable material, covering the widest range of interests: poems which the individual had saved and memorized; speeches and sermons he thought expressed his belief in religion, politics, ethics, and other subjects of deep import to him; articles which gave his ideals of love and parenthood; and descriptions of natural and local events which held his interest. The selection of materials in the scrapbooks of members of the ethnic groups clearly showed their ambivalent feelings about participation in the larger community. Interviews based on items from these sources greatly enhanced their value.

E. Genealogies and Kinship Charts

Genealogies and kinship charts proved valuable since they gave us a precise statement of the relations of individuals and, when supplemented by interviewing, elicited attitudes about approved and disapproved behavior of various kin relations. The relations found within the immediate family were directly observable, and public documents were available which gave us the membership of individual households. However, the extended kinship relations which bring together the smaller units into a larger interactive system could be defined systematically only by the use of the genealogies. Since the community is an old and settled one, a large number of the families had their genealogies in written form, but in many cases it was necessary for the researcher to collect the kinship relations by interviewing and constructing his own genealogical charts. The extended kinship relations of all groups in the community were sampled in great detail, and charts were made which demonstrated the interconnectedness on a kinship basis of hundreds and sometimes of thousands of people. These charts clearly demonstrate that kinship in our own society, far from being the moribund type of relationship of which many have accused it, is a vital structure which organizes much of the lives of the members of the community and gives them a firm place in the total society.

Not all of the genealogical records in Yankee City are those of human beings; the "old houses" also have their "genealogies." A house is often spoken of as though it were a person and is given a social position by referring to the prominent families who have owned it. Since many houses go through successive generations of kin, the house genealogy is something more than a mere analogy.

F. Documentary and Other Written Material

Documents of several types were collected: lists, directories, the records, rules, and histories of institutions, the regulations governing the community, and the like. Material of a documentary character was gathered for the following social groups and institutions: the general community and its government, the several ethnic groups, the economic organizations, the family, the schools, the churches, lodges and other associations, the library and the theater and cinema. Membership lists of the several hundred associations were systematically collected as were those of the several churches. Lists of pupils, voters, customers of stores, and city officials were compiled. All the names of those persons buried in the several cemeteries were gathered and compilations were made of the members of several ethnic groups. The editors of most of the current periodicals and magazines were solicited for a list of their subscribers in Yankee City; all but two of them sent us this valuable material. The lists of subscribers to all the Boston newspapers and to the local paper were also collected.

Lists of members of formal groups and of persons engaged in the same activities are exceedingly valuable since they make possible the exact placement of individuals in a variety of social relations. When this procedure is systematically carried through for all institutions of all the types, the task of socially placing the members of the total community is greatly facilitated. Such lists ordinarily give the researcher but one kind of information about the individuals represented: they include all these persons in, and exclude all others from, a particular direct relation.

Directories such as the city directory or the poll-tax book give more information than do ordinary lists. In addition to the names of the members of a group, a directory locates these individuals ecologically. Directories frequently give additional information, e.g., as to family membership and the sex, age, and occupation of the adults. With a knowledge of residence, the full name of the individual, his probable family relations, and his sex and age, the chances of error due to the confusion of identical first and last names are greatly lessened, and the information collected by interview from informants about other individuals can ordinarily be correctly identified.

The records of the various institutions are even more complex. They usually give information about both the individual and collective activities of the members of a group during a particular period of time. Our economic records, for instance, include the employment and pay cards of several large factories. They provided us with occupation and income records over a long period of time, by the week and by the season, of a large number of the gainfully employed of Yankee City. The working certificates given to subadults also yielded much information about employment and occupation, as did the unemployment records of the state. The census of the Federal Government, although very useful as a guide in helping us estimate the sizes of various groups, was of little use otherwise since it did not give the names of individuals and since it covered only one of the political units of Yankee City.

The annual reports of the departments of the city government, including those of the mayor, the council, the assessor, the health and school administration, were surveyed. The assessor's records gave us data as to the value and legal ownership of the real and personal property, enabling us to determine, for example, who were the landholders. The records of the public-welfare office told us the income of certain individuals and families and when this information was assembled for a number of previous years, certain families were isolated as permanent paupers or parasitic groups. When these data were later related to the discharges of employees from the factories during the depression, we knew which industries depended on the bounty of the community to support their employees for them during periods when the industry did not want them.

The health office gave us detailed records of the incidence of various diseases, including syphilis, gonorrhea, smallpox, diphtheria, typhoid fever, and measles. From this source, also, we were informed of the infractions of rules for the regulation of various enterprises such as restaurants, butcher shops, slaughterhouses, and dairies. The records of one of the minor industries, that of clamming, were available from the health office. The complete vital statistics of marriage, births, and deaths were collected for a three-year period, then for the same span of time at ten-year intervals back to 1900, and from there for less frequent intervals back to 1840. Their use in placing people in their family relations supplemented our other genealogical material and greatly aided us in building up our knowledge of the extended kinship structure.

The police records over a seven-year period, which were also collected, included information on those who had broken the law and the disposition of their cases, as well as on the kinds of crimes committed and on individual recidivism. The age and sex of the offender were given; hence juvenile delinquents could be distinguished. When the material from these records was correlated with information from the police and other sources, it became possible to discover how criminality was defined in Yankee City. The relation of liability to arrest, for certain actions, to the social status of an individual, and to his ethnic membership was determined by such means. The records of the truant officers, when supplemented with interviews, police records, and newspaper material, told us who the delinquents were, what gangs they belonged to, and what their social place was in the larger community.

The records of school attendance placed the younger individuals in the educational system and related the sex and age divisions to the formal school structure. In addition to these school records, the routines of the classroom were observed; and the private estimates which some of the teachers had written on the social and moral qualities of their students were obtained. The attendance records of the churches and the commemorative volumes of the hundredth anniversary of several of them provided invaluable information on these institutions.

The reading habits of the community were studied, not only from magazines and newspaper subscription lists, but also by securing the titles of all the books loaned at the local library during a given period of time and obtaining the names of all the borrowers for the preceding year. The records of the book and reading clubs were also gathered and, to complete our study of reading habits, the newsstands were watched to see who bought what papers and magazines.

Records of individual attendance at the movies were made for different periods of time, with names, addresses, and sex and age distribution. The box-office receipts of the theaters told us how many people had gone to the movies and at what times. A list of the motion pictures shown with a brief digest of each told us the kinds of pictures the people saw. Advertisements were culled from the local papers and classed according to the appeal made. The plots of the plays presented by high school and other local groups were also collected and analyzed. We found that the plots and their dramatic presentations clearly conformed to the standards of the local group. The same was also true of many of the motion pictures, but not all of them, and the failure of the pictures to express accurately the sentiments of the community created a problem for the group to face and the research to study.

The three-hundredth anniversary of the state had just been celebrated when our research began, and records of the parades and other dramatic rites were obtained from the scrapbooks which the directors in the city had carefully compiled.

The written rules and regulations of the several institutions studied constituted in many ways the most valuable documentary material we found. They defined the formal relations which were expected of the members of the group, and indicated the sanctions applicable to the infraction of rules. From the intensity of the sanctions it was possible to estimate the relative importance of the various rules. Many documents, indeed, expressly explained why certain rules were important.

The classified laws of the state provided the legal regulations regarding the behavior which was approved and disapproved in all institutions, especially, however, in the family, economic institutions, and the several political structures. The ordinances and laws of the local government were also gathered, as were those which pertained to the formal organization of the departments of education, health, taxation, etc. A similar analysis was made of the rules governing the various churches and associations, including those regulating rites and ceremonies. In many cases these gave an official explanation of the sacred mysteries.

During the long period of Yankee City's existence, a number of histories have been written, mainly by local authors, about certain aspects of the life of the community. They are replete with the names of families, people, and institutions of the town, and tend to emphasize selectively those persons in the past who are of significance to the members of the present society. This selective tendency frequently gives the researcher very valuable information on the movement of certain families up or down the social ladder and on the appearance, development, and disappearance of various social institutions. A partial history of certain ethnic groups has been written by interested members of these communities.

G. The Newspapers

The daily newspaper of Yankee City, which has a purely local circulation, usually consists of some eight pages of news and advertising. A large part of its news is gathered from the town itself, for the newspaper is largely concerned with intracommunity affairs. At the beginning of the research, a number of the issues of the newspaper were gone over by our research group and temporary classifications of various items in the paper were made. Each item was then dated; if it covered several subjects, cross references were made. The items were then cut out, placed in folders, and filed in alphabetical order. The classification used was not a sociological one but was entirely pragmatic and empirical. For example, although we had a folder marked "associations" which covered a large number of the smaller clubs, there were also individual folders for the American Legion, Rotary, Knights of Columbus, and other associations on which the news columns carried a large amount of material. A random sample of other headings included automobiles, banks, Chamber of Commerce, classified advertisements, health, jails, and courts. Under these headings was assembled concrete material where the news information was obviously reliable, e.g., on the meetings and activities of the various lodges and of the city council. Above all, they gave us invaluable leads for interviewing.

During the first year of the research project, every item in the newspaper was clipped, including local and national advertisements and syndicated columns (the daily short story and a gossip column on New York). At the end of this period, all items were once more examined and reclassified to conform to the general view we had achieved by that time of the society as a whole. This enabled us to evaluate the usefulness of all material with knowledge of the society as criteria. This process materially reduced the number of categories. We stopped collecting the syndicated "boiler-plate" material and a large part of the advertising, since we believed that a year's collection of these data was sufficient for an analysis of the total content of the paper. Some two hundred categories remained. The paper was clipped and analyzed for three years, at the end of which time the thousands of items collected were finally classified in conformity with our analysis of the social structure of Yankee City.

Our files included 18 subcategories on the family, 47 on economic organization, about 150 on associations, some 40 on the city government, 25 on the churches, and 16 on sports, as well as a small number of miscellaneous categories. The family file consisted of items on births, engagements, weddings, anniversaries, birthday parties, divorces, and deaths. The news items usually gave the kinship relations of the various people involved, their addresses, and their occupations, as well as the names of the other members of the society who were their immediate friends. On the whole, such material was factual and contained little or no implicit bias since it did not express the social, economic, or religious points of view of the editor.

The associational material gave us a daily account of when and where the associations met and what they did when they were in session. Frequently we were able to supplement our material on membership by the lists given in the newspapers and also to add newly discovered groups to the hundreds we had listed and studied. The political news was very detailed and included the crime and court reports and all the behavior involved in the meetings of the mayor and city council and the several boards. This information often expressed the bias of the editor and the part of the society in which he participated.

The editorial columns as well as certain other parts of the paper provided us with the point of view of one segment of the society on a great variety of subjects. We knew, by the use of the interview, the social position of the editor, the people with whom he was identified, and those to whom he was opposed. The "facts" furnished by the editorials and certain news items were not the concrete verifiable kind referred to in our earlier definition of social facts, but often reflected the attitudes, sentiments, and biases, conscious and unconscious, of the editor. When used to supplement our detailed interviews, and particularly to suggest subjects of discussion, the biased statements of the paper were of great service in the research. We also found the reception given these articles by different classes of people in the community to be highly significant.

In addition to the respectable daily paper, a weekly journal was started while we were in Yankee City. Its purpose was to attack the older paper and, in part, to serve as an organ of expression for one of the important local politicians. All of its news was "highly colored" and very definitely expressed the opinion of the editor. Since we had over a thousand pages of material directly focused on this one person and his behavior, we had, in this paper, an invaluable source of information on how the editor-politician and, in large part, his kind felt about the various classes of people and events in Yankee City. A quotation such as the following, while it does not present a verifiable sequence of "facts," unquestionably expresses certain of the sentiments and attitudes of the editor:

Councillor H at a meeting called Mayor S, while in Detroit, a cur. The Mayor understood that a cur is some kind of a dog. The Mayor doesn't mind being called anything by Councillor H, because Mayor S's father was John J. S of Grand River, West Prince Edward Island, Canada, and his mother was Mrs. Nora C. S, a resident of this city for 45 years and very well known.

The Mayor wonders whether H is a cur or not?

The following clipping, representative of a type, not only gave us the sentiments of the editor but provided us with many research leads:

JUSTICE?

This morning in court the battle of the X manufacturing company had its ending. Mr. James Y, the unfortunate victim of a cowardly assault, was made to sign an agreement that he would not prosecute. If he did, he would be fired! N, K, and E, supposed to be men of standing in the X company, would not let Justice take its course.

Mr. Joseph O should well be ashamed of himself, when he would hit Mr. Y WHILE Y's HANDS WERE OCCUPIED. It shows POOR JUDGEMENT on the part of Judge E's court to allow SUCH a case as this to go without the PROPER COURSE. But what can you expect of E?

In summary, the newspaper served the field research because it provided us with (1) descriptions of the events which took place in the community, (2) indications of the sentiments and attitudes of certain groups, (3) research leads for interviewing, and (4) materials for the study of the paper as a mechanism of communication.

H. THE SURVEYS

A number of surveys were made after the two which opened the research. The geographic distribution of certain phenomena in the community was studied to determine their spatial rather than their social distribution. The houses of Yankee City were classified by several criteria to work out their types and to locate these types in the different areas of the city. Representative houses of the several types were photographed and their architectural features studied.

An airplane survey of the community and its environs was made. The whole of the city was photographed from the plane and the overlapping edges of the pictures were fitted into a mosaic which, when completed, showed in pictorial fashion the physical relations of the community to the world around it and the relations of the several areas of the city to each other.

1. Techniques of Analysis and the First Integrations of the Diverse Materials Collected.

a. The Problem of Collaboration in a Social Research. The constant flow of material gathered by the various field techniques shortly accumulated huge quantities of data, and it became necessary to analyze them for present and future use. The problem was not one of scientific analysis alone but was also one of the collaboration of a large number of people on a single project. All the researchers had to have access to the materials which each of them gathered individually. To make them available, therefore, each interview and set of observations were recorded in duplicate by dictaphone. One copy was kept by the researcher for his own use and the other was filed for the use of the rest of the research staff.

Since the work was divided among various fieldmen, each with his special subject, it was necessary to devise some method of keeping each member informed of what the others were doing and to integrate the work generally. This was one of the principal functions of the director of the research. General conferences were held once a week at which one of the members of the research group presented a report concerning the material thus far gathered on his particular subject. His work was criticized and commented on by the other members of the group. The task of giving a report before his fellows operated to keep each research man active and alert and to stimulate him to keep his interviewing program and materials organized and presentable. At these weekly meetings general instructions were issued by the director, new work was assigned and old work temporarily abandoned, and, all in all, the labors of a clearinghouse were performed. At some meetings specialists from other disciplines were invited to speak on topics bearing upon the research. The director also held weekly conferences with the individual fieldworkers to discuss the problems of the research and lay out new projects. At these individual meetings all the reports which were to be given in the general conference were discussed and criticized by the director. In a work of this kind it was necessary to keep up the group's morale. Unless a high quality were maintained in the reports, the members might become uncertain of themselves and lose interest. There is no doubt that the simple device of preliminary individual conferences helped maintain the confidence and interest of the group to the end.

In addition to the weekly reports, each researcher submitted a yearly report of progress, and also wrote a complete report when other duties took him from the Yankee City research. Thus the earlier integrations of materials on the several ethnic groups, the schools, and the associations were available for the use of the newer recruits to the research and provided material for checking the changes which accompanied the gradual shifts in and clarification of our theoretical system.

The documentary material was indexed and filed according to a classification similar to that described for the ordering of the newspaper files. When the field work closed, all lists, records, and other documentary material were indexed and filed according to a detailed outline we had made for the purposes of preparing our material for publication.

b. Social Personality Cards. Of the various methods employed in assembling our field data, the most important was that which involved the use of what we have called the social personality card. Each individual in the community (except infants) was represented by a card. On these cards, which ultimately totaled nearly 17,000, were entered data abstracted from the original interview sheets and references to the location of pertinent material in the files. This method was carefully adjusted to the general theoretical framework of the whole research. The use of the cards made it possible to check constantly what we were doing in any part of the research and to relate in a meaningful way any new material collected to that which had already been gathered. The personality card was designed to give us a general, but at the same time detailed, view of the total participation of each individual in the society. By a series of cross-indexing devices, it gave the interrelations of each individual with those who were in direct and sometimes indirect relation with him. Usually many of the events occurring in the relations were also entered. While the field work was in progress, an examination of the cards made it possible at any time to compare persons of similar status and contrast those occupying different social places and thus arrive at quick but approximately accurate generalizations. Such tests greatly added to our working knowledge of various parts of the society and guided us as we made further inquiries by interview and observation into the life of the community. When such analyses of a selected set of cards informed us that a specific item of behavior or a set of relations seemed to be of high importance in the society, we used the schedule as a rapid method of gathering material.

At first the cards were made out for each of the several field studies and placed in the general file, but as a result of overlapping in the work, the cards were afterwards filed in alphabetical order. It was impossible to put all the material of the interviews and documents on the cards, and to have done so would have made them too unwieldy for analysis. Selection was necessary and as a consequence the interviews, at the end of the field work, were indexed according to the same outline as the cards.

A brief resumé of the principal items placed on a social personality card will serve to describe and define it as an object and as a technique for analysis. The full name, residence, age, sex, social status, and occupation were entered on the cards of all individuals. The maiden name of the wife and the names of the children were also placed on the card of the husband and father, and the cards of the wife and children were ultimately filed with his. In addition, each card was indexed to make it possible to relate the cards of spouses to those of their siblings and parents living in the community.

On the card of each individual were indicated his memberships in cliques and associations, his church affiliation, his residence and the type of house, the newspapers, magazines, and books he read, and the motion pictures he attended. The physician called in case of illness was noted as well as the undertaker who officiated at funerals in the family. The indexing of the budget material on the card gave the researcher a complete statement of the income and items of expense of the several individuals in the family. A reference to the assessor's records told us whether a person owned or rented his home and, if he owned it, whether he possessed other land in the city.

In the case of the subadult, the card told us his place in school, or, if he had a certificate to work, what kind of work he did and the name of his employer. If the family was dependent upon the public welfare associations because of the unemployment of the head of the family, if any of its members had been arrested in Yankee City between 1927 and 1931, or if any of the children were delinquent, the personality cards noted the fact.

A comparison of the wife's and husband's cards told us if they had married out of their ethnic groups and what the age differential was between them. Comparisons with relatives showed whether an individual had moved up or down in social status. Such comparisons frequently raised significant questions which further research or analysis alone could answer.

c. Statistical Analysis. Once we had decided on the use of statistics, we had to begin a systematic treatment of the material that we had collected in order to secure as large a series of individuals in various categories as possible. The first step in such a process was to make out an inventory of everything that we had and to list in this inventory all the kinds of information, and location thereof, in our social personality cards, lists, and other records. With this complete inventory as a basis, we proceeded to outline the possible ways in which the materials could be specifically treated. Upon the advice of Dr. E. B. Wilson and Dr. Karl Doering of Harvard University, we prepared a tentative statistical code. First, we set up the factors we wanted to measure as column headings, giving each column a title. In each column were listed its divisions, each represented by a hole on a punch card. Next we stated the problems to be solved in each column. Finally, we listed all correlations with other columns in the statistical code which promised to contribute to the solution of problems in the specific column.

The process may be clarified by a few concrete examples. The statement of problems in the ethnic column, for instance, follows:

What is the distribution of the individuals in ethnic groups? How are the ethnics distributed in number among the fixed classes? What are the comparative ranges within the social stratification of the different ethnic groups, and what are the proportions of an ethnic group in a given class?

A second illustration is taken from the column on the age of individuals:

We are interested in age not only as a biological phenomenon—the biological composition of Yankee City—but also as a principle for organizing social relationship. In this and other kinds of age columns, we will attempt to examine the age-graded structure from the point of view of the biological age range. We want to examine the relation of this age-graded structure to social stratification and to see what relation, if any, exists between the age-graded structure and the ethnic groups, and to study the interrelationship of social stratification, ethnic groups, and age-grading structures.

A last example may be taken from the statement prefixing the column dealing with kinship:

We are interested in finding out the relation between the social stratification of ego and the social stratification of the kinship personality in his family of orientation and procreation. In other words, how much social mobility is there in the family and in what type of relationship does the greatest amount of it occur? We are trying to find this out for the various social classes and the ethnic group. (Note: We can treat only those individuals who have relations within the family who live in Yankee City and can thus be stratified.)

The last quotation illustrates a practical problem which had to be overcome. Our data, being centered on individuals, lent themselves readily to the statistical compilation and correlation of the attributes and relational characteristics of individuals. Difficulties arose, however, when it became necessary to compare one relation between individuals with another, e.g., kinship structure with class stratification.

To measure such kinship relations as those of father to son, for example, in reference to the class position of each, new statistical devices had to be developed to conform to the limitations of our system of punch cards. The social class of a child could readily be compared with that of the father, of course, if we had one column for the social status of the person represented by a particular card and another column for the class position of his father. The reverse procedure, namely, the comparison of father with child in respect to class position, presented a difficulty in the case of a man who had a number of children. It would have been possible only to have lumped all the children together, giving the number of higher, equal, and lower class. Our resolution of the problem, however, was to decide arbitrarily not to study the relation in these terms. Even in correlating child to parent in terms of their relative class position, there was the difficulty that the tabulation would show as many parents as there were children, e.g., indicating six fathers in a family with six children. This difficulty was overcome by introducing a column giving the number of siblings. Thus a sample result would show, for example, that in siblingships of seven there are so-and-so many individuals of the same social class as their father.

In what was probably the most important and interesting aspect of the entire research, we worked out empirically, by direct observation of a fairly large sample of the total population, the existence of six stratified social classes.[7] The problem then arose of ascertaining the class position of the rest of the population on the basis of the data available concerning their social personalities. We had already noted that the membership of certain associations had a well-defined class range. The N Club, for example, included no members lower than the lower-upper class in the social scale; the Z Society none lower than upper-middle; the C Club none below lower-middle; and so on. When individuals not in our original sample belonged to several of these class-limited associations, it proved possible to place them fairly accurately in the class structure.

In dealing statistically with the class position of husbands and wives, another problem arose. Our detailed knowledge of individuals frequently indicated a different class position for husband and wife. Interviews and observation, however, showed that when a man or a woman who had married into a lower class continued to be accepted by the members of his own class, the spouse was ordinarily accepted as well. We therefore intro-

---

7. Upper-upper (UU); lower-upper (LU); upper-middle (UM); lower-middle (LM); upper-lower (UL); and lower-lower (LL). See chap. v for an explanation of how we determined six classes.

duced the convention of treating husbands and wives, for statistical purposes, as belonging to the same social class. In order to have a measure of class movement through marriage, we introduced a special column for the social class of the spouse's father, which could be correlated with ego's own class position. This convention enabled us to avoid many controversial questions of class placement in individual cases of hypergamy.

Other adjustments were necessitated by the fact that our material was collected over a number of years, specifically, from 1930 to 1934. All ages were adjusted to a single base, the year 1934. Obviously, moreover, our total number of individuals, 16,785, do not correspond to the population of Yankee City at any one time, but are somewhat larger owing to increments and decrements through birth, death, and changes of residence.

The columns in the code include data of two principal kinds. The material in many columns may be said to be of a symbolic nature, that is, indirectly rather than directly connected with the relationships of individuals. Examples would be the columns dealing with magazine subscriptions, wages, rent, value of property, and type of house. The material in other columns bears directly upon the relationships of individuals. In some instances the relationships are defined with considerable precision, as in the columns dealing with the family, kinship, class position, age, and sex. More often, however, as in the columns dealing with ethnic group, church affiliation, clique membership, location of residence, and occupation, the social relations, though indicated, are not precisely defined. For example, although we may be informed of an individual's church affiliation, we do not know whether he is a minister, a deacon, an ordinary member, or even a nonmember affiliated through his family or parish relations.

A few columns present information about certain time aspects of relations. Thus we have data on length of employment and whether rent is paid by the week or by the month, which can be related to occupation, class position, ethnic group membership, etc. A time element is also revealed in many correlations, e.g., the comparison of son and father in respect to class position. On the whole, however, the data bear upon synchronic rather than diachronic relations.

IV
GENERAL DESCRIPTION OF YANKEE CITY

YANKEE CITY is situated on a harbor at the mouth of a large river in New England. The pilot of an airplane looking down some 10,000 feet might see the harbor as the dark hand of a giant with its five fingers reaching for the sea, and the river flowing through the brown land toward the white sandy shores as an arm extended straight back from the hand and then bending sharply some few miles from the sea. The streets of the town run along the banks of the river for a few miles up from the harbor until they almost reach the bend in the river.

In shape the town is a long thin rectangle which bends at each end. Near the center of the rectangle at the bank of the river is a square around which the business district is located. The residential area covers the two ends of the rectangle as they extend up and down the river. From the two ends of the town square a highway runs out along the water front for the full length of the town. This river street is paralleled, on the other long side of the rectangle, by another broad street which runs along a ridge of high ground from one end of the city to the other. In the center of the city the residential area projects beyond the outline of the rectangle for a few blocks, and a number of dwellings are found outside the rectangle at either end, but, generally speaking, the population is concentrated within the few blocks of streets between the river and the broad street which parallels it on the ridge. The town sits on high ground with a river on one side and flatlands on the other.

The two long avenues are connected by a large number of side streets which cross several short streets as they climb from the river to the summit of the hill. A highway, one of the more important motor roads connecting southern with northern New England, crosses the center of Yankee City and leaves it over a large bridge. A railway line parallels this highway and has a station in the town.

Along the river are a large number of wharves and shipyards which were once employed in the sea trade but which were abandoned when the town turned to manufacturing. Most of the factory sites are in and near the business district, but a few are situated in each arm of the rectangle. The residences tend to be larger and better kept on the Hill Street than on the River Street side of the town. There are six cemeteries in the community and one fairly large park and a few small ones.

Several smaller towns are situated in the surrounding countryside. Yankee City maintains its own economic life and is not a satellite community to a large city. It does, however, look to Boston as its metropolis, and movement to and from Boston by automobile and train is frequent. Some of its citizens look ultimately to New York, but none of them would admit it; a very few of them look to Europe for their social centers, and all of these admit it.

Yankee City has some 17,000 people.[1] There are a few more women in its population than there are men. Slightly over 50 per cent of the population were born in or near Yankee City; 23.50 per cent were foreign-born; and the remainder were born elsewhere in the United States. The first impression one gains of the town is that it has a living tradition inherited from generations of Yankee forebears. Yankee City is "old Yankee" and proud of it.

About one fourth of the employable population are in the shoe industry. The other principal but smaller economic activities are silverware manufacturing, the building trades, transport, and electric shops. The clamming industry, the only remaining economic activity of the town which depends on the sea, employs about 1 per cent of those who work for a living.

1. The reader will notice as he goes through the pages of this and the following volumes that our samples of the population vary according to the subject under investigation. The census reports for Yankee City give but 15,000 people, but these reports cover only the incorporated large town of Yankee City and do not include the population of the several areas outside the incorporated community which are a part of the town. In addition to the people who live in near-by areas and who are part of the social system of the community, many people come in from outside communities such as Boston and even New York and are a part of the social system. This volume on the class system includes some 16,785 people for its largest sample. The volume on the status system includes more people since we were able to add to our list members of families and associations who came into the city for social purposes.

The semiskilled workers constitute the largest group (46.19 per cent) in our occupational sample. The workers in the factories compose the great bulk of this group. Only 5.28 per cent are classifiable as unskilled.[2] The professional,[3] proprietary, and managerial group comprise a seventh of those economically occupied; wholesale and retail store managers and similar proprietors, 7.92 per cent; clerks and kindred workers, 14.90 per cent; and skilled workers, 11.37 per cent. When the unemployment study was made in 1933, 50.73 per cent of those who were employable had jobs at which they were working,[4] 30.61 per cent were employed part-time, and 18.66 per cent were without work. A little over 13 per cent of the total population were recipients of relief.

According to ethnic affiliations, the Yankees comprised 53.80 per cent (9,030) of the 16,785 individuals represented in our study, and the nine other ethnic groups, 45.55 per cent (7,646).[5] There were 3,943 Irish, 1,466 French Canadians, 397 Jews, 284 Italians, 677 Poles, 412 Greeks, 246 Armenians, and 141 Russians. The Negroes, with 80 individuals, constituted the smallest group in the population. The Irish are the oldest ethnic group in Yankee City, other than the Yankees, and the Jews next in order of age. The Russians, Poles, Greeks, and Armenians are comparatively recent migrants.

Yankee City is one of the oldest Yankee cities in the United States. It was founded early in 1600 and by shipbuilding, fishing, and sea trade grew into one of the most prominent of the colonial New England communities. It quickly became a city of several thousand inhabitants. After certain fluctuations in size it attained approximately its present population and has succeeded in maintaining but not in adding to it. At one time

---

2. This sample is somewhat biased because when we studied occupation we did not get as full a census of the unskilled as we did of those who were semi- and fully skilled, since a smaller proportion of the latter were in the factories which we studied. However, Yankee City, being an industrial town where skill, as it is ordinarily defined, is more useful than elsewhere, has a higher percentage of skilled workers than most communities.

3. U. S. Bureau of the Census. Alphabetical Index of Occupations by Industries and Social-Economic Groups, 1937. Prepared by Alba M. Edwards, Ph.D., for use in the National Unemployment Census, Washington, U. S. Government Printing Office, 1937.

4. The total sample for the unemployment study was 5,005.

5. There were 109 whose ethnic affiliations were unknown.

the town was of sufficient commercial importance to compete on equal terms with Boston in its trade activities. The histories of the state in which it is located tell of its importance politically and socially and of the role it played in the life of New England at a period of its greatest prosperity. While still an important shoe and silverware manufacturing center, Yankee City is no longer of the same comparative importance; with the general growth of population and industry throughout the United States, like many other New England communities it has not grown but maintained a stable population in a stable society.

The city's earlier farming and shipping industries have largely gone. They helped employ the early Irish immigrants, but with the appearance of the factory the Irish and new immigrant groups were recruited for less skilled jobs in the shoe, textile, and other industries. The older ethnic groups have moved into varying occupations, and some of them have succeeded in climbing to the top of the occupational ladder.

Economically and socially Yankee City is organized very much like other American industrial towns. Its business district is supported by the residential area which surrounds it, and the residential area is supported, at the base at least, by workers who are largely maintained by the wages and salaries of the factories. The town has a city government with a mayor and council; city officials, boards, and committees direct such activities as the school, police, and fire departments. The mayor, council, and school board are elected by the voters.

There are a number of grade schools, parochial and public, and one public high school. There are a large number of Protestant churches, the principal ones belonging to the Congregational, Presbyterian, Unitarian, Baptist, Methodist, and Episcopalian denominations. The two Catholic churches are staffed primarily by Irish and French-Canadian priests and nuns; the congregation of the largest Catholic church is Irish, and of the other, French-Canadian. The Jews have one synagogue in the community and the Russians and Greeks have remodeled a Protestant church into a Greek Orthodox house of worship. There are thousands of members of lodges, secret societies, and fraternities, and of organizations such as the Rotary, Kiwanis, and Chamber of Commerce.

Yankee City is an American town. Its people live a life whose values are in general as understandable to Middle Westerners as they are to men from the Pacific and Atlantic coasts. Specific differences are present; certain kinds of behavior are more definite and more highly developed than elsewhere in the United States, and other ways of life are not quite so heavily accented in Yankee City as in the South or in the West. But while it is important, for a full understanding of the community, to know these differences, it would be erroneous to emphasize them and to forget the fundamental similarity to other American towns.

V

HOW THE SEVERAL CLASSES WERE DISCOVERED

WHEN the research of Yankee City began, the director wrote a description of what he believed was fundamental in our social system, in order that the assumptions he held be explicitly stated and not become unconscious biases which would distort the field work, later analysis, and ultimate conclusions. If these assumptions could be stated as hypotheses they were then subject to criticism by the collection of data which would prove, modify, or disprove them. Most of the several hypotheses so stated were subsumed under a general economic interpretation of human behavior in our society. It was believed that the fundamental structure of our society, that which ultimately controls and dominates the thinking and actions of our people, is economic, and that the most vital and far-reaching value systems which motivate Americans are to be ultimately traced to an economic order. Our first interviews tended to sustain this hypothesis. They were filled with references to "the big people with money" and to "the little people who are poor." They assigned people high status by referring to them as bankers, large property owners, people of high salary, and professional men, or they placed people in a low status by calling them laborers, ditchdiggers, and low-wage earners. Other similar economic terms were used, all designating superior and inferior positions.

All our informants agreed that certain groups, of whom we shall soon speak, were at the bottom of the social order, yet many of the members of these groups were making an income which was considerably more than that made by people whom our informants placed far higher in the social scale. It seemed evident that other factors contributed to their lower positions.

Other evidences began to accumulate which made it difficult to accept a simple economic hypothesis. Several men were doctors; and while some of them enjoyed the highest social status in the community and were so evaluated in the interviews, others were ranked beneath them although some of the latter were often admitted to be better physicians. Such ranking was frequently unconsciously done and for this reason was often more reliable than a conscious estimate of a man's status. We found similar inequalities of status among the ministers, lawyers, and other professional men. When we examined the business and industrial world, we discovered that bankers, large manufacturers, and corporation heads also were not ranked equally but were graded as higher or lower in status. An analysis of comparative wealth and occupational status in relation to all the other factors in the total social participation of the individuals we studied demonstrated that, while occupation and wealth could and did contribute greatly to the rank-status of an individual, they were but two of many factors which decided a man's ranking in the whole community. For example, a banker was never at the bottom of the society, and none in fact fell below the middle class, but he was not always at the top. Great wealth did not guarantee the highest social position. Something more was necessary.

In our efforts to find out what this "something more" was, we finally developed a class hypothesis which withstood the later test of a vast collection of data and of subsequent rigorous analysis. By class is meant two or more orders of people who are believed to be, and are accordingly ranked by the members of the community, in socially superior and inferior positions. Members of a class tend to marry within their own order, but the values of the society permit marriage up and down. A class system also provides that children are born into the same status as their parents. A class society distributes rights and privileges, duties and obligations, unequally among its inferior and superior grades. A system of classes, unlike a system of castes, provides by its own values for movement up and down the social ladder. In common parlance, this is social climbing, or in technical terms, social mobility. The social system of Yankee City, we found, was dominated by a class order.

When we examined the behavior of a person who was said by some to be "the wealthiest man in our town," to find out why he did not have a higher position, we were told that "he and his family do not act right." Their moral behavior was "all right," but they "did not do the right things." Although they were Yankees by tradition and not members of any ethnic group, we were told that "they did not belong to the right families" and that "they did not go around with the right kind of people." Our informants further said that the members of this family "didn't know how to act," and that they were not and could not be members of the "right" groups. The interviews clearly demonstrated, however, that all the members of the family were regarded as "good people," and their name was always a lure when marriage was contemplated for a young woman "of good breeding," even though there was some danger that she would be looked upon as "lowering herself" by such a marriage. Similar analysis of the industrial and businessmen who occupied lower positions brought forth the same kind of information.

Interviews about, and with, people who were ranged socially high by our informants but had little money or occupational status brought out the opposite kind of information, supplying further confirmatory evidence for our first tentative theory of a class system. These interviews revealed that "you don't need but a little money in Yankee City to do the right thing," or as it was sometimes said, "you have to have a little money but it is the way one uses it which counts." Questions about such people often brought out such statements as: "John Smith belongs to the X group," followed by remarks to the effect that "Henry Taylor and Frank Dixon and other prominent men who are at the top also belong to it." These same people, we were informed, "went around with the Fred Brown clique" or "went with the Country Club crowd," which were small groups of close friends.

In these interviews certain facts became clear which might be summarized by saying a person needed specific characteristics associated with his "station in life" and he needed to go with the "right kind" of people for the informants to be certain of his ranking. If a man's education, occupation, wealth, income, family, intimate friends, clubs and fraternities, as well as his manners, speech, and general outward behavior were known, it was not difficult for his fellow citizens to give a fairly exact estimate of his status. If only his social participation in family, clique, and association were known, he could be placed to the satisfaction of all the better informants by the process of identifying his social place with that of the others who were like him.

While making these observations on the criteria of class and attempting to locate people in the class hierarchy, we made a valuable discovery. In the expressions about wealth and occupation to which higher and lower valuations were attached, we noticed that certain geographical terms were used not only to locate people in the city's geographical space but also to evaluate their comparative place in the rank order. The first generalization of this kind which we noticed people using in interviews was the identification of a small percentage of the population as "Hill Streeters" or people who "live up on Hill Street," these expressions often being used as equivalent of "Brahmin," the rarer "aristocrat," or the less elegant "high mucky-muck," or "swell," or "snoot." The term Hill Streeter, we soon learned, was employed by people both within and outside of this classification. Whenever an individual was called a Hill Streeter, all of our evidence showed that he was near or at the top of the hierarchy.

Another geographical term with a strong evaluative class meaning was "Riverbrook." When a man was said to be a "Riverbrooker" or to live in Riverbrook, he was felt to be at the bottom of the social hierarchy. Interviews showed this generalization to be true regardless of the informant's place in the social scale. Riverbrookers were contemptuously referred to by all, their sexual morals were considered low, and their behavior was usually looked upon as ludicrous and uncouth. An obscene story concerning the seasonal activities of the Riverbrook fishermen was told scores of times by our male informants, usually with amusement, and one heard much about incestuous relations and homosexual behavior among them. These deprecatory stories were told despite the fact that it was easily verifiable that they were no more true of Riverbrookers than they were of other classes. The Riverbrooker was often a good and highly skilled worker in the shoe factories. He frequently earned a good wage by clamming. Usually a good family man, he was but one of the many variants of what is called the typical Yankee. The "low" behavior was attributed to him (as it usually is in similar social situations) because of his low social position, and these beliefs helped subordinate him when expressed by those who felt themselves above him.

With the acquisition of the terms Hill Streeter and Riverbrooker as designations for the two extremes of class, our next problems were (1) to find out to whom the expressions did and did not refer, (2) to learn what distinctions, if any, were made to differentiate other groups than these two, and (3) to discover who used any or all of these terms.

A descriptive expression which appeared with considerable frequency in our interviews was "the classes and the masses." This expression was seldom used by the people referred to as "the masses" but quite frequently by those who considered themselves "the classes." The lower members of the community sometimes spoke of those in the higher statuses as "the upper classes," and when this expression was used by them it was ordinarily synonymous with Hill Streeter. We soon found, however, that when "the masses" was used, not all the people who were so designated were Riverbrookers, and that most of them were believed to be higher in status. A distinction was made within the masses between Riverbrookers and people of somewhat higher status.

Another geographical expression which frequently appeared in the interviews was "Side Streeter," used in contradiction to Hill Streeter. In some contexts a Side Streeter was anyone who was not a Hill Streeter, but more careful interviewing indicated that to a Hill Streeter a Side Streeter and a Riverbrooker were different. "People who live in Riverbrook are at the bottom" and "of course Side Streeters are better than Riverbrookers" were frequently explicitly stated by the better informants. A Side Streeter was one who was not on the social heights of Hill Street nor in the social depths of Riverbrook. He was somewhere in between. Living along the streets connecting the river area with Hill Street, the Side Streeters were socially as well as territorially intermediate.

All Side Streeters were not the same, we discovered. Some were superior and others inferior, the former being commonly called by another geographical term—"Homevillers." The Homevillers were "good people," but few of them were in any way "socially acceptable." Certain informants placed all of them in "the classes." Homeville is a fairly definitely defined area in Yankee City at the northern end of the community. The Homeville people, we roughly estimated at the time, were people in the mid-section of the social scale but on the whole nearer the top than the bottom. The term "middle class" or "upper-middle class" was often used as equivalent for Homeviller. The Homevillers and their like, it developed through our later associational analysis, were graded ordinarily into two groups (upper-middle and lower-middle classes) and separated from a lower stratum of Side Streeters who were too much like the Riverbrookers in many of their characteristics to be classed with the Side Streeters of high status. The distinctions between the lower group of Homevillers and this lowest group of Side Streeters were not so clearly marked as the others.

At this point we saw that Hill Street was roughly equivalent to upper class, Homeville to at least a good section of the middle class, and Riverbrook to the lowest class. We perceived, too, that these geographical terms were generalizing expressions by which a large number of people could be given a class designation but which nevertheless did not define class position explicitly. When the people classed as Hill Streeters were located on a spot map it soon developed that not all of them lived on Hill Street and that not all the people living on Hill Street were Hill Streeters (upper class). Many of the people who were by class Hill Streeters lived elsewhere in the city, and some of them were fairly well concentrated in two areas other than Hill Street. We found a similar generalization to be true of the Riverbrookers and Homevillers. This discovery further demonstrated that these designations were terms of rank employed by the members of a "democratic" society to refer obliquely to higher and lower social statuses in the community.

Careful interviewing among people who were called Hill Streeters showed that the members of this group divided the general upper class into a higher and a lower subdivision. Our informants made frequent references to people of "old family" and to those of "new families." The former were individuals whose families, it was believed, had participated in upper-class behavior for several generations and who could trace this behavior through the father's or mother's line or both for three or more generations. An upper-class genealogy of this kind has been called a lineage for the purposes of this report. Long residence in Yankee City was very important, but length of residence by itself did not establish a family at the apex of the class system since in all of the six classes later established we found families with written and attested genealogies which went back two hundred and in some cases even three hundred years to the founding of the community. Some of the lower members of the upper class could also trace their genealogies well back, but their recent mobility upward if they had "come up from below" was enough to prevent an immediate claim to such a lineage. Their recent ancestors, unlike those of the uppermost members of the upper class, had not participated for a sufficient period of time in the forms of behavior and the social position which were ranked as upper class by the community. With the separation of the upper-upper from the lower-upper class, and the upper-middle from the lower-middle, we had distinguished five classes clearly and a sixth less definitely. We knew at this time that the sixth class fell somewhere in between the middle and the lowest class, but it was still possible that it might be not one but several classes. Eventually, however, we were able to establish the existence of six classes: an upper-lower and a lower-lower class in addition to the upper and lower subdivisions of the middle and upper classes.

The amount of membership in associations is comparatively larger than that in most of the other social structures of Yankee City. Despite their size, associations tend to segment the society into separate groups, and some of them help to maintain higher and lower ranking in the community. With this knowledge, we were able to place with greater exactness than we could by the use of the geographical classification a large sample of the members of Yankee City society.

Certain clubs, our interviews showed, were ranked at such extreme heights by people highly placed in the society that most of the lower classes did not even know of their existence, while middle-class people showed that they regarded them as much too high for their expectations. A very few of them, indeed, were looked upon as so exclusive that some of the Hill Streeters might be excluded on family grounds. Of other clubs, whose members were mainly Hill Streeters, it was felt that any Hill Streeter was eligible for membership if he had the other necessary qualifications (such as being a male of a certain age or interested in certain kinds of hobbies). These clubs, however, were considered too high for the vast majority of the people in Yankee City to aspire to, and it was clear that many, if not most, of the lower classes did not know of their existence. It was also felt that others did aspire to them but were not chosen because "they did not belong socially."

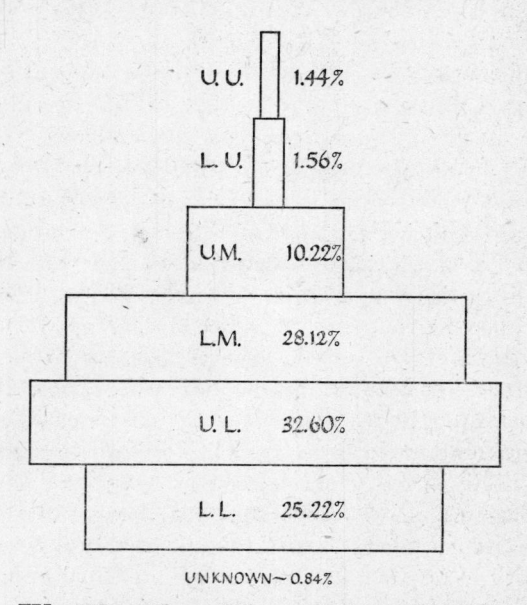

```
          U.U.  | 1.44%
          L.U.  | 1.56%
          U.M.  | 10.22%
          L.M.  | 28.12%
          U.L.  | 32.60%
          L.L.  | 25.22%
        UNKNOWN~ 0.84%
```

IV. *The Class Hierarchy of Yankee City*

Below this last level of clubs were other associations which included Hill Streeters but also had members "from further down" who were "not acceptable socially." There were still other associations where these same individuals who were not accepted socially were members and were considered to be at the top of the membership, and all other members were felt to be below them. Some associations of this kind were sufficiently high so that there were members of the community who were too low to do more than aspire to membership. There were other associations too low for Hill Streeters to join and still others which the two middle classes refused to enter. While interviews demonstrated that certain associations or clubs were believed to contain only the "best people," others mostly the "best people" but with additions, and still others only the "lowest people," some associations did not seem to be graded in class; people "of all kinds" were said to belong to them.

From a later understanding of associations, we discovered that members of the three higher classes belonged to associations which we named social clubs. The three lower classes did not. All three of the upper classes belonged to associations organized for charitable purposes. Certain of these clubs had only female members, others only male, and still others were mixed. Several female clubs included women of the three uppermost classes, but interviews showed that their lower members had some difficulty in entering them. Some female clubs refused to admit "ordinary better-class people," and some members said, "We will have only our own kind."

Ordinarily Hill Streeters did not belong to occupational associations, but Homevillers did. Hill Streeters tended to avoid fraternal organizations, secret societies and insurance orders, and associations with formal age grading. Members of the upper-middle class also tended to stay out of fraternal orders and associations with auxiliaries. On the other hand, members of the lower-middle class favored fraternal orders and semi-auxiliaries. The upper-middle people, moreover, were allowed into and favored charitable organizations, while the lower-middle members were excluded from or refused to join them. The breaks in association behavior of the members of the two middle classes greatly aided us in making our classification and in separating members of the two groups.

Lower-middle-class people did not participate in female and mixed social clubs, and since women were very conscious of class in Yankee City, the knowledge of this fact greatly aided us in our interviewing. If a person was a member of several charitable organizations, a social club or two, and possibly an occupational association, but not of a fraternal lodge, and he was not considered a member of the new or old families of Hill Streeters, it was more than likely that he was upper-middle class. A small amount of interviewing soon demonstrated whether this was true or not. Ordinarily he had a family and was a member of a few cliques; usually we possessed information about their members; often some of them had been placed by earlier interviews. With this information it was not too hard to locate this individual in his exact place in the class system.

Associations were of great value in placing large groups of people in a fairly exact status within the class system. But because these people belonged to other social structures, such as the family and clique, which made much finer status discriminations, it was possible to place them with even greater exactness. Our study of family membership demonstrated that the vast majority of families had but one class represented in their membership. Although there were very minor rank differences in family membership, the members of a family ordinarily participated as a unit in their place in the social structure. Ultimately, we estimated that 95.15 per cent of the members of the upper-upper class belonged to families in which there were only upper-upper-class people; that 87.26 per cent of lower-upper persons belonged to families confined to their own class; and that the corresponding percentages for the other classes were 91.36 for upper-middle; 90.17 for lower-middle; 86.33 for upper-lower; and 95.98 for lower-lower.

Cliques tended to include two or even three classes in their membership, but on the whole they, too, drew fairly sharp class lines. Of the upper-upper class, 36.59 per cent belonged to cliques in which there were only upper-uppers; 20.74 per cent of the clique members in the lower-upper class, 20.12 per cent in upper-middle, 14.47 per cent in lower-middle, 15.68 per cent in upper-lower, and 24.64 per cent in the lower-lower class belonged to cliques confined to their own class.

All of the types of social structure and each of the thousands of families, thousands of cliques, and hundreds of associations were, member by member, interrelated in our research. With the use of all structural participation, and with the aid of such additional testimony as the area lived in, the type of house, kind of education, manners, and other symbols of class, it was possible to determine very quickly the approximate place of any individual in the society. In the final analysis, however, individuals were placed by the evaluations of the members of Yankee City itself, e.g., by such explicit statements as "she does not belong" or "they belong to our club." Naturally there were many borderline cases. A class system, unlike a caste or any other clearly and formally marked rank-order, is one in which movement up and down is constantly taking place in the lives of many people. At the time of our study, for example, some people were moving into the lower-upper class from the upper-middle. Our interviews showed pressure on these mobile people from those above them and the development of new social behavior and memberships among them. It was a problem in these and similar cases from other classes where such people should be placed. In order to make a complete study, it was necessary to locate all of them in one of the six classes, and this we did to the best of our ability on the basis of the entire range of phenomena covered by our data.

Distinctions between the upper-upper and lower-upper, old family and new family, groups are quite clear. Differences between the upper-middle people who were not new family but who belonged to associations like them, and who were of the "better class" in Homeville and similar areas, are quite easily observed. The separation of the upper-middle from the lower-middle class is clear and distinct, but that between the lower-middle and upper-lower is less clear and, in certain respects, the least distinct of all. The distinction between the lower-lower and upper-lower class is easily made by finding out to whom the expressions, "he is a Riverbrooker" or "he is the same as a Riverbrooker," apply.

It must not be thought that all the people in Yankee City are aware of all the minute distinctions made in this book. The terms used to refer to such definitions as are made vary according to the class of the individual and his period of residence. The terms Hill Streeter, Side Streeter, Homeviller, and Riverbrooker would be known to all classes. Occasionally such terms are used only in their geographical sense, but far more often they are applied as terms of status and rank.

VI

CLASS AND SOCIAL STRUCTURE

1. *The Family in the Class System*

THE maintenance of a family's social position in any hierarchal society through an extended period of time is, in large part, dependent upon the vertically coordinate social positions of the marrying pair. If the society is organized on the principle of caste, the males and females of two uniting families must be members of the same caste; they express by the marriage their social equivalence and help maintain the continuing location of their families' place. All the values and sanctions of a caste help to enforce such equivalent marriages.

In a class system, however, there is an ambivalent situation, for only part of the values and sanctions of class act in this way. A positive sanction is placed on bettering oneself, making a "fine marriage," and a negative sanction on the opposite of "lowering oneself" or "marrying beneath oneself." Those opposing tendencies are normally resolved in a class system in such a way that these people maintain an approximation of their premarital positions by and after marriage. Nevertheless, despite the pressure to marry at one's own level, a certain number of people marry above and below their own social position. Such behavior is a part of the general situation in a class society, the reason being that there are relatively few methods available for imposing either physical or social segregation which might prevent upward or downward marriages.

The Yankee City class which has the best chance to express its social distance is the upper. This class has more mechanisms to express social distance, and often it can and does translate social distance into geographical and spatial distance. The private school, large grounds, nurses for children, large houses, and infrequent use of public conveyances all geographically express and help maintain distance between the members of this group and those who might want to become socially nearer to them.

The problem of marriage in a class system, when social position is to be maintained, is one in which there must be an equivalence of place not only for the marrying pair of one generation but for the many generations which succeed each other. In class, unlike caste, there are three possibilities of marriage instead of the one in caste. As Chart V demonstrates, a person may marry above, below, or evenly. Thus the maintenance of a given position is much more difficult since the generations of marrying pairs must maintain repeating cycles of equal marriages. The maintenance of the same position by the members of several generations of one line of descent (a patronymic group in Yankee City) through the use of the marriage mechanism is illustrated in Chart VI. It translates the descending generations which begin above ego and continue on through his own generation into those which succeed him by a line which extends laterally and is composed of arrows and signs of equality to show that the same position is maintained not only by descent but also by marriage.

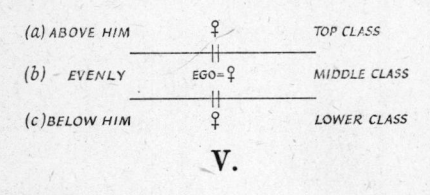

(a) ABOVE HIM — ♀ — TOP CLASS
(b) EVENLY — EGO=♀ — MIDDLE CLASS
(c) BELOW HIM — ♀ — LOWER CLASS

V.

In our interviews certain "old families" were repeatedly referred to as the uppermost group in Yankee City, and among these families a certain few were felt to be higher than all others. Representatives of these topmost families were interviewed not only to discover how they lived and thought but also to determine what families they placed in the old-family, or upper-upper group, and what they put in the new-family classification, or lower-upper category. The same was done with the other groups beneath them. From such groupings of families as we obtained by our interviewing, it was possible to work out a continuous vertical extension of members of families from the top to the bottom of the Yankee City society and to place each individual in one of the several classes. Family histories were examined and the behavior of living descendants analyzed in an effort to discover why they occupied the positions they did in the class hierarchy. To indicate the kind of material that was collected and to present the reader with the evidence for the development in our methods for the study of class, summaries of a few cases in the upper-upper group are given below.

Let us look first at the Z family. R. Z, according to the testimony of our informants and of historical documents, was a lawyer who came to Yankee City from Connecticut. First mentioned in the local history around 1800, he was a prominent

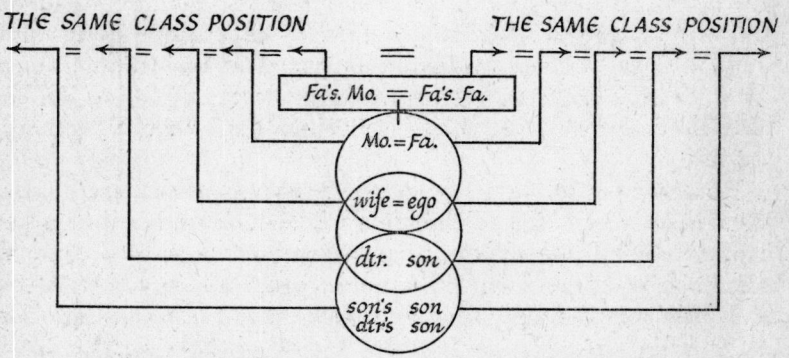

THE SAME CLASS POSITION   *THE SAME CLASS POSITION*

Fa's. Mo. = Fa's. Fa.
Mo. = Fa.
wife = ego
dtr. son
son's son
dtr's son

VI. *Marriage, Family Descent, and the Maintenance of Class Position*

official of the town—chairman of the selectmen, representative to the Grand Council—and was sufficiently important to make the public welcoming addresses when President Monroe, General Lafayette, and other prominent people came to Yankee City. From our historical vantage point, he seems to have been one of the early New England capitalists. He was interested in building canals and locks in the river and his company became the corporate overlord of a great industrial city of the state. He helped organize the Atlantic Stage Company, one of the important transportation systems of the day, and he was also concerned with the toll bridge across the river. He had two sons, D. Z and M. Z, the latter an Episcopalian minister and the successor to a famous divine of New England. D. Z was the largest owner of ships in Yankee City at a time when shipowning was of paramount importance to the town and to New

England. He was also president of the oldest and most respected bank as well as of another important bank in the community. He married Miss T who belonged also to a leading family. He was called "Lord Z" by his contemporaries in the community and stories are still told which illustrate his imperious attitude.

D. Z had three sons, D., R., and S., and a daughter who later married a member of the local aristocracy. D. married an "outsider" and had one daughter who married a manufacturer. This union was blessed with two sons and a daughter. The sons are in the manufacturing business, and the daughter married Dr. K, a surgeon with an upper-class practice in Boston. D. went into the wholesale lumber business in Boston and failed. This was his only business venture. He went into politics and became a high-ranking Federal official in Cleveland's administration.

R. Z went into the wholesale drygoods business with two of his upper-upper friends and failed. He then became a note broker and "hired money for people who wanted it largely for cotton mills, and from there went into the bond business." S. Z, the third of the three sons, went into the brokerage business with a friend of his father's. He never married. As administrator of the will of his aunt (the wife of M. Z), he gave $250,000 to a Yankee City hospital; and out of the income from another $250,000 he distributed one fifth to a dental clinic, two fifths for the treatment of tuberculosis, and two fifths for a community-welfare center in Yankee City.

R. Z married the daughter of a local upper-upper who was a "brilliant" newspaperman and soldier. He had, by this marriage, one son, N., who married a wealthy woman. He is in business with his father. The "show place" of Yankee City is now owned by his father whose present wife is of an aristocratic Philadelphia family. R. Z (the father) is one of the three wealthiest men in the state and has an estate of over 3,000 acres near Yankee City and a place in Boston. "He is the only native who has made money outside of town (this is believed, but is not true) who has spent it here and he has a great regard for Yankee City."

Let us now turn to the Y family. There were two Y's who were prominent in the Revolution; both were members of the

Council of the Colony at Massachusetts Bay and one became its president. B. Y was a brigadier general in the Mexican War, a famous attorney, an early mayor of Yankee City, one of the first ministers to China, attorney general of the United States, represented the United States in regard to the *Alabama* Claims, and almost became chief justice of the Supreme Court. (He was defeated in this—after he had been nominated by the President, so the story goes—by a senator who was a former citizen of Yankee City and who came from a family which lived on the "side streets.") B. Y had two half-brothers, N. and M. They were shipowners in the East India and Calcutta trade. M. married a local aristocrat and had two sons and two daughters. Both he and his brother N. lived in the same house. N. had one son and three daughters. His son C. went into the East India trade with other leading merchants of Yankee City but the firm was broken up shortly after.

C. Y thereupon took over the direction of one of the older banks and became director of the T Fund (an educational foundation created by a Yankee City person) for giving local men training in technical colleges. C. Y was also a director of the leading bank in the community and president of the association owning the cemetery where many of the upper-uppers buried their dead. His unmarried sister A. lived with him. One daughter married L. O, an upper-upper who had a salary of $40,000 a year. This couple had three children: N., who did not marry; G., who died; and S., who married three wives, each of whom was wealthy. The wives were related to a large number of the members of the upper-upper families in Yankee City and in the surrounding communities. C. died while the Yankee City research was in progress, and left a sizable fortune to his unmarried sister.

The X family. The members of this family have long been famous as silversmiths, there having been an uninterrupted line of craftsmen in the family since the late 1600's. M. X, the founder of the lineage in this country, was born in 1602 and came to Yankee City in the late 1630's. His son was called M. and the son of M. was called H. Since that time there has been an alternation of the names of M. and H. on a generation basis. The present M., last of the line, lives in one half of a house built by his great-grandfather; his married sister lives in the other half. "His father left him some money and M. didn't have to work after that." He has a brother D., who is a jeweler and well-known horticulturist. His brother's daughter lives across the street with a common first cousin. The family of the first cousin is related to a large number of upper-upper families in Yankee City.

The W family. Colonel W of New Hampshire married into one of the well-known upper-class families of Yankee City. His wife's father was a wealthy merchant and president of two prominent and powerful local banks. The W's had three boys and a girl. The first son married the daughter of a wealthy broker, the second became an officer in the Marines, and the third lives in Yankee City with his sister E., who is in charge of the children's guidance society in one of the larger communities in Massachusetts. The W's are related to many families of upper-upper status in Yankee City.

The V family. The Reverend D. V was the minister of the Oldtown Church in Yankee City for about fifty years, from the early 1800's to the middle of the century. Of his four sons, one went to Illinois, one to Vermont, one to New York, and one remained in Yankee City as editor of the local paper. The last son had three sons and two daughters. His wife was H. E, daughter of Squire E. Squire E was first cousin of the father of H. Y. E, who was one of the oldest and most respected members of the topmost class. Their oldest child later became a lawyer in Honolulu; the second son, a genealogist in London; and the third son, also a lawyer in Honolulu. This last son lived in Yankee City until he was about fifty. D. V, a son of the editor, was an important official in one of the investment companies in the community and, with another member of the upper-class group, reorganized one of the large turnpike companies which he later sold for what was said to be a large sum.

The T family. The T family, whose prominence in the community goes back to the seventeenth century, made their fortune in shipping. They are intermarried with a number of the upper-upper-class families in Yankee City. "There has been money in the T family for over one hundred years and they have made many bequests" to the town of Yankee City. The present generations of this family have, according to the testimony of some of their own group, "married beneath themselves." Their father went into the textile business but found that he could make more money speculating in the market. His brother, now dead, was a consulting electrical expert in partnership with another upper-upper. Their first cousin, S. T, is an inventor. "He has never worked very hard at anything. He is the only T who has kept his money."

In these brief family histories there is a wide range in wealth and occupation and in the number of generations that a family has been in the community. The Z's and Y's are the only very wealthy families; the X's are fairly well-to-do; and the others have but a modest income. It is commonly thought in Yankee City that all old families are descendants of sea captains and that social classes as presently constituted are based upon the earlier division into captains, mates, and seamen. Obviously, this simplification will not hold water.

It will be remembered that the X family were silversmiths; their occupation has very high prestige because the S silver, which bears the family name, is now to be found in such famous collections as that of the British Museum. The first Y was a minister; the second, an editor; the first Z was a lawyer.

The significant thing to note in these histories is that for over one hundred years these families have been among the most prominent in Yankee City. Their occupations have always been those of high social value although they have changed in character with the changing technology. A woman of the upper-upper class contrasted the "new people" with a family like that of the Y's. She said of the latter, "They have a fascinating family history." This characterization would be true of all the family histories of those who belonged to the upper-upper group. Whether as sea captains, merchants, bankers, lawyers, capitalists, or intellectuals, they have been the dominant families in the town, a position which they still retain.

From our investigation of the upper-upper families we concluded that a family was in this class if it had participated in *general* upper-class behavior for several generations. Only through time could a family move from lower-upper to upper-upper. The participation by the families' ancestors for several generations in the two upper strata, and ultimately in the upper of the two, gave it a lineage. A lineage we defined as an unbroken line of ancestors who could be traced through the father's or mother's line, or both, and who would be members of the upper class.

An informant who had definitely formulated her ideas of what factors were involved in class behavior declared, "You have got to have family to get anywhere in Yankee City and you have got to have some money. Not very much, but enough to do the right thing." In other words, money is of importance only as it enables one to carry out the behavior which is felt to be inherently appropriate to the upper-class configuration; and this behavior, it is believed, must have been performed by the former members of a family as well as by its present members. It must be emphasized that the present-day families go back before the American Revolution; and some, like the T's and S's, were prominent almost from the beginning of the settlement.

A New England historian, writing of the "great period" of New England's maritime history, has drawn a picture of Yankee City which will add to our understanding of what this continuity of family prominence means to the members of the community.

. . . [Yankee City] boasted a society inferior to no other town on the continent. Most of the leading families were but one generation removed from the plough or the forecastle; but they had acquired wealth before the Revolution and conducted social matters with a grace and dignity of an old regime. When General Gore made a state visit to . . . [Yankee City] where he had once studied law he came in a coach and four with outriders, uniformed aides, and a cavalry escort; and when the town fathers informed his ancient benefactress, Madame K, that his Excellency would honor her with a call the spokesman delivered his message on his knees at the good lady's feet. We read of weekly routs and balls, of wedding coaches drawn by six white horses with liveried footmen in this town of less than eight thousand inhabitants. When personal property was assessed several Yankee City merchants [the upper class of the day] reported from one thousand to twelve hundred gallons of wine in their cellars.

One of the important facts about lineage as we have defined it in American society is that it is usually bilateral; descent is reckoned not necessarily through the male line alone. When lists were compiled by our informants of the names of those families who were included in the upper class, certain names were not included which we definitely knew to be upper class. Of the members of these families it was said that they belonged to the Y family or Z family, that is, that these individuals traced their descent through the mother rather than the father in order to maintain the height of their position. These people were looked upon as upper-upper, but they were thought of in terms of the lineage and connected with a patronym which was upper class. In a generation or two their present names will be absorbed into the group and will become the names of a lineage in their own right. The authoritative informants in the upper-upper group often spoke of the P's as an old family. Actually their patronym was second generation in Yankee City, but further interviewing showed that the first of the P family married the daughter of Captain Jonathan N, a member of the upper-upper, and since the system of descent in a lineage in Yankee City is bilateral, the P's are now a continuation of the older lineage. Apparently it takes at least two generations, and sometimes more, for one name to supersede another. N. E, granddaughter of Y. Y. E, speaks of the S's (a new lineage) as an old family, but in the generation of her grandfather they were spoken of as Z's (an old lineage).

In the upper-upper group there are a number of definitely known lineages which are recognized by members of this group and by the members of the lower-upper group. These lineages are regarded as a single linked group through a belief in their general superiority to the other groups in the community. This belief is expressed in a common behavior pattern which helps maintain the social distance of those who use it. Mrs. O said, "My husband told me when I came here that the one thing you couldn't do in Yankee City was mix social classes." Another upper-upper informant declared that the old families never had accepted the new people into their group. The members of the topmost group frequently use a kinship terminology in ordinary address, even when they are not related as kinsmen; for example, the term "cousin" is often used when there is no traceable relationship. This was explained by one informant in these words: "She is my cousin not because she is an actual cousin but because my mother and father grew up with her." There was strong evidence that the upper-upper class in Yankee City behaved as a biological kinship group to express their mutual feeling of social proximity to each other and, obversely, to express social distance from those with whom they did not use such terms.

Although this relation of kinship in the upper-upper class is sometimes a fiction based upon membership in a common group, it is nevertheless a definite extension of the family. The class is highly endogamous and practically everyone is related in some fashion to the other members. As one of the oldest and best-informed members of this group commented, "I haven't an ancestor that landed here [Yankee City] after 1650. The farthest any went for a wife was to X [a suburb of Yankee City] and only two went there; so you can see what a community you have struck. All marriages are inside the community." Often these relationships are very distant, but each member of the class endeavors to link himself and his family with the others on a kinship basis. One of our most trusted informants, when speaking of his wife, said, "I didn't know that she 'existed' until I was twenty-one. I then found out that her great-grandfather and my great-grandmother were brother and sister." The first thing he and his wife did was to compare genealogies.

This brief analysis demonstrates the complicated and often distant kinship ties which link these people together. At times a distant or fairly close kinsman may be quietly disowned because he does not belong to this group. There is a standing feud in Yankee City between the members of two families who have the same patronym because one individual who belongs to a lower class insists that he traces his lineage back to common ancestors and, to clinch the point, calls his son by the Christian name of the original ancestor of the upper-class family. There is a relationship between the members of the two families but through a different line. It was felt by the upper-class family that their vested rights were being used and that the lower-class family was attempting to augment its social prestige by attaching itself to an upper-class lineage. There can be little doubt that this is what was being attempted since the members of each family were thinking within the social context of Yankee City.

In this semiendogamous group, marriage with a first cousin is quite frequent and there is very little or no taboo upon it. Micajah X married his first cousin and when he died, another cousin, an N, came back to the community and married the widow. Tracing the lineages of many of the upper-upper-class families is extremely complicated since they have been intermarried for generations and there is a definite feeling of pride on the part of the members of the group in the closeness of the marriages. X. Y. Z, a member of this group, said, "My wife is some relation to the T's in the same way I am; my children are descended from the 'original immigrant' of the T's in sixteen different ways, nine on the mother's side and seven on the father's. That is how intermarried we are around here."

Since the class is largely endogamous, and since males are more apt to leave the city, the necessity to marry within the class has left many females single. Many of our informants spoke of so-and-so's remaining single because she would never marry below her—"she was too high class for that." S. S, upper-middle class, one of the most respected capitalists in the community, was in love with a woman of the upper-upper group when he was a young man, but "of course, she would have none of him." Such marriages occur but rarely, and when they do, it becomes necessary for the person of lower rank to assume the behavior of the upper group.

An examination of the membership of the lower-upper families presents a very different situation from that of the upper-upper. When we examine the lives of the outsiders who have come to Yankee City to live, several things become evident about their family structure. Most of the outsiders consist of single families of parents and children; that is, the adults who come to Yankee City are essentially in families of procreation, because their parents ordinarily remain in their home communities. Associated with leaving the home community is the fact that the primary control of the old superordinate generation is removed, and at the same time, these individuals are ordinarily separated from their siblings and other kin and tend to be isolated as kindred when they arrive in Yankee City. In addition to their kinship isolation, they also tend to have few social relations with the members of the community. For some little time after arrival their direct relations are primarily those associated with the occupation of the husband and father. Ordinarily they have certain people in the community who act as sponsors for them. Failing such sponsors, it is possible for the family to remain in almost permanent isolation, and instances are cited of people leaving the community because they were not accepted. If the "immigrant" family has been properly sponsored, and if it has the other necessary requirements, it is possible, after a few years, for its members to become a part of the lower-upper class.

Not all of the lower-upper individuals are newly arrived persons from outside the geographical limits of Yankee City. Many of them, born in the community, are recently arrived from a lower position in the social scale. Such people, on the whole, occupy a position similar to those who have come in from the outside since, although they are not separated from the parental generation and their larger kinship group physically, they tend to be separated almost as definitely. A similar lack of relations tends to exist between the older generation and the younger one which has augmented its social position.

One of the most characteristic aspects of the lower-upper class is the unstable situation within the family which, as we have said, arises in part from the lack of control of the superordinate generation and the submission to initiated standards taken over from the class into which they have recently entered. The family arrives, by social mobility, in the lower-upper class where the standards that the members of this family have been taught in their youth are looked upon as vulgar, cheap, and demeaning. They have no older generation on whom they can rely for support. The very elaborate and detailed modes of behavior which are considered marks of their new position cannot be learned by growing into them but must be acquired from a group which is in part hostile to these new members. What they learn they feel is from outside them, and to some extent the adopted behavior is always felt by them to be external and strange. The largely hostile class environment makes it difficult for them to participate with ease and to acquire freely the kind of behavior necessary for them to have in order to consolidate their new positions. They are continually on the defensive. By contrast, a member of the upper-upper group offers his opinions easily and freely even though they may be divergent from those held by other members of his group. He can afford to criticize and to be criticized.

In the lower-upper group, however, there is a tendency to perfect a part of the total behavior expected of an upper-class person, and this part of the behavior frequently becomes for them a substitute for the whole. For example, A. N, a young man of the lower-upper class, owned a large plane which became, according to his own view, the very center of his existence. He spent large sums of money on it, displayed it frequently, and devoted a great amount of his time to overseeing its maintenance. It became to him a symbol of his position, and when he sold it, he said "he felt as though he had sold his bride" or as though "someone in the family had died." While he was in possession of the airplane he was often subjected to the ridicule of the members of the upper-upper group.

Although the upper class is divided into these two groups, the children of the same age grades go to the same schools and, on the whole, participate in the same activities when they are together. This creates a skewed situation between the two generations and the two classes. In the upper-upper, the children are definitely subordinate to the older group and their position is one of great subordination to the parental generation in comparison to that of the younger generation within the families of the classes beneath this group. The adults in the lower-upper class are subordinate to the adults of the upper-upper class and, in relative social place, they are subordinate to the children of the upper-upper class. The lower-upper children, however, are friends of the upper-upper children and frequently assume a higher position than their parents because of their association with the upper-upper children. The continual association between the growing members of the upper-upper class and those of the lower-upper class helps the latter rise in the social scale while, at the same time, it acts to increase the social distance between the parents and children of the lower-upper group.

2. The Family in the Home

An upper-class home in Yankee City contains anywhere from eight to twenty or more rooms, all of which play a definite role in the lives of the individuals who occupy and use them. The living room serves as the focal point in organizing the face-to-face relations of all members of the family group. Most living rooms have fireplaces which, possessing more than utilitarian value, serve as symbols of the unity of the family group. Each individual in the household, moreover, has a specific room of his own, and, in many instances, a private dressing room and bath as well. From these private rooms emerge the specific individual personalities to join the other members of the family in their common activities. Children and servants are usually quartered on the top floors; rooms used by the entire family are generally on the ground floor; and the specialized rooms of adults and more important members of the family are located on the second floor.

There are, of course, variations in this general rule; but the two rooms in which the family spends most time as a group are without question the living and dining rooms. Frequently the living room is divided into two rooms, the smaller and more intimate being set aside for family use, and the other, a parlor, used for the entertainment of guests. If outsiders are invited to such a function as tea, for instance, the larger living room is used; but if the guests include only more intimate friends, they are received in the family living room. The larger living room is seldom used by the family alone.

The dining room is usually restricted to the more intimate participation groups and is rarely used for larger functions except for formal dinners. Meals in the home have different values which depend upon the social status of the family. The upper-class family, for instance, spends more time over its breakfasts and endows this meal with more group significance than do families in other classes.

In upper-class families there are generally servants to perform a large part of the secular household ritual through their daily rounds of tasks and duties which keep the house in order. The mistress of the house ordinarily superintends the activities of her servants, but she does not herself do any of the actual work. However, she and other members of the family perform definite ritual acts which top off the work of their paid employees: arranging flowers, carving at table, lighting the fire, and pouring at tea. Maids serve at the table according to a strictly formalized routine, while the food is prepared by a cook hired especially for that work. Maids are outfitted in uniforms of different types according to the time of day and the specific duties in which they are engaged, their dress symbolizing their subordination to and separation from the family whom they serve. The leisure time accruing to the family that can maintain servants allows more frequent performance of ritual acts outside the home, the women participating in various social activities which bring them conspicuously to the attention of the remainder of the community, and the men indulging in a variety of sports, intellectual interests and hobbies, and community activities by means of which they express and constantly reaffirm their social position.

All of the activities which surround the preparation of the table and the serving and eating of the meal are demonstrations of ritual relations between members of the family, the servants, and objects which have esthetic and traditional value in the house. They are also expressions of the meal as a family communion. Nonmembers of the immediate family—such as collateral kin and clique members—who are invited in to eat at the family table may be said to participate in the "private communion" of the family and household, a secular but highly organized ritual. These ritual elements surrounding the daily life within a household tend to increase in number and intensity of function with the height of the stratification of the family. As household ritual becomes more elaborate, larger and larger sums of money are necessary to maintain it. Most families, however, do not have sufficient income to support a large staff and many of them hire servants for the day or on a part-time basis; a few have no servants at all, but so long as the house is maintained properly, the absence of servants in no way reflects on the social position of the family. There is a certain minimum, of course, which must be met, but anything above that is mere elaboration.

People of the lower-upper class, the so-called new families, adopt the more elaborate ritual in order to demonstrate that they know and follow the behavior patterns of the upper-upper-class people. The elaborate ritual of the upper class in general is associated with strong feelings for property and its correct handling. An upper-middle-class person, in speaking about the Christmas season activities of local charitable associations, said, "Hill Streeters can well afford to give toys because their children are not destructive; they have more intelligence and are made to respect things, and toys are treated just like furniture; there is a definite place for a thing and their children are taught to put it there." In other words, there is a definitely recognized household arrangement which each child is brought up to respect and the parts of which he must treat with almost ritual care. In this pattern, the antiques, heirlooms, and other properties which have been handed down from the past are the important centers around which other house furnishings are arranged. The inheritance of ritual objects from the past and their use by living lineal descendants provide the members of the upper-class group with a symbolic apparatus which ties the sentiments of the living with those of the dead. The house, its furnishings, and the gardens thus become symbolic expressions of the relations not only between household members but also between the living and the dead.

Many of the houses themselves, as previously mentioned, may be said to possess lineages of their own. Those which do not have less value, however old or beautiful they may be. A house with a distinguished lineage is concrete evidence of upper-class status. Although the spatial arrangements of the rooms and their specialization of function help to impress an elaborate ritual on the occupants, the spiritual presence of the ancestors, as experienced through the use of ancestral rooms and furniture, is more important in maintaining a disciplined continuity in the minds of the inhabitants. One of the upper-upper-class families was forced to sell its house to a comparatively wealthy upper-middle-class Irish family. A member of the upper-class family, commenting on what had happened to her old home, said:

When the N's bought the place, we thought it was awfully nice. He had lots of money to take care of it, which we couldn't, but then they tore out everything: all the walls, all the woodwork, and all the fireplaces. The only thing they didn't touch was the third floor. It used to be my brother's room up in that back room there. When I saw the house after the N's came in, it felt like the family had been massacred. It was nothing against them, I suppose; they're nice people and all that. They just don't understand and they can't appreciate good things. You know that wisteria blooming in the front yard? Well, my sister planted that over forty years ago. The N's came in and even chopped that down.

The implicit assumption in this statement was that the house was not simply a habitation, but a place which had a certain character about it that demanded a particular kind of ritual treatment, which treatment (the N's not being in the upper-class tradition) had been neglected.

The possession of "a house" is a prime requisite for social mobility; after several generations, the "new people" who live in these houses and who have adopted upper-class behavior will become members of old families and enter the upper-upper class. The value of an old house is so high that even an individual who is a member of an old family is open to criticism if he does not possess a house which is deemed a suitable setting for upper-class behavior. Mrs. W, when referring to a new dwelling purchased by the daughter of one of the community's most prominent men, said, "It is deadly to buy a house like that in Yankee City." When asked to explain, she answered, "It has no background."

Many of the objects in these houses are definitely connected with specific personalities in the past and therefore have an even greater value to the members of the family and class than those objects which are only generally related to antiquity. The linkage of specific personalities with material objects is particularly well revealed in the case of the house of Miss K, a living member of an old lineage. Associated with nearly every object and part of the house is a whole cycle of stories relating to various members of the family. The objects are associated not only with past and present members of the family, but with future owners as well. In fact, so great is the general and historical value attaching to antiques connected with distinguished lineages that there is a concerted effort made by their members to prevent others from purchasing them. L. Y, for instance, a member of a prosperous lower-upper-class family, was able to buy only a few pieces from one of the upper-upper families who sold its antiques to people outside of the community. Mrs. T, an upper-upper who had fallen into straitened circumstances, sold her antiques to a Boston dealer with the proviso that he come to collect them at night. There is a definite feeling that these objects should not pass to the mobile lower-upper group; this attitude, of course, also helps to prevent the downward mobility of the old families. It seems likely, moreover, that selling these objects to an outsider for purely economic reasons lessens the likelihood that the spiritual value of the family heirlooms will be transferred to the purchaser.

The plants, flowers, and ornamental objects in the gardens are also associated with personalities. Many of the valuable flowering shrubs are connected with the dead members of a family. When the gardens of Yankee City were opened for public inspection, the ones chosen were those which had lineage connections. "The garden of Mrs. E. D, once visited by President Monroe and Lafayette"; the garden of the Y's—"has an historic and patriotic record and is unique in New England with its air of an Old World manor." In all the gardens, the plants pointed out were very old and hence had been in the lineage a long while, or else they could be traced back to an English original which had been transported to America by the ancestors of the present owners of the garden. Thus the garden, like the house and its furnishings, functions as a lineage symbol.

It was mentioned earlier that one of the characteristics of the lower-upper class is an overelaboration of one particular aspect of upper-class behavior. From the upper-upper point of view, these elaborations are artificial and "not really a part of the person" because they have been acquired late in life. Consequently they are open to criticism. These attitudes help to keep lower-upper-class persons subordinated and allow the upper-upper group more freedom in conforming to a set pattern of behavior.

3. The Clique in the Class System

A. Discovery of the Clique

The discovery of the clique and the determination of its great significance as a social and structural mechanism came rather late in our field investigation in Yankee City. In our interviews we had long been aware of the importance of such designations as "our crowd," "our bunch," "the Jones's gang," "the ring we go in," and "our circle," but we had not focused our attention on the theoretical implications of such terms as descriptive of a special type of social relations. It soon became apparent, however, that such statements as "that crowd's snooty as hell," "she's not so hot, she goes around with the X crowd," or "he thinks he rates because he plays with that Y gang," and other evaluations derisive or laudatory, and all referring to particular cliques, were of the highest importance in assigning people to their actual social positions in the status hierarchy of the city. We eventually became convinced that the cliques were next in importance to the family in placing people socially. Thus it devolved upon us to define the clique as a social group as carefully and precisely as we had the family and to analyze our materials again according to the principles implicit in this form of social structure for whatever further light they might shed on the total society of Yankee City.

B. The Clique as a Structure

As we define it, the clique is an intimate nonkin group, membership in which may vary in numbers from two to thirty or more people. As such it is a phenomenon characteristic of our own society. When it approaches the latter figure in size, it ordinarily breaks up into several smaller cliques. The clique is an informal association because it has no explicit rules of entrance, of membership, or of exit. It ordinarily possesses no regular place or time of meeting. It has no elected officers nor any formally recognized hierarchy of leaders. It lacks specifically stated purposes, and its functions are less explicit than those of the family, the association, or the institution. The clique may or may not include biologically related persons;

but all its members know each other intimately and participate in frequent face-to-face relations.

Despite the lack of explicit rules of entrance, exit, and membership behavior, the clique does have very exacting rules of custom which govern the relations of its members. In-group feelings are highly charged, and members speak of others in the community as outsiders. Feelings of unity may even reach such a pitch of intensity that a clique member can and does act in ways contrary to the best interests of his own family.

A person may belong to several cliques at the same time. The clique may or may not be age graded, although the smaller ones ordinarily are. It may also be unisexual or bisexual, depending on its general character. Its activities vary according to the social position and relative wealth of its members. It may be composed of employees of a factory, an ethnic group, the adolescents of a neighborhood or school, or of the members of a fraternity, political organization, or church.

The life span of a clique tends to be short in comparison with that of other social structures because, unlike a formal association, it does not provide for continuity over long periods of time. Cliques, it is true, do accept new members and older ones drop out, but the changes which take place under such circumstances frequently disrupt the structure. The span of existence of a clique, therefore, is highly contingent on the longevity of its members or the continuation of their common interests.

C. The Clique as an Instrument for the Measurement of Class

As we have stated previously, a person may be and frequently is a member of several cliques. He may also be the only member of a given clique who belongs to others, or he may be one of several members of a named clique who belong to others. Such overlapping in clique membership spreads out into a network of interrelations which integrate almost the entire population of a community in a single vast system of clique relations. Consequently the use of the clique concept as a tool of social analysis becomes imperative. The manner in which it was employed by us will now be given. We began by constructing from our interviews several clique structures whose membership had been previously determined. Wherever the members also belonged to other cliques, this fact was noted. Our interview material attested to the fact that all cliques fell into an interlocking vertical hierarchy which crosscuts the entire society. This is represented schematically in Chart VII. Using Clique 12 as an example, we may note that its membership overlaps with that of Cliques 11 and 13, the former being the higher in status. Actually this is a somewhat oversimplified representation, and is more adequately portrayed in Chart VIII. The vertical extension of the clique system is represented by the line TB, and the lateral extension by the line LR. The lines TB and LR divide the circle, which represents Clique 12, into four segments. The interlocking half-circles represent other cliques, part of whose members belong to Clique 12. The cliques above LR are superordinate to the cliques below, and those to the left and right of TB are co-ordinate. (Co-ordinate relations of lateral extension will be discussed more fully below.) This detailed arrangement of the membership of interlocking cliques provides an exact method for implementing social placement by other techniques.

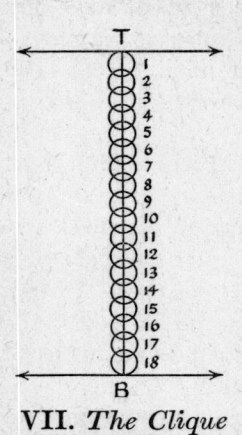

VII. *The Clique Vertical Axis*

4. The Association in the Class System

A. THE FIRST HYPOTHESIS OF THE PLACE AND FUNCTIONS OF ASSOCIATIONS

From near the beginning of the Yankee City research the formal association was studied as a separate structure, with a distinctive organization of its own, and as a mechanism for placing people in the class hierarchy. The formal association differs from the clique in having explicit and definite rules (usually written) of entrance, membership, and exit as well as rules governing payment of fees and ritual procedure. The association differs from economic groupings in the manner in which it relates its members to one another and in the types of activities in which it engages. Whereas economic organizations have ordinary members and officers in a similar structural sense, the association derives its authority, ultimately, from the members themselves rather than accepting it as handed down from a permanent control group.

Social anthropologists have frequently pointed to Melanesian

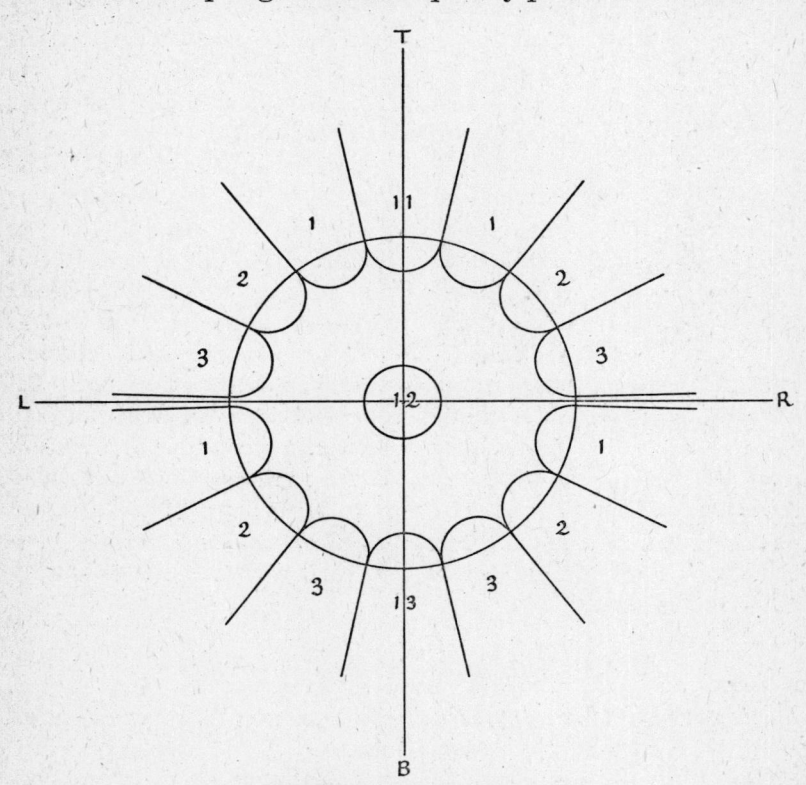

VIII. *The Clique Quadrants*

and West African societies as the outstanding examples of organized groups exhibiting a great proliferation of associations. In so doing, they have passed over far richer material on associations right in our own society, as we learned in our research in Yankee City. Yankee City, in fact, possesses a larger number of these voluntary groupings than any society yet examined by social anthropologists. In view of the importance attached to them in this community, we believed that a careful analysis of their workings and structure would shed considerable light on the underlying mechanisms and principles which operate generally in our social behavior. Consequently we made a wide survey of the social anthropological and sociological literature on this particular subject but found little to assist us in the way of usable theoretical formulations. Our own hypothesis, which was derived from the Yankee City data, was that the function of an association is to integrate the larger structures of the society to the community. The members of each larger inner structure meet antagonisms with other members of the community when they attempt to integrate their behavior to the total society. The association, as an adjunct to such a structure, helps resolve these antagonisms of the larger community to such a structure (e.g., a church, a school, a factory, etc.), and it also acts to organize the antagonisms of the members of the structure to the membership of the larger community.

This general function can be divided into a number of subtypes which are best described with a chart and brief explanations. The first subtype is represented by Diagram A of Chart IX which shows one large inner structure, for example, a factory or a church, being integrated to the total community by associations. Subtype II is represented by Diagram B which shows two larger inner structures being articulated to each other and integrated to the total community (for example, the Y. M. C. A. and Y. W. C. A. help articulate the schools to the churches and relate both of them to the community).

Diagram C of Chart IX shows two communities or cities being tied together by associations such as the mayors' club, school superintendent associations, and local lodges which belong to larger intercity organizations.

While we were examining the general structure of the associations, we also attempted to determine how they fitted into the general class hierarchy. The evidence we had collected pointed to their conforming to the class hierarchy, as had the family and the clique, but the association conformed to this general recognition of class by definite modifications of the place occupied by the family and the clique. In our first analysis of the

Class and Social Structure 115

functions of associations in class, we separated those associations which prevent social mobility from those which aid it. Diagram D of the same chart represents the associations which prevent social mobility. The rectangle representing the community is divided into lower, middle, and upper class, and there are several squares running along the upper side of the line

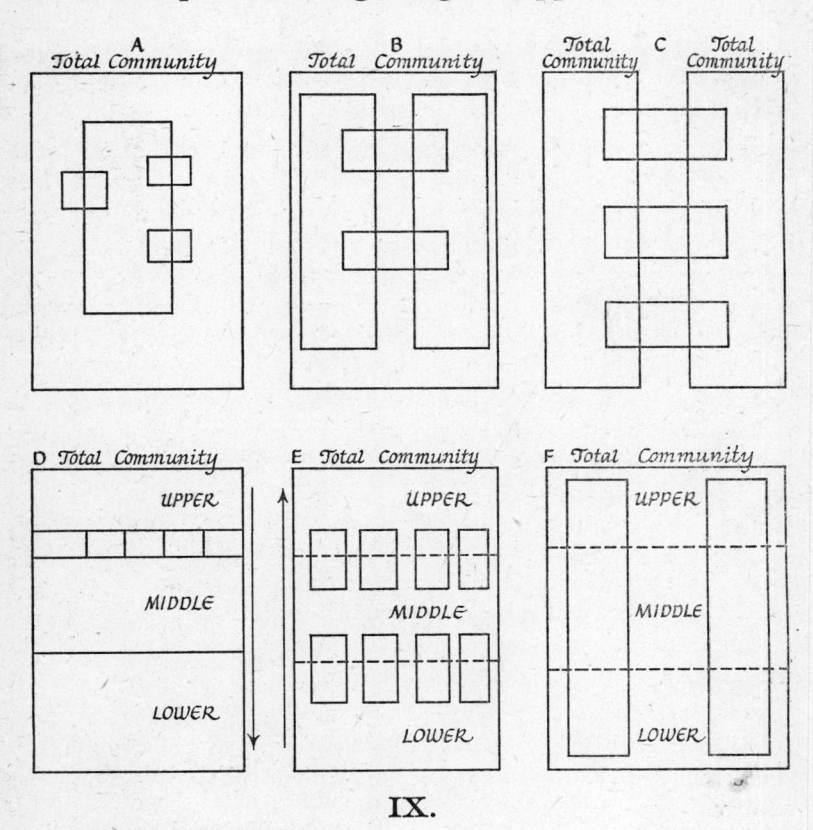

IX.

which divides the middle from the upper class. These squares represent associations which impede movement out of the middle class into the upper. Such associations as those organized for the purpose of preventing cruelty to children and animals, discussion groups, and certain recreational types, such as the country club, perform this function. The arrow which points downward, at the right of the rectangle representing the total community, symbolizes the effect of these associations on social mobility.

Diagram E is divided into lower, middle, and upper classes by horizontal lines. The small rectangles which overlap the two lines represent the associations which function to organize and regulate upward mobility in Yankee City. Associations which are designated by such general terms as lodges and secret societies were thought to function in this capacity.

Another type of association found in Yankee City is represented by Diagram F, which represents the associations crosscutting all three classes and helping to integrate the members of all three classes in the total community. Such associations as the American Legion and certain other patriotic societies fit into this category. These associations frequently have rituals which tie the living community to that of the past and are in many ways similar to the so-called "cults of the dead" found in other cultures.

This earlier hypothesis of the function of the association to integrate the class system and the larger structures of the society into the total community was later modified when it became evident that any association could function both to help and to hinder the social mobility of an individual. If a man were accepted by one of the upper-class clubs, his position in the society became higher and more secure. However, this same association by refusing to admit certain individuals who wished to join it might prevent their rise into a higher part of the society than they at that time occupied.

The study of the association's place and function in Yankee City society led to further developments in using the association for measuring class position. As stated earlier, we had sought simple mechanisms by which the members of the society generalized the place of a large number of individuals, and by so doing, separated vertically the places of the bottom and top groupings. An analysis of the membership of certain types of associations soon demonstrated that certain of these organizations functioned in this manner in the total community.

While an analysis was being made of the newspaper clippings and interviews which described in detail the activities and meetings of the members of the associations, a difference was noticed in the principles of naming the individuals who participated. This difference suggested that the name variation might also mean a difference in social place. (A good example of what is meant here is the custom of using the title "Mr." and "Mrs." in Southern society only when addressing the whites, no matter whether they be poor whites or aristocrats, the use of the title Mr. among the whites exclusively being a symbol of social [e.g., caste] position.) In the upper-class organizations which were composed in part or entirely of women, the woman was spoken of in the newspaper accounts by her husband's name. This was particularly true for any list of officers. Certain exceptions occurred, but it was discovered on further examination that these were widows whose husbands had died some time before and who now were being called by their given first names. In the case of several widows this was not true, for they still were called by their husbands' names even though the husbands had been dead for a long period of time. Among these names were a number of people we had already identified as belonging to the upper-upper group. A quick survey of most of the associations demonstrated that there were a number which followed this practice of naming, and that all of them had members who were definitely upper class.

When we came to associations in which we knew that a good percentage of the members were lower-class or lower-middle, quite a different situation in the naming of women was found. In all cases the officers were given by their own feminine first names and very frequently without the use of the title Mrs. A survey was made of a number of associations which we knew to be largely lower-class and the naming principle was found to operate in the case of all members in all the associations. Certain associations which seemed to spread through a number of classes varied from the two groups just described and here lower-class officers were called by their feminine names while upper-class officers were known by their husbands' names, and in some cases, a woman was known by both her husband's name and her given name.

Our observations seemed to indicate that the upper-class woman participates in the society or at least in the associations primarily as the wife of her husband; that is, she is thought of in terms of her husband all through his lifetime, and at his death, if she is sufficiently upper-class, she is not removed from that category. The lower-class woman, however, seems to be much less dependent upon her husband's social place. On the whole, the upper-class woman does not belong to auxiliaries of her husband's associations, and the only auxiliaries of which she is a member are those connected with churches. The upper-class woman's status seems to depend more upon her place in the family than her place in other organizations, while the lower-class woman's social personality is less dependent upon her husband's place, and she relies not only on the family but on associations such as auxiliaries for her status.

Certain other associations seemed to contradict this naming principle. One of the women's clubs, for example, employed the female first name frequently, as did an art club. Further examination of this latter organization showed two types of members: among the first type were those who had a definite musical talent which they used for entertaining the members at the various meetings; the second type did not take an active part but merely had the privilege of entertaining the club in their homes and listening to the programs. In the club's published booklet, the associated members who only entertained were spoken of by the names of their husbands, while those who were more active were given their feminine names. It seemed evident that the members of the talent group in this association were attempting to maintain a separate social personality for themselves. The same was true for the talented members of the Woman's Club.

The upper-class women's associations were largely charitable and philanthropic, and the women took the roles of patrons but never equals. This meant that, for them, one of the chief ways of delimiting the classes was by considering whom one would invite to one's home, rather than with whom one had friendly relations in associational activity.

It was noticed that certain types of associations were peculiar to certain classes; for example, the insurance orders were not found in the upper class, and the members of the patriotic orders were generally lower-middle and lower class except for the total community types. Many of these associations of the lower classes were of the auxiliary type. This type of organization, both male and female, is organized on the pattern of the family. It utilizes family relations to preserve the group solidarity of the formal association. The auxiliary organizes the women into a group and brings them into definite and ritual relations with the male group. There is noticeable here a sharp sex dichotomy, found in all classes but much stronger in the lower ones.

Although the pattern of the auxiliary type of association prevalent in the lower class is built on the family, it seemed that the family in the lower groups is much weaker than in the upper groups, particularly because of lack of high social position on the part of the father and also because any upward thrust of the individuals who make up a family causes a severe strain on the structure itself, "the family tradition" being weaker in the lower classes. Sexual solidarities are very strong in the lower groups. In almost all cases where there were formal ritual relations between the two sexes, joint installations were examples of the more serious types of such rituals, while mock weddings, meetings at Hallowe'en, Valentine's Day, and birthday parties were often used to organize ritually the two sexual groups.

The upper-upper woman does not have to belong to auxiliaries or clubs because her social position is at the top and she can go no higher, but the lower- and middle-class women have to find means to rise with their husbands and to bring the other members of the family along with them. (The children could rise by "proper" education, purchased with the money from the father's business success.) The differentials in social mobility between the husband and wife explain the theme of certain modern "triangle" novels which are very popular in Yankee City. The man rises and the wife stays in the position which she occupied when she was married. The husband, because of his changed behavior, meets women of the upper class and forms an attachment to one of them. Often the opposite situation is exploited by popular novelists in which the woman, through social mobility in certain societies, gains a higher position than her husband, or, because of her husband's rise, goes outside the family and achieves a similar position for herself and by so doing maintains the family solidarity.

The so-called total-community type of association was of further import to the theoretical development of the research since a number of the associations which were included in this type were patriotic associations. The activities of such associations led to the development of a hypothesis that associations which are organized around total-community crises, such as wars, ordinarily include in their membership the representatives of all classes; that the activities of such groups tend to be highly ritualized; that such rituals are a part of a general ceremonial which resembles the "cults of the dead" found in other societies. The several churches organize the relations of the different church groups to the sacred and spiritual world, but the association organizes the members of all varieties of church belief into membership groups whose cohesiveness depends upon sentiments which surround the dead of the total community rather than upon the ideology of any one denomination of church thought. The Jewish, the Catholic, and the various Protestant sects are integrated by these patriotic organizations; and the Memorial and Armistice Day rituals, expressing sentiments which are larger than sect or class, cover the whole community.

The American Legion was organized around the crisis of the World War, a period when the community euphoria was at its highest. Many of its activities serve to restate ritually the behavior which occurred during the World War crisis. Other activities are of a more practical nature but they again are integrated upon warlike activities. They may be summarized under the headings of preparedness and include the formation of rifle clubs, support of various adolescent military groups, a watchful attitude toward the welfare of the army and navy, etc. The wearing of uniforms, the use of flags, dedications of cannon as memorials, and a variety of patriotic ceremonies all serve to remind visitors coming to Yankee City that "we did our share during the World War."

The membership of the Legion is drawn from all three classes but there are significant differences in proportion of members and in the amount of their participation, the lower classes having by far the largest number of members. The real strength of the Legion is due in great measure to the fact that it serves to relate the living members of the society to the dead. It gains added prestige by serving those members of the community who died in its defense in the crises around which the

Legion is organized. Associated with this general interest in the dead are such activities as the care of disabled veterans and orphans, the care of the veterans' graves, the furnishing of flowers and supervision of burial details for funerals, and many other activities of a similar nature. Since its position in the society is strengthened by the fact that the dead are looked upon as part of the whole group, it tends to extend its ritual relations with all the dead, and on Memorial Day, when representatives of the whole society participate, it and similar patriotic associations perform the main ceremonial for the society. For the Legion, Armistice Day is almost equally important since it is the ceremonial day specially set aside for the celebration of the participation of the United States in the World War crisis.

The Memorial and Armistice Day ceremonies bring complete participation of all the patriotic societies, and their rituals symbolize the expression of the various social structures in this total-community ritual. The function and importance of the various societies are demonstrated by the part they play in the ceremonies and parade.

B. Structural Analysis of Associations

The formal associations were studied to determine the distribution of the membership by class, age, sex, ethnic group, and religion. They were also analyzed to ascertain how they were related to each other and to the other internal organizations of the community. In addition to this, a detailed analysis was made of the activities of all of them to discover what activities were engaged in the most and the least, and then to see how the various activities were related to the different class-types and to the different sex and age associations. After we had made an exhaustive study, we discovered that our earlier hypothesis—that the associations were used to relate other larger structures to the larger society—was only in part true.

It became clear that we had to deal with two fundamental types of associations: (1) those in which there were no formal affiliations with any other organizations; and (2) those in which there were formal connections with other institutions including the church, economic organizations, etc. The associa-

122   *The Social Life of a Modern Community*

tions which were connected with other organizations were divided into subtypes including satellites and those which incorporated a number of smaller associations into one unit. The satellites were redivided into the type of institution with which they had connections. There were no divisions of the second subtype. Satellites included such forms as auxiliaries and Boy Scout organizations which were sponsored by other organizations such as the church and the American Legion. The type of association which grouped a number of separate ones together was usually called a league and was a formal organization which allowed various associations to compete in athletic or other activities.

There were 357 associations for which we had complete or almost complete lists of memberships. Of these, 143 had only males, 110 had only females, and 104 had both males and females. Many of these associations were divided into older and younger groupings or, if the associations consisted of older people, they excluded the younger people from membership. The combination of age and sex factors produced nine different types of associations. Many of the associations included only male adults; others, only female adults; still others, male subadults or female subadults. In addition to these six types of associations, there were also those in which there was no age bifurcation and the membership list went through from the very young to the very old. Such associations were often found affiliated with the various churches of the community. As we have already said, many associations allowed both sexes to become members.

The accompanying chart (Chart X) represents the possible types of associations on the basis of age and sex in the Yankee City study. Associations 1 and 3 are adult male and adult female respectively; 7 and 9 are subadult male and subadult female respectively; 2 and 8 are types of associations in which males and females are found; types 4 and 6 are those in which both adults and subadults are members. The lines A and B which run at right angles to each other represent age bifurcation and sexual bifurcation. Types 4 and 6 overlap both the adult and subadult sections; 2 and 8 overlap the sections which belong to the males and females; and 5 overlaps all four of the sections, which indicates that it is a type of association in which are found all ages and both sexes.

After the associations had been structurally classified by sex and age, we then turned to the distribution of the membership among the six classes. It was discovered that the members of the 357 associations were distributed through 19 class types.

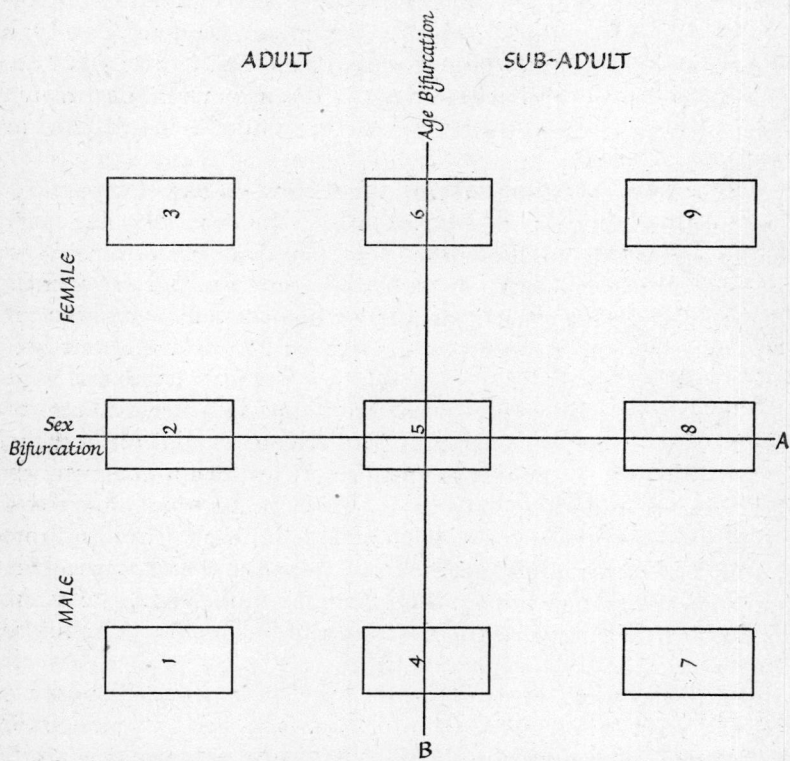

X. *The Divisions of Age and Sex and Associational Types*

There were (1) those associations in which there were only upper-upper members; (2) those in which there were only upper-uppers and lower-uppers; (3) those in which the members were distributed from the upper-upper group through the upper-middle; (4) those which ran from upper-upper through lower-middle; (5) those which were distributed from the topmost group down through the upper-lower; and (6) those which ran all the way from the top to the bottom.

These were followed by associations whose membership was distributed from the lower-upper through the upper-middle (7); those which ran from lower-upper through lower-middle (8); those from lower-upper through upper-lower (9); and those from lower-upper through lower-lower (10).

Certain associations (11) had members who were only in the upper-middle and the lower-middle classes. Others (12) had members who were distributed from the upper-middle through the upper-lower; and there were certain associations (13) which ran from upper-middle through lower-lower. A few associations (14) had only lower-middle members; certain associations (15) had members in lower-middle and upper-lower; and others (16) had members from lower-middle through lower-lower. There were a few associations (17) which had only upper-lower members; a fairly large number (18) which had upper-lower and lower-lower; and a very few (19) which had only lower-lower members.

There was only one association found in which there were only upper-upper members. There were no associations in which there were only lower-upper members or upper-middle members. There were four associations in which there were only lower-middle members; one association in which there were only upper-lower members; and three associations in which there were only lower-lower members. The largest number of associations, some 90 of them, were those which ranged from upper-middle to lower-lower. This type of association was followed by associations whose members were distributed from lower-middle to lower-lower. There were 61 of these. The type of association which ran from upper-middle through upper-lower had a total of 32 associations. There were some 27 associations whose membership was distributed from lower-upper through lower-lower and 25 whose membership was distributed from upper-upper through lower-middle. Of the 357 associations, 21 had a membership which ran from the upper-upper through the lower-lower.

Whereas the membership of the family tends to be distributed in but one class, and that of the clique tends to be in not more than two classes, the associational membership is usually distributed in three or four classes, and the kinds of class relationships involved are very different from those found in the membership of the family or of the clique. Let us now examine the association in the same way that we have the family and the clique in an effort to show how the association differs.

Of the 269 associations in which there were upper-upper members, only 1 had members confined entirely to the upper-upper class. In 81 of these associations there were upper-uppers and lower-uppers; in 77, upper-uppers and upper-middles; in 57, lower-middles and upper-uppers; in 32, upper-lowers and

TABLE 1

A Measurement of the Interconnectedness of the Several Classes in their Associational Relations

	UU No.	UU %	LU No.	LU %	UM No.	UM %	LM No.	LM %	UL No.	UL %	LL No.	LL %	Total No.	Total %
UU	1	0.40	81	30.10	77	28.60	57	21.20	32	11.90	21	7.80	269	100.00
LU	81	19.50	0	0.00	120	28.90	99	23.80	68	16.30	48	11.50	416	100.00
UM	77	10.10	120	15.80	0	0.00	237	31.10	190	24.90	138	18.10	762	100.00
LM	57	6.60	99	11.50	237	27.50	4	0.50	267	30.90	199	23.00	863	100.00
UL	32	4.20	68	8.90	190	24.80	267	34.90	1	0.10	208	27.10	766	100.00
LL	21	3.40	48	7.80	138	22.40	199	32.20	208	33.70	3	0.50	617	100.00

upper-uppers; and in 21, lower-lowers and upper-uppers. To state these relations by percentages: 0.40 per cent of the associations in which there were upper-uppers had only upper-uppers; 30.10 per cent had lower-uppers; 28.60 per cent had upper-middles; 21.20 per cent had lower-middles; 11.90 per cent had upper-lowers; and 7.80 per cent had lower-lowers. (See Table 1.)

Of the 416 associational relations which existed between lower-upper members and members of their class or members of other classes, there were 19.50 per cent which had lower-uppers and upper-uppers; none which had only lower-uppers; 28.90 per cent which had upper-middles; 23.80 per cent in which there were lower-middles; 16.30 per cent in which there were upper-lowers; and 11.50 per cent in which there were lower-lowers.

There were 762 associational relations in which upper-middles participated. Of these, 10.10 per cent had upper-uppers also; 15.80 per cent had lower-uppers; none had only upper-middles; 31.10 per cent had lower-middles; 24.90 per cent had upper-lowers; and 18.10 per cent had lower-lowers.

Of the 863 associational relations in which lower-middle members were to be found in direct relation with members of their own class or members of other classes, 6.60 per cent had upper-uppers in them; 11.50 per cent had lower-uppers; 27.50 per cent had upper-middles; 0.50 per cent had lower-middles; 30.90 per cent had upper-lowers; and 23.00 per cent had lower-lowers.

Of the 766 associational relations in which upper-lower members were to be found in direct relation with members of their own class or members of other classes, 4.20 per cent had upper-upper members in them; 8.90 per cent had lower-uppers; 24.80 per cent had upper-middle members; 34.90 per cent had lower-middle; only 0.10 per cent had upper-lower alone; and 27.10 per cent had lower-lowers.

There were 617 associational relations in which lower-lowers participated. Of these, 3.40 per cent had upper-uppers in them; 7.80 per cent had lower-uppers; 22.40 per cent had upper-middles; 32.20 per cent had lower-middles; 33.70 per cent had upper-lowers; and 0.50 per cent had lower-lowers.

VII

PROFILES FROM YANKEE CITY

THE present chapter introduces some of the human types who are members of the six classes. The several sketches which follow are intended to do no more than illustrate how the several social levels appear to the observer and how it feels to live in the class system of Yankee City. The people described, as well as their families, cliques, associations, political and economic institutions, are presented as examples of what the researcher observes while doing his field work.

Each person, each institution, and each incident in each essay is a composite drawing. No one actual individual or family in Yankee City is depicted, rather the lives of several individuals are compressed into that of one fictive person. The personnel of all families has been changed. In the "New Family" story (Section 4), for example, the Phillip Starrs are an amalgam of many individuals who are socially like them. The Patriotic Order of United States Veterans of All Wars is not one but a number of organizations and the events assigned to it are a composite of happenings from many associations. The justification for these changes lies in our attempt to protect our subjects and to tell our story economically. We have not hesitated to exclude all material which might identify specific persons in the community; and we have included generalized material wherever necessary to prevent recognition. The people and situations in some of the sketches are entirely imaginary. In all cases where changes were introduced in the reworking of our field notes, we first satisfied ourselves that they would not destroy the essential social reality of the points of the original interview. Only then were such materials included in our text.

This chapter relates some of the more critical or revealing happenings in the lives of typical Yankee City people. Successful and unsuccessful upward mobility within several classes is illustrated. The methods of including and excluding people from significant class groupings are portrayed. The outward symbols of class are given; and the negative and positive evaluations of the several classes are expressed in the actions and words of the participants. The upper classes are treated first, followed by the middle and lower ones. (The reader should consult Chart XI at the end of this chapter whenever names of organizations are mentioned in the text.)

1. They All Came

ON that autumn evening Mrs. Henry Adams Breckenridge was sitting in a large wing chair by the fireplace whose dying embers occasionally flared and lighted her pale face and white hair. Behind her, numerous used teacups were scattered on the table. Of her fifty-odd guests all but two had departed. Their automobiles, which had spread out along Hill Street and overflowed down the side streets, had disappeared.

The home of Mr. and Mrs. Henry Adams Breckenridge (UU) where the tea had been given is a square white house which sits well back from the street. It has three stories and is topped by a captain's walk which increases its height. During most of the year large trees and a tall thick hedge obscure the house from the street. A gravel drive cuts through the center of the hedge and, passing the front of the house, continues to a large barn (now a garage) one hundred yards to the rear. In front of the house the drive forms a circle almost too sharp to allow automobiles to turn. Mrs. Breckenridge has often commented that the "circle" was made for carriages and should now be enlarged to accommodate automobiles; "but I like it the way it is and I won't have it changed."

The lawn runs from the hedge back to the barn. The garden stretches one hundred yards from the front circle on one side of the house to the adjoining property, owned and occupied by Mr. Breckenridge's brother and his family (UU). The latter grounds are also well kept, but they do not have an elaborate garden.

There are many old rose bushes in the Breckenridge garden, in which Mr. Breckenridge shows some interest. He occasionally picks off dead flowers and sprays the roses with a homemade solution to kill the rose bugs. Mrs. Breckenridge very rarely cares for the garden although she enjoys walking through it and telling visitors about the flowers. Back of the barn lie apple orchard and meadow. The trees are sprayed occasionally, but little effort is made to make them produce.

For years Mrs. Breckenridge and her sister drove about the town in horse-drawn carriages as did their friends, the Marshalls (UU). Mrs. Breckenridge's chief girlhood interest, in fact, was in horses; and she is still so fond of them that she grudgingly accepts the automobile as a necessary convenience.

Inside the house "very good colonial furniture" is mixed indiscriminately with mid-Victorian. This is a common occurrence in the houses of families whose means made it possible to add furniture during the period when the Victorian superseded the earlier colonial style. There are no reproductions. A few family portraits—two signed by famous artists—have prominent places.

When inspecting the shiny appearance of a new house built by a lower-upper, Mrs. Breckenridge said that one of the things she liked about her own home was that it always had the feeling of having been lived in. This is perhaps the first and most lasting impression that one has of the Breckenridge residence.

"It was nice of you to stay on," she said to the woman and man who sat with her by the fireplace. "I find these large teas a little exhausting. I always hate to give them but I couldn't get out of this one. Several of the members of the committee had given teas and they were afraid that Mrs. Starr [LU] would try to give the last one. She always gives the most perfect and elaborate ones but I am afraid everyone talks about them because they're just a little too-too. She was the one that you saw sitting in the library telling John Alton [UU] about sailing ship days. It was amusing to listen in on that. I confess I eavesdropped on some of it. As you know, John belongs to one of the oldest families in Yankee City, and John's great-grandfather built and sailed more ships out of this harbor than almost anyone."

"Of course, the Starrs are new shoe people," said Mrs. Wentworth (UU). "No one ever heard of him until he made his fortune manufacturing shoes."

"All of John's knowledge about the days of the sailing ships," remarked Mrs. Breckenridge, "came from his father and his grandfather. And I suppose he heard some of it from my father [UU] and from my Uncle George [UU]. You could tell that all of what Mrs. Starr said she had learned from books she had read. Somehow it annoys me. I just can't help it. You could almost see her memorizing it all so she could use it on people like John and my brothers. I wouldn't mind so much if I thought she really cared about such things, but I know that she doesn't. She thinks it will help her socially to talk to them about things in which they have a genuine interest.

"Mrs. Starr is a social climber. I don't think that the fact of her recent arrival in Yankee City has anything to do with it. She is too aggressive—she is a social climber. She can be very nice, though, and her children are nice. Some of them are very good-looking, but the daughter isn't so much now because she is beginning to look like her mother."

Mrs. Breckenridge continued, "Mrs. Starr is very pushy and she tries to get into everything. I don't dislike her just because she's new. Everybody in the House and Home Club [UU-LU] hates her. If it hadn't been for Miss Churchill [UU] she would never have got in, but she was always very nice to Miss Churchill. When we started the club and sent out invitations, Mrs. Starr was not included; and when I was having it at my house, she called up just as if she were a bosom friend of mine, which she never was, and asked if she could come. I was embarrassed to death and I said, 'Why, no, Mrs. Starr. Mrs. Marshall started the club, and I don't feel I have any right to ask anyone, but if you would like to send in your name you may.' She said, 'All right, very well,' and she sent in her name. Everyone objected, but they all liked Miss Churchill so they said all right."

"When Mrs. Sinclair [UU] had the meeting last year," said Mrs. Wentworth, "Mrs. Starr called up and asked if she might bring her daughter; whereupon the daughter and her friends went to the club and Mrs. Sinclair was simply furious, and she said, 'What sort of person is this that you have in the House and Home Club?'

"When Frederica Alton [UU] started a bridge club, Mrs. Starr called her and asked why she wasn't invited to the club and attempted to get in. She is just like that in everything that she does.

"Mrs. Breckenridge said that Mrs. Starr 'was certainly

smart. She was right on the spot. We were so mad that we had to let her into the House and Home Club, but you can just bet that none of her friends will get in.'[1]

"The things the Starrs do sometimes are unbelievable," Mrs. Wentworth went on. "You know, they have the most valuable ship model in Yankee City. It used to belong to the Altons; Mr. Starr bought it when Frederica Alton needed money and sold some things after her husband died. Frederica took them up to Boston and sold them on the quiet so no one would know about it and so people like that wouldn't get them. But Mrs. Starr's dealer sent her word that he had acquired these things; and do you know that Phillip Starr [LU] went into Boston and actually bought the model? Everyone was annoyed, but Frederica said, 'What could you expect?'

"I've always made fun of birth and old families, but they do mean something. Mrs. Starr has learned a lot from her books and by being on the *qui vive;* but breeding is something that doesn't come out of a book or by imitating your betters."

"You should have learned a lot about our city this afternoon," the hostess said to the man. "All sorts of people were here. People one hardly knows. Wouldn't you know, not one of the women on the committee or their husbands stayed away. They all came. The Camps [UM], the Frenches [UM], and the Flahertys [UM] were here. They were the people who stood off in one corner pretty much by themselves. They were the ones who were so polite when you tried to talk to them. They always agreed with everything you said. You know, I was just thinking that this is the first time that any of those three women has ever been in my house."

"Yet," said the second woman, "with the exception of Mrs.

---

1. All the above evidence demonstrates how an ambitious, socially mobile person can manipulate an associational structure for the purpose of climbing in the community. It also shows how a given association can be used by an individual to climb and by the society to prevent further mobility. In the case of Mrs. Starr, there was a definite progression in the associations which she joined as she moved upward in the social hierarchy. She was at first active in an organization which included the three uppermost classes. As she became more successful in achieving social status, she lost interest in this association. She later joined another organization which had a smaller number of UM people and finally became a member of an organization which had no one outside of the two upper classes. Her interests decreased in the first two organizations and increased in the last.

Flaherty, they were born and reared here. But, you see, at this time an election is too important."

"Yes," the hostess said. "Aunt Caroline saw the governor at Uncle Ned's the last time she was in Boston, and he said that the election was going to be very close. That awful Mr. Meaghan may get back in again.

"Diane, did you notice how those Kimbles [LU], Waltons [LU], and Starrs patronized the Frenches and the Camps? It was really funny to see how snooty some of those new shoe families can be when they're talking to people who haven't got as far as they have."

"Those poor Starr children [LU] were here," said Mrs. Wentworth. "Katherine was looking a little beaten and worn and Johnny apparently was suffering from a hangover. I don't care what people say. I can't dislike them. I always remember when they were growing up how badly they were treated. I've actually seen people turn their backs on them when the two of them came in. It's not as bad as that any more, but it's bad enough. This town does something to children like them."

"We invited the Flahertys [UM] because they are the nice type of Irish," Mrs. Breckenridge remarked. "My grandfather remembered when Flaherty's grandfather came here and worked as a common laborer, but they've always been a good honest family. We once had an Irish maid, and she called them 'lace-curtain Irish.' Fred Flaherty put himself through school. He went to Boston College when he failed to get into Harvard. He was very ambitious and he later went to law school and came back here to practice. Uncle George said that he has one of the best practices in town."

While they talked, the man smoked and added appropriate remarks and seeming assent whenever necessary. The second woman left. The man accepted an invitation to stay a bit longer and have a drink.

"You know," the hostess continued, "every time Diane Wentworth and I talk like that I'm just a little ashamed afterward but somehow that's the way I honestly feel when I do it. I wish someone like Sinclair Lewis would write up this town. I am afraid it would be like washing our mouths out with soap but it would do us good.

"I always think of the chapter in *Babbitt* after gossiping

the way we've been doing.[2] Babbitt invited the *nouveau riche* McKelvey family to dinner; and they treated him so terribly that he and his wife were miserable. And then the Babbitts reversed it all by doing the same thing to the little people who were socially below them and made them feel miserable. Have you ever read *Babbitt?*"

The man said that he had.

"Don't you think that it is something like we are here?"

Her companion said that there were many resemblances, but that *Babbitt* was set in a Middle Western town.

"I am afraid we feel ourselves superior. In fact, I sometimes think this town feels superior even to Boston and London. No one here would admit that New York is better than we are. New York is a good place to make money in and that's all. You hear people talking of Middle Westerners as though they were country cousins. Many of us here have never been west of the Connecticut River. Somehow we're proud of it.

"The people of Yankee City are peculiar. They don't seem to be interested in anyone but themselves. Sometimes new people come in here and leave town before anyone knows about them. I remember a very nice family who were here for over a year, but no one knew them. And they met the wrong people. People say they left because no one picked them up. That's always happening here. You need the right kind of sponsors when you come into this town."

While she continued talking, Mrs. Breckenridge searched among the books which filled the shelves on the wall opposite the fireplace.

"Yes, I know that Babbitt's Zenith is Middle West. We people in Yankee City like to think ourselves superior to the Middle West, and it pleases us to laugh at those people when we read Mr. Lewis' books; but fundamentally we are very much like them. Middle Westerners like to think they are much more democratic, but I think Sinclair Lewis has them absolutely right.

"The Babbitts and their crowd were socially below the McKelveys and their circle, and the McKelveys felt inferior to what Lewis calls 'the Old Families' of Zenith. Then, Babbitt

2. The part of *Babbitt* to which she refers is chap. xv. In it Lewis outlines several of the social levels of Zenith.

was above those little people where the Babbitts went to dinner.[3]

"We speak of old families here in Yankee City, too. People like the Breckenridges and the Marshalls, the Wentworths, the Treppingtons, some of the Talbots [UU], and my own family, for that matter, are old family here; and people like the Starrs and the Waltons [LU], the Tolmans [LU], and those other new people belong to the *nouveau riche* crowd like the McKelveys in Lewis' *Babbitt*.

"And there are scores of Babbitts here. Some I like and some I don't. Ezra Rodgers [UM] and Alexander French [UM], for instance. They were here this afternoon.

"Mr. Ezra Rodgers was that odd little man who sat in the love seat all the time. As plain and simple as he can be. He and his wife are just what they are. They're not trying to push in where they're not wanted. They're good solid Homeville and don't want to be anything else. He's awfully well liked by the men. All of them say that he is always doing something worth while for our town. He belongs to everything, but I must confess he sometimes embarrasses me with his booster spirit. He's a Rotarian. He's in the Chamber of Commerce. He belongs to all of the civic associations and all of the improvement associations. And he's very active in the Baptist Church. I believe he's a member of the Lowell Club.

"He's just the opposite of Alexander French. Alec and his wife [UM] are 'pushers' and climbers. They're always scheming to get into your house by being on a church committee or by being more Republican than anyone else on the committee. We had to have them here this afternoon and, believe me, if there's a Babbitt in this town, he's the one. He actually believes all of these things that you read in the Boston *Herald* about our businessmen being superior to anybody else. I think he's still surprised there's not any grass growing in our streets now that Roosevelt is in.

"Then there's the Camps [UM], the Flahertys, and the Joneses [UM]. They all seem to know each other and stick together at large teas like this."

3. It is quite clear that "the McKelveys" are similar to "the new people" of the LU class in Yankee City, and that the old families—to whom they feel inferior—are what we have called UU. Babbitt and his crowd are UM, and they admit inferiority to the LU McKelveys.

2. All the Men Have Left

WHEN the male visitor had finished his drink, he looked at his watch and remarked that he would have to hurry to catch his train for Boston. His hostess said that her daughter Elizabeth was driving in and would be glad to take him. Elizabeth Breckenridge was a graduate of Smith, and, although twenty-eight, she still lived at home. During the hour's ride she discussed some of her personal problems with her passenger whom she had known and confided in before.

"This may sound queer to you but it's a familiar one in Yankee City," said Elizabeth Breckenridge. "My problem is a simple one. There's just no one in this town for a person like me to marry. All of the young men have left. My younger brother, Henry, is in New York. When he graduated from Harvard he was offered a marvelous opportunity in one of the large law offices in New York. One of the senior partners is a friend of father's—they were in the same class at Harvard. Father says that Henry may not be a genius but that he is sensible and thoroughly dependable; and father's friend told him that Henry was just the kind of man they wanted. He said that they could hire all of the smart young Jewish lawyers they wanted to do the dirty work, but they needed men of character to take over when it was time for the older men to retire.

"Henry's engaged to a girl who is a sister of a classmate of his. He met her years ago when he was at school at St. Paul's. Both of our families are for the marriage because, well, it's sort of funny. You may not believe this, but New Yorkers look up to us New Englanders. We may not have much money, but we do have something that you can only get by being born into a long line of distinguished families—of people who just know instinctively how to do the right thing. That may be snobbish, but breeding does count. My father says it's too bad that the word 'gentlewoman' has gone out, but thank God we can still use 'gentleman' and have it mean something.

"My father sits in his study and reads nineteenth-century English novels and studies old English ballads. He retired when he was thirty-five. Some people thought that was wrong for a man with a New England heritage but Dad didn't say anything in reply. He's always said to us, 'Never defend what you do after you've done it. Other people's standards are never any better than yours and seldom as good.' You know, I somehow believe that.

"My contemporaries are all gone and now all of Henry's are gone, too. There are no large families in Yankee City any more. Two or three children are about all. My old beau is in Honolulu. That place is run by Boston and Yankee City people. The McIlraiths are also out there. Sometimes they come back for the summer and live in one of the old family houses. They all like to get back. People of my father's generation believe them when they say they would like to stay here, but I know better. The younger people respect us and admit our social position, but they prefer New York. Some of them even like San Francisco and Los Angeles.

"The men have always gone away from here, and the women have stayed home. I always remember my two aunts when I think of my own mess. They are old ladies now and neither of them has ever married. They live in lonely respectability in a house they inherited from father's great-aunt. They cared for their two brothers and their grandfather until their brothers married and the grandfather died. I have heard stories about Aunt Elizabeth and Aunt Janice wanting to marry young men who were 'beneath them,' but they say 'their mother ruled them with an iron hand and stopped them from making a bad marriage. It wasn't that the young men weren't nice, you know, but they were just a little common.'"

This was the background against which she would have her confidant view her present, most pressing problem. She had "somehow become involved" with an older man who had been divorced. Her father had warned her about being mixed up with such a person; yet her father's two best friends had been divorced. She knew that if the man she was interested in had been in the same "station in life" as her father, very little would have been made of his divorce. The divorce was simply a convenient peg on which her father could hang his criticism of the man's lowly status.

The car drew up before the entrance of a downtown hotel in Boston.

"Well, come again," she said. "I'll tell you the rest of the story of my life—if there is ever anything more to tell. Nothing like being well-behaved and maintaining your reticence."

3. Old Family

MR. and Mrs. John Aldington Breckenridge (UU) left the tea earlier than the others. They refused several offers to be driven the short distance home, declaring that they needed the exercise.

John Aldington, elder brother of Henry Adams Breckenridge, was a tall rugged man, and when he walked down Hill Street people said he looked as "straight as the mast of a sailing ship." His white mustache and beard glistened in the late afternoon sunlight. When the people of the town saw him they bowed respectfully and commented among themselves on how well he kept his age. His detractors said he was "so lofty" that he was like the Lowells and spoke "only to God." But, to those who knew him, he was "a directly spoken person who always said what he believed to be the truth."

Mrs. John Breckenridge was a lady who had reached her seventh decade. She managed her home and family with great efficiency and quiet tact. She had not married until after she was thirty, but had borne her husband three children.

Many generations had lived in their large Hill Street house, and not a few of the great names from New England's and the nation's history had known its hospitality. The furnishings of the house were simple and included the accumulations of the several generations of Breckenridges who had inhabited the place. Oliver Wendell Holmes, who had sometimes driven by to talk about genealogical matters and to discuss the names of the well-remembered dead, was remembered by his cherished gift, a silver inkstand.

From his study, Mr. Breckenridge could see up and down Hill Street. From memory he could recount the names of all of the families who lived in the houses on each side of the wide street. Each house "worth remembering" had a name. There was the "Captain Brown house," built in 1810 by a famous captain in the China trade; or the Littlefield house—"he was said to be the best orator the old Presbyterian Church ever had, even in the days when every pew in the Church harbored a captain and his family." When he talked about the houses, those present symbols of the living past, he usually commented on some of their occupants. For many of the houses he knew the names of all of the former occupants but not of the present ones. "It's one of those new Irish families, you know, and I don't know much about them"; or, "Those people may be the ones who are doing something out at the silverware factory, but I'm not sure."

Mr. Breckenridge was thumbing through a fat genealogical record of his family when his dinner guest arrived—a New York painter who was staying for a few weeks at the Yankee City Inn.

"I was checking a point in the family history," he said to his guest. "I had an argument at tea about it with Caleb Marshall." He put a marker in the book and placed it on the library table.

"My children say I think more of that book than I do of my Bible—and you know I think they're right."

At dinner the conversation continued on the topic of the history of Yankee City. And the history of Yankee City to Mr. and Mrs. Breckenridge was largely the history of the old families.

"There are only a few of the old families left," she informed her guest. "Many people who are now considered by some to be old family were not when I was a young girl. There are all of these new shoe people—who are nice people, but they don't belong with such families as the Leveretts, the Wentworths, and the Breckenridges. They all seem just a little new to me, and while undoubtedly they are very nice, they are not old family. My sister Louisa says that they probably think we're a bit queer, too, just as we think they're somehow a little odd; and probably we're both right."

The visitor to the City observed that everything seemed to be judged by its comparative age in Yankee City.

"You see," Mrs. Breckenridge explained, "we people who have always lived here remember a great deal. We go back a long time. All the things my little grandmother used to tell me are as fresh in my mind as yesterday. I can remember walking in the cemetery with her while she put flowers on her mother's grave. She was always so sensible and told me all about the people who were buried there. I felt as though I knew them all. She told me about all her own people. And as I grew older I learned some of the untold secrets of our family and, I am afraid, some of the gossip about the other families.

"I got to know those people better than almost anyone living. Sometimes I still go over there, not just because of duty but because it is somehow satisfying.

"Modern people hate graveyards but they seem places of peace to me. When I walk through now, each gravestone reminds me of someone I knew or someone grandmother knew and told me about.

"Yankee City is the home of people scattered all over this world. I know several members of old families who live out in Honolulu. They are very prominent people there. Ever so often they come back and take a place here; 'just to come home again,' they say. Some of the houses of Hill Street are only open in the summer time when their owners return from New York, Philadelphia, and Washington.

"In one sense, our lovely houses aren't our homes. It may seem odd, but for those of us whose people have always lived here, the cemetery is truly our home, for there live all of our people. All of them. The men and women who lived in these same houses. You see how we feel and why people come home. I could name a number of families who have not lived here, except in the summer, for the last generation; but when they die all of them are sent back here to be buried. To be in a permanent home.

"I honestly feel sorry for the new people. They can't feel the same way we do about such things."

Mr. Breckenridge had interrupted her with a few confirmatory remarks while she spoke. When they left the dinner table he took up the burden of the conversation.

"The old families aren't as powerful as they used to be. The sons don't follow in their fathers' footsteps. New people keep coming in. They're the ones who get control. Not we. Old families used to run this town but not any more."

Yet that very day, while walking to and from his office (where he had spent some four hours saying "yes" and "no" to people who were attempting to translate their decisions into economic reality) Mr. Breckenridge had been stopped by five people, each with a question to submit to his judgment and authority.

What did Mr. Breckenridge think about the new schoolhouse?

"Well, the one we've got is good enough. This is no time to be spending our money on a new building."

That night the questioner advised his lodge brothers to work against the building of a new schoolhouse because "this is no time to be spending our money on a new building."

"Mr. Breckenridge," another asked, "what is your opinion about the Newtown real estate projects?"

"Much too high, and I can't see what they think they're doing out there. This town doesn't need new dwelling houses."

His inquisitor that evening called his friend in Newtown and informed him that he had postponed buying a lot out in Newtown. He thought prices ought to come down.

The president of one of the banks (UM), thinking of advising some of his local clients in their investments, inquired about the possibilities of certain new utilities offerings. He was told by Mr. Breckenridge that the investments were worthless. The next day the president of the bank informed his clients that after careful investigation he believed it was unwise to put such stocks and bonds in their portfolios at that time.

As Mr. Breckenridge continued down the street he was stopped by a young Pole, Paul Stanley (UL), whose father had once worked for him as a yardboy. The young man tipped his hat and said "sir" when he started speaking.

"Mr. Breckenridge, I would like to get married, but I want to buy a house. Would you tell me what to do?"

"How much have you saved, Paul?"

The young man told him.

"But that's not enough to get you a house, Paul."

"That's what I wanted to see you about, Mr. Breckenridge. I thought maybe you would tell the bank I was okay."

He looked at Paul for a minute.

"Certainly, I will. You're a good risk."

Paul Stanley got back in his coupe and drove down to the region of the small houses to announce their good fortune to the girl to whom he was engaged. (See Section 13, "Going Up in the World.")

And finally, as he was turning into his gate, one of the ushers of his church (UU) stopped Mr. Breckenridge.

"What did you think of Rev. Ainsley's [UM] sermon last Sunday?"

"I thought it was no better and no worse than the first one he gave three years ago. I knew then he was muddleheaded. He doesn't understand this town. James, we made a mistake in him. We should have waited until we could have found someone like Sutterfield [UU]."

They both agreed that the appointment of Rev. Mr. Ainsley had been a mistake. The Rev. Mr. Ainsley's duties as shepherd of his flock became increasingly difficult. As the months passed, he had an uneasy feeling that the bishop did not seem quite so friendly as before. He and his wife discussed the advantages of taking a parish in a poor neighborhood of some large city where they could do more effective work.

4. New Family

THE Phillip Starrs drove home from the tea in an oversized, custom-built limousine. John Alton had once remarked sarcastically that if Phillip ever lost his money he could put his stove in his car and camp out for the winter. And his hearer is reported to have said, "Or install a calliope in it and join the circus."

The Starrs were one of a small group of families who recently had purchased Georgian houses in one of the more handsome sections on Hill Street.

The large, square house is one of the old ones on Hill Street. Two well-known architects have declared it to be "one of the most beautiful surviving examples of Federal architecture." Several members of certain old families admitted that it was a beautiful home, but they said, "She's made a museum out of it. It's too perfect. She spent thousands of dollars to remodel it and make it a perfect example of Federal architecture. The trouble with her is she imitates and always overdoes it." Only a few feet of well-clipped grass separate the house from the sidewalk, but in the rear an expansive lawn, flanked by meticulously tended gardens, glistens in the sunlight. Some people feel that the gardens are overcared for, that the gardener has been too scrupulous, and that the house has been so frequently painted that it shines just a little too much.

Mrs. Starr's furniture had been purchased with the aid of an expert on New England antiques. There was nothing in her house that was not called "authentic Adams," or "a perfect example of Queen Anne." And her garden, one soon learned, had won numerous prizes.

The garden parties, teas, and dinners Mrs. Starr gave were said by the gossiping members of the older families to be "too elaborate," "too perfect," and "done for effect." Her defenders (many of them trying to be equally perfect) said it was lovely that she could do such nice things and loved entertaining because she did it so well.

Mr. and Mrs. Starr went into the library and waited dinner there before an open fire. Mr. Starr read the editorials of the Boston *Transcript* and re-examined the financial pages of the Boston *Herald*. He found nothing in the editorials but "good sound sense." He said it was "too bad that more people didn't read them." The financial pages of the *Herald* were somewhat upsetting, for Mr. Starr's income from the sale of one of his shoe factories had been invested in the bonds of several large national and international companies.

Mrs. Starr looked over the magazines on the library table. Those of her husband and son were arranged in a neat row on one side. They included *Fortune, Time, National Geographic,* and *Sports Afield*. Mr. Starr kept the *Saturday Evening Post* by his bedside and Mrs. Starr read the *Pictorial Review* in her own room. Such magazines, not considered fitting symbol's of one's social place and intellectual level, were kept away from the view of casual—perhaps critical?—guests.

Mrs. Starr glanced idly through the magazines to which she and her husband subscribed: *Atlantic Monthly, House Beautiful, Harper's,* and *Vogue*.

Their son Johnny, however, bought *Film Fun* at the local store, and their daughter Katherine sometimes read the movie magazines; but they knew better than to subscribe to them and always gave them to the maid later.

After dinner Mr. Starr took his own car and drove down to

the Lowell Club (UU to UM). The Lowell Club was called the "House of Lords" in local speech, while the Out-of-Doors Club was known as the "House of Commons." This was one way of saying that the Lowell Club was "more choosy" about its members—"no Catholics, and only the best people" are allowed in; but "the House of Commons takes in more fellows from the side streets."

The clubhouse of the Lowell Club had been the home of one of the old families. When Mr. Starr entered it that evening, he met many of the men whom he had seen at the tea. He talked with a broker, a manufacturer, and a banker about investment problems and found out from them what Jonathan Wentworth (UU) and John Breckenridge, the directors of several large institutions, had said on the subject. Mr. Wentworth and Mr. Breckenridge did not belong to the Lowell Club. Mr. Starr listened to Alexander French who talked about what the "classes and the masses" were going to do in the coming election. He heard Mr. French express surprise that there was social "class consciousness now among the people." French said that "the solid people like the men in the Chamber of Commerce and the Rotary Club and our own club can be depended on, but one can't always tell about some of the fellows in the Antlers (UU to LM) and the Caribou (UM to LL). And most of those foreigners down on River Street are the ringleaders in the unions, and they'll vote the other way."

Jackman (UM), owner of one of the shoe factories, said that his foreman had told him that even the Riverbrookers were now joining the unions.

French agreed with Jackman and then told about the last election held by the United States Veterans of All Wars. He prefaced these remarks by saying, "Don't misunderstand me now, because I like that organization. It has a good influence on the town, and I think it is a duty of all of us to support it; but, you know, it's got everybody in it from the clam flats to Hill Street, and now and then some of those fellows from down there go too far. They get us into a jam, and some of us have to get back in and straighten them out.

"Most of our crowd hardly ever goes. Tim Pinkham [LM] and people like him and the bunch from the Antlers [largely LM] and the Three Mast [LM to LL] run it. It got so bad that they had some strip tease dancers down from Boston. Brooks Sinclair [UU] got us all together, and we put on a quiet little campaign and elected Paul Foley [LU]. Paul didn't want to run, but he agreed to when we convinced him that the better people in town should clean things up and raise the standards."

Everyone spoke approvingly of the outcome and of Sinclair's campaign.[4]

While this conversation was in progress, Mr. Starr looked at his watch and said that he would have to hurry on or he would be late to the meeting of the February Club (UU to LU). When he stood up to go, Jim Whitecotton (LU) and Cyrus Jordan (LU) arose and departed with him. Alec French stayed on. He was quiet for a moment after they left, remembering what Jordan's wife had told his wife in a burst of confidence: that when his, Alec's, name had been put up before the February Club he had been blackballed, and Mrs. Jordan had said it was because everybody thought "Alec was too young." Alec knew that there were men in the club who were younger than he. He had once been indignant when he had heard an Irish doctor, who lived just off Hill Street, declare that the men in the January (UU to LU) and February clubs thought they were "Lowells and Cabots." But on occasions such as tonight he found it difficult to refrain from harboring similar sentiments himself. Mr. French was still trying to get into the club. Jordan had told him after the last country club dinner when they were having a few drinks together that he was working on Starr and Walton (LU).

Alec had said to forget it all, but he said it in such a way that Jordan knew that he should try again.

Mr. Starr and his companions, on leaving the Lowell Club, drove to the home of Mr. Arthur Walton. The Walton residence was located in the same cluster of houses with that of Mr. Starr. Several members of their discussion group were already present when they arrived, including active or retired owners of several factories, bankers, lawyers, doctors, ministers,

---

4. All of the people to whom French was speaking were UM, LU, or UU. He had once said to an interviewer in reference to the same incident, "That's the way it is around here. Things reach a certain point in these big organizations when we people up here have to take a hand and do something."

a professor, and a writer. All graduates of universities, they were known as "the heads of prominent families in the country." Except for two Democrats, all were Republicans; but those two were both old family. One was from one of the oldest and most respected families in the community. He once said, "The trouble with most of those fellows is that they forget that the Roosevelts were aristocrats and had money in the family before the Revolution. Most of the people who talk are about two generations from gatekeepers. They spend the rest of their lives trying to forget it."

The February Club was a discussion group. The paper of the evening, fittingly entitled "The History of a Yankee Ship," told how the author, a member of an old family, had spent a recent three months in the Dutch Indies in Malaya. He had searched through certain records in Singapore and had come across the tale he was about to relate that evening. It was shortly after the beginning of the nineteenth century when the clipper *East Wind,* sailing under Capt. John Breckenridge and owned by the captain's father, had run into a great typhoon. The captain had more than won his right to his title during the struggle to keep his ship afloat. After the storm, the ship's crew picked up three survivors of a wreck. One of these was Lord Nelson Wellington who later became prominent in the Napoleonic campaigns and the English leader who, many authorities declared, had saved the British Empire.

After the paper, the discussion brought out the facts that Captain Breckenridge was the great-grandfather of John and Henry Breckenridge; that the chief mate was Jonathan Marshall, the lineal ancestor of the Edward Marshalls; and that the builder of the boat, Frederick Alton, was an ancestor of both John Alton and the wife of Elliot Nash. All these names were connected with the club or were old family and intimate friends of its members.

Anecdotes which usually began: "My father told me that the *East Wind* . . ." or "My Uncle John knew old man Cartwright . . ." were told by some of the older members. The members of the new families present referred more often to history books or asked questions of the others.

At the last meeting, Mr. Starr had given his paper. He

had talked on "Henry Ford's Contribution to American Industry." At the meeting before that, Mr. James Whitecotton's paper had not been too well liked. It was called "The Place of Modern Philanthropy in a Modern World."

When Mr. Starr returned home he found none of the family there. Mrs. Starr, he learned, had gone to pick up Margaret Churchill. Miss Churchill lived in the downstairs of an old mansion sadly in need of repair. Her income (from her dead brother's will) was enough for her to maintain herself in simplicity but not sufficient to allow renovation of her home or more than a modest scale of living. Everyone said, "I don't see how she does it," and "She never says a word but doesn't she always give the nicest little teas?"

Mrs. Starr had dropped by Margaret's to invite her to see some old silverware she had bought in London and to look at her new clothes from Paris. She had not been able to call Miss Churchill on the telephone because Miss Churchill, regarding this new invention as an unnecessary waste, had never had one installed.

Miss Churchill inspected the silverware and clothes and was pleasantly surprised by gifts of expensive underwear, stockings, and gloves. "They're so cheap over there, my dear; I got them for nothing. I'm glad you think they are beautiful. I thought of you as soon as I saw them."

When Miss Churchill said that she must go, Mrs. Starr suggested that they take a short drive down to the sea. While they drove through the sand dunes, Mrs. Starr adroitly turned the subject to the possibility of her daughter's getting into the House and Home Club. She herself had achieved this eminence because her friend, Miss Churchill, had threatened to resign unless the members who opposed Mrs. Starr agreed to allow her in. The members of the club were still bitter about it, but they blamed "that social climber who took advantage of Margaret" rather than Miss Churchill herself.

Miss Churchill told Mrs. Starr it would take time to accomplish this because Mrs. Walton, Mrs. Jordan, and Mrs. Whitecotton (all LU competitors of Mrs. Starr's), were still in the club. Mrs. Starr dropped the subject. (Her daughter has not yet been invited into the club.)

After dinner, Johnny Starr had left immediately and had

driven up to see the Travis Uptons (LU). It was a familiar sight to see his new Packard, which he drove at fifty miles an hour, racing up Hill Street. The local police had asked his father to request John to drive more slowly because it was dangerous. Whenever Johnny "got too tight" and the police found him, they always drove him home; but he had yet to be arrested. He and his friends laughed about the night when they were all tight and had to stop down there by one of the wharves on River Street to sober up. "A cop came up and started to bawl us out, and he was getting ready to arrest us; but when he saw it was John Starr he said, 'Oh, I didn't know it was you, Johnny. Now you just move over and keep quiet and I'll drive you home.'" Johnny said if the cops had run him and his friends in every time they'd found them drunk their record would have been longer than that of the town drunk.

Johnny had studied music in Rome after he had flunked out at Princeton. "I spent all of my time in New York—at the Astor and in the speaks in the 50's. And I never cracked a book while I was at Princeton." The three years in Rome had broadened his knowledge of human sexual behavior, increased his interest in modern painting, sculpturing, and architecture, and taught him enough music to make it possible for him to get a job with one of the wholesale music houses in Boston.

Johnny had returned home from Europe very suddenly, immediately after a friend (LU) of his had committed suicide. This friend was a son of a wealthy hat manufacturer in Yankee City who had accompanied Johnny to Rome "to learn how to write." He took his own life when a blackmailer had threatened to expose certain peculiarities of his career. Johnny himself was considered psychologically unstable and had once talked of going to a psychiatrist to "get all these complexes ironed out."

The Travis Uptons were not exciting people to Johnny. The example of Travis was always being thrown in Johnny's face by his father to show him what he might have done had he, Johnny, followed his father's advice. He wanted to see Travis and his wife about the coming Country Club dance. They were all on the arrangement committee.

Travis was the highly respected son of C. I. Upton. People in his own set always said, "Of course, he can't hold a candle to his father, but he's dependable and a hard worker. It's too bad his wife's a climber and mistreats him, but that's not his fault."

Travis belonged to the Rotary, the Lowell, and January discussion group. The last club closely resembled the February Club in its social composition. His wife belonged to the Women's Club, the Garden Club, and the House and Home Club. She was on the board of the library, the Y. W. C. A., and the S. P. C. C. Except for the Country Club, Johnny Starr belonged to no local organizations. Indeed, he professed contempt for those who did.

When Johnny arrived at the Upton's, he found that they had a couple new to Yankee City as dinner guests. They were from New York and "were dear friends of the Cartwrights and the Putnams, you know." By remarks adroitly dropped in the conversation, it soon developed that the husband was Yale '23 and the wife Vassar '26, and that he had come to Yankee City as the manager of one of the large companies.

While drinks were being mixed, Johnny said, "Well, I feel sorry for you because you've come to a funny town." Everyone laughed politely.

"I don't know," the new lady said, "I think it's all so beautiful, so old, and so lovely."

"It's old all right," Johnny said. "The last novelties came into this town when Victoria was alive, and most of the women who still live here are of the same vintage. The people who run this place haven't had a new idea since General Grant died."

The newcomers continued to laugh politely.

"Don't you believe him," said the hostess. "It's not as bad as he says. They are conservative here. You will find it a little hard to get to know people and everyone will tell you the sad story about the very nice couple that stayed here a year, and no one called on them so they moved away."

"We haven't found them that way. So many nice people have called," said the new lady.

"Of course they will with you because everyone knows who you are. But most people are conservative here," Mrs. Upton continued. "I mean particularly the old families. They take pride in it, I guess. My family have been here only a generation, and we still don't really rate being old family. And the older they are the more conservative they are."

"Yes," said Johnny, "the Wentworths don't even have a bathroom. And they still have an outside privy. They won't install a toilet because if the house was good enough the way their ancestors had it, it's good enough for them. Do you know that there are old families here who won't even put in electric lights? They say they're new and not worth having."

Again everyone laughed politely. Mrs. Upton once more took up the conversation. "It takes time, Mrs. Ainsworth [LU], to get used to this place. I agree with you, it is beautiful. Even Salem's Chestnut Street is no more beautiful than our Hill Street. And, Johnny, you're just wrong about it all. You had too good a time in Rome, and I am afraid you met too many ladies there whose morals were not what they should have been."

While Johnny fixed himself another drink, he commented, "Lord, she's always trying to find out what we did in Rome. But let me get back to my favorite theme. What I can't understand about this place is why all these people are so proud of it all. They talk about this one or that one being a descendant of a family that was in the 'Calcutta trade,' you know. That always burns me up. Why, my father is a successful shoe manufacturer. He worked hard, and he made a lot of money; and he acted smart in saving it. Maybe we should act snooty about that. He sent us kids to good schools, and he's given a lot of money to help this town; but when they say I am the son of a shoe manufacturer that means that we Starrs are too new to count. Take my advice, dear lady, and go far far away."

"If that's the way you feel about it, why do you stay?" said the host. He had entered the conversation after a quiet discussion of business matters with his male guest.

"I don't know; I can't help it. But I keep staying on. I swore I would never come back when I went to Rome, but I did. I am always planning to get out. Sometimes I dream of going down to Tahiti, but somehow I always come back here. My mother says whenever I used to get pushed around I always clung to her. I guess that's it. I can't leave mamma, and I can't leave home."

After having two more highballs, Johnny left. He drove down to River Street and stopped near a small shack where he bought a pint of rye from a Pole. He drank a large part of it by upending the bottle. Then he drove to the interstate highway and started for Boston. On the way, he telephoned a girl who danced at a Boston night club. He always grinned when he spoke of her and said he liked her because "she's just a little depraved."

After he called the girl he telephoned his mother and said that he had a business call from Boston and wouldn't be home that night. At the night club he finished his rye and bought some more. He never finished it, however, for he passed out and was driven in his car by the girl to her apartment. In the morning she said to him: "Johnny, I can't understand why you always want to pass out. It's no fun to get drunk that way."

Johnny replied, "Nuts! That's the only way to drink. A very wise guy once said, 'I consider it the end of all wisdom to be drunken and go to the dogs.'"

When Mrs. Starr drove over to pick up Miss Churchill, her daughter Katherine walked down to the Y. W. C. A. building to attend a council meeting of the Girl Scouts. She had become interested in them because Mrs. Upton had invited her to one of the meetings and she had seen how these "eager youngsters were taught better ways to live." The children were impressed with the virtues of cleanliness. They learned good manners, and their speech improved, and it was so very flattering to have all the "little dears look up to her." Most of the little girls were from "those awful little houses down in the clam flats. Some of them are the children of those Greeks and foreigners who live down on River Street."

Katherine's interest in the Girl Scouts was heightened by the breakup of her clique. Three of the five girls who composed it had married, but she and another friend had not.

"There just aren't any males around any more."

Occasionally young men came down from Boston, but none of them had become serious. At an earlier period in Katherine's life her mother had tried to do something about it but had quietly admitted failure.

Katherine wanted a husband "who didn't have to possess money. Of course, it would be nice if he did. But anyhow papa could help us." There were lots of ordinary boys in town. Sometimes she saw them on the streets, boys she had gone to high school with. She said she always felt funny when they spoke.

"The other day I saw a man in a mail carrier's uniform. He spoke to me and called me 'Katherine.' I looked and it was Fred Smith [LM] who used to be in high school with me. I said 'hello' and walked on. I never know what to do, and that happens ever so often."

On the way home from the Y. W. she stopped in to see the unmarried girl (UU) who belonged to her clique.

"Sometimes it seems a little too futile," she confided. "One goes down there week after week and tries to teach those kids how to behave. And while you're doing it you can tell that their minds are only on one thing, and that's boys. Tonight I was instructing them on how to give a tea party. But their boy friends were outside playing baseball, and whenever the ball would hit the wall they would all giggle. I'm sure most of them were there so that they could get away from their parents and have a chance to see their boy friends. I know that their parents would not let them out unless they were going to something like the Y. W., and I know none of them is allowed to date."

"Maybe it's not a bad idea at that," her friend replied. "After all, a boy friend is a boy friend. Think how nice it would be if we had a whole host of men around waiting for us the way they have."

They both laughed and lit another cigarette.

Once Katherine had liked the son of the manager of a chain store in a near-by town. "You know," she said to her friend, "he was tall, dark, and handsome, and I really fell for him; but I must confess he had funny manners. When mother heard how things were and that he was an Irish Catholic, she raised Cain. Dad checked up on him and discovered that he had no prospects. Well, I got a trip to Europe out of that one.

"One time in a fit of confidence, I told Mary Cartwright [UU] about what happened, and I guess I cried a little when I told her. She told me about the time when she had been crazy enough to turn down a young farmer over in Oldtown because his manners upset her and because her parents acted like mine. She said it was the greatest mistake in her life."

When Katherine left her friend's house she went home. She picked up the current copy of the *National Geographic* and took it to bed with her. As she idly thumbed the pages and looked at the pictures of Egypt and the Near East, she wondered if she could get her father to pay for a Mediterranean cruise. It would be swell to get away from all this, and maybe she would meet someone she liked. She soon went to sleep.

Later in that same week, however, she wrote a letter to a well-known school for social work and asked for their catalogue. After a row with her father about funds for tuition, she went away for special training in social work. But the following year saw her back in Yankee City. She told her father she guessed he had been right. She joined the S. P. C. C., the Y. W. C. A., the advisory board of the Y. M. C. A., and became active in the women's philanthropic organizations of the Episcopal Church.

5. Homeville

As Mr. and Mrs. Alexander French drove home from the Breckenridge tea, each reviewed in silence the events of the afternoon. Mrs. French had been very busy talking to Mrs. Starr, whom she disliked, and Frederica Alton, whom she admired. When she had felt herself being edged out by other ladies who engaged these two in conversation, she had sought out one of her cliquemates, Mrs. William Camp, and discussed the details of the coming Women's Club play. They were both to have parts in it. Mrs. Starr and Mrs. Alton had made it rather difficult to enter into their conversation because they were repeating some of the things that were said at the last meeting of the House and Home Club (UU to LU). Mrs. French would have liked to belong to the House and Home Club, but all her efforts in this direction had met with failure —just as her husband's hope for membership in the February Club had never been fulfilled.

On the way home they passed a new Buick car, driven by a rather pretty girl.

"There goes Suzie Rodgers [UM]," said Mr. French. "Why wasn't she at the tea?"

"I know she and her parents were asked. They're odd people. They act as though they never wanted to be anything."

"You would never know it, but her father's one of the wealthiest men in this town. I can't understand why some of these boys don't marry her. Why, she's the best catch in this town. Maybe it's because she doesn't put on enough airs."

"The Rodgers don't act like the snooty Starrs," said Mrs. French, "and Suzie didn't have a coming-out party like some of them, but there's no better family in Homeville."

"Her old man," said Mr. French, "has done more in this town than anybody else—not just making money either. He puts his own time in on it. He's been president of the Community Center and the Chamber of Commerce. There's not a better Mason in town, and he organized all those meetings to help the unemployed. You won't see him at the January or February Club, and he never goes to the Country Club. His wife isn't in the Garden Club. But when it comes to public spirit and doing good nobody can beat Ez Rodgers."

"Ezra's wife is in the Women's Club," said Mrs. French. "She's always organizing committees to make this town a better place to live in."

"Suzie's beyond me," said French. "I can't understand her. I can't understand her whole family. Wouldn't you think that her father would have wanted to see to it that his children had the best of everything? At least Jerry Rodgers [UM] should have gone to college; but, no, he stops when he graduates from high school."

"They didn't even send him to a good prep school, something with a little class," said Mrs. French.

At a recent meeting of the Women's Club, Mrs. French had overheard Mrs. Ezra Rodgers talking to the wife of the Congregational minister. She had said:

"Mr. Rodgers and I have tried to rear our children so that they would value the finer things in life. We have had to set them an example. We have the money to live in any one of the finest houses in this town, but we like the one we have and we want our children to like it. It's not pretentious, but it's comfortable and we like it. We want our children to be good Christians, and I think they both are. Jerry's a fine clean boy, and I am glad he's going to marry the girl he's engaged to. Neither he nor Suzie is socially ambitious.

"My husband could buy and sell most of the husbands of the women in the House and Home Club who put on all of those airs and pretend to be so much more than they are. You would think they were all millionaires the way they act . . ."

"Suzie goes around," said Mrs. French, "with the most uninteresting people. And Jerry doesn't even know how to carry on a conversation. You remember when we invited them both to a Country Club dance last year? I was a little surprised when they came."

"But they wouldn't take a drink," said Mr. French, "and they danced only a little. You could see that they didn't have a good time and they left very early. No one wanted to invite them to be members."

"I guess it's their business," said Mrs. French, "if they want to be like that. But I should hate it."

At that particular Country Club dance, Marion Upton, wife of Travis Upton, said, "Look, Suzie and Jerry Rodgers are here tonight. God help them! They're with those awful Frenches."

Her dancing partner replied, "Are they as wealthy as people say?"

"Sure, but you can't rate them tops just because they have a lot of money. The Rodgers don't act right, and they don't seem to want to go around with the right people. They're nice and everybody seems to like them, but most of the people I know can't understand them."

Mr. French turned his car into his driveway and the two of them got out. The Frenches live in a modern six-room colonial house just off Hill Street in Homeville. It is a house with all of the most modern plumbing and mechanical conveniences built into it. There is a stained-shingle exterior which does not have to be repainted or stained again. The trim around the windows is white with blue blinds. The walk to the front door from the sidewalk is concrete as are the front steps. This use of concrete is a departure from what is approved of by members of the higher classes. The middle-class Frenches follow out the same social pattern as others of their status and mix the latest of modern improvements with the old or with reproductions of the old.

The living room has polished hardwood floors and bright paper with a green background on the walls. Mr. French is very proud of several pieces of old furniture, but his pride seems to consist in how much they are worth and how much he could sell them for. Most of the pieces are reproductions of antiques. The bellows hanging by the fireplace are new and an improvement on the old models. The lawn has small well-cut evergreen trees planted in front of the house and the small shrubs are carefully trimmed.

6. These Bones Shall Rise Again

MR. CHARLES WATSON (LM), the superintendent of the cemetery, squatted on his haunches while he supervised the pick-and-shovel activities of his two workmen. It was hot. He had removed his blue serge coat and laid it carefully over a gravestone. He loosened his tie and opened the collar of his white shirt. Dirt rose from the dry earth. While Sam Jones (LL) broke the soil on one side of a burial plot, Tom Green (LL) shoveled the already loosened earth from the opposite side of the plot.

The burial lot where these operations were proceeding was down on the flat ground in one corner of the cemetery. The headpieces were stone and rather small. Next to and just below this flat part of the cemetery was the area of wooden headpieces. Many of them had fallen and lay rotting on the ground. On the other side of the cemetery, the stone headpieces were larger and increased in size until they reached the hill section where there were some elaborate funeral urns. In this area a whole burial lot was often bordered with white marble.

The shoveler stopped his work and lit a cigarette.

"I can't understand that guy," he said. "Why the hell can't Phil Starr leave his old man and old lady rest in peace? Why, they've been down in this here grave for thirty years, and now, by God, he's digging them up and running all over town with them. I say, once they're buried, let them stay buried. The dead ought to be left alone, and they ought to rest in peace."

The pickman stopped and wiped his hands on his overalls.

"What makes me sore is it ain't because the old bastard had to get them out because of something else, like a new road being put through or city improvements, but he's doing it on purpose because he's got to be a big shot. Why, my own mother is buried right over there by that rosebush. It's good enough for her and there wasn't a better woman ever lived than she was."

The other picked up the conservation.

"Why, I remember the time before he made his dough in the Neway Shoe Factory when he didn't have a red cent. Why, that guy—"

"I think you men," said the superintendent, "aren't seeing this thing right. Mr. Starr is only showing his love for his father and mother. When they were alive he had yet to make his money, and he was unable to do the things for them he would have liked. If he had had the money when they were alive, he told me, he would have moved them out of that little shack they had down there in the flats and up to his house on Hill Street. That's natural. Anyone who's worth his salt would want to do that for his pa and ma, especially when he's able to do it. But, you see, they died too soon.

"He told me just the other day he wanted to give them the best place to rest in that could be found in the cemeteries in this town. I tried to show him one of our better lots up on the hill but 'no,' he said, 'only Elm Hill Grove will do.' He's putting them in a grave up there on the highest hill next to the Breckenridges and the Wentworths and all of those other old families. It's going to be his own lot. He's a-doing this for his pa and ma. Just what any decent American would do for his."

"Oh, yeah?" said the shoveler.

"That sounds okay," said the pickman, "but he ain't worried about this place not bein' good enough for his pa and ma. He's worried about it not bein' good enough for him. I bet that son and daughter of his don't like to come down here with him to decorate their grandpa's and grandma's grave."

"Sure," the shovelman continued. "It makes those kids remember that their old man is just one jump from the clam flats. Why, hell! Old Grandpa Starr and my old man grew up together. Old lady Starr and my mother was in and out of each other's house every day. My mother told me old lady Starr used to borrow flour from her so that Phil Starr could eat enough to stay in school. Phil was a few grades ahead of me at the Smith School. He and my brother used to learn their lessons together. My brother and me quit school, and he went on through high school.

"He got to runnin' around with Cy Jordan and his crowd in high school. When that happened even his own folks weren't good enough for him then. Cy's old man gave Phil a job helping to take care of the books for the shoe factory. He was smart and learned fast. When he got out of high school he went into the factory, and in a little while he was Mr. Jordan's right-hand man. The next thing you know he's out on his own and partners with Jim Whitecotton. That old Neway factory made those fellows a fortune. When they shut up, old man Starr puts his in stocks and bonds. He got on the board of a lot of banks, and there he sits on his ass in the old Cartwright house and tries to act like he'd been born in it.

"Did he go down to the flats to see his ma and pa then? He did not. He tried to get them to move, but old man Starr told his wife he would beat the hell out of her if she even talked about it again. Old lady Starr wanted to move up with her son, but I can tell you that Phil's wife put a stop to that. You can just imagine those two living in the same house."

"My brother," said Jones, "used to work for him as a cutter over in the Neway Shoe Factory. Fred said that Starr was the hardest man to deal with in the world. He was always up to some trick to cut wages or to get longer hours. He may be tops now, but I don't think so. I bet you none of the people like John Breckenridge or the Wentworths or any of those fine people will have a goddamn thing to do with him."

"Yeah," said his companion, "and that goddamn Mick in the chlorination plant! They're both just the same. One's a Yankee carpetbagger, and the other is lace-curtain Irish; but you can't tell them apart. They're just the same."

"I think you men are wrong," said Mr. Watson, "I sometimes see Mr. Starr at the Antlers. He always stops and speaks. Last time he saw me he said, 'Charlie, how are you?' and I said, 'I'm fine.' 'How's your missus?' says he, and I said, 'She's okay, too.'"

The two workmen said nothing. They resumed their work. Mr. Watson went back to his small office. After he had gone, Jones spoke:

"Christ, Charlie'd kiss anybody's ass for a quarter."

They went on digging. They were about waist deep when they rested again.

"Sam, I was just thinking some more about Phil Starr, and then I thought about Ez Rodgers. Now, there's a man for you. Different as day and night from that other bastard. I guess

Ez Rodgers has more money than anybody else in this town, but to look at him you wouldn't know he had a cent, and he acts as common as an old shoe. A hard bargainer. He works his help hard but he treats them fair.

"His family is just the same way he is. Why, they don't even live up on Hill Street. They don't have one of those big houses, and the car he drives is only a Ford. That girl of his still goes around with the same kids she knew in high school. She went out West to some college for a couple of years, but she didn't like college. When she came back she acted just the way she always had. There's nothing high-hat about her. Ez's old lady still lives in the same house with them. And Ez still listens to what his ma has to say. And, believe me, she bosses those grandchildren of hers like they was her own.

"Ez says he wants his kids to act sensible. He says he wants them to keep their good names. You know they all go to the Baptist Church every Sunday. And Rev. Garner say there's no family in his church that's as charitable as the Rodgers, and you know I think that's true."

7. *You Can't Mix People*

THE lady speaking was the former Mrs. Edward Wentworth (LU) late of Yankee City. She was seated at a luncheon table at the Waldorf-Astoria in New York. Her companion was a middle-aged man who had just returned to New York after a short visit in Yankee City. They had spoken the names of mutual friends and had had their second cocktail when the lady said:

"I must tell you the truth. I know you like Yankee City, but I hate that place. Edward [UU] and I used to go there in the summer because of his fondness for it. I always told him that he liked to walk down Hill Street and know that he belonged to the Wentworth family and see those poor eggs around him bend their knees when he walked by. I prefer him the way he was when we were out in Cleveland. He's a damn good lawyer there, and he has his place because of what he has done, not because of what his family has been. We lived out in one of the nicer suburbs in Cleveland and went around with friends who were like Edward and me. And what's more, we were free to pick and choose our friends. But in Yankee City we would go to tea at Aunt Betty's house, and there we'd see Edward's three maiden aunts, his two old-maid cousins, and all of the other unmarried virgins. And for all I know, one or two married ones. That's the way it looks to me. I used to think it was because all of the men went away that these women didn't marry. But now I sometimes think they prefer to remain virgins rather than to put up with husbands of the kind that they would get in Yankee City. I didn't use to think like that, but that place has done something to me and, I am afraid, to my child.

"When I met Edward I was studying voice in Paris. I had gone there from Kansas City and had been there for a year and a half and knew a lot of people. One night a mutual friend —an American—introduced us at a cocktail party. We were all a little high. Some of the other men began to show their liquor but Edward went on drinking quietly and saying pleasant things in his dry Boston accent. Edward and I left the party and took in all of the bars and did all of the things that we Americans used to do when prohibition was on and we were in Paris. We arrived home pretty tight and he made a few passes and kissed me a few times. He told me I was beautiful, and I believed him. I told him he was a big bad male, and he believed me. It was fun. During those few weeks, we weren't always as proper as we might have been either. As a matter of fact, we would have been less proper, but his conscience, and not mine, was our guide.

"Anyhow, before we left we agreed to marry if we felt the same way when we got back to America. I saw him in Cleveland when I came through, and he came up to Kansas City some time later to meet my family. Mother, of course, was for him because she spotted immediately that his family was tops in and around Boston; and mother, God bless her, is a social climber. To tell the truth, I wasn't unaware of the social benefits of marrying into the Wentworth family. My father had been very successful in business and made a lot of money and had managed to keep it; but I must say that we had no pretensions to high society.

"After we married in Kansas City we came back to Yankee City. God, I'll never forget that first day as long as I live. It was ghastly. Among other things, there was a reception. All his family were there. Dozens of maiden aunts a thousand years old. The younger people, not less than fifty years old, stood while the older women sat. They all looked me over. I've never been so uncomfortable in my life. Several unmarried women of my own age were there. They literally glared at me. I knew what they were thinking—I had got something that belonged to them.

"There was an old dowager there called Cousin Winifred [UU] who acted like Queen Mary. Everybody treated her with deference. I was told that her family was one of the most distinguished in Yankee City and, believe me, she acted as if she spoke for her whole line of distinguished ancestors every time she opened her mouth.

"She looked at me and said, 'So, you're the girl who married our Edward. And you're from Kansas City, aren't you?'

"Then she said: 'Kansas City is famous here for its big slaughterhouses. My, it seems a long way to go for a wife.'

"Then came this one, 'You know, we older people always feel that our men should marry Yankee City girls.'

"I mumbled something and tried to keep my temper. Edward said nothing. Then came the crowning blow. She said, 'You will forgive an old lady when I say this, but I suppose our unmarried girls must take comfort in the refrain of the old song that they are rich in ancestors rather than gold.' Well, that's a sample of what it was like while I was in Yankee City.

"That night when they had all gone I went up to Edward's and my room and had a good cry. I was mad and hurt. Just who the hell did they think they were, anyway? They forget that they made their money selling rum to the Negroes in Africa, and then they shanghaied them while they were drunk and sold them in the slave trade. Now they are clipping coupons on the money their great-grandfathers invested for them.

"Well, anyway, Edward came upstairs and asked in that detached way of his, 'What's the matter, dear?'

"I said, 'You can tell that Cousin Winifred of yours for me that she and all her ancestors and your ancestors can go to hell.'

"Edward said, 'Dear, you haven't it exactly right because she isn't really my cousin. She's just a very intimate friend of mother's family.'

"I said, 'My family isn't New England, and thank God they

aren't, but they're just as good as your family.' I said that although my father came over here when he was a boy and we weren't all American, we could trace our family back to the early nobility of France. I told him that just because they didn't come over here in the *Mayflower* to get out of paying their debts or to keep from going to jail there was no reason to look down on them. I said I would match my ancestors with his any day. I said that Cousin Winifred's crack about rich in ancestors rather than gold didn't mean a thing to me and that I was proud that my father had started as a butcher in a meat-packing house and had enough brains to be a manager and part-owner of it before he quit. I have yet to see one of those people turn down a dime in Yankee City if they could get their hands on it.

"That should have been Edward's and my first fight, but it wasn't because Edward wouldn't fight. We didn't sleep in the same bed that night because Edward said that he had a headache and slept in another room.

"When I started going around with the Uptons and the Starrs, my sister-in-law put all the pressure she could on me. She always said, 'You can't mix people here in Yankee City. It just doesn't pay.'

"Then one night I drove into town with Johnny Starr. I liked him. He knew what was going on and wasn't dead mentally. Next morning the whole town was buzzing. You'd have thought I'd spent the night with him.

"Edward said, 'That man has been in one divorce scandal,' and I said, 'So have some of your friends,' and he said, 'But those people are different,' and I said, 'Yes, I know you mean you can't mix people here in Yankee City.'

"I thought maybe the arrival of our baby would help, but things only got worse. I finally went out to California and established residence. I'm certainly glad to get out of that."

8. *Niece Delgracia*

MRS. JOHN TREPPINGTON (UU) had come from one of the larger cities of Iowa. She went around with only the best people in Yankee City. Her newly acquired name was one of the best in the community. Generations of Treppingtons (UU) had lived in the city, and their fathers and grandfathers before them had distinguished themselves as shipping merchants, lawyers, bankers, and doctors, as well as in the political and military services of their country. A few had risen to national prominence and served their country in the diplomatic service. Mr. Treppington, a retired banker, still served on the boards of a number of large companies, of a bank or two, and of several highly regarded philanthropic organizations.

The house was one of the oldest of the Georgian mansions; its broad lawns sloped down to Elm Street, and ancient elms filtered sunlight against its white walls and famous carved doorways. Most of the furniture had been inherited from earlier generations of Treppingtons and had a distinguished history. Pieces were referred to as "the Treppington chairs" or "the Graves table."

Mrs. Treppington's son was in one of the better New England preparatory schools where a High Church atmosphere and classical tradition were rigidly maintained. Mrs. Treppington's daughter Delgracia had entered Vassar because "everyone I know is going there and, you know, Mother, Smith isn't what it was twenty years ago."

An examination of Mrs. Treppington's smaller and more intimate cliques showed that her personal friends were upper-upper; her larger cliques extended down to include only members of the lower-upper class. She belonged to the famous Knife Club, a semiformal group which used bridge as the *raison d'être* of its meetings but spent most of the time gossiping about the other members of Hill Street. The name of the club had humorous implications but with overtones of fear, particularly for those who were the objects of the group's interest.

In speaking of Mrs. Treppington, younger people, particularly, said that she came from Boston and that her relatives had connections in Yankee City. Only a few older women, who were mature when Mrs. Treppington married into one of Yankee City's "oldest families," knew that she came from the West. Her history is told because it is a story of successful upper-class mobility by a woman from outside the community.

Mrs. Treppington's father, Mr. Flood, had been the owner of one of the largest newspapers in Iowa. But instead of becoming a great editor, he turned his high intellectual talents to making money, and when he retired shortly before he died, he had made a large fortune. At the State Agricultural College he had been a good trackman, editor of the college paper, and a leader in his class. He had come from a small farm in the southwestern part of the state. He did not make a fraternity until his junior year; in fact, as a sophomore he had led the "barbarians" against the fraternities. This political conflict brought him into prominence and led to his election as class president. The men in the fraternity he finally joined (he said later) were largely sons of "the State's more prominent people."

In his sophomore year he met the girl who was later to be his wife, the daughter of a wealthy merchant in Des Moines. He once said that he started watching his "p's" and "q's" and took an interest in being somebody and getting places when he first met his wife. That year he started going to the dances at her sorority and began to meet the fraternity crowd. The following summer her father got him a job that paid well, and "a mysterious friend" gave her father the money to loan to him to keep him in school for the next two years. During the summer he met the friends of his future wife's family. He bought a tuxedo and began to feel less embarrassed in the homes of the wealthy. Some of the young men he met belonged to the better fraternities of the university.

When he came back in the fall he was invited around "to the house," and he soon was a member of what was considered one of the "Big Three" Greek letter societies in the Middle West. Meanwhile, his desire to improve his English had led him into a number of English classes. A young instructor took an interest in him and said he showed talent. The instructor introduced him to the editor of the college paper; and he quickly learned the job of college reporting. In his senior year he became the fraternity's candidate for editor of the paper and by a series of brilliant political deals triumphed over his "barbarian" opponent.

He took his new job very seriously and dreamed of becoming a great editor and writer, a power for good in his state.

Meanwhile the romance ripened into an informal engagement. After graduation, it was formally announced. His future wife's father knew the owner of the city's paper and spoke of him to the owner. Serving a brief apprenticeship as a cub reporter and a longer time on the City Hall beat, he learned the ropes and ultimately became city editor.

In time he became general manager of the paper because his suggestions to the owner on advertising and on methods of cutting down expenses and increasing income demonstrated that he knew how to run a paper. A few years later, at Mr. Flood's suggestion, several local papers were bought by the owner and formed into a chain. Eventually the owner got into financial difficulties from overexpansion. Mr. Flood and his wife were able to persuade her father to come to their financial assistance. With the help of a substantial loan from the old man, Flood bought out the former owner. He quickly instituted reforms and was soon able to show a profit. He bought out and merged the opposition paper in the town. This paper had never been popular with the advertisers because it had supported Bryan and backed up the farmers against the mortgage holders. He became an ardent supporter of the Republican party and was often tempted to run for congressman, but his father-in-law (he once confessed) had told him to let the politicians run the country and they would run the politicians. His wife and he were introduced into the better set by her parents. They joined the right clubs and, as their fortune increased with the ever-present aid of her father, they built what was often called the finest home in the city. It was in the style which his daughter later referred to as "late Victorian ironic."

It was here that Delgracia Flood grew into adolescence. She attended a private school and later went away to an Eastern finishing school for a year before entering Smith ("you know it was Smith then rather than Vassar").

Her father had first objected to Smith because he thought it would be nice for Delgracia to go back to "State" and join her mother's sorority. All of his lingering doubts disappeared when he and his wife visited their daughter during a business trip to New York and met some of the parents of girls at the finishing school who were planning to go to Smith.

Delgracia, her mother said, had always acted old for her age. She was socially precocious and quickly learned at the finishing school who the other parvenus were. She cultivated the daughters of New York's and Boston's better families and, with the exception of two girls from Chicago (Winnetka), avoided everyone from her own region. While at Smith, the Chicago girls proved useful when she visited their homes and dated some of the boys who belonged to families that had made their money in farm machinery, hotels, packing houses, iron and steel, and railways. Such boys were attending Harvard, Yale, and Princeton. Many of them brought their classmates and club members home for the holidays. All of these boys were Easterners. Delgracia greatly enjoyed meeting them and continued to be what was called a social success. The families of her newly acquired friends had the great virtue of having made their fortunes a generation before her own family had started its spectacular rise. (She had found herself speaking less of her father and more of her mother's father when she made her claims to social prestige. The money her father had made was a little too "new" for comfort.)

At Smith, Delgracia's career continued successfully. Several of the girls she had known at finishing school had decided to go on to college, and many of the boys whom she had known attended the proms. She was invited to several coming-out parties of those of her classmates who had not gone on to college, and she was soon a welcome guest in the homes of some of the better Boston and New York families. Delgracia was always careful to be particularly attentive to the wishes of the older people, and she never competed too openly with any of her friends for dates with some of the more attractive boys in the sets in which she participated.

She had the great advantage of not being a fortune hunter. Being an only child, she would inherit her adoring father's wealth. She felt economically secure and intended to be socially secure, as well; but now she felt inferior to girls whose families had far less money than her own. There were girls at finishing school and at Smith who were in attendance through scholarships or the quiet philanthropy of their remote kin. Yet all of them she knew to be socially superior to herself. She often loaned them money, took them to shows, let them borrow her clothes; but she did it unobstrusively, and this prevented criticism and gave her a reputation for generosity. She made it plain that her clothes were borrowed not because the girls needed them but because she had such excellent taste. All the girls assured her of this when they asked her for them. It was always thought to be nice to go to the theater with Delgracia because she always knew what the best shows were.

Delgracia's social career was greatly strengthened by her feeling secure in the path she had chosen. This security came from a knowledge of her parents' complete sympathy with her aims and gratification in the success of her efforts. She knew that they hoped she would marry one of the boys she had met at school or college. She had learned during a summer that they felt none of the local young men was eligible. The experience had been painful. When she remembered it in later years the episode sometimes caused her heart to beat faster, not because she still cared for "that funny boy" but because it would have been "the most terrible mistake of my life."

The funny boy was up from a state college. His father and hers were old friends. He was very masculine, and she thought him very handsome; and somehow his blond looks, his well-formed chin, and his curly hair made her feel just a little queer and uncertain of herself. It was the way she sometimes felt when she saw her favorite matinee idol.

He later confessed to her that he felt a little funny when he first saw her. And they soon were agreed that it was love at first sight. He was at the house a great deal, and Delgracia often found herself going around with his crowd, a group she had long since given up. At these times she always knew she must somehow and in some way get out of it. But when she reached home and sat on the davenport before the fire and he kissed her, she forgot social realities. She neglected to answer letters from her friends and from an Eastern boy who was currently fond of her; she turned down an invitation to a week-end party at a north shore estate. She knew she wasn't acting right and felt a little helpless. Her mother, increasingly alarmed, said that Delgracia was not herself.

Her mother had a heart-to-heart talk with her and told Delgracia that she should be awfully careful not to be silly enough to fall in love and marry before college was over. There would be time enough then. Delgracia agreed and said that it really didn't mean anything, that she was just amusing herself while at home. Her mother's apprehensions then took another form.

"I do hope you have remembered all I have told you. A girl can't be too careful about her reputation."

Delgracia insisted that the whole affair was nothing and, by indirection, told her mother that she still retained her virginity. She decided, however, to get away—she would go East to visit a friend on Long Island.

That night when the boy came and after her parents and the servants retired, she sat in the chair beside the fireplace to avoid the temptations of the davenport. She tried to tell him she was going East but found it too difficult to say. She knew that she didn't really want to go. With many tears she found herself beside the boy and in the morning she said she had decided to stay. Her father and mother expressed great anxiety by their silence. She resolved then to give the boy up and was able to hold to her resolve because it "was his fault," and because he "started it in the first place."

She returned frightened, yet still attracted by the boy at home. Supposing, she thought, supposing she had given in and married him. She would have been sorry all her life. In time, her friends in New York and Boston would have dropped her. No matter how hard they had tried the boy would not have been able to fit into their world. Her fear of the possible moral condemnation and concomitant social ostracism and of being dropped from the crowd she had cultivated coalesced into an overwhelming anxiety. She had learned her lesson. She knew now she could do what she had to do. She knew she must keep her self-control if she were to get the things she wanted. Her position wasn't strong enough to marry someone beneath her. She had to marry into Boston or New York or she would be doomed in time to being quietly forgotten by all the people she cared about.

She occupied all of her time in studying hard and going to every "right" place where she was invited. The college doctors said that her developing nervousness was due to overwork. They advised her to quit school for the semester and go home. She quit and spent the time with great-aunt Agnes, in Boston. The woman was not an actual relative but someone whom Delgracia had carefully cultivated and who had established doubtful, remote kinship with Delgracia because certain of their cousins shared the same surname and came from Boston.

Great-aunt Agnes, wise to the folkways of Boston, had through the years allowed her friends to believe Delgracia to be a near kinswoman. She always referred to her as "niece Delgracia." It was while she was living on Beacon Street with her aunt and going about with the best people that she met her future husband.

Under the careful tutelage of her great-aunt and with her wise advice, the early romance blossomed into a formal engagement. The wedding was arranged in such a way that the kinship bonds of "niece Delgracia" and "Aunt Agnes" were emphasized by receptions and parties, all carefully sponsored by the aunt. After a honeymoon in the South, the newly married couple returned to Yankee City. They lived in the house that had been in the Treppington family for generations.

9. *All Men Are Born Free and Equal*

THE Patriotic Order of the United States Veterans of All Wars (UU to LL) was in session. The people of Yankee City said there were members from all walks of life in the Order. They ranged from the old families at the top down through the several layers of Sidestreeters to the veterans from the clam flats of Riverbrook. It was the night that new officers were to be elected. The active campaign had been going on for weeks and everybody was there.

A few weeks earlier a scandal had broken and gossip had spread through the city. The background of the incident which had aroused the members and many of the citizens is of considerable interest. Money in the treasury was low. The members were attending in smaller and smaller numbers. The incumbent administration was blamed for the lack of interest. It was decided by some of the officers to hold a series of smokers. "Let the boys tell a few jokes and import a little talent, you know, a few gals from Boston."

The first smoker was a success. Outsiders were allowed to come to the other sessions which followed. The small admission fee they paid helped fill the treasury. The officers were congratulated by some of the members for getting such good turnouts and solving the financial problem. "It's all right," they said, "to have a few evenings with patriotic speakers; but they get dull after a while, and we need something like these shows to pep the boys up."

No one from Hill Street had come to the smokers, but "those Hill-streeters never come anyway." They paid their dues and came through for extra assessments. They were always active when called upon to see that the needy members and their families were remembered at Christmas. It was an ever-present hope that some of them, sometime, might help contribute enough money to build a veterans' hall.

People like Mather Blaisdail (UU), Brooks Sinclair, and Travis Upton never came, and people like Alec French and William Camp came very infrequently. When French came some of the brothers said it was because he was trying to rent a house or catch some sucker for an insurance policy. Most of the men who came regularly to the meetings were fellows like Tim Pinkham, who was the president of the Order, some of the fellows from the Antlers and the Caribous (UM to LL), and many of the workers from the shoe and silverware factories, and a few clammers. Men like Tim Pinkham ran things and attended the meetings; and men like the shoe workers and clammers were run by them.

But this meeting was different. There was suppressed excitement. Blaisdail and Travis Upton had entered the large hall and sat down near the center of the room. Even Edward Marshall Jr. was there.

"That's the first time Mr. Marshall's been to one of our meetings since I can remember."

The president got up and went over to where Mr. Marshall was sitting.

"Glad to see you here, Mr. Marshall," he said.

"Glad to be here, Tim. I don't get out to enough of these meetings. I believe all of us should come at least for elections."

Mr. Marshall invited the president to sit beside him. Mr. Pinkham offered Mr. Marshall a cigarette which the latter accepted. They both lit their cigarettes from Mr. Marshall's match.

Meanwhile, Mr. Upton, young president of the Booster

Club, Fred Flaherty, and Brooks Sinclair arrived with a group of the town's prominent business men. They waved their hands to a number of men they knew.

At one side of the hall in the seat across the aisle sat a score or more of men. Among them were Sam Jones, Tom Green, and Frank Tyler (LL). Many of them had sweaters on and were without ties. They smoked, told jokes, and engaged in horseplay.

After looking at his watch, the president walked to the front and called the meeting to order. A simple ritual was performed. It symbolized the "sacrifice" made by the members of this organization in all wars for their flag, their country, and their homes. It referred to the self-evident fact that all men were born free and equal and that our democracy guaranteed these things to all of us. It spoke of the comrades who had fought and died on foreign fields and assured them that they had not made these sacrifices in vain; for the Patriotic Order of the United States Veterans of All Wars was a living expression of those great ideals for which they had shown this last measure of devotion.

Routine business matters were quickly settled. When it was announced by the treasurer that he was glad to report a considerable increase in the Order's current funds no one said anything. The nominating speeches began. After a number of them had been made, Edward Marshall stood up to speak.

"I too seldom meet here with you comrades of former days and present members of this splendid organization. I came tonight because I believe it my duty to be here to cast my vote for my good friend, Paul Foley [LU]. I was delighted when your former president and great leader, William Camp, nominated him. Paul's a man we all know. He's a living example of what the Order stands for. He proves that race and creed [Foley was Catholic] have nothing to do with a man attaining the highest office our encampment has to offer. He is a good citizen, a good husband, a splendid businessman, and a loyal member of our Order. He is a good democrat—democrat with a small 'd.' "

He smiled, and the crowd laughed.

"During this coming year, many grave problems face us. We must solve them if we are to go forward. Yankee City must solve such questions as getting new industries in order to keep all of our men fully employed. We must have work for our people whether they are employed at the bench or in the business office. We must pull together. There's no organization in this community that better represents the best of our city than our own Order of the United States Veterans of All Wars. There's no man better qualified to lead this order than Paul Foley.

"The other candidates are good men. We can't miss on any of them. Our present president has a good record—one to be proud of. I wouldn't hesitate to vote for any of them. But when the time comes to solve such questions as getting money for a building for our new organization, Paul's the man to do it. I am going to vote for Paul. This is a free country. Our votes are our own. Since each man has only *one* vote, we are all equal. I am going to cast my *one* vote for Paul."

He sat down. After the other speeches were made and the votes taken, it was announced that over half of the members had voted for Paul Foley. On the way out, Edward Marshall took occasion to speak to each of the defeated candidates and their friends. They joked about small matters and some of them called him "Ed," but most of them said "Mr. Marshall," and they were all called by their first names when he spoke to them.

Outside the hall, John Burke (LM) asked Flaherty if he wanted to go with some of the boys down to the Caribous for a bottle of beer. Flaherty said "no," he couldn't because he had another engagement. He started toward his car and was stopped by Mather Blaisdail (UU) who invited him to come up to his house on Hill Street for a highball. Flaherty accepted. He, Foley, Marshall, Blaisdail, and a few others stopped their cars in front of the Blaisdail house.

Patrick Donaghue (UL) and Tim Kelley (UL) drove by shortly afterwards on their way out to Littletown. Kelley said, "These guys up here on Hill Street certainly stick together, don't they?"

Inside Blaisdail's house Scotch highballs were being served. They drank to the new commander and kidded him about how they were going to show him proper respect and asked if he would still speak to them now that he had arrived.

"Don't drink to me," said Foley. "Brooks Sinclair is the man to be congratulated. We all know that he put this thing over. Tell them how you did it, Brooks."

"I didn't do anything," Sinclair replied. Everyone laughed and glanced knowingly at each other.

Flaherty said, "Why, Brooks, I just told somebody the other day that if I wanted to show how this city was run I would draw a lot of lines from all over this town and they would all point to your house."

"Well, to tell the truth," said Sinclair, "I did call up a few people. I wanted to straighten things out and make sure that the Order didn't get into a mess.

"Mather, the last time we were at the February Club the Reverend John Frank Foreman [UU] came to me and said at the last meeting of the ministers' association [UU to UM] they raised hell about those strip tease, hootchy-kootchy gals the boys had at the smoker. I had heard all about it before, but I am ashamed to say I pretended I didn't. I wasn't quite sure how to act. I never had liked the idea of a show like that being run by the Order, but I remember the time when we were in New York, Mather, when we got a little high and went down to Minsky's. I remember all of the laughs we got. When I thought of that it made me feel a little like a hypocrite."

Blaisdail replied by commenting on how he had feared he wasn't going to get Paul out of the show because of the blonde on the end.

Sinclair continued: "But I began to see this thing was serious. I heard from all over that people were sore. And several of them said it would hurt the good name of our town if this got around.

"After I talked to a few of you, I got hold of the Reverend and asked him to tell the others to give us a little time because he could trust me to take care of the situation. Well, to make a long story short, I got Flaherty to get ahold of the boys at the Knights of St. Patrick's and swing them into line. He told them Paul was going to run and some of the better citizens were giving him their support. Alec here went down to the Caribous and Fred to the Antlers and got them lined up. Of course, the good word was passed on to the ministers, and Mather here lined up everyone on Hill Street.

"The point about all of this story is our people are sound at heart. Why, I bet even the Riverbrookers voted for Paul after Ed Marshall spoke. Well, you can see I didn't do anything. It was easy."

After Flaherty had refused his invitation, John Burke, in the company of Tim Pinkham, Fred Milkton (LM), and two other fellows, Will Carlton (UL) and Tom Rafferty (UL), drove down to Caribou Hall. They had had their first bottle of beer when John said:

"You know, the thing that happened tonight is what I like about this town. Everybody from top to bottom comes out to vote at a meeting of the Order. Old Ed Marshall was just as interested in the outcome as any of us. There may be differences between our people, but this town is run democratically. It did make me a little sore, though, when Alec French came down here to the hall the other night. It's the first time he's been down at this place since he rode the goat. I knew he was up to something when he came. I'd 've been sore if he hadn't told me the whole story about some of those dry balls raising hell about the smokers. He told me enough to let me see that we had to do something. He said that the better elements of this town had to get together and get a new crowd in or the Order was likely to have trouble. I was going to vote for somebody else until he told me that, but he convinced me that we had better have Foley because it would look better."

Somebody said: "Hell, none of those dames had any class. They wouldn't lead nobody astray."

Somebody else made a few anatomical remarks, and another told a story about a traveling salesman and a highly persistent old maid. They had more beer, and the conversation turned to the topic of the layoff at the Neway Factory. Shortly after their second bottle, they left.

After the meeting, Sam Jones, Tom Green, and Frank Tyler stopped at Sam's house. Sam came out with a pint of alcohol. They rode down to the Three Mast Hall [LM to LL] where they found a crowd of shoe workers from the Neway Factory with some clammers and several men on relief. They ordered some near-beer and mixed it with the alcohol. They discussed the Neway layoff and the bad treatment that the workers got over at the P. O. Factory.

Green said: "That goddamn kike they got there now! Why, they say he won't have a girl in the plant that he can't screw. How the hell can a girl keep decent making the wages she gets now with those bastards around? My daddy belonged to the American Order of Mechanics. They hated kikes."

Jones said: "Well, none of my family ever joined a union but I guess I'm a-goin' to this time. Things are too tough. Maybe they're right. Maybe we should stick together."

The three of them were joined by a Greek who worked in their plant. He had a slight accent. They "didn't like no foreigners but Johnny [LL] was a good guy," and he had taken out his papers. They invited Johnny to have a drink and to catch up with them. He drank one quickly. The talk returned to the layoff.

Johnny said: "See me, I ain't got a goddamn cent now. Well, you all remember when I used to have a store. I made a little money, and I had a nice house and a garden for the missus and the kids, and now what have I got? Nothin', that's what I got. I'm back cutting shoes again."

Jones said: "Well, Johnny, cutters don't come no better than you."

"Yeah, I know, but I only been working once a week, and now we are all laid off. I say, there's something wrong, somewhere. Look, I watch those sons-of-bitches drive down from Hill Street. They go along like they're crazy in their big cars. They drive fifty miles a hour. Do they care if they kill one of our kids? Like hell they do. It's those guys who cause this trouble. They got most of the money but they ain't satisfied. They want all of it. Us guys down here ought to do something."

Somebody asked if he had joined the union.

"Well, I wasn't going to tell you 'cause I know how you guys feel about unions, but I have. We got to do something."

Jones, Green, and Tyler agreed that something had to be done. Johnny called out to a man who was better dressed than they were. It turned out that he was a union organizer, and he was invited to sit down at the table. He pulled a bottle of gin out of his pocket. They all had a drink from his bottle. They liked him. He had his veteran's pin on. He said that he belonged to the Order and was proud of it.

Tyler said: "We had an election tonight. Got ourselves a

new president. When I seen French and Upton and all of those other bastards lining up for him I wasn't going to vote for him, but when Ez Rodgers said he was okay I changed my mind. I never liked Pinkham anyway. He's always been snooty around here. He never comes down to the Three Mast. He's a member all right, but he just thinks he's too goddamm good to 'sociate with guys like us. I could tell election time was around when he came in the other night. He thinks clammers and shoe workers ain't good enough for him."

Johnny interjected: "The goddamn rich people up on Hill Street."

Jones snorted and said: "Hillstreeter, hell, he's no Hillstreeter. Why, he lives over there in Littletown. He ain't got a pot to piss in."

Johnny said, "He don't do no work, does he?"

"Hell, no, he sells insurance. Did you see how he kissed French's ass tonight?"

"Why, it's just like being in the army," said Jones. "The doughboys had to kiss the asses of sergeants like Pinkham, and all of those goddamn non-coms stood around just looking for a chance to kiss a shavetail's ass."

The union organizer observed, "Yeah, that's how it is."

They asked him to tell them about the shoe workers' union. He told them about how bad conditions had been over in New Hampshire and how his union had cleaned things up. They said they guessed they would follow Johnny and join up. Right now it was getting pretty late and they'd better be getting on home. The men parted under the sputtering arc light. Tyler was apparently anxious to prolong the talk, but meeting only the fuddled yawns of his friends he turned down the river road toward the flats and home.

Jones and Green left. They walked down the road along the river toward the flats.

Johnny walked up the road toward the square on River Street. He climbed up several flights of dark stairs. He was a little drunk and stumbled as he went along. As he passed each floor he was cursed in Greek by those he awakened. He opened the door. Two other Greeks were asleep on the bed. He took his shoes off and got in under the army blankets on his cot. He was soon sound asleep.

The next morning Mr. Blaisdail awakened late. He had a light breakfast because his doctor had told the cook to keep him on a diet. He ate at the breakfast table. Mrs. Blaisdail had not made her appearance, for she was to have her glass of orange juice and cup of coffee served in her bedroom at half-past ten. Just as Mr. Blaisdail was completing his careful perusal of the financial page of the Boston *Herald*, the telephone rang.

The maid who answered said it was his secretary, and he told the maid to tell the secretary he wouldn't be down until later. He drove down to his office. He answered his mail and prepared to drive in to Boston to see his broker about certain investments. Phillip Starr met him following an hour spent at the factory conferring with his manager. They both had the same broker, and they planned to have a late lunch together at the Union Club with John Aldington Breckenridge's son who was vice-president of one of the large banks in Boston.

Alexander French went down to his office where he telephoned a number of people about appointments. Two of his salesmen reported a few sales and a number of rentals. He dictated several letters. At noon he had lunch with his fellow Rotarians. Blaisdail and Starr did not belong to this society. French and the other members of the Rotary sang "America the Beautiful." They heard a talk on "America Looks Ahead" by a visitor from Boston who stressed the need for businessmen to realize that the pioneer spirit was not dead; that just as Daniel Boone had led the way for the sturdy men and women who followed the trail he had blazed in the wilderness, so modern businessmen must blaze the trail for other Americans to follow.

Timothy Pinkham walked to the small office he shared with two other men. Each of them said it was foolish to have a separate office and pay all that money just for being swanky when one office for all of them served just as well. Pinkham typed several letters on the mutually owned typewriter and got in his car and called on several prospects for life insurance. He went home at noon for what he called dinner. His wife had spent the morning "fixing up the house."

They lived in a two-family house rather close to the street.

A concrete walk led to the street entrance at one side. A small but well-kept garden covered the ground between the street and house. It was protected by a wire fence which separated it from the sidewalk but permitted passers-by to see that the Pinkhams had a nice garden. Mr. and Mrs. Pinkham did all of the gardening from the heavy spading to weeding and watering, and the repair work around the house was done by him. Mrs. Pinkham did all of her own work; she sent the washing out and did her own ironing. The kitchen was used more than any room in the house. Except when they had company, it was there that they ate their meals. The furniture throughout the house was of the Grand Rapids variety. There was a large cabinet radio and a number of Maxfield Parrish reproductions in the living room.

The Pinkhams were ambitious to improve the house by installing mechanical improvements such as new plumbing, radio, washing machine, and electric refrigerator.

Mrs. Pinkham was preparing to go to a meeting that afternoon of the Woman's Auxiliary (LM to LL), in which she took a prominent part and held office. The women in the Auxiliary always looked up to her. She had a nicer house than most of them and always seemed to dress better than they.

There were some thirty or forty members in the Auxiliary. Mrs. Pinkham and three other ladies were the only members who belonged to the Art Club (UU to LM). They sometimes discussed the affairs of the club before the other members of the Auxiliary. They did this with a certain feeling of satisfaction since the Art Club, they believed, was "one of the most refined" organizations in the town. They never discussed the Auxiliary before the members of the Art Club. When they attended the meetings of the Art Club they sometimes felt ill at ease. Once, while at the movies, Mrs. Pinkham had eavesdropped on Mrs. Travis Upton, a member of one of the new shoe families, and she heard her making fun of the Art Club. Mrs. Pinkham felt uneasy because Mrs. Upton was a member of the club and it was disloyal for her to talk like that. She always felt uneasy and outmoded around Mrs. Upton anyway, and spoke very grammatically because Mrs. Upton had a very broad "A." (Mrs. Pinkham did not know that Mrs. Henry

Breckenridge had once said she was sure that Upton woman had probably got her English "A" from a broken-down English actor.)

Mrs. Pinkham was vaguely conscious that Mrs. Upton had been to one of the better women's colleges whereas she had only finished high school and studied a year at the Boston Business College.

Next morning Mr. Carlton went down to the silverware factory. His wife had packed his lunch, and he had left long before Mr. Blaisdail or Mr. Starr had eaten their breakfasts. He had helped his wife cook his breakfast. His son had got up earlier to turn up the heat to get the house warm before his parents had awakened. The boy had then left and gone to several houses in Homeville and Hill Street where he performed the same operation for a small fee. Mr. Carlton was proud of his son. The boy got good marks in high school. He was ambitious and said he was going to college.

After Mr. Carlton had departed, his wife awakened the other four children in time for them to wash their faces and have their breakfast while she mended several tears in their school clothes.

Mr. Carlton had worked in the factory for years and was respected by everyone.

"He's got one of the best paying jobs in the whole place" was a frequent remark by other workers in the factory. He was considered an expert on one of the machines making flatware.

10. Clam Flats

Going home after he had said goodnight, Jones crawled in bed beside his wife and the springs sank in the middle. Three small children were asleep on a mattress in the corner of the room. Two adolescent daughters slept on cots next to the wood stove in the kitchen.

By morning, it had suddenly turned bitter cold. Seven persons were crowded around the iron stove in a small kitchen. There was no central heating in the house because it was too expensive and perhaps "unnecessary." The kitchen table was still littered with the remains of the evening meal. Mr. Sam

Jones was smoking his pipe. He and his family had eaten a good meal of bread, potatoes, and clams. Mrs. Jones's brother had given them the clams, a part of the results of his hard diggings on the clam flats that morning. They were the last of the season. He had said, "The damn chlorinating plant's taking all the profit out of clamming. There ain't any money in it any more, and it's hardly worth a man's time to go out there and freeze to death on the flats."

The potatoes had come from a supply which Mrs. Jones had bought when they were cheap. The half-empty gunny sack sat in one corner of the room. She had made the bread they had eaten, and her husband had said it was 'a damn sight better than that store bread.'

Later in the day Sam Jones went out to see about doing a little road work for the city. Maybe if he could get a good steady job he would get "off the relief." He always came home angry every time he went to the relief office anyway.

"Those bastards are nosy. They always ask questions that are none of their business." He wished times were like they used to be. A man was his own boss then. He could clam a little and fish a little and earn a little extra money at the shoe factory, and when he got tired he would go hunting ducks. Why, he remembered the time when little Tim Jones had come into the factory where they were working and told his father the ducks were lighting over on the west pond, and all ten of the cutters from Riverbrook in his room had quit right then and gone hunting.

"Now, goddamn it, you had to join a union to keep a measly job."

After some inquiries, he heard there were no municipal jobs to be had, nor were there jobs at any of the shoe factories. He came home and lay down on the unmade bed. He took yesterday's copy of the Boston *Record* out of his pocket and glanced at the box scores. He then began a story in an old copy of *Cosmopolitan* magazine. Someone knocked at the door, but he didn't answer. He was afraid it might be the S. P. C. C. girl, or the truant officer, or the relief worker, or someone from the veterans' bureau, or from the church which gave him coal, or just someone who would try to tell him what to do. After a brief period the knocking ceased and the unknown caller went away.

His life was filled with people like that. Jones went on with his story; but before he had finished the magazine dropped from his hands. Sam Jones snored.

They lived in a region of the town where two or more families crowded into one small house, where people seldom owned their own homes, but rented a few rooms. The houses were run-down and needed paint. Toilet facilities were limited. A garden was rare, and there was little or no attempt to keep a lawn.

One of the most noticeable characteristics of lower-class housing is the lack of space. Heating usually comes from the coal stove in the kitchen, which in cooler weather turns into the dining and living room as well. Several beds are often found in the one bedroom, and the overflow sleeps on cots in the kitchen-dining room. In rare instances there is a living room with some cheap overstuffed furniture.

The first American ancestors of the Joneses, the Greens, and the Tylers settled around Yankee City and in near-by villages coincidentally with the founding of those communities. Like the ancestors of their fellow citizens on Hill Street, they plowed the rocky soil a very little and fished the shores and sailed their boats to make a living. Legends tell of the ancestors of certain of these Riverbrook families being washed ashore at a near-by town on log rafts when a great storm swept them in from a mysterious southern land; but genealogies and the testimony of gravestones indicate that the Riverbrookers are of good old English stock, that "these degenerate Yankees" are the living descendants of "those who came to America to worship God," to get rich, and "to escape the unpleasant circumstances of their English homeland."

Long before his son was born, the father of Sam Jones had watched his lobster pots in season, helped his brother William, when the clamming was profitable, and worked as a stitcher in the P. O. Shoe Factory "when the spirit moved him." Sam's father was the last man, his son said, to take shoes by contract. After him, shoes were no longer made in the home but manufactured in the factory.

The Joneses were faced with a problem. That day that very "fresh" girl had called on them again. She had the truant officer (LM) with her. ("One of those goddamn Catholics who liked to show his authority.") She had also visited the Frank Tylers. They had both asked Mrs. Jones why her children were not in school. She had wanted to tell "that Mick" it was none of his business but she was afraid he might take her children or do something equally unpleasant in retaliation. The truant officer had said that "unless those kids come more regularly to school, I am going to have you up in front of Judge Black [UM]." This frightened her because her brother's two boys had been sent to reform school when this same cop had snooped around and caught them and some other boys selling a few things they had taken from a store.

The girl was from the Society for the Prevention of Cruelty to Children (UM). Mrs. Jones smelled cigarette smoke on her, and any woman who would smoke would do anything. What right had she to come around asking questions about a body's own children, a-hintin' that her girls were misbehavin' with some of the boys up at the Smith School? Only yesterday she had beaten the tar out of both of them for this very thing. And she didn't think it did any good. She had tried before and it didn't work. Anyway, the boys weren't foreigners, and if worse came to worse she knew their folks.

Mr. Jones had listened to his wife's account of the incident and said, "Well, Bessie, let's take the kids and get out of this town. Let's go back across the river. This city welfare here is just as nosy. When Johnny broke his leg across the river he had to go to the hospital in an undertaker's wagon, but the doctor over there don't try to tell you how to bring up your kids."

Mr. Jones said he guessed he'd go and talk it over with Frank Tyler.

When the girl from the S. P. C. C. and the truant officer drove away in her shiny new coupe, they rode over to see the principal of the Smith School. The truant officer found Principal Oldfield (UM) out in the schoolyard. He said to him, "The S. P. C. C. gal is in your office. We've just been down to Sam Jones's and the Frank Tylers. I thought she was going to puke when she went into their kitchens. It did smell pretty terrible."

Oldfield came into his office. He greeted her by saying:

"Well, how do you like our Riverbrookers? I hear you've been calling on Mrs. Sam Jones and Mrs. Frank Tyler."

"Why do people have to be so filthy?"

"Because that's the way they like it. Keep them all clean for six months and it would kill them. They cause me more trouble than all the rest of the kids put together. They're dumb and not interested. They don't want to learn anything. But what can you expect when their parents don't want them to either?"

"I suppose delinquency rates must be higher in your school?" she said.

"Delinquency rates! Don't make me laugh! Delinquency rates! Why that little trollop, Bessie Jones, alone rates about one delinquency a day, and that day they caught her over there behind the old tire factory with those four boys. Well, I'd imagine it was at the rate of every ten minutes. Isn't that right, Fred?"

The truant officer who had taken a subsidiary role and was largely ignored when the principal and the S. P. C. C. girl began their conversation said:

"They keep me busy. Not only on sex crimes. They're easy. But they have no respect for property. They'll steal anything. I've just broken up my third gang this year."

Oldfield looked at the truant officer in a vague way.

"But most of those kids weren't Riverbrookers. Some of them were your own breed of cat."

"Yeah, I know. Some of those shanty Irish are just the same as Riverbrookers. Those new foreigners, some of those Poles and Greeks—give me time and I'll get them all over to the reform school where they'll learn something useful."

"Well, in my small way," said Oldfield, "I keep a lot of them out of trouble. I always advise them to take the commercial and stay out of the Latin and scientific courses in high school. That means they learn a little something useful. I see no use in people like that taking courses that would prepare them for college. Too many people are going to college anyway."

"Are any of them bright?"

"Yes, some are. But they don't last long. They soon peter out."

Frank Tyler, Sam Jones's sister's husband, was retired on a small veteran's pension. He lived with his wife and children on River Street not far from the Joneses. His brother, a man of thirty or so, lived with them and shared the pension. The brother was a clammer when he was working. He had a reputation for being "lazy and good-for-nothing." The Tylers' home consisted of four rooms on the ground floor of a large run-down house. The rest of the house was in such bad condition that it couldn't be occupied. The living room, which was also a bedroom, was located in the front of the house where Frank could keep an eye on what the rest of the Riverbrookers were doing and not have to get out of his chair. The room was heated by a small cheap, parlor stove, and an easy chair had been improvised by throwing a couple of blankets over a wooden chair. The chair was largely the handiwork of Frank. It was originally a store chair, but he had cut it down and otherwise altered it to fit his own needs.

There was a half-finished dish of oatmeal on the parlor stove being kept warm for the next meal. The kitchen was small. It was not much more than a good-sized pantry with a small coal stove in it for cooking and probably was not used except for cooking.

Frank criticized the morals of his neighbors, and they told tales on him. When his wife was not present he called them "Riverbrookers" as a term of derogation since he had not been born "in the flats," but all of his companions were of this stock and he was thought to be a Riverbrooker by everyone else who knew him in the community. He sometimes pointed to fat Mary Green and Maisie Docker as they walked by.

"They ought not to give out relief to those people," he said. "Both of those women are living with fellows up the street and taking care of them. Mary's husband got tired of her so he kicked her out. And now he's got another woman living with him, too. None of them don't do nothing but they still get their relief money."

His daughter, Annie (UL), had deserted her family when she was fourteen. She had obtained a job as nursegirl in a house on Hill Street. When she refused to live at home he tried to get the police to interfere, but after conferring with some of her employers, the police warned Mr. Tyler not to interfere with his daughter in her new home.

11. There Are No Better Christians in This Town

THE minister (UM) of the church attended by most Riverbrookers, his friend and clique mate, the doctor (UM), who had taken a deep interest in these people, and two friends of theirs (LU) were discussing their favorite topic.

"I've known these Riverbrookers—man and boy—well, I guess I've known them all my life," said the doctor. "You've heard people call them "broken-down Yankees" and accuse them of all the crimes on the calendar. People are always asking me if they all sleep with their daughters. Because there have been one or two cases of homosexuality among them, everyone in Yankee City thinks that all of the Riverbrookers are homosexual. They are always being accused of being lazy and spending all of their time doing nothing. Of course, you've heard the old one about 'their fishing et cetera in the summer but they can't fish in the winter.' This is told you by everyone who uses the little four-letter words.

"Now, as a matter of fact, there's no more incest here than up on Hill Street, and I've heard of very little up there. People up there do get involved in rather strong emotional ties inside their families which sometimes interfere with their marriages. I suspect that aristocrats are more likely to be homosexual than lower-class people."

"One's always hearing that these lower-class kids are said to be more delinquent," said the minister. "I think about all that such a statement means is that the police catch them more often and they get less protection from the police than the people do up on Hill Street."

Phillip Alsop (LU) interrupted, "I agree with you. Tim [LU], do you remember the time when we broke into the old Breckenridge house when they were away for the summer and stole their silverware and took all of those things out of their living room? After we had done it, we were all so scared we buried everything out in the pond in the Common."

"I certainly do. I often think of that and all of the other things we did when I hear about these foreign kids and the kids in the clam flats being arrested for stealing."

The minister said, "Why a mother of an adolescent daughter, you all know her—she lives on Hill Street—was complaining to me the other day about the morals of her children and their friends. Some of the children today in Yankee City behave in a way that frightened her. The group her daughter went around with were not acting well at all. She said she knew that some of them were indulging in sexual play. That's not the first time I've heard of our better-class children's morals. Some of the children in the high school, I hear, are doing all sorts of things which they shouldn't be. They are always talking about necking, and I guess a few of them go much further than that. Some of these kids are from good families, too."

Said Phillip Alsop, "I remember when I was playing around before I got married. All my attention to the girls did not come out of pure love. Not by a long shot. We had fun. I don't think these kids today are any worse than we used to be."

"Well, Phil," said the doctor smilingly, "I've heard that you didn't show much interest in the loaf of bread part of Omar's little piece of poetry."

The minister continued, "There are no better Christians in this town than the Riverbrookers. They help each other. They share their food and whatever they have with each other. They don't lose their self-respect and independence because some of them receive charity. I like them. I like them a lot more than some of my parishioners from Hill Street."

12. Going Down in the World

WILL CARLTON (UL) was busy that Saturday afternoon painting his back fence. He had repaired it and put two strands of barbed wire along the top. Mr. Carlton and his sons had painted the house themselves a couple of years ago, and they had always done practically all of the maintenance work inside and outside: plumbing, carpentering, and painting. Mrs. Carlton does all of the cooking and most of the laundry for her family of five. The kitchen is the most lived-in room in the house, and the children share the bedrooms—with two in each and three in the largest room. Mr. and Mrs. Carlton did not finish high school. "We had to get jobs."

When the eldest daughter married, she and her husband moved into the attic bedroom and contributed to the household expenses. The children are ambitious to "buy our mother a washing machine so she won't have to work so hard on wash days."

The living room is the only one in the front of the house. It is small and crowded with furniture—an old upright piano, a cheap cabinet-type radio, gaudily figured overstuffed chairs, and pictures of the family. The windows are covered with lace curtains. This room is never used except for company whom the family are anxious to impress. More intimate friends rarely sit in this room. There is no dining room and all meals are eaten in the kitchen.

"Those damn kids from next door," Mr. Carlton said to his friend, Sam Dixon (UL), who had come over to help and gossip. "You can't have anything nice around here. They've ruined my fence and my garden. Maybe it's not their fault. It's the way they've been raised. Will you look over there in that yard? It looks like a junk heap. They're all clammers. They was born clammers, and they'll always be clammers. If I could sell out I'd do it in a minute. I get so goddamn mad sometimes I could kill them. I tried to sell this place to my brother, Art [LL], but you know my brother. Why he's got worse than these Riverbrookers. He knows better'n to live like they do. But there he is down on River Street a-livin' with that two-bit whore.

"I went down to see him the other morning just to have a heart-to-heart talk with him. First time I'd been there for almost a year.

"You know, I was really ashamed to go in, and he's my own brother. The place looked like a pigpen. Their yard had an old broken-down bedstead in it, and the fences was pushed over, and the backyard was full of old tires and automobile parts. Just like over there across this fence. I went inside and there sat that woman [LL] he's got now. No shame at all. She ain't the first one he's had. She had on a dirty kimona that had big yellow flowers all over it. She looked just like a two-bit whore to me. She's one of those peroxide blondes and she's got a chassis on her that sticks out a foot in front and two feet behind. She was stirring some oatmeal on the stove. Dirty dishes was all over the table. And things were so dirty I hated to sit down.

"She said hello but I didn't say anything.

" 'Oh,' says she, 'So you think you're too good to speak to me, do you?'

"I didn't say nothin'. About that time I heard Art getting up putting on his clothes. He came out of the bedroom buttoning up his clothes.

"I stuck out my hand and said 'Hello, Art' 'cause I could see he was mad. We shook hands.

"Then he says, 'What do you want?'

"I said, 'I'd like to talk to you.'

" 'Well, talk away,' he says. 'There ain't anything to stop you.'

"Then, this blonde cracks, 'Your brother thinks he's too good to speak to me.'

"Art says to her, 'Take it easy.'

"We walked out in the backyard and sat down on an automobile seat. I said, 'Look here, Art, I don't never butt into your business, and you've never butted into mine. But, Art, you're my brother and I've got to talk to you. You ain't actin' right. You know damn well that pa and ma never taught us kids to live the way you're doin'. All the relatives are talkin'. Everybody knows that you are livin' with that woman. I'm tellin' you, it ain't right. An' no Carlton exceptin' Uncle Ned ever acted like you're doin'.'

"He says, 'Don't say nothin' against her 'cause she's a good woman.' But he won't look at me while he's sayin' it. I said, 'Art, why don't you get Annie [LL] back? She was a good wife to you. Why don't you clean this place up? You ought to fix it up inside and out. I can get you some paint, and it won't cost you nothin'; and I'll be glad to help you fix up the fences and paint your house. We can take my trailer an' haul all of the junk you've got away some place. You can have some of ma's old furniture I got put away. Why, you can live like ma and pa taught us if you want to.'

"He didn't say nothin'. I could see I'd got at him. Then he says, 'Look, Will, I'll take what you say 'cause you're my brother and I guess 'cause it's the truth. Your wife told Annie the same thing you said. She told Annie to fix things up, but you know how Annie's people raised her. Annie told your wife she couldn't see nothin' the matter with the way we lived. 'Course

I knew the difference. When we split up, me and Helen in there got together. Don't say nothin' against her 'cause she's a good woman. I guess that's all there is to it. I'm stayin' here with her.'

"I didn't say nothin'. We walked around the side of the house and I got in my car. I says, 'Art, goddamn it, you was raised to be somethin' better'n one of these clammers.' But I made up my mind right then and there that I'd had enough. It was kinda hard with him bein' my brother, but I got my wife and family to think about."

13. Going Up in the World

WHEN Paul Stanley (UL to LM and still moving) was in high school he played football well enough to gain a reputation which brought him several offers of scholarships. He chose Eastern College because there he would have less competition and would be sure of being subsidized for his four college years. After finishing he sought to enter Harvard Law School but his college record was not sufficiently good to be passed by the board of admissions. He chose a less difficult, professional law school in Boston and in time received his law degree. Meanwhile, he had supported himself by working in the law office of John Bates (UM).

Mr. Bates was a loyal alumnus of the local high school. He once said to Mr. John Breckenridge that "Paul Stanley's a good sound boy. Hard worker and knows people. He's a fellow to watch."

Paul's father and mother (UL) had come over from Poland with their respective parents when they were still children. After they had met and married they settled in the Downtown region of Yankee City where Paul, their first child, grew up. They both had worked in the shoe factory and gone to an "Americanization school" to improve their English.

The Stanleys were proud of their home. They owned it outright, and the husband and wife had planted the flower garden. Mr. Stanley had painted the house and fences with two coats of white paint. He placed cast-off tires in appropriate places in the front yard and had given them a coating of white paint. After Mr. Stanley had spaded the ground inside the tires, his wife had planted petunias. Rows of hollyhocks grew beside the white fences. The smaller sons had collected flat stones and made a walk from the sidewalk to the door. Mr. Stanley dug a trench on each side of the stone walk. Here he half-buried empty beer bottles in neat rows so that they formed a glistening border to the path that his boys had fashioned.

The family was proud of its flower garden and pleased at the returns from the vegetable garden in the backyard. They kept chickens and ducks penned in a small coop in one corner, next to the garage where Mr. Stanley housed his second-hand car. (He had purchased the car from a fellow who had also bought it second-hand.)

Mr. Stanley watered and weeded the lawn and kept it well fertilized with manure from the stables owned by a teamster friend. He also considered himself something of a wag. "You know," he said, while he scattered manure about the garden, "I think those people in the Garden Club should see my garden. I bet they would elect me president. My wife says I'm a better manure spreader than any of them. Maybe they'll give me a prize for that."

Mr. Stanley always appreciated this little joke, but once when Paul heard him telling it he informed him that only peasants talked like that.

He looked down on his neighbors. Not one of them on his street cared for his house and yard as he did. They weren't clean and neat. He had learned all of the current folklore about the Riverbrookers and believed it all. He retold all of the sexual jokes he had heard about them, and at the same time warned his children to keep away from the children of Riverbrookers. He liked the derogatory jokes about Riverbrookers because they put into words what he felt about "some of these Americans."

"Not all of these Americans are so hot. Some of the Yankees are no better than the greenhorn Poles, and you can't blame those greenhorns for acting like pigs because that's the way they were forced to live in the old country."

On his son, Paul, he lavished the greatest affection. When Mr. Stanley wanted to expand and demonstrate how he had gone up in the world since coming from Poland, he first talked of his son's college education and then spoke of "my beautiful white house." He then made comments about "all these Yankees who have lived here forever and never got any place." But now it was different because his own Paul wanted to marry one of those Riverbrookers.

When his wife first started "yelling about that Tyler girl" Mr. Stanley had thought little of it, because the boy, Paul, was doing what everybody else did—having a little fun with a Riverbrook girl. He had an Irish friend who ran a small store up the street who always bragged about how he had screwed lots of them; it was fun because you didn't have to marry any of them. That had amused Mr. Stanley before, but now Paul wanted to marry one of them.

When he tried to talk to his son about it he found it very difficult. It was always difficult to talk to Paul. It shouldn't be that way, but he couldn't help feeling that Paul was somehow or other above him. The first time the subject was mentioned, the boy had told his father that it was none of his business. He had said that Annie (starts LL, climbs to LM, and still mobile) was a fine girl. She had gone to high school, and she was no Riverbrooker because she had left her family—to get away from them—and had earned her way while she went through high school. She had been a nursegirl for the Joneses and had learned how to act.

She didn't dress like the others in her family; she didn't act like them; everybody who knew said she had "class"; she was good-looking, and she talked refined and used correct English. Paul had overwhelmed his father with these arguments, reducing him to impotent silence.

Annie Tyler had belonged to the same high school girls' club as Paul's sister. All of her friends said she ought to have credit for what she had done for herself. After a long pause, the father could only say:

"Well, they tell me, 'once a Riverbrooker, always a Riverbrooker.'"

Paul's mother also had quarreled with him about marrying the daughter of a clammer.

"Those Riverbrookers are no good. Now, you have a fine education," she said, "and you can marry a good Catholic girl. Those Riverbrookers are low. Their women will sleep with anybody. They live like pigs."

After a long talk with Mr. Breckenridge, Paul got in his

small car and drove down among the small houses on River Street and stopped at the home of Frank Tyler. He knew that Annie, whom he wanted to see, was visiting her parents. She had come down from Hill Street to see her mother on her day off. He started to knock, when he heard the mother and girl quarreling inside. The daughter had asked her mother why she didn't keep the house clean and make her little brothers wash. She said she was very embarrassed when the truant officer had stopped her on the way down and asked her if she would see to it that the boys stayed in school.

The mother had said that the boys were helping their father, and it was none of that nosy truant officer's business if they weren't in school. They were getting old enough to help their father.

"Your brother, Joe, is just as smart as the next one. I want to tell you, young lady, there ain't nothing the matter with him. He ain't aiming to set the world on fire, and he will be as good a shoe worker as the next one. He will be just as good as those kids who go all the way through high school. If things keep on getting bad we'll move across the river 'til they let us alone. We make a pretty good living making shoes and doing a little clamming. The Joneses and Tylers always have and always will. That boy can figure as good as anybody now and he can read whenever he wants to.

"None of the Tylers or Joneses have ever gone beyond grade school exceptin' you and now you act like you was too good for your own folks.

"Why, I went as far as the fourth grade, and your pa went to the fifth. We can read and figure and write all that's needed, and that's enough for anybody. If that officer keeps on botherin' us, we'll move over to the other side of town. We don't have to take nothin' from nobody."

Paul waited for Annie Tyler to come out and then she and Paul walked up to where Annie worked. After he had told her about getting Mr. Breckenridge's approval, they discussed the date of their marriage. When they arrived at the Smith office where Annie was employed they announced the good news to Mr. Smith and arranged for Annie to have the week-end off.

They "ran away and got married." It was so much easier. They both thought it was too difficult to have the relatives there. The wedding caused an open split in Annie's family. They said she had married a "damn foreigner" and "a fellow who was a Catholic." The new Mrs. Paul Stanley found it expedient to widen the break first made by her parents because it meant she wasn't embarrassed by her relatives' visiting her new home. They might have come at times when friends were there, or neighbors might see them; and she didn't have to face going down to visit the dirty homes of her relatives. She wanted children and she didn't want them to be like her own brothers and sisters.

They seldom saw Paul's father and mother, but his sister was a frequent visitor. She usually met her beaux at their house, and Paul and Annie were pleased that his sister had a chance to meet a better class of people in their own home.

When younger, Paul had been proud of the home of his parents. It was the nicest house in their neighborhood. But now he saw it not as the nicest house in the neighborhood but in the larger context of the whole town, and this made it appear just a little ridiculous. He became a little ashamed of the white tires and the rows of glistening beer bottles. The house he bought was over in Newtown. He wanted to raise his family away from everything which would make them think of what he had gone through. He wanted a nice new house—"one of those cute little bungalows with a big lawn in front and a concrete sidewalk on the street with new curves and a high-class name."

He had been flattered after graduating from law school when some members of the Caribous had invited him to join their organization. There were only a few Poles in the Caribous and most of the members were Yankees. They were all good fellows.

Before he had left the bank after negotiating with some of the officials for his money, he had been congratulated by several of the bank employees on acquiring the new house. They had kidded him about his coming marriage. A few evenings later one of the bank clerks told a clique mate of his, the manager of a hardware store, that Mr. Breckenridge thought very highly of Paul Stanley. At the moment he was talking, they were enjoying a glass of prohibition beer at the hall of the American

Order of Antlers. The Antlers, they felt, had "everyone who counted in Yankee City" as members.

"Paul Stanley's come a long way," he said, "and he's come the hard way. And what's more, he's going a lot further. Nobody who's got what it takes and who's got the backing of Mr. Breckenridge can help but succeed. You know, I think Paul would make a swell member of the Antlers."

"That's a swell idea," his companion replied.

Within the year, Paul was a member in good standing of the Antlers, and he played Bridge there several nights a week. He still belonged to the Caribou, but some of the members of the latter organization were beginning to complain that he didn't come around any more.

The Stanleys were now in a clique with Mr. and Mrs. Tim Pinkham, Mr. and Mrs. Dick Jones (LM), and Mr. and Mrs. Jerry Thomas (LM), but people like the Camps, the Frenches, and the Flahertys, whom Paul knew at the Antlers, never invited them to dinner, nor did any of the "nice ladies from Hill Street" ever call on Annie. It is possible that this occasionally worried them, but there is more evidence that their past success was still a pleasant reward and that the present filled them with hope for the future.

"And anyway," they said, "we're going to see to it that our children have every advantage."

Paul's wife never went to the meetings of the Auxiliary. She had made new friends in her neighborhood and had attended one or two meetings of the Art Club. She was not yet a member of this organization, but she was pleased, she told her husband, to be "introduced to several of the nicest ladies in Yankee City."

14. Learning How to Act

MR. SAM DIXON (UL) was repairing his car. It was a four-year-old model and needed his constant attention. He had it jacked up in the backyard of the two-family house in which he lived, on the river side of the Downtown area.

"This neighborhood's not Hill Street, but it's respectable. There ain't any Wentworths or any Breckenridges living down here," continued Mr. Dixon, "but the people are good solid Americans who stay off relief and work for an honest living.

Now next to me, for instance, is Fred Jones [LM] and he's got a good job in the post office. Then there's Al White [UL] and he's got a good job down at the silverware factory. And across the street is Henry Allen [LM] who works in an office uptown. My work's not steady at the Neway Factory, but I manage to keep the kids in school. They're smart and ambitious and out to help themselves. Bill and Elsie are both in high school.

"We've got a good high school here. Our children have certainly liked it. I don't know exactly what it is that they study, but they both want to go to college and they're studying for that. I told them to get ahead, but I can't help them any longer than high school. I would like to, but I haven't got the money.

"Travis Upton stopped me in the street the other day. He asked me if I was Bill's dad. He said for me not to worry about Bill because he was too good a football player not to go to college. Bill told me that they invited him to come up to Amherst to see the place. I guess Bill's set all right.

"He's already grown so I hardly know him. I never see him any more anyway. He's always up to his friends' houses. 'Cause everybody likes him. They tell me he's a great hit with the girls. But he never has any of his friends down to our house."

Bill went in a clique of three boys and three girls. All of the boys were prominent in school athletics, and the girls belonged to one or more of the letter clubs. The cliques of the girls ran from lower-middle to upper-middle, and the male cliques, from upper-lower to lower-upper.

Most of Bill's clique friends were the children of families one or two classes above his own; only a few of the families of his friends were in the same class as his parents; and none had parents who were clique mates of his parents.

Bill's expanding social world was becoming a constellation wherein he met girls who were above him and from whom he could learn how to act when he met more of their kind when he reached the age of marriage. He learned how to express deference to their parents and to engage in pleasant small conversation which won their approval. It seems likely that Bill was unconscious of most of this, but it is certain that he knew it was a good thing and that he liked it. He had only contempt for "those fellows who don't know how to act and care less."

His sister, although less experienced, was learning the same lessons which would give her a passing grade when later social examinations finally decided her "station in life."

Miss Florence Henderson (UM), teacher at the local high school, was very proud of Elsie Dixon.

"Elsie's parents," she said, "are nice simple people. The wrong side of the tracks, of course. They live in the Downtown area. They're the kind that's ambitious for their kids, not like the Riverbrookers. Elsie catches on quickly and has been taken up by Elaine French and Fay Camp and their crowd. I think it's nice that they invite her to their houses where she can learn how to do things and improve herself.

"I felt sorry for her and had her over to my house. She asked all sorts of questions about everything. Nothing impudent, you know, but you could see she wasn't missing anything.

"I arranged to have her stay with my mother when my brother and I are away. She and my mother have got so they talk about everything. And mother says that no one could have higher moral standards than Elsie. She told mother that she liked to have boys take her to nice places. She said that no boy was going to kiss her until she had got through college and was ready to get married. She wants to be a social worker like my sister in Boston, and she says she's going to marry a doctor.

"When she came to high school she entered the commercial course because her father wanted her to learn something useful. I hear that Oldfield down at the Smith School advised her to take the commercial course, but at the end of her freshman year she changed over. She borrows mother's fashion books and uses the money she gets from us to buy materials to make new dresses. She and her mother make them.

"Of course, her brother's prominence in high school helps her. He's the pride and joy of Coach Black. Several prominent men have taken an interest in him, too. They think they can get him a scholarship for Dartmouth. He's not dumb. His average is about a 'B,' and he can sure play football.

"He's liked by everybody, too. Both of those kids are ambitious but they're not pushy and people like them. Bill belongs to several of the 'letter clubs' and is president of the senior class. He says he wants to be a civil engineer when he grows up."

Elsie went with very few people, and all of them were superior to her in class. These two young people were already participating above the class of their parents, who were even at this time learning to subordinate themselves to their children. The children were still partly identified with the status of their parents because of their partial economic dependence on them, living in the same house and neighborhood, and because they were still known as the children of Sam Dixon. They had yet to consolidate their higher status.

The several foregoing sections need little analysis. Only the more general and obvious points shall be spoken of here since the details of status are treated systematically in Volume II.

"They All Came" describes the members of the three upper classes in primary interaction. There are indications that these people would have felt it inappropriate to have invited people from the lower strata. Furthermore, members of the three lower classes would have felt uncomfortable had they been present. The first sketch presents some of the significant class values and class attitudes of the upper-upper category. The methods used by members of this class to subordinate the people of the class below it are also depicted. Some of the actions of the social climber, Mrs. Phillip Starr, illustrate the upward and downward pressures operating between the two orders. The outward symbols of wealth are a little more conspicuously displayed by the lower-upper members than by the upper-upper members, and their dependence upon such displays appears in the "New Family" sketch. The rather typical social frustrations of the grown children of lower-upper people who try to stay in the community are shown in the daydreaming of both Starr children. Their unsatisfactory escapes from their own "insoluble" problems by attempting to flee (Rome, Tahiti, a Mediterranean cruise), by studying art, studying social work, getting drunk, or becoming active in the problems of the lower classes show how the class system can operate in the personalities of the younger generation.

The marriage problems of the girls in both the upper classes are defined by the same rules of behavior (Sections 2 and 4). The Homeville people who were mobile (Section 5) and those who were nonmobile illustrate how two families in the same class can define their situation in almost diametrically opposed ways. It is also apparent how such definitions affect their personalities and their behavior with other people. The mobile Frenches use their social positions in the upper-middle class to attempt the next step upward. They are not succeeding and, meanwhile, they are arousing the antagonisms of the people who are above them (Section 1 and 3) as well as those who are below them (Section 6).

The exhumation of the bones of Phillip Starr's parents (such a practice is found in other mobile classes) becomes explicable when matched with Mrs. Henry Breckenridge's graveyard meditations and Mr. Breckenridge's genealogical reckonings which are embedded in the facts of the dead. The stability and satisfactions provided for the Breckenridges by their status in the social system may be placed over against the instability and insecurity of the Starr's position. An individual reared in a maladjusted family who grows to maturity in the lower-upper class is much more likely to "crack up" mentally in later life than one coming from a similar maladjusted family who belongs to the upper-upper class.

In the contrasting stories of Mrs. Edward Wentworth and Delgracia Treppington (Sections 7 and 8) successful mobility into the upper class is achieved by Mrs. Treppington and failure is recorded for Mrs. Wentworth. There is clear evidence that each was mobile. Mrs. Treppington came from a highly mobile family and had, in fact, been taught how to be mobile before coming to Yankee City. It is also clear that Mrs. Wentworth had not learned this lesson. Delgracia Treppington used the kinship fiction in addition to her other techniques to fit into the system. Her greatest asset was the knowledge she had learned through painful past experiences of how to subordinate the demands of her own individuality to the necessities of acquiring the status she sought. In common parlance, she knew what she wanted, had the money, and was willing to pay for it.

Mrs. Wentworth refused to meet the demands of the upper-upper status and terminated her marriage as a way of solving her problems. In her situation, there was a conflict between what she, as an individual, wanted to do and the demands of her new status. Negative sanctions were used against her when she tried to consolidate her position while still maintaining her personal freedom. It is highly likely that a long life history of her and of her husband would demonstrate that each of them defined divorce as a personal failure rather than something that happened in their lives because of their status.

In "All Men Are Born Free and Equal" (Section 9), we see men of all classes of societies meeting together in a small crisis. The problem of how a very small number of upper-class people can control the large number from the lower ranks is well illustrated here. The ritual and speech are symbolic expressions used by all the classes when they meet in a situation where it is important to ignore differential status. The groupings formed before and after the meeting indicate how the members organize along class lines and how their attitudes and sentiments shift because of the different social context in which they are participating.

"Clam Flats" and "No Better Christians" (Sections 10 and 11) give two reports on a part of the lower-lower class. These reports contradict each other. Our own evidence shows that the doctor and minister were more nearly right than the truant officer, teacher, and S. P. C. C. agent. A favorite device in all ranked societies is to attribute immoral behavior (that which is socially disapproved) to the lower classes. It is an easy method of subordinating them and of feeling superior. In one of these sketches the school system is seen functioning to maintain the lowly status of the Riverbrookers through more than one generation. A child inherits its lowly position and the school, although an obvious instrument of social mobility in our society, is failing to function in this capacity for most of the Riverbrook children.

The last three sections on upward and downward mobility illustrate how people in the lower classes rise and fall. "Low" moral behavior associated with the refusal to maintain the secular rituals contributes to Art Carlton's downward mobility. Paul Stanley's career tells the story of the upward mobility of a Yankee and an ethnic and demonstrates how the intervention of an upper-upper individual aids his social rise. This boost in his status reflects not only the loan for Stanley's house but also the changes in his cliques, associations, family relations, and the area in which he lives. It shows that upper-upper control is something more than preventing the people below them from doing the things they want, for it also includes helping many people in the lower classes to rise.

The Dixon children (Section 14) are in the critical adolescent period of their lives trying to use the school system to

XI. *Certain Groupings Discussed in Chapter XVII*

1. Breckenridges, Churchill, Alton, Marshall, Sinclair, Wentworth, Treppington, Blaisdail
2. Foley, Starrs, Kimbles, Waltons, Tolman, Whitecotton, Jordan, Upton, Mrs. Edward Wentworth
3. Camps, Frenches, Flahertys, Rodgers, Oldfield, the S.P.C.C. girl, Florence Henderson, Jones
4. Watson, Pinkham, Burke, truant officer
5. Donaghue, Kelley, Stanley, Carlton, Dixon, Annie Tyler
6. Jones, Green, Tyler, Art Carlton, the Greek

climb above the status into which they were born. They are obviously succeeding and doing it in a way which is socially approved.

A casual analysis of the interview material from which these several sketches have been drawn clearly indicates that there is a recognized rank order where people are striving for social recognition. Their values differ in the several strata and within the same social levels. Certain simple generalizations are possible, however, which tell us something of how these people evaluate themselves and others in the world around them. It is clear that the upper-upper class believes in the efficacy of birth and breeding, and the individuals of that class possess each in varying degrees and with proportionate feelings of security. Money is important, but its chief importance is to allow one to live properly.

The lower-upper class also believes in birth and breeding. They cannot use their money to buy birth, but they can spend it to acquire the proper upper-class secular rituals which they hope will secure them the high rank they seek. Money is very important to them, but they are willing to spend large portions of it to secure proper recognition for themselves or their children and to marry their children into the class above them.

The upper-middle class believes in money, but many of them also believe in what they call comfort. Some of them know that money is not enough to be at the top. Nevertheless, most try to get more money to gain higher status. More money is always important. Many of them want money for its own sake and because its mere accumulation has value.

The lower-middle class also wants more money and more comfort. They believe that money and morals are the keys to all of their problems. They are more secure, however, than the two lower classes, and most of them have greater psychological security than the people of the upper-middle class.

Individuals in the upper-lower class tend to be ambitious. They want money, but they are trying to acquire the symbols of higher status such as "nice furniture," "pretty yards," and "a good education." Such things differentiate them from the class below and make them more like the people who are just above them. They are much nearer the bare struggle for existence than the lower-middle class, but they utilize their money for neat-looking clothes, good magazines, and to "give our children a better education than we had."

The lower-lower class cares little for education. Money is important because it shuts the door on the ever-present wolf of want, but it is not of such importance that a parent would force his children to go to school that they might acquire an education in order to get better jobs. Money is to be spent and not saved.

These oversimplified summaries are manifestly inadequate. Our social structure is too complex to be described with such simple generalities. Too many people in each of the several classes do not fit into these categories.

Furthermore, the composite life histories, the social crises, and descriptions of the personal behavior of the members of the several classes are inadequate. They tell part of the truth, and they are designed to allow the reader to understand how it must feel to be in some of the several classes, and to know how the members of the classes appear to the investigator; but again the picture is oversimplified and subject to the unconscious biases of the writer.

The chapters which follow are devoted to a statistical analysis of class similarities and differences. The many statistical tables demonstrate that there are fundamental differences in the social characteristics of the several social strata. By this quantitative analysis, we will find out in just what way and how much the classes differ. For example, we will find out how much the upper-upper class is composed of old people and of unmarried women, and how it differs in this respect from the other classes. We will look at the incomes of these people and determine how they spend their money. We will examine the proportionate number of people in the several classes who have large and desirable houses and who have small and undesirable houses. We will discover what books and magazines and newspapers each of the several classes reads, and we can investigate many other factors in our efforts to see how the different social ranks behave. The remainder of this volume is concerned solely with this quantitative problem.

VIII
BIOLOGICAL COMPOSITION OF THE SIX CLASSES

1. *Sex and Age*

THE social structure of a community arranges its biological aggregate into varying social groupings in accordance with normative rules and cultural values associated with the physical characteristics of the population. Yankee City differentially evaluates such physical characteristics as sex and age, number of people in a group, and the circumstances of such physical events as birth and death. The biological characteristics of the population of the total community remain relatively constant and approximate the normal conditions found in most communities. The physical characteristics of the internal social groupings, however, vary enormously.

A knowledge of the physical characteristics of the total community and all classes provides us with basic evidence by which we can compare each class with all other classes and with the total community. The knowledge gained by such analysis tells us something of the fundamental relations of each class and how the social controls in each operate. In the first part of this chapter we will examine the size, age, and sex of each class; and, in the second section, the place of birth of the total population and of each class.

The most significant facts about the distribution of the population by class are that over 85 per cent of the people are dispersed, rather evenly, in the three lowest strata, and that only 3 per cent are found in the two highest strata. The three lowest classes are from two-and-a-half to three times as large as the upper-middle class and over twenty times as large as either of the two upper ones. The sharpest breaks in number and percentage of class members occur at the junctures upper-middle–lower-upper and lower-middle–upper-middle, indicating that movement into and out of the upper-middle class is rela-

TABLE 2
Distribution of Population by Class

Class	Number	Per Cent Total Population
UU	242	1.44
LU	262	1.56
UM	1,715	10.22
LM	4,720	28.12
UL	5,471	32.60
LL	4,234	25.22
Unknown	141	0.84†
Total	16,785*	100.00

* This is the largest sample used for general statistical analysis for the characteristics of social behavior in Yankee City. In Volume II a still larger sample is used which was accumulated after further analysis of our field data. It must be emphasized that not all of these people live within the legal boundary of the two political units which make up the larger part of the whole community. The larger political unit is the focal point for part of the population of neighboring villages and towns who come into the city to work, trade, play, and partake of the community life. For most purposes in the study of human interaction in a social system, they are sociologically indistinguishable from those who actually reside within the legal limits of the city. Again it seems well to restate that the data here presented are not directly comparable either to the figures of the United States census for 1930 or to other censuses of this community. Two other discriminations must be made about the statistical material of this research: (1) We estimate that there are approximately 1,000 more subadults residing in the Yankee City we studied than our enumeration shows. Our tabulations were based on social personality cards which were prepared for each individual participating in the society. For a proportion of the subadults of a very young age, separate cards were not made and these individuals were not counted (more of them appear in the analysis of the social structure in Volume II). Their names for this part of their analysis were entered on the social personality cards of their parents. (2) The number of individuals tabulated was affected by a time element. Since our material was collected over a five-year period, all ages were adjusted to one base year; persons who had been studied but who had died before this year were not eliminated from the records. All ages were brought up to the base year. The same adjustment was made for children born during the period.

† A few persons (141 or 0.84 per cent) could not be placed definitely in the class hierarchy on the basis of data available. We know, however, that none of these was in the two upper classes.

tively less than in the other classes. The distribution of the population in the six classes does not conform to the "pyramidal" form into which the class population is usually thought to fall. The upper-lower class is largest of all classes and the lower-lower class is the smallest of the three lowest and largest strata. The population of the classes of Yankee City is greatly influenced by the high proportion of skilled workers and low proportion of unskilled ones in the silverware and shoe factories.

The small number of individuals at the top conforms to the usual hierarchical distribution of people in stratified societies found elsewhere in the world. The unequal representation of the population by class in no way reflects the relative influence of one class as against another. The evaluation and control of class symbols are the means through which influence is maintained.

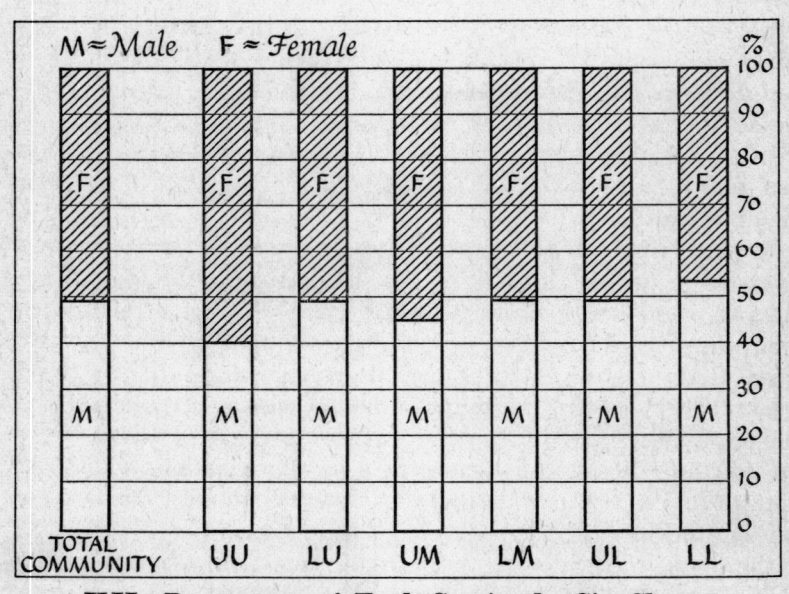

XII. *Percentage of Each Sex in the Six Classes*

The sex composition of the six classes differs considerably. There is a slight excess of females in the community (51 per cent). In Chart XII this is shown in the rectangle marked "total community" at the left. All classes except lower-lower (47 per cent) have more women than men. The upper-upper class (60 per cent) and the upper-middle (55 per cent) have a greater excess of females than found in the general population; the other classes approximate the sex ratio found in the total population. The figures running at intervals of ten at the right of the chart represent the percentage of men and women in each class and in the whole community.[1]

The comparatively large number of men in the lower-lower class is accounted for by the high proportion of immigrant men who are not ordinarily accompanied by their wives and womenfolk. Although the upper-lower class has more people of ethnic derivation than the lower-lower, its people have been here long enough to establish families.

The young men from the three highest classes tend to leave town to find employment. The young women are more likely to stay home. This explains the high percentage of women in the upper-upper and lower-upper classes but does not explain the fairly even sex distribution in lower-upper. The lower-upper men do leave like the upper-upper, but the lower-upper people are somewhat like the lower-lower for they are often "immigrants" into their class. These "new people" frequently are men who have been mobile from families below that class in or out of the city.

In analyzing the age composition of the community, we first divided the people into two major categories: adults (twenty-one and over) and subadults (below twenty-one). These major groupings were further subdivided into the age categories listed at the top of Chart XIII. An examination of this chart reveals the following significant facts. About 80 per cent of the population are adults, the various groups of whom show but few significant differences in age and sex. The excess of females in the two groups between twenty-one and thirty-nine can be attributed to the emigration of younger men, while that in the group sixty years and up can be accounted for by the high percentage of widows and old maids. Between the subadult age levels neither sex nor age differences are significant.[2]

Age distribution by class differs considerably from that of the general population. Chart XIII clearly indicates that with

---

[1]. See Volume VI, *Data Book for the Yankee City Series*. A large number of the tables on which many of the summaries in this and the remaining chapters of this volume are based could not be included. The results of many tables are not given. The demands of space and clear narration prevented it. All such tables have been placed in Volume VI. In the chapters which follow, frequent references to this material will be made by footnotes. Most of the tables in the *Data* volume are of interest to the specialist.

[2]. Cf. *ibid*.

206 *The Social Life of a Modern Community*

few exceptions there is a fairly steady increase in the percentage of subadults, and a fairly steady decrease in the percentage of adults, from the upper-upper class right down through the lower-lower class. Undoubtedly, differential birth rates and ethnic infiltrations are the major factors producing these variations.

XIII. *The Age of the Members of the Six Classes*

In general we may say of sex-age distribution (see *Data Book*) that the upper-upper class contains relatively few subadults and few adults between the ages of twenty-one and thirty-nine; it contains an excess of females; and it is marked by a low birth rate. The lower-upper class shows a fairly even sex ratio in all age groups except that of sixty years of age and over which has an excess of females. The upper-middle class contains a predominance of females in all age groups, as does the lower-middle class, except in the subadult group and in the adult group from forty to forty-nine. The upper-lower class contains many subadults and also has an excess of females in the age range of forty to forty-nine. The lower-lower class is the only one which has a preponderance of males in all age groups.

In summary, the class system tends to put more women at the top and more men at the bottom. This will continue to be true for the lower-lower class until all immigration ceases and our communities become more stable. It seems unlikely that there will be any great change in the high number of women in the old-family group. Furthermore, there will be more old people at the top than at the bottom.

2. Birthplace

THE high positive value associated with place of birth, particularly among the upper classes, and the negative value generally placed on foreign birth by people of Yankee City clearly indicate that birth is an accidental characteristic of great social importance to the community. To determine something of the significance of a person's birthplace, statistics were gathered which threw light on the problem for all six classes and for the whole community.

We did this by using the following fivefold classification based on the relative distance of the birthplace from Yankee City: (1) those born in Yankee City; (2) those born outside the city but within a radius of ten miles; (3) those born in New England outside of regions 1 and 2; (4) those born in the United States outside of New England; and (5) those born in foreign countries. The results of this classification, about which a number of significant statements may be made, can be readily seen by consulting Table 3. At the left side of the table the age categories are found. This column is first divided into subadults and adults. The adult population is redivided into ten-year periods. The title of the column on place of birth is found at the top of the table.

Of the people generally, over 75 per cent were born in America (see Table 3) and about 40 per cent were born in Yankee City. A higher proportion of the subadults (69 per cent) than adults (34 per cent) were born in Yankee City. Of those born in all other areas, the ratio is just reversed. This is particularly noticeable in the foreign-born group, which shows a markedly higher proportion of adults than subadults. The increase of foreign-born is to be expected in view of the facts

TABLE 3

Birthplace of People of Different Ages

Birthplace	Yankee City		Contiguous		New England		Rest of U.S.		Foreign-Born		Total	
Subadults	30.52	69.44 / 834	11.01	6.99 / 84	15.03	17.74 / 213	13.69	3.00 / 36	2.14	2.83 / 34	17.75	1,201
Total Adults	67.17	34.49 / 1,836	84.66	12.14 / 646	81.17	21.60 / 1,150	80.23	3.96 / 211	93.09	27.80 / 1,480	78.68	5,323
21–29	25.03	51.31 / 684	25.95	14.85 / 198	21.31	22.66 / 302	14.83	2.93 / 39	6.92	8.25 / 110	19.70	1,333
30–39	15.95	34.38 / 436	20.97	12.62 / 160	20.47	22.87 / 290	20.15	4.18 / 53	20.69	25.95 / 329	18.74	1,268
40–49	9.44	24.00 / 258	12.06	8.56 / 92	16.80	22.14 / 238	18.63	4.56 / 49	27.55	40.74 / 438	15.89	1,075
50–59	4.35	19.64 / 119	9.17	11.55 / 70	8.05	18.81 / 114	10.27	4.46 / 27	17.36	45.54 / 276	8.96	606
60–over	12.40	32.56 / 339	16.51	12.10 / 126	14.54	19.79 / 206	16.35	4.13 / 43	20.57	31.41 / 327	15.39	1,041
Unknown	2.31	26.03 / 63	4.33	13.64 / 33	3.80	22.31 / 54	6.08	6.61 / 16	4.77	31.40 / 76	3.57	242
Total		40.39 / 2,733		11.28 / 763		20.94 / 1,417		3.89 / 263		23.50 / 1,590		6,766

that immigration has been restricted since 1924 and that the foreign-born group, as before mentioned, contains a high percentage of single men. Among the adults, as age increases (see 21–29 to 50–59) there is a constant decrease in the proportion of each age level born in Yankee City and an increase of those of foreign birth. Furthermore, the proportion at sixty years and over of those born in Yankee City greatly increases while

TABLE 4

Birthplace of the People of the Six Classes

Social Stratification	1 Yankee City	2 Contiguous	3 Rest of New England States	4 Rest of U.S.	5 Foreign-Born	Total
1 UU	0.84 / 52.27 / 23	0.39 / 6.82 / 3	0.56 / 18.18 / 8	3.80 / 22.73 / 10	—	0.65 / 44
2 LU	2.09 / 50.44 / 57	1.83 / 12.39 / 14	1.06 / 13.27 / 15	9.89 / 23.02 / 26	0.06 / 0.88 / 1	1.67 / 113
3 UM	8.12 / 48.06 / 222	7.86 / 12.99 / 60	8.75 / 26.83 / 124	11.41 / 6.49 / 30	1.64 / 5.63 / 26	6.83 / 462
4 LM	29.89 / 48.89 / 817	24.51 / 11.19 / 187	26.11 / 22.14 / 370	26.62 / 4.19 / 70	14.28 / 13.59 / 227	24.70 / 1,671
5 UL	32.97 / 41.38 / 901	25.95 / 9.10 / 198	25.76 / 16.77 / 365	20.53 / 2.48 / 54	41.45 / 30.27 / 659	32.18 / 2,177
6 LL	25.06 / 31.38 / 685	38.93 / 13.61 / 297	33.17 / 21.52 / 470	26.24 / 3.16 / 69	41.64 / 30.33 / 662	32.26 / 2,183
Unknown	1.02 / 24.14 / 28	0.52 / 3.45 / 4	4.59 / 56.03 / 65	1.52 / 3.45 / 4	0.94 / 12.93 / 15	1.71 / 116
Total	40.39 / 2,733	11.28 / 763	20.94 / 1,417	3.89 / 263	23.50 / 1,590	6,766

the number of foreign-born decreases. The high proportion of old people in the upper class accounts for a large part of the increase in people over sixty who were born in Yankee City. Only minor differences in regard to place of birth are noticeable between the sexes, the only exception being that the number of foreign-born men in the community greatly exceeds the number of foreign-born women. (For further data see Chapter IX.)

Table 4, an analysis of birthplace by class, reveals a number of important points. First, as class status increases, the proportion of those born in Yankee City increases; and, obversely, as class status increases, the percentage of the foreign-born decreases; (the upper-upper class contains no foreign-born; the lower-upper, only one, whose parents held American citizenship); third, the highest percentage of foreign-born is located in the two lowest strata, the greatest relative disparity occurring at the juncture upper-lower–lower-middle, beyond which ethnic mobility is slowed down; fourth, a high proportion of those born in New England (outside of Yankee City and the contiguous area) fall into the middle classes; and, finally, the two upper classes contain a relatively higher proportion than the other classes of people born in the United States outside of New England.

These last two points offer some clues regarding the process of social climbing in the class system. Of the people born outside of the community but in the United States, those born at some distance seem to have greater chances for mobility in the upper classes than those born close at hand. One of the probable reasons for this is that family connections—the most important single criterion of exclusion from the upper classes—are more readily traced for those born near at hand. Moreover, the fact that the people of the upper classes travel more doubtless increases the probability of their returning to Yankee City with spouses and children born in other sections of the country.

IX
THE ETHNIC MINORITIES OF YANKEE CITY

1. Who They Are

ACCORDING to the United States census of 1930, approximately half the population of Yankee City is either foreign-born or native-born of at least one foreign parent. The census classifies these individuals under twenty-nine categories "according to country of birth." Our research, however, divided the population of Yankee City into ten groups, each of which had certain distinctive features. These groups are: (1) Native, or Yankee; (2) Irish; (3) French (French Canadians); (4) Jewish; (5) Italian; (6) Armenian; (7) Greek; (8) Polish; (9) Russian; and (10) Negro.

These groups, with the exception of the first, we have called "ethnics."[1] The term "ethnic," as used in this study, does not refer simply to foreign birth. Rather, it has a wider meaning. An individual was classified as belonging to a specific ethnic group if (1) he considered himself or was considered by the Yankee City community as a member of the group, and (2) if he participated in the activities of the group.[2]

Our purpose in using such a broad definition was to facilitate a study of the ethnics in their relation to the larger community, to discover the nature of the social organization of the various ethnic subcommunities, and to evaluate the prevailing beliefs, attitudes, and sentiments concerning ethnic individuals. Early in our stay in the community we were made aware of the force of these ethnic distinctions, of how these distinctions conditioned behavior by limiting and enlarging the participation and the social personality of the individual,

1. We ordinarily do not speak of the natives, or Yankees, as an ethnic group. This is simply a device to avoid terminological difficulties.
2. A more extended discussion of the terms "ethnic" and "ethnic group" will be presented in Volume III, to follow.

and of how quickly and directly barriers were set up on the basis of ethnicity.

Thus it became evident that many individuals, despite the fact of their birth in the United States or even in Yankee City, were nevertheless regarded by the native group as "foreigners" and were constrained to this role in certain areas of social relations by the pressure of Yankee opinion.

A factor which caused this research to adopt the broader definition of the term ethnic (rather than the narrow and misleading concept of "country of birth") grew out of a preliminary survey of the ethnic population which revealed that many of the ethnic groups isolated by this research were drawn from several countries. Interviews taken in the ethnic communities indicated, for example, that the Greeks, Armenians, and Poles each had several countries of birth. Moreover, the Jews, although not listed as a separate group by the census, nevertheless exist in Yankee City as a distinctive, organized community. Although predominantly from Russia and Poland, they claim seven different countries of birth. In view of these facts, it was impossible to attempt an adequate sociological analysis of the ethnic population according to the classification established by the census. Only with a broad definition based on community attitudes and the participation of the individual in the activities of his ethnic group could the social realities of the situation be understood.

Another problem of definition and classification arose early in the study. In our efforts to determine membership in the various ethnic groups, and the relative size of each, we faced the problem of how to classify persons born of mixed marriages. Not only was intermarriage between natives and ethnics found to be of frequent occurrence, but also intermarriage between members of different ethnic groups. For purposes of tabulation, an arbitrary rule was followed: in cases of mixed marriage, the child was assigned to the ethnic group of the father; if the father was native and the mother ethnic, however, the child was assigned to the ethnic group of the mother.

In following this arbitrary rule, it was not possible at the time to take into account the question of whether or not the individual so classified was actually participating in the group with which we identified him. However, a greatly detailed analysis of the complex mass of ethnic data was then in progress and part of this investigation was devoted to tracing through the several ethnic generations back to the original immigrant group. This material, which appears in the volume on ethnic communities, not only takes into account the facts of the intermingling of the ethnic groups but also the facts of the individual's participation or lack of participation in the communal activities of the ethnics.[3]

The numerical strength of the natives in Yankee City is 9,030 individuals, 53.80 per cent of the total population. The great majority are descendants of colonists of British stock who sailed westward across the Atlantic and settled in New England and Yankee City in or after 1635. The exodus from England began in the early seventeenth century and continued through the nineteenth century.

Included in the group of people designated as native, or Yankee, are a small number of individuals who stem from non-English societies. A few French Huguenots and German Jews settled in the City early in its history, when it was at the peak of its maritime glory. The descendants of these scattered families were assimilated into the native group and today are regarded as natives by the community. Their ethnic past has been effectively forgotten and the individuals themselves are not behaviorally distinguishable from the Yankee group.

Another, and larger, group of persons, recently immigrant, are regarded by the community (and therefore by this research) as natives. These are the Canadians, English, North Irish, and Scotch, whose foreign birth presents no barriers to free participation in the Yankee society.

The native group in its interaction with the ethnics represents the American type of social system and the American

3. In this volume, a great emphasis is placed on descent as a criterion of ethnicity. Because of more extensive work in tracing descent and the analysis of the ethnic generations, differences appear between the totals for ethnic population and the ones presented in this volume. This volume attempts to "account for the ethnic factor, however diluted, as far as it carries in the line of descent," an attempt not made in the tabulation of data. Moreover, in cases of intermarriage this volume applies the test of relational participation in the communal activities of the ethnics. For the criteria of classifications, see Chapter II of the volume on ethnic communities.

214   *The Social Life of a Modern Community*

culture. Predominant in numbers, the native group also dominates the economic, political, and social structures of the community.

The combined numerical strength of all the ethnic groups in Yankee City is 7,646 individuals, 45.55 per cent of the total population.[4] Chart XIV represents the percentage of ethnic

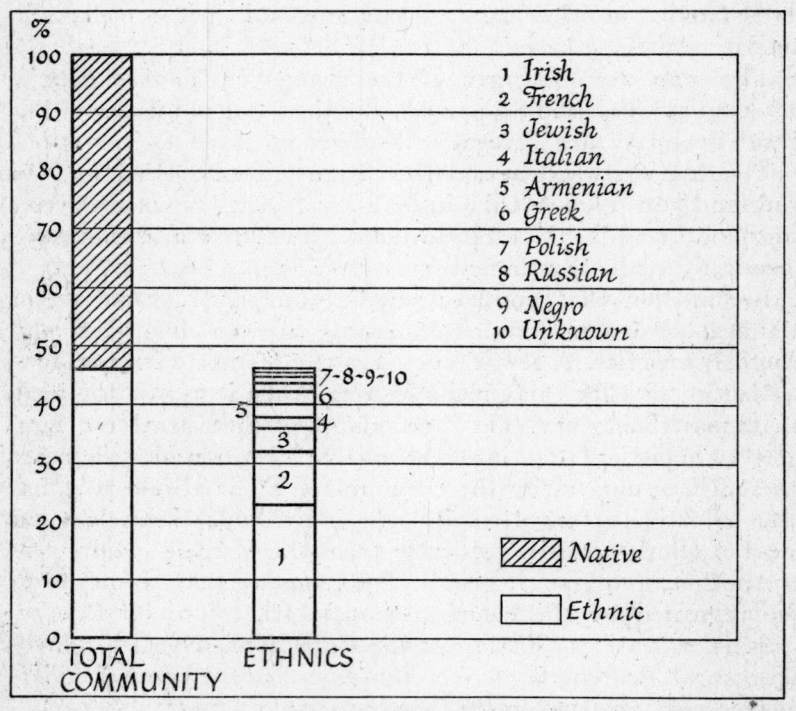

XIV. *The Percentage of Ethnic Groups in the Total Population*

groups in the total population. The oldest and easily the largest group in the city is the Irish. A smattering of Irish Catholics was living in the community in the early days of the nineteenth century, but the influx of Irish in significant numbers did not begin until 1840. In the first Yankee City directory, published

4. For 109 individuals, 0.65 per cent of the total, native or ethnic affiliation could not be determined.

in 1850, 104 Irish families were listed. Today they number 3,943 individuals.

The Irish, forced out of Ireland by famine conditions, augmented the steady stream of emigrants from England and Scotland and formed the first culturally divergent group in the community. Although they ordinarily conformed to the Yankee City social system linguistically, they nevertheless differed from it in other fundamental respects. Yankee City was almost entirely Protestant; the Irish were Roman Catholic. Yankee City was then an important seaport with its economic life geared to shipbuilding and maritime commerce; the Irish were rural and agricultural in background.

The ethnic group which followed the Irish into Yankee City was the French Canadian. A small infiltration of these people, descendants of the French Catholic colonists, was already apparent in 1880. By 1903, however, 127 households of French Canadians had been set up in the city, and now they number 1,466 individuals. Organized around the parish system and their separate Roman Catholic church, the French community today exhibits great internal cohesion. The efforts of this group to transmit its heritage and tradition to the children have been greatly helped by the parish school through instruction in the French language and the Catholic faith. The parish school also helps to preserve family solidarity for it transmits the ideal of the family pattern from the older to the younger generation. Not only is French the language of the school and of the church rituals; it is also the language of the home.

Although a few German-Jewish families came into Yankee City about the middle of the last century, the Russian-Polish Jews—who form the largest element in the Jewish community today—did not appear until the 'nineties. In 1903, fifteen families of Polish Jews were present in the city; a decade later, the number had grown to forty-four households; at the time of this study, the Jews numbered 397 individuals, forming 2.37 per cent of the total population.

The Jews who settled in Yankee City conformed both ecologically and economically to the prevailing social system of the new country. While the earlier ethnics derived from agrarian-peasant economies, the Jews were traditional city dwellers. They had a background as tradesmen, small shopkeepers, and manual workers in the urban centers of Russia and Poland. In other respects—in language, in religion, and in family and cultural tradition—they were dissimilar. While the earlier ethnics, upon entry into Yankee City, had in large measure abandoned their original callings, the Jews maintained the same occupational patterns which for centuries had characterized their life in Europe.

The Italians came to Yankee City about the same time as the Jews, adding a new Catholic element to the life of the town. Still too few in numbers to be organized as a separate parish, they are nominally members of one of the Irish churches. The Italians, moreover, are split into mutually antagonistic North and South Italian subgroups. The North Italian group was the earlier to arrive and has been partially assimilated into the general community. In all, there are 284 Italians, constituting 1.69 per cent of the total population and 3.71 per cent of the ethnic population.

The Armenian group is only a trifle smaller than the Italian, numbering 246 individuals. The entry of the Armenians into the city around 1900 is directly connected with the shoe industry. One of their number, who is employed in the largest shoe-manufacturing plant and is now foreman of one of the departments, originally secured jobs for the others, many of whom were his kin. Thus, unlike the other ethnics, the Armenians were at first exclusively employed in one industry. Today some of their number are small entrepreneurs—grocers, fruit-store owners, newsstand proprietors, and the like. The bulk are, however, still shoe workers.

The Armenian group is split along religious lines, some being Protestant (Congregational) and others Eastern Orthodox. Because of this dichotomy, the Armenian subcommunity has lacked complete integration. However, despite progressive assimilation of the younger people into the general society, the authoritarian power of the father in the family structure is very pronounced, and the group is organized largely on a kinship basis.

In 1893, only five Greeks resided in Yankee City; at the time of this study, the Greeks numbered 412, comprising the fourth largest ethnic group. Of the total population, they constituted

2.45 per cent; of the ethnics, 5.39 per cent. The greatest movement into the city occurred in the 1920's.

About two thirds of the Greeks employed are factory workers, the great majority in the shoe industry. Others are confectioners, restaurant owners, barbers, etc. Their church, the Greek Orthodox, is a powerful social agency and maintains a parochial school. Family ties are strong. For the most part, the father has maintained his patriarchal role; the mother and children are subordinated.

The Poles and Russians are the most recent ethnic arrivals. Their first appearance in the community dates back only twenty-five years to the World War. Like the Greeks and Italians, the majority of the Polish men drifted in singly from other cities of the East Coast, most of them as young adults. At first they were employed by the cotton mills, but with the collapse of the Yankee City textile industry, many obtained jobs in the local shoe and hat factories. Although Poles and Russians are antagonistic in Europe, close and amicable relations exist between them in Yankee City. This arises from a knowledge of each other's language, from frequent and informal meetings in their local provision stores, and from the smallness of the Russian group. The Poles numbered 677, the Russians, only 141. The Poles (the third-largest ethnic group) constituted 4.03 per cent of the population; the Russians, 0.84 per cent.

Negroes have been present in Yankee City from the days of the New England slave trade. During the Civil War they were sent to the battlefields as "bought substitutes" for members of prominent families. At the time of this study, the Negro group had dwindled to eighty individuals, only 0.48 per cent of the total population. The caste barrier or color line, rigid and unrelenting, has cut off this small group from the general life of the community.

2. The Biological Characteristics of Each Group

IN SEX composition, the combined ethnics differ little from the natives: the native group has a slight excess of females while the sex ratio among the combined ethnics is evenly balanced.[5]

5. The native population consists of 4,400 males and 4,630 females; the combined ethnics, of 3,800 males and 3,846 females.

However, if the ethnic population is broken down into its component groups, definite variations appear.

All ethnic groups, with the exception of the Irish, contain a preponderance of males. It is significant that the Irish is the only one which has an excess of females, and that this preponderance of females is even greater than among the natives. Interview material offers an explanation. Upon investigation we found that the natives, both men and women, are leaving the city but at a differential rate: the men are departing more rapidly than the women. However, in recent years the women, too, have sought a chance to leave. The prevalent feeling among them is that "there is nothing to do in Yankee City." Undoubtedly, to the girl of native stock who feels herself above the status of a factory hand with the "foreigners," Yankee City has little to offer. Moreover, she feels her opportunities for a good marriage with someone of her own social class slipping away. So she leaves Yankee City, not only in search of economic advancement but in search of a proper husband.

The Irish ethnic group, however, has advanced farther in the class hierarchy than any other; but it feels keenly the barrier of exclusion from the upper ranks on the one hand, and the economic pressure of the newer ethnics on the other. Hence the men are leaving while the women remain, feeling stranded. The Irish women, who occupy positions of lower social status than native women and are not stigmatized by factory work, have found jobs in the shoe industry in significant numbers.

In age composition, the ethnics as a whole are sharply differentiated from the natives. This is clearly shown in Table 5, below:

If we subdivide the adult population into different age groups and compare the natives with the combined ethnics, we find that the proportion of native adults below forty-five years of age is smaller than the proportion of ethnics in that age range. While 54.40 per cent of the ethnic adults are under forty-five, only 42.24 per cent of the natives are in this age bracket. Here again it is the more recent groups with a great preponderance of population in the younger age brackets which account for the variation. However, the most striking difference in age composition shows up at the other end of the age scale, in the percentage of persons sixty and over. Here

TABLE 5
Distribution of Ethnic Groups by Age

	Adult	Below 14	14–17	17–20	Unknown	Total
Native	56.98 / 82.45 / 7,446	41.96 / 8.55 / 772	40.28 / 4.29 / 387	44.39 / 3.90 / 352	59.35 / 0.81 / 73	53.80 / 9,030
Total Ethnic	42.35 / 72.39 / 5,535	57.55 / 13.85 / 1,059	59.10 / 7.43 / 568	54.73 / 5.68 / 434	40.65 / 0.65 / 50	45.55 / 7,646
Irish	23.45 / 77.73 / 3,065	24.51 / 11.44 / 451	24.45 / 5.96 / 235	22.07 / 4.44 / 175	13.81 / 0.43 / 17	23.49 / 3,943
French	7.84 / 69.86 / 1,024	12.93 / 16.23 / 238	11.55 / 7.59 / 111	9.84 / 5.32 / 78	12.20 / 1.02 / 15	8.73 / 1,466
Jewish	2.04 / 67.26 / 267	2.93 / 13.60 / 54	3.85 / 9.32 / 37	4.67 / 9.32 / 37	1.63 / 0.50 / 2	2.37 / 397
Italian	1.59 / 73.24 / 208	2.28 / 14.79 / 42	1.56 / 5.28 / 15	2.14 / 5.99 / 17	1.63 / 0.70 / 2	1.69 / 284
Armenian	1.44 / 76.43 / 188	1.85 / 13.82 / 34	1.35 / 5.28 / 13	1.01 / 3.25 / 8	2.44 / 1.22 / 3	1.47 / 246
Greek	1.79 / 56.80 / 234	4.95 / 22.08 / 91	5.10 / 11.89 / 49	4.41 / 8.50 / 35	2.44 / 0.73 / 3	2.45 / 412
Polish	3.08 / 59.54 / 403	6.09 / 16.54 / 112	8.95 / 12.70 / 86	8.70 / 10.19 / 69	5.69 / 1.03 / 7	4.03 / 677
Russian	0.60 / 55.32 / 78	1.90 / 24.82 / 35	1.77 / 12.06 / 17	1.26 / 7.09 / 10	0.81 / 0.71 / 1	0.84 / 141
Negro	0.52 / 85.00 / 68	0.11 / 2.50 / 2	0.52 / 6.25 / 5	0.63 / 6.25 / 5	/ / 0	0.48 / 80
Unknown	0.67 / 79.82 / 87	0.49 / 8.26 / 9	0.62 / 5.50 / 6	0.88 / 6.42 / 7	/ / 0	0.65 / 109
Total	77.86 / 13,068	10.96 / 1,840	5.73 / 961	4.72 / 793	0.73 / 123	16,785

220 *The Social Life of a Modern Community*

the relationship is reversed. Of the native adults, 26.44 per cent are sixty or more years old; of the combined ethnics, only 14.74 per cent.

As has been previously stated, the concept of ethnicity is not based simply on place of birth. The natives as well as the ethnics contain a foreign-born element, but in a widely varying proportion. Obviously the foreign-born ethnics greatly outnumber the foreign-born natives, actually almost five to one. Of the native group, 280 persons or 8.37 per cent were born outside the boundaries of the United States. This group consists of the English, North Irish, and Scotch mentioned above who are regarded as native by the community.

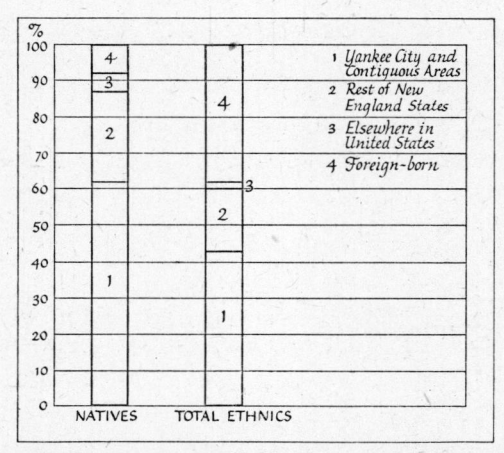

XV. *The Birthplace of the Native and Combined Ethnic Groups*

Chart XV (The Birthplace of the Native and Combined Ethnic Groups) presents a contrast in the birthplaces of the two groups. It shows that a relatively large proportion of the ethnics were born in Yankee City or elsewhere in the United States and that a small percentage of Yankees were foreign-born. It demonstrates that well over half of the Yankees were born in Yankee City itself or within ten miles of it and that less than 15 per cent were born out of New England.

Table 6 (The Birthplace of Ethnic Groups) tells the detailed story for all these cultural groups. It is a table of significance (mean square contingency). The ethnic groups are found in the left-hand column and the birthplaces head the columns at the top of the table. The natives were born in significantly higher numbers in all areas in the United States. The Irish and Greeks were the only ethnic groups who were not born in significantly high numbers in foreign countries. The natives and the Irish were the only groups who were born in significant numbers in Yankee City; all others except Negroes and French Canadians were significantly low. The low Irish population born in the city explains the high percentage of local ethnic births found in Chart XV. The French Canadians in Yankee City came from their homeland or from other parts of New England. The Negroes migrated to Yankee City from other parts of Massachusetts and from the South.

TABLE 6

The Birthplace of Ethnic Groups

H — Significantly High
L — Significantly Low
— — Non-significant
O — Not Present

	Yankee City	Contiguous Areas	Rest of Mass.	Rest of New Hampshire	Maine	Connecticut and Rhode Island	Rest of U. S.	Foreign-Born
Native	H	H	H	H	H	—	H	L
Irish	H	L	—	L	L	—	L	—
French	L	—	H	H	H	—	—	H
Jewish	—	L	—	—	L	O	—	H
Italian	L	L	—	L	—	O	—	H
Armenian	L	L	L	L	O	—	—	H
Greek	L	L	—	—	—	O	L	—
Polish	L	L	L	L	L	H	L	H
Russian	L	L	L	L	—	—	O	H
Negro	L	—	H	—	O	O	H	L

3. *The Ethnic Groups in the Class System*

In their relation to the class structure of the community, the ethnics present a remarkable picture, one which clearly reveals how the system works. Their story is one of class-mobility-in-time, for the length of time a group has been established in the community bears a definite relationship to its average class status. In general, the oldest groups have risen highest in the class hierarchy. Chart XVI represents the class affiliations of the ethnic and native groups in Yankee City today.

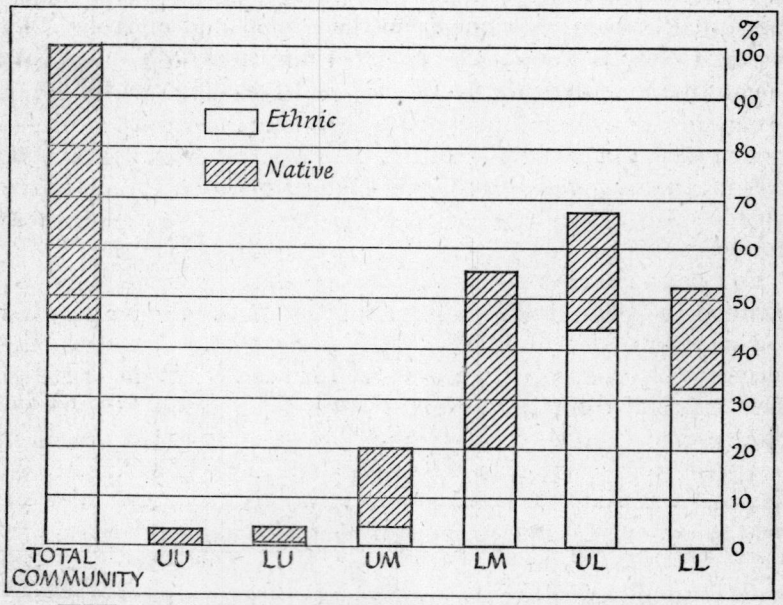

XVI. *The Ethnic Composition of the Six Classes*

The incoming ethnics were faced with the problem of adjusting to the Yankee scheme of things. This meant taking on the behavioral patterns and values of the established group, the Yankees, and the concomitant sloughing off of peculiarly ethnic traits, ideas, and attitudes. To the extent that individual members of the ethnic groups were successful in doing this, their upward mobility was facilitated. As they adjusted to the society, submerging the qualities which differentiated them sharply from the natives, and as the classes higher in the social stratification began to shape up to them, they gradually could select behavioral forms which would make upward mobility an assured fact. But rising in the class hierarchy is a slow process. Although the class system per se requires mobility, nevertheless the rate is slow; for otherwise the system could not maintain itself. Certain rigidities based on the principles of exclusion from each class require time before they can be overcome.[6]

Here we can give only a glimmering of the fundamental and all-pervading changes which upward mobility imposes on the individual. The changes cover every phase of his life: he must manipulate every possible device with consummate skill. To rise in the class hierarchy, economic advance alone is insufficient; basic acceptance by the people in the class above is the minimum. The social personality of the individual changes even in such details as his reading habits. The neighborhood he lives in, the church he attends, his family relationships, and his friends—all gradually shift as he gropes his way up the class ladder.

For the roughest sort of index of ethnic mobility, let us examine the class range of participation of the various groups and compare them with the natives. First and foremost, the natives comprise the only group in the society whose range of class participation is complete, stretching from the lower-lower class to the very top of the class structure. No person is accepted by the upper-upper class as one of them unless he is a Yankee, and that in a special sense. His family origins must go back to persons of note in the maritime period of glory early in the city's history; the person must fit in the New England tradition and measure up, genealogically, to its important values.[7]

From the viewpoint of the ethnic composition of each class, we find that the upper-upper class is the only one which is homogeneous, comprising only natives. The lower-upper, on

6. For an extended discussion of ethnic mobility, particularly an examination of the rate at which the process takes place in the different ethnic generations, see the volume on ethnic groups in this series.
7. A few persons not of English origin have made their way into this class. Today, these persons have intermarried with the natives, are members of the Protestant church, and are characterized by all other upper-upper-class behavior traits. Their origins have been largely obscured by time.

the other hand, includes a few Irish. In the upper-middle class, all ethnic groups save the two most recent ones and the Negroes have a representation. The lower-middle class and the upper-lower include members of every ethnic group except the Negroes. In complete contrast to the top class in the society, the lower-lower contains members of every ethnic group to be found in the city.

Table 7 gives exact information on the class representation of the several ethnic groups.

Let us now examine it from the viewpoint of each social class in order to compare relative ethnic composition. The vertical figures on the left list the percentage of natives in each class. It will be seen that, with the exception of the lower-lower class, the percentage of natives decreases from the top to the bottom of the class hierarchy. The entire upper-upper is native; the lower-upper contains a small proportion of ethnics. Better than four fifths of the upper-middle is native, but the proportion drops to two thirds in the lower-middle. The lower-lower has a greater percentage of natives than the upper-lower; in the lower-lower is included a sizable group of Riverbrook clam diggers who are often regarded as different and apart and as the dregs of the society.

In summary, the facts bear out our hypothesis associating the average class status of a group with the length of time it has been in the city. Two groups, the French Canadians and the Jews, are the only important deviants.

It will be recalled from our discussion of the age composition of the ethnics that the proportion of adults in the native group (82.45 per cent) is greater than among the combined ethnics (72.39 per cent). The dearth of older persons, accompanied by a high birth rate among the newer groups, accounts for this.

Not only is the percentage of native adults higher in the general population, but it is also higher within each class. Thus in the lower-lower class native adults comprise more than three fourths of the native group while ethnic adults form only two thirds of the total ethnics. In the upper-lower, natives of adult age form 81.62 per cent; ethnic adults, only 73.78 per cent. Similar differentials appear in the middle classes and in the lower-upper.

The proportion of adults to subadults is not only higher for

TABLE 7
Class and Ethnic Group

	UU	LU	UM	LM	UL	LL	Total
Yankee	100.00 / 2.69	95.42 / 2.78	83.44 / 15.93	67.10 / 35.26	38.00 / 23.15	42.80 / 20.19	53.96
Total Ethnic		4.58 / 0.16	15.69 / 3.55	32.78 / 20.39	61.49 / 44.33	56.57 / 31.57	45.58
Irish		4.58 / 0.31	13.42 / 5.89	22.74 / 27.52	38.33 / 53.75	11.54 / 12.53	23.43
French			0.82 / 0.96	4.05 / 13.15	10.69 / 40.29	15.64 / 45.60	8.72
Jewish			0.70 / 3.02	3.52 / 41.81	3.45 / 47.61	0.71 / 7.56	2.39
Italian			0.06 / 0.35	0.83 / 13.73	2.18 / 41.90	2.95 / 44.02	1.71
Armenian			0.17 / 1.22	0.93 / 17.89	2.28 / 50.81	1.75 / 30.08	1.48
Greek			0.52 / 2.20	0.47 / 5.37	2.69 / 35.85	5.48 / 56.58	2.46
Polish				0.11 / 0.74	1.21 / 9.78	14.27 / 89.48	4.06
Russian				0.13 / 4.26	0.66 / 25.53	2.34 / 70.21	0.85
Negro						1.89 / 100.00	0.48
Unknown			0.87 / 19.74	0.12 / 7.89	0.51 / 36.84	0.63 / 35.53	0.46
Total	1.45	1.57	10.30	28.36	32.88	25.44	

the natives than for the ethnics of similar class status, but class differentials are apparent within each group. In general, whether we are speaking of the natives or of any ethnic group, the proportion of adults increases as class status becomes higher. The French provide an illustration, although any other group might be used. The percentage of adults in the various classes is as follows: upper-middle, 78.57 per cent; lower-middle, 73.94 per cent; upper-lower, 71.77 per cent; lower-lower, 68.03 per cent.

By and large, the pattern holds for every ethnic group whose class range permits comparison. Evidently, as class status improves, the birth rate tends to fall.

In conclusion, the ethnics play an important role in the class structure of the community. Much of their behavior and attitudes can be understood only in relation to their varying positions in the class hierarchy and to their mobility since their arrival in the city.

X
ECOLOGICAL AREAS OF YANKEE CITY

1. *The Twelve Areas*

ON the basis of such criteria as the size and condition of the house, the amount and payment of rent, class membership, property values, crime and delinquency, percentage of foreign-born, distribution of ethnic groups, and recognition by the members of the community (which will be severally discussed in the chapters to follow), we divided Yankee City into twelve ecological areas, as shown in the accompanying map (Map 1).

Oldtown (area 11), the original settlement—still having a separate town government, lies at the easternmost extremity of the town; while Newtown (area 10), the most recently developed residential area, lies at the westernmost extremity. These two areas are connected by Hill Street (area 1), on the north side of which most of the other areas are located. The Business District (area 6) conveniently divides the residential section into two halves. In this study the area called Across the River (area 12) has also been included, because a large number of its people have sufficient participation with the residents of Yankee City to make them socially a part of the town.

Of the areas most clearly defined by the inhabitants, Hill Street and Riverbrook are outstanding: the former is considered "the best part of town"; the latter, the "lowest part of town." The remaining areas, except Homeville, which is believed to be composed of "good solid Americans," are less distinct. But they vary considerably as we shall see upon further analysis.

At this point we must refer the reader to a number of tables. The first (Table 8) is an analysis of the ecological areas in terms of the general population and in terms of sex. Since the areas vary considerably in geographical size, there seems to be no great significance attaching to the general population figures. A glance at this table also indicates that there is no sig-

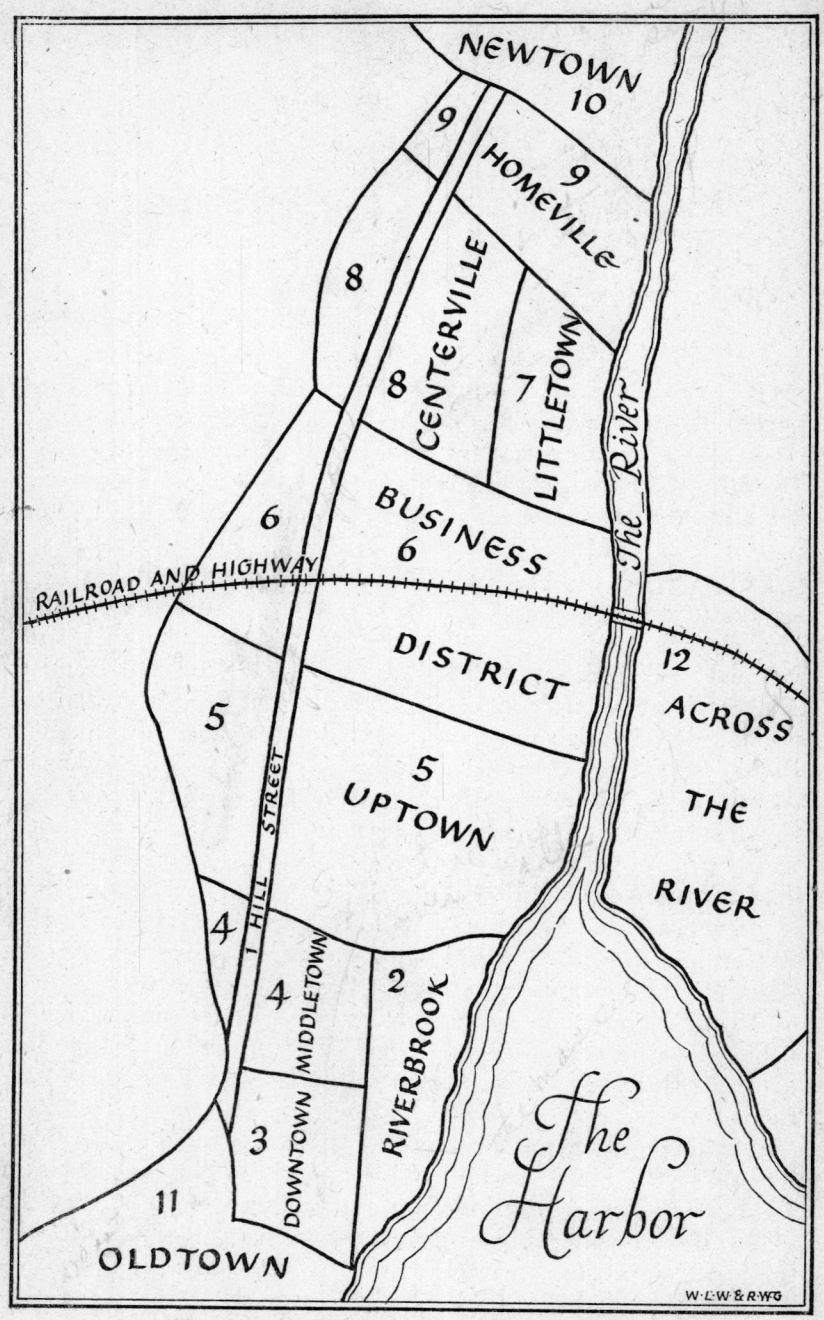

The Ecological Areas of Yankee City

TABLE 8

Population of the Twelve Areas

Sex	1 Hill Street	2 Riverbrook	3 Downtown	4 Middletown	5 Uptown	6 Business Area	7 Littletown	8 Centerville	9 Homeville	10 Newtown	11 Oldtown	12 Across the River	Unknown	Total
Male	5.22 431 43.40	8.82 728 48.79	10.34 853 49.28	13.88 1,146 50.11	10.26 847 50.75	9.78 807 48.18	7.78 642 50.39	6.01 496 48.34	10.86 896 47.71	3.35 276 48.42	5.03 415 49.46	2.47 204 53.12	6.20 512 48.94	8,253
Female	6.59 562 56.60	8.95 764 51.21	10.29 878 50.72	13.37 1,141 49.89	9.64 822 49.25	10.17 868 51.82	7.41 632 49.61	6.21 530 51.66	11.51 982 52.29	3.45 294 51.58	4.97 424 50.54	2.11 180 46.88	5.33 455 51.06	8,532
Total	5.92 993	8.89 1,492	10.31 1,731	13.63 2,287	9.94 1,669	9.98 1,675	7.59 1,274	6.11 1,026	11.19 1,878	3.40 570	4.99 839	2.29 384	5.76 967	16,785

TABLE 9
Weekly and Monthly Rentals by Area

	Weekly		Monthly		Total	
Hill Street	1.64	32.80 / 41	5.79	67.20 / 84	3.16	125
Riverbrook	12.13	73.08 / 304	7.72	26.92 / 112	10.51	416
Downtown	13.53	72.44 / 339	8.89	27.56 / 129	11.83	468
Middletown	18.00	64.80 / 451	16.88	35.20 / 245	17.59	696
Uptown	13.37	64.55 / 335	12.68	35.45 / 184	13.12	519
Business District	11.61	57.62 / 291	14.75	42.38 / 214	12.76	505
Littletown	10.85	71.77 / 272	7.37	28.23 / 107	9.58	379
Centerville	5.95	63.40 / 149	5.93	36.60 / 86	5.94	235
Homeville	9.38	58.60 / 235	11.44	41.40 / 166	10.13	401
Newtown	1.12	38.36 / 28	3.10	61.64 / 45	1.84	73
Oldtown	1.00	69.44 / 25	0.76	30.56 / 11	0.91	36
Across the River	0.16	80.00 / 4	0.07	20.00 / 1	0.13	5
Unknown	1.28	32.32 / 32	4.62	67.68 / 67	2.50	99
Total		63.33 / 2,506		36.67 / 1,451		3,957

nificant difference in the sex ratio of any area except Hill Street, which contains a significantly high proportion of women. Inasmuch as there is in this area a heavy concentration of the upper-upper class, part of the disparity can be accounted for on the class basis.

The next table (Table 9) is an ecological analysis of renters who pay by the month, as against those who pay by the week. The figures indicate that a relatively high proportion (over 60 per cent) of the renters of Riverbrook, Downtown, Middletown, Uptown, Littletown, Centerville, and Oldtown pay rent by the week; a corresponding proportion of the renters of Hill Street and Newtown pay rent by the month.

TABLE 10

Median Monthly Rentals for Each Area

Area	Median Monthly Rental
Hill Street	$28.93
Homeville	19.62
Uptown	19.54
Business District	19.42
Middletown	18.93
Littletown	18.49
Centerville	18.21
Downtown	17.42
Riverbrook	17.06
Newtown	16.13
Oldtown	14.31

In this connection the median rentals of the various areas are also important. The median rental for all areas is $18.77. The highest rentals were paid in Hill Street, Homeville, Uptown, and the Business District; the lowest, in Newtown and Oldtown areas. These last two areas tend to be high in social prestige despite the low rentals. Their low rentals are in part due to their peripheral location.

The median rentals of the various areas are listed in Table 10.

2. Ethnic Distribution in the Twelve Areas

WHEN each area is examined as a cultural unit, certain ethnic living patterns become apparent. A close reading of Table 11 (Ethnic Distribution in the Twelve Areas) clearly demonstrates this point.

Hill Street is an area characterized by a high concentration of Yankees and, with the exception of the peripheral Greeks and Negroes, a low concentration of all other ethnic groups. Riverbrook contains a high percentage of French Canadians and Russians and a low percentage of Greeks, Italians, and Jews. The Downtown district has a high concentration of French Canadians, Poles, and Russians and is avoided by the Irish, Armenians, and Italians. Middletown is significant for the number of French Canadians, Poles, Russians, Greeks, and Jews, and for a low distribution of Yankees, Irish, Armenians, and Italians.

The Uptown area has high concentrations of Irish, Jews, and Greeks, and is avoided by the Yankees and Armenians. In the Business District there is a significant distribution of the Irish, French, Greeks, Armenians, Italians, and Negroes, and a low distribution of Yankees, Poles, and Russians. In Littletown there is a high distribution of Irish, Armenians, and Italians, but this district is avoided by Yankees, Poles, and Russians. In Centerville the Irish, Armenians, and Italians reside in significantly high numbers; the Yankees, Poles, Russians, and Greeks, in significantly low numbers. In the Homeville area the Yankees are concentrated in significantly high numbers; the French, Irish, Poles, Russians, Greeks, Armenians, and Jews, in significantly low numbers.

The Newtown area contains a significantly high number of Yankees, a low distribution of French Canadians, Irish, and Jews, and no Russians, Armenians, or Negroes. Oldtown is comprised of a significantly high number of Yankees, and all

TABLE 11
Ethnic Distribution in the Twelve Areas

H — Significantly High
L — Significantly Low
— — Non-Significant
O — Not Present

	Hill Street	River-brook	Down-town	Middle-town	Uptown	Business District	Little-town	Center-ville	Home-ville	New-town	Old-town	Across the River
Yankee	H	—	—	L	L	L	L	L	H	H	H	H
Irish	L	—	L	L	H	H	H	H	L	L	L	L
French	L	H	H	H	—	—	—	—	L	L	L	—
Jewish	—	L	—	H	H	—	—	—	L	L	L	L
Italian	L	L	L	L	—	H	H	H	—	—	L	—
Armenian	L	—	L	L	H	H	H	H	L	L	L	L
Greek	—	L	—	H	—	H	—	L	L	L	L	L
Polish	L	—	H	H	—	L	L	L	L	L	L	L
Russian	L	H	H	H	—	L	L	L	L	L	L	L
Negro	—	—	—	—	—	H	—	O	O	O	O	O

the other ethnic groups either are significantly low or are not found here. The Yankees also form a significantly high percentage of the population Across the River, where there is a low concentration of Poles and Irish and where there are no Russians, Greeks, Armenians, Jews, and Negroes. The ethnic distribution is interpreted in the sections of this chapter on ethnic groups, class and area.

3. Class Distribution in the Twelve Areas

ALL classes seek out certain areas to live in and avoid, or are excluded from, others. A brief review of Table 12 shows that Hill Street is a region where the two upper classes and no others reside in significantly high numbers. Riverbrook is avoided by the four highest classes but it has a high concentration of upper-lower and lower-lower people. The Downtown region has no upper-upper residents, is avoided by the next three classes, but is significantly high for the lower-lower class. All classes except the lower-lower avoid the Middletown region. The two upper classes stay out of the Uptown area in significant numbers, the next three classes are neither high nor low in it, and the lower-lower class is significantly high there. All four of the highest classes avoid the Business District; the upper-lower class prefers it; and the lower-lower is there in neither high nor low numbers. Littletown has a somewhat similar distribution. Centerville is an area preferred by the upper-lower class. Homeville is the preferred region of the two middle classes and, except for the upper-lower class, is avoided by all others. Newtown's residents are upper-upper and lower-middle. All four of the highest classes live in Oldtown.[1]

4. Ethnic Members of the Six Classes in the Twelve Areas

THE members of the different ethnic groups and the various classes, as we have already seen, tend to prefer certain areas and avoid others. We may now turn to a few questions arising from this point. Do members of an ethnic group concentrate in certain areas regardless of class? Do members of the same class prefer particular areas, avoid others, and thereby dis-

---

1. Those on relief were in significantly high percentages in Riverbrook, Downtown, Middletown, Uptown, and Littletown, and in significantly low percentages in Centerville, Homeville, and Newtown.

regard their ethnic traditions? Do certain classes and certain ethnic groups follow one pattern of behavior, and other ethnic groups and classes, different patterns of behavior?

TABLE 12

Areas Preferred by the Six Classes

H — Significantly High Concentration
L — Significantly Low Concentration
(—) — Non-Significant
(O) — None Present

	UU	LU	UM	LM	UL	LL
Hill Street	H	H	H	—	L	L
Riverbrook	L	L	L	L	H	H
Downtown	O	L	L	L	—	H
Middletown	L	L	L	L	L	H
Uptown	L	L	—	—	—	H
Business Area	L	L	L	L	H	—
Littletown	—	L	L	—	H	—
Centerville	—	—	—	—	H	L
Homeville	L	L	H	H	—	L
Newtown	H	O	L	H	—	L
Oldtown	H	H	H	H	L	L
Across the River	O	O	L	—	L	H

Since the upper-upper class is all Yankee, it is impossible, by an analysis of the behavior found here, to answer these questions. A few Irish are found with the Yankees in the lower-upper class. The lower-upper Yankees are found in all but two areas of the city; approximately half, however, are on Hill Street and about one fifth in Oldtown. Nine of the ten Irish in the lower-upper class live on Hill Street; one lives in Oldtown. (See *Data Book* for ethnic, class, and area table.) These few Irish tend to obey the class rules more closely than ethnic rules, for they live in areas which are symbolic of upper-class position and significantly low for the Irish population generally.

The upper-middle class presents further evidence in answer to these questions. In this class the Yankees are again well diffused with a preference for Hill Street, Oldtown, and Homeville, a pattern of distribution also followed by upper-middle-class Irish. The upper-middle French Canadians, however, are concentrated primarily in two areas: Homeville and Riverbrook. The latter includes the area of their original settlement, while their occupation of the former represents a move into an area regarded by the Yankees as being the essence of upper-middle class. In other words, part of the French upper-middle class obey class lines, and part of them seem to be ruled by ethnic factors.

Upper-middle-class Jews are also concentrated in two areas: Uptown and Middletown. Both of these are near their original settlement in Yankee City, suggesting that they cling to ethnic sentiments in choice of place of residence.

There is a tendency for the lower-middle-class Yankees to concentrate in Homeville; otherwise they are more evenly spread throughout the several areas of the community than are the other ethnic groups in this class. The lower-middle members of each ethnic group tend to concentrate in one or two areas and are almost negligible in all others. The lower-middle Irish and French Canadians are more like the Yankees than the others. However, few of them live in Oldtown. The lower-middle-class Jews again tend to concentrate in the Middletown and Uptown areas. The lower-middle Italians are concentrated in Homeville and the Business District. The Homeville distribution indicates that lower-middle Italians are obeying class sentiments, while the Business District members still live where Italians generally tend to congregate. The lower-middle-class Armenians are located largely in Littletown where there are a high number of this ethnic group; the lower-middle Greeks are in the Business District with the rest of their group; but the few Poles and Russians in this class are in Homeville, which suggests, since this district is decidedly Yankee and middle class, that class rather than ethnic factors are in operation here.

The upper-lower-class Yankees are spread out through the

city, but are concentrated in Homeville, Downtown, Riverbrook, and the Business District. The upper-lower Irish also are well distributed throughout the city, but all the other ethnic groups in this class tend to concentrate where the bulk of their group is found. The Jews stay in Middletown and Uptown. The Italians remain in Littletown where there is the highest concentration of their population, although there is some tendency for them to move into Homeville. The upper-lower-class Armenians are found in large numbers in the Business District where the Armenians generally are located. The upper-lower-class Greeks are in the Business District and the Uptown areas. The upper-lower-class Poles are in Middletown and Riverbrook as are the others of their ethnic group, and the Russians are in Middletown with the other lower-class Russians.

The lower-lower-class Irish are like the Yankees in distribution. The lower-lower-class French are highly concentrated in Middletown; the Jews, in Uptown; the Italians, in Littletown, the Business District, and Centerville; the Armenians, in the Business District; the Greeks, in Uptown, Middletown, and the Business District; the Poles, in Middletown; the Russians, in Riverbrook, Downtown, and Middletown; and the Negroes, in the Business District. On the whole, we may thus conclude that both class and ethnic factors operate in the ecological distribution of the Yankee City population. The areas of Hill Street and Oldtown, followed closely by Newtown, seem to be the areas of highest social evaluation. Riverbrook and Downtown are those of lowest social evaluation, although they are followed closely in this respect by the area Across the River, Uptown, and Middletown. The Business District, Littletown, and Centerville are areas favored by the upper-lower class; but Centerville also contains a medium distribution of the upper and middle classes.

The reader should re-examine the ecological map with the class of the residents in mind. With the exception of Oldtown, the whole region to the right of the Business District has a concentration of lower-lower people and, on the whole, is avoided by other classes. The central region, from the Business District over to Homeville, with high concentration of upper-lower people, is higher in the social scale. Homeville goes a step higher into the middle classes, and Newtown still higher to the upper-upper class. Hill Street is a thin line of upper-class people who spread out fanwise at each end of the town into the Newtown and Oldtown areas.

XI

THE HOUSES OF YANKEE CITY

1. *Size and Condition of the Houses and Their Evaluation*

THE dwellings of Yankee City are chiefly one- or two-family houses; the community contains few apartments, almost no one lives in a hotel, and only a small percentage of the population resides in business structures. Naturally the houses vary considerably in size, in condition of repair, and in the economic and social evaluation placed upon them. For purposes of this investigation they were divided into three sizes—large, medium, and small—and each of these types was classified according to three conditions of repair—good, ordinary, and bad. (Social evaluation of the house further depended upon rent, assessor's value, and prestige statements gained through interview.) The distribution of the various types of houses, moreover, varies considerably, as we shall see later, according to ecological area, class, and ethnic group.

Of the people in the community, 46.69 per cent live in small houses, 43.38 per cent in medium-sized houses, 7.22 per cent in large houses, and 2.71 per cent in structures built primarily for business purposes.[1]

Slightly over 3 per cent of the people of Yankee City live in houses which are large and in good repair, 2 per cent are in large houses in ordinary repair, and a little under 2 per cent are in big houses which are in bad condition. (See percentages at the bottom of Table 13.)

The occupants of medium-sized houses in good repair include 9 per cent of the total population; those in houses of medium repair, 20 per cent; and those in houses in bad repair, 15 per cent.

Only 7 per cent of the people live in small and good houses,

[1]. This sample includes 12,770 individuals. The area Across the River is not included, only part of Oldtown is, and none of the houses of people who come to Yankee City from other communities is part of this sample.

whereas 16 and 23 per cent live in small houses in ordinary and bad repair.

The large houses in good condition are assessed at a median value of $3,967, the highest in the community. The large and medium are next ($3,738), and the large houses in bad repair are third ($2,717). The houses of medium size and in good condition are fourth ($2,277), and those which are medium both in size and condition are fifth ($1,982). Houses which are small in size and in good condition ($1,722) outrank houses which are medium in size but in bad condition ($1,572). Small houses in ordinary condition are assessed at $1,537, and small houses in bad condition rank last with a median value of $1,283.

As can readily be seen from the above figures, the large houses, most of which are comparatively old and of Georgian design, are most highly valued despite their condition; but the small houses which are in good condition are given a higher assessed value than those of ordinary size which are in bad condition. The high value of a large house is partly due to the fact that the size of the plot of land it occupies tends to be larger than that occupied by a smaller house.

Furthermore, large houses in good repair command the highest rentals in Yankee City. They have a median monthly rental of $32.67. The large houses in medium repair rent for less ($23.27) than houses of ordinary size and good repair ($26.19). The large houses in bad repair rank eighth ($18.80). They are topped by small houses in good condition ($22.56), medium-sized houses in ordinary repair ($20.87), small houses in medium repair, and business structures ($18.86). The house rentals of business structures outrank those of medium-sized houses in bad repair ($17.63) and the small houses in bad repair, which are last ($17.16).

The rental value of a house does not always correspond exactly to its assessed evaluation. The renter pays more for a house which is in good repair than for any other type of house. The large, medium, and small houses in good repair are ranked in that order in the highest rental group; the large, medium, and small houses in poor repair are ranked in that order in the lowest rental group; and the houses in medium condition are in the intermediate group. The only exception to this abso-

TABLE 13
House Type According to Ecological Area

Area Lived In	1 LxG	2 LxM	3 LxB	4 MxG	5 MxM	6 MxB	7 SxG	8 SxM	9 SxB	10 Business	Total
Hill Street	20.84 170 / 42.18	9.31 76 / 25.95	0.61 5 / 2.21	15.20 124 / 11.20	29.66 242 / 9.48	1.96 16 / 0.83	2.08 17 / 1.94	15.07 123 / 5.88	4.41 36 / 1.20	0.86 7 / 2.02	816 / 6.89
Riverbrook	1.97 27 / 6.70	1.53 21 / 7.17	1.89 26 / 11.50	5.17 71 / 6.41	13.83 190 / 7.45	20.01 275 / 14.62	7.57 104 / 11.87	15.72 216 / 10.32	31.15 428 / 14.30	1.16 16 / 4.62	1,374 / 10.76
Downtown	1.43 23 / 5.71	0.68 11 / 3.75	0.87 14 / 6.19	7.66 123 / 11.11	18.12 291 / 11.40	13.20 212 / 11.27	7.04 113 / 12.90	17.75 285 / 13.62	28.95 465 / 15.53	4.30 69 / 19.94	1,606 / 12.58
Middletown	1.14 24 / 5.96	3.71 78 / 26.62	2.57 54 / 23.89	6.52 137 / 12.38	14.56 306 / 11.99	22.17 466 / 24.78	2.66 56 / 6.39	15.08 317 / 15.15	30.64 644 / 21.52	0.95 20 / 5.78	2,102 / 16.47
Uptown	2.74 36 / 8.93	2.82 37 / 12.63	2.06 27 / 11.96	8.00 105 / 9.49	17.15 225 / 8.82	17.45 229 / 12.17	7.09 93 / 10.62	10.98 144 / 6.88	22.03 289 / 9.66	9.68 127 / 36.71	1,312 / 10.27
Business District	2.90 38 / 9.43	4.05 53 / 18.09	4.97 65 / 28.76	6.04 79 / 7.14	23.22 304 / 11.92	12.07 158 / 8.40	4.05 53 / 6.05	16.65 218 / 10.42	22.84 299 / 9.99	3.21 42 / 12.14	1,309 / 10.25

TABLE 13 (Continued)

Area Lived In	1 L×G	2 L×M	3 L×B	4 M×G	5 M×M	6 M×B	7 S×G	8 S×M	9 S×B	10 Business	Total
Littletown	2.11 / 24 / 5.96	0 / 3.75	0.96 / 11 / 4.87	7.11 / 81 / 7.32	23.42 / 267 / 10.46	20.79 / 237 / 12.60	7.72 / 88 / 10.05	12.19 / 139 / 6.64	20.88 / 238 / 7.95	4.82 / 55 / 15.90	1,140 / 8.93
Centerville	2.34 / 21 / 5.21	1.22 / 11	1.67 / 15 / 6.64	11.02 / 99 / 8.94	23.95 / 215 / 8.42	17.38 / 156 / 8.29	6.01 / 54 / 6.16	10.80 / 97 / 4.63	25.39 / 228 / 7.62	0.22 / 2 / 0.58	898 / 7.03
Homeville	1.10 / 19 / 4.71	0 / 2.04	0.52 / 9 / 3.98	14.76 / 254 / 22.94	24.06 / 414 / 16.22	6.86 / 118 / 6.27	12.32 / 212 / 24.20	23.30 / 401 / 19.15	16.73 / 288 / 9.62	0.35 / 6 / 1.73	1,721 / 13.48
Newtown	3.30 / 15 / 3.72	1.32 / 6		6.81 / 31 / 2.80	21.10 / 96 / 3.76	1.98 / 9 / 0.48	18.90 / 86 / 9.82	32.08 / 146 / 6.98	14.51 / 66 / 2.21		455 / 3.56
Oldtown	20.00 / 6 / 1.49			10.00 / 3 / 0.27	6.67 / 2 / 0.08	16.67 / 5 / 0.27		23.33 / 7 / 0.33	23.33 / 7 / 0.23		30 / 0.23
Across the River									71.43 / 5 / 0.17	28.57 / 2 / 0.58	7 / 0.05
	3.16 / 403	2.29 / 293	1.77 / 226	8.67 / 1,107	19.98 / 2,552	14.73 / 1,881	6.86 / 876	16.39 / 2,093	23.44 / 2,993	2.71 / 346	12,770

lute ranking—by condition and by size—is that large houses in medium repair receive higher rentals than small houses in good condition. There is still a tendency for largeness to be given high value. The renter is primarily interested in condition, secondarily in size, while the assessor tends to value large houses (and their surrounding land), regardless of condition, above smaller-sized houses and lots.

2. Where Good and Bad Houses Are Located

THE good and bad houses of Yankee City are unequally distributed through the city. Table 13 demonstrates this quite clearly. The house types are listed at the top of the page and the areas at the left. In the first column we notice that almost 21 per cent of the people of Hill Street are in large and good houses while less than 2 per cent of those of Riverbrook are of this type; on the other hand, less than 5 per cent of Hill Street's houses are small and bad, but over 30 per cent of those in Riverbrook are of this least-desired type.

Let us briefly review the facts about the house types of each area. Hill Street has more large and good houses than would be expected by chance. It also has more large houses in medium condition and medium-sized houses in good or medium repair. It has fewer people than would be expected who live in houses which are of all three sizes but in bad condition. It has fewer people who live in business structures or in small houses in good repair.

Riverbrook, on the other hand, is an area where there are more houses than would be expected by chance which are small and in bad repair or of ordinary size and in bad repair. It is an area avoided by people who live in large houses in good condition or ordinary-sized houses in good or in medium condition. It is also an area which lacks business structures which serve as dwellings.

In the Downtown area, people do not have houses which are large, no matter what their condition, but show a preference for small houses (which are in need of repair) and for business structures. The Middletown area evinces mixed preferences: it shows high preference for small, medium, or large houses in bad repair, but also for medium-sized houses in ordinary repair.

The Uptown people rent or own business structures and

houses in bad repair and of medium size. They avoid in significant numbers medium or small houses which are in ordinary repair.

The Business area likewise demonstrates mixed preferences. Large houses in medium or bad repair and medium-sized houses in ordinary repair are those in which people live in significant numbers. They then favor medium-sized houses which are in good or bad repair or small houses which are in good condition. The Littletown area favors business structures and medium-sized houses in medium or bad repair. These people do not show a preference for large or small houses in medium repair. The people of Centerville live in houses which are medium in size and in good or medium repair, and they stay out of business structures and small houses of medium repair.

The Homeville inhabitants prefer houses medium in size and medium or good in condition or houses which are small and in good or medium repair. They avoid houses which are large no matter what their condition, business structures, and medium or small houses in bad repair.

In summary, Hill Street is an area of good housing, Homeville is an area of medium and small houses in good repair, Riverbrook and Downtown are areas with bad housing, most of the Middletown houses are bad, the Business area tends toward large size but ordinary to bad condition, Littletown and Uptown have medium-sized houses with condition from ordinary to bad, Centerville has houses medium in size and tending from medium to good repair, and the houses favored by Newtown are small but from ordinary to good condition.

3. What Classes Get What Houses

JUST as the house types are disproportionately divided among the several areas, so they are unequally distributed among the six classes. Chart XVII represents the distribution of houses among the six classes. As usual, the six classes and the total community are depicted by columns. The percentages of people living in each type of house are in the left-hand margin. The numbers (see legend) refer to the ten house types. We note that large parts of the upper-upper and lower-upper columns are given to Type 1 and that almost none of the lower-middle, upper-lower, and lower-lower columns is so listed. On the other hand, large sections of the lower-lower and upper-lower columns are given over to Type 9, small and bad houses, while none of the upper-upper column is. This chart gives the reader the approximate percentages. (See *Data Book* for details.)

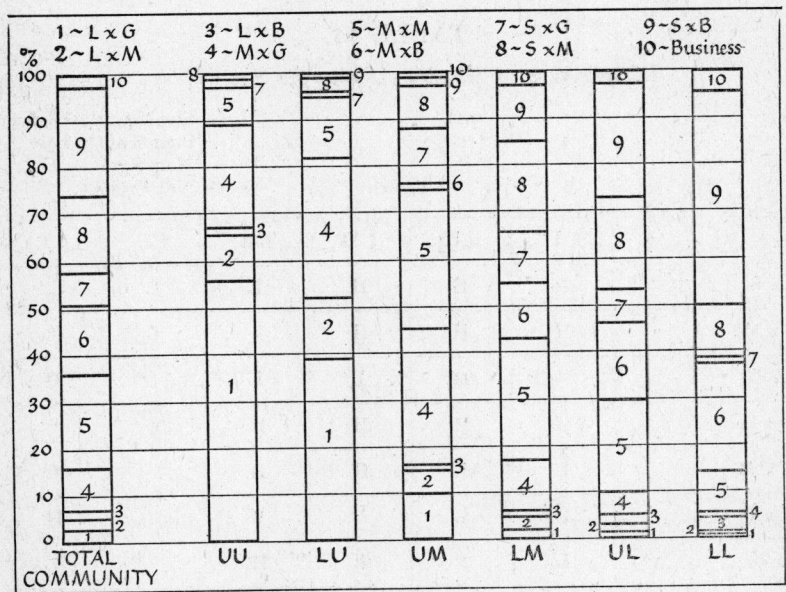

XVII. What Classes Get What Houses

Table 14 gives further support to the above conclusions. This table of significance shows that houses which are in good or medium repair are of high significance (H) in the three highest classes and of low significance (L) in the three lowest levels. It demonstrates that the intermediate types of houses (M x G, M x M, and S x M) are favored by the two middle classes and by no other stratum; that whereas the upper-middle class is significantly high and the lower-middle significantly low for large and good houses, the reverse is true at the other end of the scale of preferred houses, for the upper-middle class is significantly low and the lower-middle significantly high for the small and medium houses.

This table demonstrates another important fact: that bad housing, whether the place be large, medium, or small, is a characteristic of the lower-lower class but of no other, for the lower-lower group is significantly high for all three of those types and no other class is. Moreover, the lower class does live in significantly low numbers in all types of houses which are in good repair.

TABLE 14

Distribution of Houses Among the Six Classes

H — Significantly High
L — Significantly Low
— — Non-Significant
O — Not Present

	UU	LU	UM	LM	UL	LL
L x G	H	H	H	L	L	L
L x M	H	H	H	—	L	L
L x B	—	O	L	L	—	H
M x G	H	H	H	H	L	L
M x M	L	L	H	H	—	L
M x B	L	L	L	L	L	H
S x G	L	L	L	H	—	L
S x M	L	L	L	H	H	L
S x B	L	L	L	L	—	H
Business	O	O	L	—	—	H

In brief, as one descends in the class order the type of house becomes smaller and less preferable, and as one ascends the house tends to become larger and better. The upper classes get the better homes; the middle classes, the ordinary houses; and the lower classes, the poor ones.

The various types of houses are also unequally distributed among the ethnic groups of Yankee City, as shown in Table 15. The Yankees and Jews are the only ethnic groups that occupy large and good houses in significantly high numbers. The French, Poles, and Greeks, on the contrary, are significantly low in this respect.

TABLE 15
Ethnic Group and House Type

H — Significantly High
L — Significantly Low
— — Non-Significant
O — Not Present

	L x G	L x M	L x B	M x G	M x M	M x B	S x G	S x M	S x B	Business
Native	H	H	L	H	—	L	—	—	L	—
Irish	—	L	—	—	H	—	H	H	L	L
French	L	—	H	L	—	H	L	—	H	—
Jewish	H	H	H	L	—	H	L	L	—	H
Italian	O	O	—	—	L	—	L	—	—	H
Armenian	—	H	H	—	L	—	L	H	—	—
Greek	L	L	—	L	L	H	L	—	—	H
Polish	L	L	—	—	L	H	L	—	H	—
Russian	O	O	—	O	L	—	—	—	H	O
Negro	O	O	O	O	—	—	O	—	H	—

The foregoing tables of class and ethnic occupation of houses demonstrate that the upper classes get the good houses, and the lower classes get the bad ones; and that certain ethnic groups, particularly the old Yankees, get a larger share of the good houses and a smaller share of the bad ones than can be accounted for by chance alone. Certain significant points stand out when we interrelate these two analyses. Although there are slight differences in housing conditions depending on the ethnic group, these are not very great, and what differences there are depend largely on the fact that an ethnic group has reached a better class in such small numbers that the differences in house on first sight appear greater than they actually are.

There is no ethnic group other than Yankee in the upper-upper class; only Yankees and Irish are found in the lower-upper class. The Irish in the lower-upper class exhibit almost identical housing with the natives. In the upper-middle class, however, the Irish have a higher concentration than the natives of large and good houses. Because of their ethnic characteristics many of the Irish have been prevented from entering higher classes, but they have been able to buy the proper symbols.

The upper-middle-class natives are slightly better housed than the other upper-middle-class ethnic groups. In the lower-middle class, all the ethnic groups are much the same; however, the Yankees, Irish, French Canadians, and Jews reside in the large houses. The newer ethnics, on the whole, possess poorer housing facilities than the ethnic groups just listed who have been here much longer. Here there is an ethnic difference within the class. In the upper-lower class, the Irish are better housed than all other groups—even better than the Yankees. In the lower-lower class, the Jews have the worst housing and vary from all other groups.

Within each ethnic group, there is a great variation in housing, depending upon class. Class is far more significant in housing than is the ethnic position of an individual. In the upper-upper class over 56 per cent of the Yankees live in large and good houses, in the lower-upper class 37.59 per cent, in upper-middle 7.16 per cent, in the lower-middle 2.18 per cent, in the upper-lower 0.83 per cent, and in the lower-lower 0.16 per cent (see *Data Book*).

The Irish, whose highest class is the lower-upper, follow this same proportionate distribution. Over 45 per cent of the lower-upper-class Irish live in large and good houses, 20.11 per cent of the upper-middle Irish, 2.60 per cent of the lower-middle Irish, 1.15 per cent of the upper-lower Irish, and none of the lower-lower Irish. The highest members of the French-Canadian group are upper-middle class. None of them lives in large and good houses. In the lower-middle class 1.31 per cent of the French occupy large and good houses, in the upper-lower class 1.09 per cent, and in the lower-lower class none. The French Canadians seem to be less influenced by class in their housing than any other group.

The highest class in which the Jews are found is the upper-middle. Approximately 42 per cent of the upper-middle-class Jews live in large and good houses, 2.90 per cent of those in the lower-middle class, 2.78 per cent of those in the upper-lower class, and 5.62 per cent of those in the lower-lower class. Of the other ethnic groups, no Italians, Poles, Russians, nor any Negroes live in large houses; six Armenians in the lower-lower class and one Greek in the upper-lower class live in large and good houses. Although the fact that no Italians, Poles, Russians, and Negroes live in large and good houses might appear to be due entirely to ethnic influence, it must be remembered that all of these groups are at the bottom of a class hierarchy. In time some Italians, Poles, and Russians are certain to rise, and the change in their class position will bring about a corresponding change in their housing. This is predictable because of the way in which other ethnic groups such as the Irish and Jews have been able to acquire better housing as they have risen in class status. The Negroes, however, because of their caste position, symbolized by their physical variation, are likely to remain in the lowest position and be excluded from houses of the preferable kind.[2]

Over 31 per cent (31.28 per cent) of the Yankees in the upper-middle class live in medium-sized houses in good repair, 11.99 per cent of those in the lower-middle class, 3.44 per cent of those in the upper-lower class, and 0.39 per cent of those in the lower-lower class.[3] Over seventeen per cent (17.39 per cent) of the upper-middle-class Irish live in medium-sized houses in good condition, 11.21 per cent of the lower-middle Irish, 7.18 per cent of the upper-lower Irish, and 1.23 per cent of the lower-lower Irish. In the upper-middle class 27.27 per cent of the French Canadians live in houses of this type, in the lower-middle class 2.61 per cent, in the upper-lower class 5.46 per cent, and in the lower-lower class 0.56 per cent. The lower-middle-class Jews are the only ones of their group who occupy houses of this type (1.45 per cent). None of the upper-middle-class Italians lives in such houses, 25.93 per cent of the lower-middle Italians, 8.24 per cent of the upper-lower Italians, and 4.60 per cent of the lower-lower Italians. None of the upper-middle Armenians lives in medium-sized houses in good repair, 41.18 per cent of the lower-middle Armenians, and none of the two lower classes in this group. In the upper-middle class, 55.56

2. The statistics for house type of all ethnics in all classes have been worked out, but because they bulk so large it will be necessary to give only samples.
3. In the two upper classes, the Yankees are not given because they are not important in a comparison for this type of house with the other ethnic groups.

per cent of the Greeks dwell in houses of this type and 10.53 per cent of those in the lower-middle class. None of the Greeks in the two lower classes resides in such houses. The highest Poles in the community are lower-middle class. Twenty-five per cent of the Polish middle class, 16.07 per cent of the upper-lower-class Poles, and 5.76 per cent of the lower-lower-class Poles occupy medium-sized houses in good repair; none of the Russians or Negroes lives in such houses. In the lower-lower class 55.57 per cent of the Yankees live in such houses, in the upper-lower class 29.52 per cent, in the lower-middle class 11.77 per cent, and in the upper-middle class 1.72 per cent.[4]

In the lower-lower class 42.01 per cent of the Irish live in small houses in bad repair, in the upper-lower class 20.61 per cent, in the lower-middle class 11.21 per cent, in the upper-middle class 2.17 per cent, and in the lower-upper class none. Of the French in the lower-lower class 40.11 per cent live in small houses in bad repair, in the upper-lower class 23.80 per cent, in the lower-middle class 15.03 per cent, in the upper-middle class none. In the lower-lower class 73.68 per cent of the Jews live in such houses, in the upper-lower class 22.22 per cent, in the lower-middle class 15.22 per cent, and in the upper-middle class none. Thirty-four and forty-eight hundredths per cent of the Italians in the lower-lower class, 20.00 per cent in the upper-lower class, 22.22 per cent in the lower-middle class, and none in the upper-middle class occupy the poorest housing facilities. In the lower-lower class 38.46 per cent of the Armenians reside in small houses in poor condition, in the upper-lower class 24.14 per cent, in the lower-middle 2.94 per cent, and in the upper-middle class none. Of the Greeks 29.41 per cent in the lower-lower class live in small and bad houses, 25.23 per cent in the upper-lower, 10.53 per cent in the lower-middle, and 44.44 per cent in the upper-middle. In the lower-lower class 33.33 per cent of the Poles live in such houses, in the upper-lower class 19.64 per cent, and in the lower-middle class none. In the lower-lower class 47.44 per cent of the Russians live in small and bad houses, in the upper-lower class 37.50 per cent, and in the lower-middle class 16.67 per cent. Of the Ne-

---

4. It might be noted here that none of the Yankees in the two upper classes lives in such houses.

groes, all of whom are in the lower-lower class, 50.88 per cent reside in small and bad houses.

For all ethnic groups except the Greeks in the upper-middle class and, to a lesser extent, the Italians in the lower-middle class, there is a steady diminution of the number of people living in small and bad houses as the rank of the members of each ethnic group increases; and, correspondingly, a steady increase in the number as rank decreases.

Yankee City houses are thus symbols of status in the society. The cultural differences in the family life of the several classes are reflected in house type and symbolized by it. The house is, moreover, the paramount symbol of the unequal distribution of the valued things of life among the several classes.

XII

MARRIAGE AND THE FAMILY IN YANKEE CITY

1. Marital Status in Yankee City

AT first observation the family system of Yankee City appeared to be one and the same in all six classes, but a detailed analysis demonstrated definite differences. The ethnic groups also manifested considerable variation. The structure of ethnic families will be discussed in the volume on ethnic minorities.

XVIII. *Marital Status of the Members of the Total Community*

The age at marriage is in direct relation to the status of an individual. If upper class he will marry late; if lower class he will marry young. After marriage, if upper class he will have a small family; if lower class, a large family. Class factors thus influence family life in a variety of ways; family, on the other hand, is a potent mechanism for maintaining the class system. Class as it is now organized could not endure without the auspices of the family which maintains its values and organizes the relations of its members.

Marriage and the Family in Yankee City 253

Approximately one third of all Yankee City people fifteen years of age and over have never been married. A glance at Chart XVIII shows that about half of the single people are women and half men. The married group, consisting of both married and divorced persons, constituted about 58 per cent of the total. There were more women in the widowed group than men. (See *Data Book* for marital percentages by age.)

The number of unmarried persons in the native group is significantly low, while in several of the ethnic groups—Irish, French, Poles, Greeks, Jews, and Italians—the number is significantly high. Conversely, the number of married persons is significantly high for the natives and significantly low for the Irish and Poles. The widowed group shows a significantly large number of natives and a significantly small number of French, Greeks, Italians, and Jews.

XIX. *Marital Status of the Ethnic Groups*

In contrast to the total ethnics, the native group has a smaller proportion of single persons and a larger proportion of married and widowed individuals. The ethnics tend to have a larger number of single people in their population than the natives (see Chart XIX) partly because many of them are recently arrived from their homeland, and ordinarily such immigrants come as single individuals.

Although the ethnics as a whole have a smaller proportion

254   *The Social Life of a Modern Community*

of married persons among their numbers than the natives, three of the ethnic groups show a higher percentage of married individuals. These three groups are the Negroes, the French Canadians, and the Russians. The Greeks also have a very high proportion of married persons, but somewhat smaller than the natives. The smallest proportion of married persons is found among the Irish.

The median age at the time of marriage in Yankee City is 24.40 years. For women the median age is 23.18 years; for men, 25.92 years. One fourth are less than twenty-one years of age at the time of marriage. The great majority of these are women; less than 200 are men.

XX. *Age at Marriage of Men and Women*

The percentages of men and women who marry at the several age levels are indicated by Chart XX. The percentages of subadult males are far smaller than those of subadult females; on the other hand the upper end of the columns shows that men marry between the ages of thirty and forty much more frequently than women.

In Yankee City 71.67 per cent of the men are married to women younger than themselves, 10.75 per cent have wives of the same age, and 17.58 per cent have wives who are older.

A glance at Chart XXI will show that in all classes except the upper-upper more than half the population of fifteen years

Marriage and the Family in Yankee City 255

or over are married. The figure for the upper-upper class is slightly under 50 per cent. The percentage of those widowed in each class decreases with the class scale. When it is remembered that the percentage of old people, mostly female, is highest in the upper classes, part of the high percentage of widowed people in the upper classes is understood. The newer ethnic groups at the bottom of the class hierarchy have relatively few older people. For example, among the Poles less than 1 per cent is sixty-five years or over, while among the natives this age group constitutes 19.25 per cent of the population.

XXI. *Marital Status of the Six Classes*

The median age for marriage for all classes, as we have said earlier, is 24.40 years; but it becomes higher as class status increases. The figures for the six classes are as follows: 27.90 years for the upper-upper class, 26.60 years for the lower-upper class, 26.10 years for the upper-middle class, 25.10 years for the lower-middle class, 24.40 years for the upper-lower class, and 23.20 years for the lower-lower class.

XIII

ECONOMIC LIFE OF THE COMMUNITY

1. Workers in the Various Industries

THE largest and most important industry in Yankee City is shoe manufacturing. The second most important is silverware manufacturing which provides employment for a large group of highly trained workers. At the time of our study most of the workers classed as auto-body and cotton textile employees were unemployed since these industries had left the city and surrounding areas. Farming, moreover, is a negligible pursuit in the economic life of the town, and those who follow the sea have been reduced to a few clammers, insignificant in number, but nevertheless important in the life of the community.

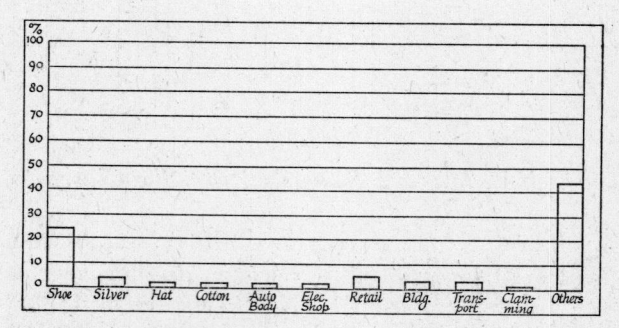

XXII. *The Percentage of Workers Employed in the Several Industries*

Of the 6,155 workers in Yankee City, 71 per cent are male and 29 per cent female. The male workers are concentrated in significantly high numbers in hat and auto-body factories, in building trades, in transportation, and in clamming, and in significantly low numbers in the shoe industry. The female workers are employed in significantly high numbers in the shoe industry and in electric shops, and in significantly low

Economic Life of the Community 257

numbers in silverware factories, auto-body works, building trades, transportation, and clamming. (The percentage of workers employed in each industry is represented in Chart XXII.)

Over 51 per cent (51.54 per cent) of those employable are Yankees and 47.88 per cent are members of the other ethnic groups.[1]

In half of the major industries there is a higher percentage of ethnics employed than Yankees. These industries are shoe manufacturing, hat manufacturing, cotton textile manufacturing, retail stores, and transport. The industries in which there is a higher proportion of Yankees than of the other ethnic groups combined are silverware, auto-body, electric shops, building trades, and clamming.

The natives were significantly high (see Table 16) in the silverware factories, the building trades, and in clamming (for percentages see the *Data Book*). They were also significantly high in "other" economic activities. They were significantly low in the shoe factories, hat, and cotton textile factories, and in the retail stores. The Irish were significantly high in transport, and in "other" economic activities. There was a significantly low number of Irish in the silver factories, the building trades, and in clamming. There was a significantly high number of French in the shoe and cotton factories and a significantly low number in the silverware factories and in "other" economic occupations. The Jews were significantly high in the retail stores and significantly low in the building trades and transport. There was a significantly high number of Polish workers in the hat and cotton industries and a significantly low number in "other" economic activities. The Russians were

1. Of the workers, 26.04 per cent are Irish, 8.98 per cent are French, 2.45 per cent are Jewish, 1.84 per cent are Italian, 1.64 per cent are Armenian, 2.23 per cent are Greek, 3.56 per cent are Polish, 0.73 per cent are Russian, and 0.41 per cent are Negro. The ethnic affiliation of 0.58 per cent of the workers is unaccounted for. The rank order of the percentage of workers of each of the ten ethnic groups corresponds to the rank order of their numbers in the general population. The natives have the highest percentage of the workers in all industries except cotton manufacturing, in which they rank third, the Irish being first and the French and Poles second. The Irish rank second for the percentage of workers in all industries except cotton manufacturing and clamming, in which they rank third. The French rank third for all industries except cotton manufacturing, retail stores, and clamming. In the retail stores they rank fourth.

TABLE 16

The Ethnic Groups in the Various Industries

Ethnic	Shoe	Silver	Hat	Cotton	Auto Body	Electric Shop	Retail Stores	Building Trades	Transport	Clammers	Others	Never Worked
Native	L	H	L	L	—	—	L	H	—	H	H	L
Irish	—	L	—	—	—	—	—	L	H	L	H	—
French	H	L	—	H	—	—	—	—	—	—	L	H
Jewish	—	—	—	—	—	—	H	—	—	—	—	—
Italian	H	—	H	—	—	H	—	L	L	—	—	—
Armenian	H	—	—	—	—	—	H	—	—	—	L	—
Greek	H	—	—	—	—	—	—	—	—	—	L	—
Polish	—	—	H	H	—	—	—	—	—	—	L	—
Russian	—	—	H	H	—	—	—	—	—	—	L	H
Negro	—	—	—	—	—	—	—	—	—	—	—	—

significantly high in the hat and cotton industries and low in "other" economic activities. The Greeks were significantly high in the shoe factories and significantly low in "other" economic activities. The Armenians were significantly high in the shoe factories and the retail stores and significantly low in "other" activities. The Italians were significantly high in the shoe and hat factories and in the electric shops.

In summary, no ethnic group had a significantly high number of workers in any industry where the natives did except the Irish in the general economic activity called "others"; and no ethnic group was significantly low in any activity where the natives were significantly low. The French, Greeks, Armenians, and Italians were significantly high in the shoe industry where the natives were significantly low; and the Poles, Russians, and Italians were significantly high in the hat industry where the natives were significantly low; the French, Poles, and Russians were significantly high in the cotton textile factories where the natives were significantly low, and the Armenians and the Jews were significantly high in retail stores where the natives were significantly low.

The French and Irish were significantly low in the silverware factories where the natives were high. The Irish and Jews were significantly low in the building trades where the natives were significantly high. The Irish had a low number of workers in the clamming industry where the natives had a significantly high number; and the French, Poles, Russians, Greeks, and Armenians had a significantly low number of workers in "other" economic activities where the natives and Irish had a high number.

2. *The Six Classes in Industry*

THE lower-lower class had a higher proportion of its workers than all other classes in the shoe factories, the hat and cotton industries, the electric shops, transport, and in clamming. The upper-lower class outranked all others for the proportion of its workers in the auto-body factories.

The lower-middle class outranked all others for the proportion of its workers in the silverware factories, the retail stores, and the building trades. The upper-upper class outranked all others in the proportion of its workers who were in "other" economic activities.

The lower-lower class had a significantly high number of workers in the shoe, hat, cotton, transport, and clamming industries. There were a significantly low number of lower-lower-class workers in the silverware factories, the retail stores, and in "other" economic activities. There were a significantly high number of upper-lower-class workers in the shoe factories and in the auto-body factories. There were a significantly low number of them in the silverware factories and in "other" economic activities. There were a significantly high number of lower-middle-class workers in the silverware factories, in the retail stores, and in "other" economic activities. There were a significantly low number of them in the shoe factories, in the hat and cotton factories, and in clamming.

There were a significantly high number of upper-middle class in retail stores and "other" economic activities. There were a significantly low number of them in the shoe, hat, and cotton factories, and in the clamming industry. There were a significantly high number of the upper-upper and lower-upper classes in "other" economic activities and a significantly low number of the lower-upper class in the shoe factories.

Looked at from the point of view of the industries, the two lower classes were highly represented in the shoe factories, and the two middle and the lower-upper classes were significantly low. The upper three classes reverse the order of the two lower classes. In the silverware industry, the lower-middle class was significantly high, and the two lower classes, significantly low. Once again the highest class, which is significant, reverses the two lower ones. In the hat and cotton textile industries, the two middle classes had a significantly low number, and the lower-lower class, a significantly high number of workers. In the auto-body factories the upper-lower class was significantly high, and the lower-middle was significantly low. In the retail stores the two middle classes were significantly high, and the lower-lower class, significantly low in the number of its workers employed.

In the transport industry, the upper-middle class was significantly low and the upper-lower, significantly high. In clamming, the lower-lower class was significantly high, and the lower-middle, significantly low. In "other" economic activities, the two lower classes were significantly low, and the four classes above them, significantly high. In all of the industries, where the upper classes were significantly high, the lower classes were significantly low, and where the lower classes were significantly high, the higher classes represented were significantly low.

3. Occupations of the Six Classes

THERE is a high correlation between type of occupation and class position in Yankee City. If a person is a professional man or a proprietor he tends to be upper or middle class; if he is an unskilled worker he tends to be lower class. However, not all professional men are upper class and not all workers are lower class. Although clerks tend to be lower-middle class, some of them are upper class and others are lower class.

TABLE 17

Occupation and Class

	UU	LU	UM	LM	UL	LL
Professional and Proprietary	83.33	85.72	62.16	13.74	2.78	0.73
Wholesale and Retail Dealers		7.14	15.38	10.87	5.88	2.74
Clerks and Kindred Workers	16.67	7.14	15.08	28.80	9.19	3.66
Skilled Workers			5.23	17.32	12.71	4.57
Semiskilled Workers			2.15	27.12	61.53	79.16
Unskilled Workers				2.15	7.91	9.14

An analysis of Table 17 and Chart XXIII shows that professional and proprietary occupations and clerks are found throughout the six classes, and that there is a sharp drop in the first classification from the upper-middle to the lower-middle class and from the latter class to the upper-lower stratum. There is also a break in the percentage of clerks from the upper-lower to the lower-lower.

262   *The Social Life of a Modern Community*

There are no skilled or semiskilled workers higher than the upper-middle group. The day laborer, although ranging from lower-lower to lower-middle, tends to be lower class.

Chart XXIII shows that most of the lower-lower class is composed of unskilled or nonskilled workers (see 5); the space devoted to semiskilled workers steadily drops away through lower-middle to upper-middle and disappears in the two upper classes. On the other hand, most of the space in the upper-upper, lower-upper, and upper-middle columns is taken up by the professional and proprietary workers. The occupational group rapidly loses ground to the other categories in the lower-middle and lower-class strata.

Class and occupation are closely interrelated, but it is a mistake to classify all professional people at the top of the heap and all workers at the bottom; far too many factors contribute to a person's social status for such arbitrary ranking to be exact and accurate.

XXIII. *The Occupations of the Six Classes*

4. Unemployment in Yankee City

ABOUT 51 per cent (50.73 per cent) of the employable people in Yankee City are fully employed, 30.61 per cent are partially employed, and 18.66 per cent are without work.[2] Of those peo-

2. This sample includes 5,005 individuals.

Economic Life of the Community

ple employable 3,593 (71.79 per cent) are male and 1,412 (28.21 per cent) female.[3] The females are well below the general average of those unemployed, the males above it. At the time of this study there was a strong effort being made by the Federal Government, aided by private initiative, to care for people who had no income. Part-time jobs were "being made" by both the government and private industry to fill this need. The emphasis on getting jobs was to help males as "heads of household" rather than females.

Of the 2,466 people who were either partially or fully unemployed, 694 (28.14 per cent) had been out of work for six months; 599 (24.29 per cent) for a year; 499 (20.24 per cent) for two years; 319 (12.94 per cent) for three years; 202 (8.19 per cent) for four years; 90 (3.65 per cent) for five years; and 63 (2.55 per cent) for six years or over.[4]

More women were unemployed for the six-month and one-year periods than men, and fewer of them for the periods of longer duration except that of six years or over. On the left side of Chart XXIV the first column depicts the percentage of employment and unemployment in all of Yankee City. The next three columns represent the percentage of each sex involved. The three columns on the right show the period of unemployment and add the time factor to the last of the four columns on the left.

3. Of those fully employed, 72.12 per cent were male, and 27.88 per cent were female. Of those wholly unemployed, 64.35 per cent were male, and 35.65 per cent were female; and 75.78 per cent of those partially employed were male, and only 24.22 per cent were female. Of the 3,593 employable males in Yankee City, 50.96 per cent were employed; and of the 1,412 females, 50.14 per cent were employed. Of the males, 16.73 per cent, or less than the average, were wholly unemployed; and 23.58 per cent of the females, or well above the average, were wholly unemployed. Slightly over 32 per cent (32.31 per cent) of the males were not fully employed, and 26.28 per cent of the females were not fully employed.

4. Almost 70 per cent (69.31 per cent) of those who had been out of work for six months were males, and about 31 per cent (30.69 per cent) were females. Of those who had been out of work for one year, 64.11 per cent were males, and 35.89 per cent were females. Of those who had been out of work for two years, 72.95 per cent were males, and 27.05 per cent were females. Of those who had not worked for three years, 78.68 per cent were males, and 21.32 per cent were females. Of those who had been out of work for four years, 82.18 per cent were males, and 17.82 per cent were females. Of those who had not worked for five years, 80 per cent were males, and 20 per cent were females. Of those who had been out of work for six years or longer, 69.84 per cent were males, and 30.16 per cent were females.

264   *The Social Life of a Modern Community*

There were 1,190 (23.78 per cent) of the employable people in Yankee City who had worked or were working in the shoe industry: 25.80 per cent were fully employed; 46.97 per cent were partly employed; and 27.23 per cent were unemployed. There were 202 (4.04 per cent) of the total employable people working in the silver industry: 64.36 per cent were fully employed; 31.68 per cent were partially employed; and only 3.96 per cent were unemployed. The silver industry in Yankee City had a general reputation in the community for stability, while the shoe industry was felt to be uncertain and less preferable as a place to work. (See Table 18.)

XXIV. *Duration of Unemployment*

The highest percentage of people fully unemployed in any industry was in cotton manufacturing, and next in the hat industry. Both of these were declining industries in Yankee City. The shoe industry ranked third in the number of those unemployed; the building trades, fourth; the auto-body industry, fifth; the electric shops, sixth; transport, seventh; the retail stores, eighth; and the silver manufacturing industry, ninth. There can be little question that one of the reasons for the low rating of the unemployed in the silverware industry was

TABLE 18
Employment in the Various Industries

Industry	Employed	Part-Time Employed	Unemployed	Total
1 Shoe	12.09 / 25.80 / 307	36.49 / 46.97 / 559	34.69 / 27.23 / 324	23.78 / 1,190
2 Silver	5.12 / 64.36 / 130	4.18 / 31.68 / 64	0.86 / 3.96 / 8	4.04 / 202
3 Hat	1.46 / 32.74 / 37	2.42 / 32.74 / 37	4.18 / 34.52 / 39	2.26 / 113
4 Cotton	0.87 / 24.18 / 22	2.22 / 37.36 / 34	3.75 / 38.46 / 35	1.82 / 91
5 Auto Body	0.75 / 20.43 / 19	3.33 / 54.84 / 51	2.46 / 24.73 / 23	1.86 / 93
6 Elec. Shop	2.21 / 46.67 / 56	2.55 / 32.50 / 39	2.68 / 20.83 / 25	2.40 / 120
7 Retail Stores	7.72 / 75.10 / 196	2.94 / 17.24 / 45	2.14 / 7.66 / 20	5.21 / 261
8 Bldg. Trades	1.54 / 24.07 / 39	5.29 / 50.00 / 81	4.50 / 25.93 / 42	3.24 / 162
9 Transport	3.51 / 56.33 / 89	3.20 / 31.01 / 49	2.14 / 12.66 / 20	3.16 / 158
10 Clamming	0.95 / 53.33 / 24	1.37 / 46.67 / 21	0	0.90 / 45
11 Others	62.78 / 67.18 / 1,594	32.44 / 20.94 / 497	30.19 / 11.88 / 282	47.41 / 2,373

TABLE 18 (Continued)

Industry	Employed		Part-Time Employed		Unemployed		Total	
12 Never Worked	0	1.17	14.75 18	11.13	85.25 104	2.44	122	
13 Unknown	34.67 26	1.02	49.33 37	2.42	16.00 12	1.28	75	1.50
Total	50.73 2,539		30.61 1,532		18.66 934		5,005	

the intelligent planning which the manufacturers of the silverware plants conducted for the purpose of maintaining stable employment for their workers.[5]

The retail stores had a higher percentage of their people employed than any of the other types of industry in Yankee City. The silver manufacturing plants were second; transport companies, third; clamming, fourth; the electric shops, fifth; the hat shops, sixth; shoe factories, seventh; clothing manufacturing, eighth; building trades, ninth; and the auto-body plants, tenth.

The workers in the auto-body manufacturing plants led all those of all industries who had been part-time employed or unemployed; the building trades were second; the shoe industry, third; clamming, fourth; cotton textiles, fifth; hat workers, sixth; electric shops, seventh; the silverware factories, eighth; transport, ninth; and retail stores, last.

5. The industries just enumerated are the principal ones in Yankee City. The remainder of the workers were classified as belonging to other industries or as "never worked" at full-time jobs. Of these, 47.41 per cent were classified as working in other industries. Of these, 67.18 per cent were employed; 20.94 per cent partly employed; and 11.88 per cent were unemployed. Of those who had never had full-time jobs, 14.75 per cent were partially employed, and 85.25 per cent were unemployed. For 1.50 per cent of the unemployed in Yankee City we had no record of the industry to which they belonged.

The analysis just made informs us what proportions of the workers in each industry were unemployed or employed, but it does not tell us how each industry contributed to the unemployed population in Yankee City, nor does it inform us how each industry helped support the economy of the town.

Workers from the building trades, retail stores, and transport industries led all others for the longest period of unemployment. The workers in the shoe, silver, and hat factories tended to be unemployed the shortest period of time, most for not more than a year; the cotton workers, for four years and three years; the auto-body workers, from three to four years; the electric shop workers, for six months and for two years; the workers from the retail stores, six months and two years; the workers from the building trades, two years; transport, two years and six months; and none of the clammers has been unemployed longer than a year.

5. *Unemployment among the Ethnic Workers*

JEWS and natives had more of their workers employed than any other ethnic group in Yankee City, and the Negroes and Poles had fewer. The unemployed Jews led all others in the shortness of duration of their unemployment. The Jews not only outranked the other ethnic groups for their ability successfully to adjust economically, but despite their comparative recency they also surpassed the Yankees in the activity for which the members of each group most pride themselves—business. Despite the fact that the Jew has demonstrated his economic talent—a talent which is most highly rewarded in this society—he is nevertheless unable to achieve high "social" success. There is a strong likelihood that an economically successful Yankee can translate his economic success into social success, for himself and his family. But a socially ambitious Jew, if he stays a Jew, is doomed to a social career below the aristocratic class. However, he and his children, if not too deviant physically from the Yankee group, can change their ethnic affiliations, become Yankee, and climb socially.

The Negroes had the smallest percentage of their workers employed; the Poles and Italians were next. The unemployed Negroes had been without work for a longer length of time than any other group, and they were closely followed by the

Russians and Poles. The Russians and Poles are the most recent ethnic groups in Yankee City. They came in at the lowest stratum of the class hierarchy and at the very bottom of the economic system. Most of them, if not all, are viewed by the rest of Yankee City as "those foreigners" and as people who are unpleasantly different.

The Negro has been in Yankee City for generations and in this country since its beginning, yet his status, despite this fact, is most like that of the lowest of the several ethnic groups and, in fact, is worse than even the lowest of these. Not only is he most vulnerable to the vicissitudes of our economic system at any given moment in time, but he has little assurance that his children will not have to go through the same experiences. If the marriage statistics of Yankee City and those of other places are significant for predictability, the Negro will continue to marry within his own group. He will not marry out into the larger Yankee community or into the other ethnic groups. Whereas the Negro who has been here for generations is still marrying within his own group, even the newest of the ethnic groups are now marrying into the general Yankee population. One has but to look at the statistics for the ethnics who have been here a longer time to demonstrate that it is only a matter of time until all ethnic groups will intermarry freely. The Negro, by his past performance, appears certain to continue as a socially isolated individual within a socially isolated group. Despite the democratic protestations of equality that are heard in New England, the social system by which the Yankees regulate the behavior of Negroes and whites is more like that of the Deep South than it is like that of any other social system.

There was a general tendency for ethnics to be more frequently employed than Yankees, and more of the ethnics were partially employed than were the Yankees. Over 54 per cent (54.66 per cent) of the natives were employed as against 46.81 per cent of the ethnics. There were 28.91 per cent of the natives who were partially employed or unemployed and 32.44 per cent of the ethnics. There were 16.63 per cent of the natives who were unemployed and 20.75 per cent of all the ethnic workers. (See Table 19.)

The Russians, as demonstrated by Chart XXV, led all others

TABLE 19
Amount of Ethnic Unemployment

	Ethnic	1 Employment	2 Partially Unemployed	3 Unemployed	Total
1	Native	55.57 / 54.46 / 1,411	48.89 / 28.91 / 749	46.15 / 16.63 / 431	51.77 / 2,591
2	Total Ethnic	44.15 / 46.81 / 1,121	50.72 / 32.44 / 777	53.21 / 20.75 / 497	47.85 / 2,395
3	Irish	25.80 / 47.33 / 655	29.31 / 32.44 / 449	29.98 / 20.23 / 280	27.64 / 1,384
4	French	7.12 / 44.91 / 181	9.20 / 34.99 / 141	8.67 / 20.10 / 81	8.05 / 403
5	Jewish	3.51 / 72.36 / 89	1.11 / 13.82 / 17	1.82 / 13.82 / 17	2.46 / 123
6	Italian	1.30 / 37.08 / 33	2.48 / 42.70 / 38	1.93 / 20.22 / 18	1.78 / 89
7	Armenian	1.18 / 42.86 / 30	1.83 / 40.00 / 28	1.28 / 17.14 / 12	1.40 / 70
8	Greek	1.89 / 50.00 / 48	2.02 / 32.29 / 31	1.82 / 17.71 / 17	1.92 / 96
9	Polish	2.44 / 35.83 / 62	3.79 / 33.53 / 58	5.67 / 30.64 / 53	3.46 / 173
10	Russian	.67 / 47.22 / 17	.33 / 13.89 / 5	1.50 / 38.89 / 14	.72 / 36
11	Negro	.24 / 28.57 / 6	.65 / 47.62 / 10	.54 / 23.81 / 5	.42 / 21
12	Unknown	.28 / 36.84 / 7	.39 / 31.58 / 6	.64 / 31.58 / 6	.38 / 19
	Total	50.73 / 2,539	30.61 / 1,532	18.66 / 934	5,005

270 The Social Life of a Modern Community

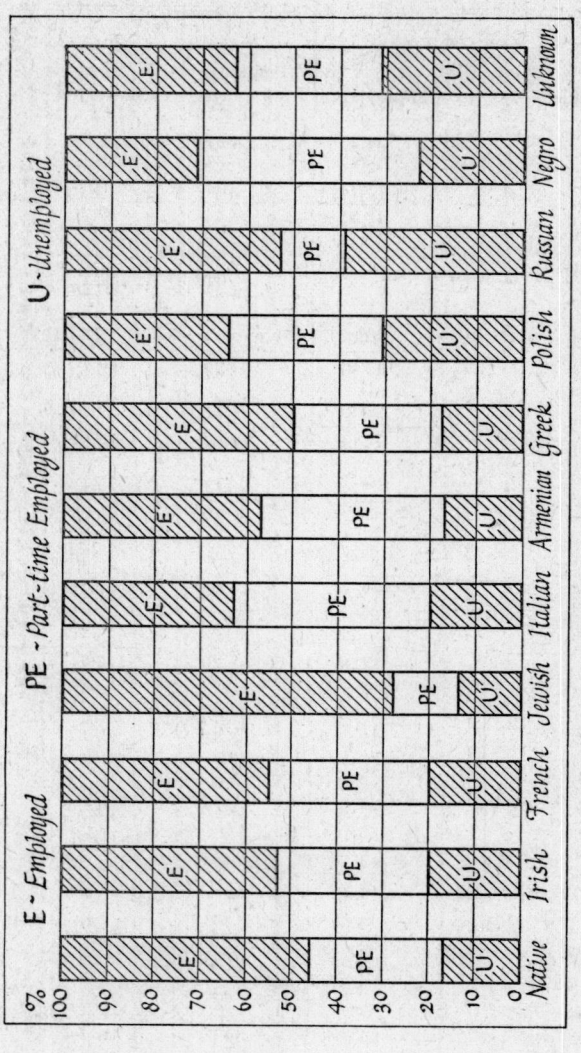

XXV. Employment among the Ethnic Groups

Economic Life of the Community 271

in the percentage of their workers who were unemployed; the Poles had the second highest percentage of unemployment; the Negroes were third; the Irish ranked fourth; and the Jews were last. More of the Jews were fully employed than any other ethnic group in Yankee City; the Yankees were second; and the Greeks were third. The Irish ranked fourth for the number of their employed. The Negroes were last.

Although the Negroes had the smallest percentage of their workers employed and ranked very high (third) for those who

XXVI. *Duration of Ethnic Unemployment*

were fully unemployed, they ranked first among all ethnic groups for those who were partly employed. The Italians were second; the Armenians were third; the Jews were last.[6]

The Negroes led all others in the percentage of their unemployed who had been without work for six years, for five years, and for two years. (See Chart XXVI.) The Russians ranked second for the percentage of unemployed who had been out of work for six years or longer; the Poles were third; the

6. Of the 1,180 Yankees who were unemployed, 29.49 per cent had been unemployed six months or less; 22.54 per cent, for one year; 20.51 per cent, for two years; 13.56 per cent, for three years; 6.86 per cent, for four years; 3.73 per cent, for five years; and 3.31 per cent, for six years or longer. Of the 1,274 members of the combined ethnic groups who were unemployed, 27.00 per cent had been out of work for six months or less; 25.90 per cent, for a year; 19.86 per cent, for two years; 12.40 per cent, for three years; 9.42 per cent, for four years; 3.61 per cent, for five years; and 1.81 per cent, for six years.

natives, fourth; the Irish, fifth; and the Greeks, sixth. The Poles were second in the percentage of their unemployed who had been out of work for five years; the Irish, third; the natives, fourth; the Italians, fifth; Jews, sixth; French, seventh; and the Greeks, last. The Russians outranked all others in the percentage of their workers who had been unemployed for four years; the Poles were second; the French, third; the Irish, fourth; the Italians, fifth; the Yankees, sixth; the Negroes, seventh; Jews, eighth; the Armenians, ninth; and the Greeks, tenth.

A higher percentage of the Irish workers had been unemployed for three years than the workers in any other ethnic group. The natives were second; the Negroes, third; the Jews, fourth; French, fifth; Russians, sixth; Greeks, seventh; Poles, eighth; Italians, ninth; and the Armenians, tenth.

Only the Negroes outranked the Italians in the percentage of their unemployed who had been out of work for two years. The Armenians were third; the Irish, fourth; the Yankees, fifth; the Poles, sixth; the French Canadians, seventh; the Greeks, eighth; the Russians, ninth; and the Jews, last.

The Armenians outranked all others in the percentage of their unemployed who had been out of work for a year; the Greeks were second; the Jews, third; the Italians, fourth; the Irish, fifth; the natives, sixth; the Poles, seventh; the French, eighth; the Negroes, ninth; and the Russians, tenth. The French led all others in the percentage of their workers who had been out of work for six months or less; the Jews were next; the Greeks, third; the Poles, fourth; the natives, fifth; the Italians, sixth; the Russians, seventh; the Irish, eighth; the Armenians, ninth; and the Negroes, tenth.

6. *Ethnic Unemployment in Each of the Yankee City Industries*

LET us now examine the problem of ethnic employment in the several industries. The question to be answered is whether the difference of employment among ethnic workers in the general community is the same in all industries, whether some industries favor one group and not the other, or whether ethnic groups are treated in each industry much as they are generally within the community? The presence or lack of difference can be tested by the comparative duration of unemployment in each industry and the comparative duration of unemployment for each ethnic group.

The Yankees who were in the retail stores led all others in the percentage of their group who were employed. (See Table 20.) Those in the silverware manufacturing plants were second, and those in the transport industry were third. The clammers, the workers in the electric shops, and those in the hat and cotton factories were, in the order named, next; while the auto-body workers, those in the building trades, and the shoe workers, in the order named, were the least employed. In manufacturing, the silver industry fully employed a greater percentage of its workers, and the shoe factories, a smaller percentage than any other industry. The hat manufacturers led all others in the percentage of Yankee workers who were unemployed. The next largest group of Yankee workers who were unemployed were in the cotton industry, and the shoe industry was third. The Yankee workers in the building trades, auto-body factories, electric shops, and transport industries, in the order named, were the highest groups of unemployed, while the retail stores and silver factories were last. The hat, cotton, and shoe industries contributed a higher percentage of unemployed workers for the community or others to support than any other industry in Yankee City, while the retail stores and silver factories contributed the least.

The Yankee shoe workers tended to be unemployed for a year or less; the silver workers, from a year to two years; the hat workers, for a six-month period; the cotton textile workers, from three to four years; the auto-body workers, from three to four years. The Yankees in the electric shops and retail stores were largely unemployed for a two-year period; in the building trades, from six months to a year; and the clammers for six months to a year.[7]

A higher percentage of the Irish workers in the electric shops was employed than in any other industry; the Irish

[7]. Although the exact percentage for the duration of unemployment for each of the ethnic groups was computed, it will not be given because of the limitations of space. Only summaries will be presented. The reader must remember that for duration of unemployment the fully employed group has been separated from the other two and the fully unemployed and the partially employed-unemployed have been grouped together.

TABLE 20
Ethnic Unemployment in the Various Industries

Industry	Employed Native	Irish	French	Jewish	Italian	Not Fully Employed Native	Irish	French	Jewish	Italian	Unemployed Native	Irish	French	Jewish	Italian
Shoe	25.15	17.82	35.22	57.14	20.00	48.30	47.74	40.88	28.57	54.29	26.55	34.44	23.90	14.29	25.71
Silver	65.46	61.36	63.64	—	50.00	30.22	34.09	36.36	100.00	50.00	4.32	4.55	—	—	—
Hat	33.33	23.08	33.33	—	50.00	27.78	53.84	50.00	—	25.00	38.89	23.08	16.67	—	25.00
Cotton	28.58	8.33	25.00	—	—	35.71	62.50	30.00	100.00	100.00	35.71	29.17	45.00	—	—
Auto Body	26.00	12.50	23.08	—	—	52.00	50.00	61.54	—	—	22.00	37.50	15.38	100.00	—
Electric Shop	45.46	62.50	18.18	—	42.86	36.36	20.83	36.36	100.00	14.28	18.18	16.67	45.46	—	42.86
Retail Stores	79.82	59.04	86.36	84.00	83.33	14.68	27.71	4.55	12.00	16.67	5.50	13.25	9.09	4.00	—
Bldg. Trades	25.21	27.59	11.11	—	—	49.58	41.38	77.78	—	—	25.21	31.03	11.11	—	100.00
Transport	60.00	59.19	35.71	—	—	22.35	34.69	64.29	—	—	17.65	6.12	—	—	100.00
Clamming	56.10	—	33.33	—	50.00	43.90	100.00	66.67	—	—	—	—	—	—	—
Others	69.47	64.14	62.70	83.58	—	19.24	23.00	25.40	5.97	43.33	11.29	12.86	11.90	10.45	6.67
Never Worked	—	—	—	—	—	15.09	21.87	—	16.67	100.00	84.91	78.13	100.00	83.33	—

TABLE 20 (Continued)

Industry	Employed						Not Fully Employed						Unemployed					
	Armenian	Greek	Polish	Russian	Negro		Armenian	Greek	Polish	Russian	Negro		Armenian	Greek	Polish	Russian	Negro
Shoe	25.71	37.50	29.41	50.00	100.00		57.15	50.00	45.10	16.67	—		17.14	12.50	25.49	33.33	—
Silver	50.00	100.00	66.67	—	—		50.00	—	33.33	14.29	—		—	—	—	—	—
Hat	—	—	34.38	57.14	—		—	—	25.00	—	—		—	100.00	40.62	28.57	—
Cotton	—	—	36.84	40.00	—		—	—	31.58	—	—		—	100.00	31.58	60.00	100.00
Auto Body	—	—	—	—	—		100.00	—	100.00	—	100.00		—	—	—	—	—
Electric Shop	66.67	—	75.00	50.00	—		33.33	100.00	—	50.00	—		—	—	25.00	—	—
Retail Stores	100.00	85.71	100.00	—	—		—	14.29	—	—	—		—	—	—	—	—
Bldg. Trade	—	100.00	—	—	—		100.00	—	100.00	—	—		—	—	—	—	—
Transport	—	100.00	50.00	—	—		—	—	50.00	—	66.67		—	—	—	—	33.33
Clamming	—	—	—	—	100.00		—	—	—	—	—		—	—	—	—	—
Others	55.56	71.43	55.55	71.43	30.77		22.22	17.86	27.78	28.57	53.85		22.22	10.71	16.67	—	15.38
Never Worked	—	—	—	—	—		—	—	9.09	—	—		100.00	100.00	90.91	100.00	100.00

workers in the silverware factories were second; and those in the transport business, third. The Irish workers in the retail stores, in the building trades, and in the hat factories were, in the order named, next most employed. The Irish workers in the shoe industry, auto-body plants, and cotton industry were the least employed of that ethnic group.

Of the fully unemployed Irish workers, the highest percentage was originally in the auto-body industry, followed by the shoe factories and the building trades. The next highest group of unemployed Irish was, in the order named, from the cotton textile factories, the hat factories, the electric shops, and the retail stores. The smallest number came from the transport industry and the silver factories. More of the Irish unemployed tended to be without work for the period of six months to a year in the shoe, silver, and hat industries; in cotton textiles, for four years; in the auto-body factories, for three to four years; in the electric shops, from one year to three years; in the retail stores, for a six-month period; in the building trades, from one year to two years; and in transport, for a two-year period.

The French-Canadian workers were most fully employed in the retail stores. They were next most employed in the silver factories and in the transport industry. The shoe workers, clammers, the workers in the hat, cotton, and auto-body factories, in the order named, were next most employed; and those in the electric shops and building trades were least employed.

Of the French-Canadian unemployed, the highest percentage came from the electric shops; the next, from the cotton factories; and the next, from the shoe factories. Those in the hat, auto-body, building trades, and retail stores, in the order named, were next. There were no French Canadians in the transport, clamming, and silverware industries who were fully unemployed.

Most of the French Canadians who were unemployed in the shoe factories had been out of work for six months to a year. Most of the cotton textile unemployed French Canadians had been out of work for three to four years. Half of the French Canadian unemployed auto-body workers had been out of work for four years; and over two thirds of their unemployed workers from the electric shops had been out of work for six months.

The Jews were most employed in the retail stores and least

employed in the shoe factories. Except for the auto-body workers (only one person) they were most unemployed in the shoe factories and least in the retail stores. The period of duration for unemployment in the shoe factories for Jewish workers was from six months to a year, and in the retail stores, for six months.

The highest percentage of Italians employed was in the retail stores; next, in the hat industry; the next, in the silver factories. The electric shops and the shoe factories had the smallest percentage of employed Italian workers. Most of the Greeks and Armenians were in shoe manufacturing. Well over a third of each group was unemployed.

7. *Unemployment among the Six Classes*

CLASS played a decided role in the employment of workers in the industries of Yankee City. If a man were a member of the three upper classes the chances of his being employed were high; if he were a member of the two lower classes, he had much less chance of being employed. But the duration of his unemployment did not follow such exact class lines. More of the unemployment of the higher classes was for six months and a year than that of the lower classes, but the differences between them were small. On the other hand the higher classes tended to have more of their people without work for longer periods of time (five and six years) than the lower ones did, but again the differences between them were not great.

In the general population, 50.73 per cent were employed, 30.61 per cent were part-time employed, and 18.66 per cent were unemployed. The percentage of the fully unemployed varies with class. Over 94 per cent (94.44 per cent) of the lower-upper class were fully employed; 90.00 per cent of the upper-upper were employed; 83.14 per cent of the upper-middle; 62.26 per cent of the lower-middle; 41.48 per cent of the upper-lower; and 27.57 per cent of the lower-lower.

In both the lower classes, less than half of the employable workers were fully employed. (See Chart XXVII.) In the lower-lower class, only about one fourth of them worked full time. Both of these groups had a significantly low number of workers who were fully employed. The highest percentage of unemployment was in the lower-lower class, and the lowest, in the lower-upper group. Twenty-six per cent of the lower-lower group were totally jobless, 22 per cent of the upper-lower class were without work, 15 per cent of the lower-middle, 8 per cent of the upper-middle, 7 per cent (only two individuals) of the upper-upper, and 6 per cent of the lower-upper. This represents three individuals. With the exception of the upper-upper

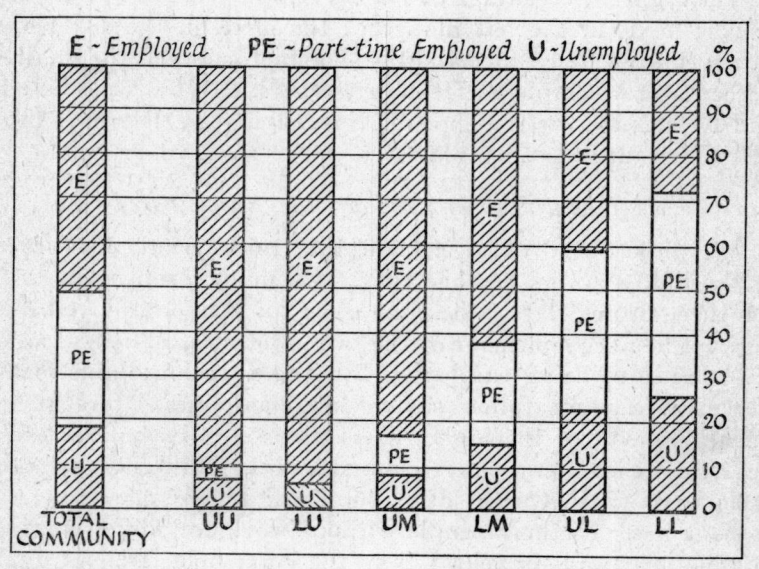

XXVII. *The Amount of Employment in the Six Classes*

class, as the rank of the class decreases, the number of employed also decreases.

The percentage of part-time workers also varies with class, the highest percentage being in the lower-lower, the lowest percentage being in the lower-middle.[8] Forty-six per cent of the lower-lower group had part-time work; 36 per cent of the

---

8. There was a higher percentage of Poles on relief than any other group: 26.88 per cent of this ethnic group were on relief; 23.06 per cent of the French Canadians were on public welfare; 22.70 per cent of the Russians; 21.12 per cent of the Greeks; 19.72 per cent of the Italians; and 12.50 per cent of the Negroes. All of the ethnic groups which have just been listed had a larger percentage of their population on relief than did the Yankees. Approximately 10 per cent (9.94 per cent) of the Irish were on relief; 4.88 per cent of the Armenians; and 4.79 per cent of the Jews.

upper-lower; 23 per cent of the lower-middle; and 9 per cent of the upper-middle.

8. *Public Support for the Relief of the Unemployed*

UNEMPLOYED individuals from the two middle and the two lower classes were supported by public funds. There were 2,234, or 13.31 per cent, of the population on relief. There was no one from the two upper groups. The percentage of those on relief rapidly increases as their status decreases and is lower in the class hierarchy. About two thirds (65.26 per cent) of the relief population was lower-lower class; about one fourth (25.25 per cent) was upper-lower; 7.61 per cent was lower-middle; and 0.58 per cent was upper-middle. In the lower-lower class, one out of every three persons was on relief (34.44 per cent); one out of every ten of the upper-lower was on relief (10.31 per cent); one out of every thirty-three of the lower-middle (3.60 per cent); and about one out of every 130 (0.76 per cent) of the upper-middle was on relief.

There were 12.16 per cent of the Yankees on relief and 14.75 per cent of the combined ethnic groups on relief. The natives, Irish, Armenians, and Jews had a significantly low number of people on relief, while other groups had a significantly high number on relief.[8]

XIV

THE CONTROL OF PROPERTY

1. *The Dollar Value of Property*

THERE were 2,911 persons who owned real estate in Yankee City.[1] Most of the real estate owned by any individual was less than $3,000,[2] the median value of all real estate possessed by each person being $2,391. Slightly over 50 per cent (50.40 per cent) of the property was owned by males, and 49.60 per cent by females.

The median value of the property of male owners was $2,238 and of females, $2,538. With the exception of males in their fifties there is a constant increase in the value of real estate owned by either sex as age increases but the value of real estate owned by females at any age level is higher than that of the males. (See Table 21.)

TABLE 21

Median Value of Individual Ownership by Age and Sex

Age	All Owners	Males	Females
60 and over	$2,564	$2,480	$2,658
50–59	2,335	2,070	2,566
40–49	2,436	2,319	2,546
30–39	2,206	1,991	2,391
Below 30 yrs.	1,588	1,358	1,759
All Ages	2,391	2,238	2,538

1. This figure covers all areas except Oldtown and Across the River. The data for the property in the other ten areas come from the assessor's office.
2. Sixty-four per cent of all the real estate was valued below $3,000; 28.21 per cent was valued by the assessor at more than $3,000 and less than $5,000; 9.10 per cent at more than $5,000 and less than $10,000; 3.26 per cent was valued at more than $10,000 and less than $20,000; and 2.13 per cent at $20,000 or more.

The Control of Property 281

Almost 60 per cent of the real property owners of Yankee City were Yankee.[3] The Armenians outranked all other ethnic groups in the percentage of their ownership which was worth more than $20,000 (see *Data Book*). They were followed, in the order named, by the Jews, Irish, natives, and French Canadians. No other ethnic groups owned real estate worth this amount. The Jews led the Armenians, Yankees, Poles, Greeks,

TABLE 22

Median Value All Real Estate by Ethnic Group

Ethnic Group	Median Value
Natives	$2,470
Total Ethnics	2,284
Irish	2,152
French	2,207
Jewish	3,864
Italian	2,938
Armenian	3,000
Greek	3,182
Polish	1,767
Russian	1,957
Negro	1,817

Irish, and French Canadians for ownership of property above $10,000 and below $20,000. No other groups owned property of this value.

3. Two thirds of the male and three fifths, or 60.67 per cent, of the female group owned property below $3,000. One fifth of the male group owned property between $3,000 and $5,000. One fourth of the female group was in this category of ownership. Eight per cent of the male group owned property worth $5,000 and up to $10,000, and 10 per cent of the female group were owners of property of this value. There were 3.14 per cent of the male group who owned property worth $10,000 to $20,000, and 3.39 per cent of the female group were owners of property of this value. There were 2.66 per cent of the male group who owned property of $20,000 or more in value and 1.59 per cent of the female group of owners who had property worth this amount.

For property worth from $5,000 to $10,000 the Greeks were first and the Jews and Armenians were next. Except for the Negroes, all ethnic groups were represented. The Italians led all others in the proportion of owners who held property worth from $3,000 to $5,000. The Greeks, natives, and Jews followed.

The Poles, Russians, and Negroes in the order named had a higher proportion of the lowest priced property (below $3,000). The Jews owned the smallest proportion of such property. They were followed by the Greeks and Armenians. No Negro owned property worth more than $5,000. No Russian or Italian had real estate worth more than $10,000 and no Greek or Pole owned property worth $20,000.

2. The Class Ownership of Property

THE median value of all real estate increases as the rank of the class increases.[4] A perusal of Table 23 shows that the higher classes tended to own real estate in the higher brackets and the lower classes in the lower ones. For example, 87 per cent of the lower-lower owners held real estate below $3,000; 76 per cent of the upper-lower; 63 per cent of the lower-middle; 38 per cent of the upper-middle; 22 per cent of the lower-upper; and 18 per cent of the upper-upper. More than one half of the three lowest classes of owners fell in this lowest category of ownership. The lower-lower class is last for the proportionate amount of real estate owned at all levels except the lowest where it is first. The upper-upper class leads for the $20,000 classification followed by the lower-upper and upper-middle classes. The lower-upper class ranks first followed by the upper-upper and upper-middle for the $10,000 and $5,000 categories. The upper-middle class is first and the upper-upper and lower-upper next in the $3,000 to $5,000 bracket. Class and property ownership show definite relationship, but nevertheless there are

4. The median value of the ownership of all real estate in Yankee City, it will be remembered, was $2,391. The median value of real estate owned by the four highest classes was more than this figure, and that of the two lowest classes, less than this amount. The median value of real estate of the upper-upper class was $5,833; of the lower-upper, $5,600; of the upper-middle, $3,555; of the lower-middle, $2,477; of the upper-lower, $1,980; of the lower-lower, $1,606.

property owners of the highest brackets belonging to the lowest classes, and property owners of the lowest brackets belonging to the highest classes.

TABLE 23

Real Estate and Class

Class	Below $3,000	$3,000–$4,999	$5,000–$9,999	$10,000–$19,999	$20,000 and Over	Total
UU	0.65 / 17.91	2.99 / 28.36	6.79 / 26.87	13.68 / 19.40	8.06 / 7.46	2.30
LU	0.97 / 21.95	3.15 / 24.39	8.68 / 28.05	18.95 / 21.95	4.84 / 3.66	2.82
UM	9.22 / 37.75	25.52 / 35.76	24.15 / 14.13	26.31 / 5.52	50.00 / 6.84	15.56
LM	33.13 / 62.72	36.22 / 23.49	36.99 / 10.01	18.95 / 1.84	30.65 / 1.94	33.63
UL	41.96 / 75.76	27.87 / 17.24	19.62 / 5.06	18.95 / 1.75	3.23 / 0.19	35.28
LL	13.21 / 87.18	3.78 / 8.54	3.02 / 2.85	3.16 / 1.07	1.61 / 0.36	9.65
Unknown	0.86 / 72.72	0.47 / 13.64	0.75 / 9.09	0.00 / 0.00	1.61 / 4.55	0.76
Total	63.69	21.81	9.10	3.26	2.13	

The value of a person's house (owned and lived in) declines as the rank of his class decreases. The only exception to this rule is that the lower-upper houses have a higher median value than the upper-upper houses. The median value of houses owned and lived in by the upper-upper class was $3,750; for the lower-upper, $4,121; the upper-middle, $2,706; the lower-middle, $1,800; the upper-lower, $1,530; and the lower-lower, $1,202.

3. The Form of Ownership

THERE were 2,411 "persons" who were recorded as owning their own homes in Yankee City. Some of them owned their homes individually, others held their property with their spouses, and still others owned their homes with some person other than the spouse. The largest number of ownerships were those where the title was held by one person: 1,397 ownerships were of this type; 880 were ownerships by husbands and wives; and 134 were those where people owned the property who were not husbands and wives. There were 777 persons who individually held title to property other than their own homes; 192 persons owned property other than their own homes in common with their spouses; and 100 persons owned property other than their own homes with some persons other than their spouses.

There was some variation by sex in the way property was owned. When ego owned his home in his own right, there was no significant sex variation although female ownership was slightly more frequent. Of persons owning their own homes by themselves, 47.60 per cent were male, and 52.40 per cent female. When persons owned property other than their own homes, the male group was significantly high: 64.61 per cent of such ownerships were male, and 35.39 per cent female. When ego and persons other than the spouse owned a home, the female was significantly high. As the age increased the amount of home ownership also increased.[5]

More than one half of all the home ownerships (56.49 per cent) in Yankee City were held by the Yankees; about one fourth, by the Irish; about 5 per cent, by the French Canadians; and less than 3 per cent by each of the other groups.[6]

---

5. These figures cannot be totaled to give the number of individuals since one individual (one ownership) may appear in more than one category because he may own one piece of property by himself and also own other property with someone else. What is being counted here is the numbers of each kind of ownership.

6. The Irish composed 24.68 per cent of the ownership of such property; the French Canadians, 5.27 per cent; the Poles, 2.90 per cent; the Jews, 2.57 per cent; the Greeks, 1.95 per cent; the Italians, 1.82 per cent; the Armenians,

The Control of Property

The natives and Irish were the only two ethnic groups whose home ownership exceeded their proportion in the population. The Jews, Greeks, Italians, Armenians, Russians, and Negroes had about the same percentage of home ownership as their representation in the total population. The French and Poles had a smaller proportion of home ownership than their proportion in the general population.

The Yankees and Jews who owned property other than their own homes exceeded their proportion of the general population. The Irish, Greeks, Italians, Armenians, Russians, and Negroes had about the same percentage of such ownership, and the French and Poles owned a smaller percentage than their representation in the total population. For all property ownership, whether it was ownership of the home or of other property, the natives outranked all others.

The Yankees and Jews exceeded their proportion of the population in the amount of all property they owned, the French and Poles fell below their proportion in the population, and the other groups formed about the same proportion in the population. The Poles, Negroes, and Russians tended to own their own homes and no other property; 86.42 per cent of the Polish ownerships were of this kind; 85.71 per cent of the Negro ownerships were of this type; and 77.14 per cent of the Russian ownerships were home ownerships. On the other hand, these three groups were last in the percentage of their ownership of property other than the home.[7]

1.82 per cent; the Russians, 1.12 per cent; and the Negroes, 0.75 per cent. There were 0.62 per cent unaccounted for.

For the ownership of other property than the home, the natives led with 55.57 per cent; the Irish were next with 22.64 per cent; the Jews were third with 6.55 per cent; the French Canadians, fourth with 5.05 per cent; the Greeks, fifth (3.37 per cent); the Italians, sixth (2.34 per cent); the Armenians were seventh (1.87 per cent); the Poles were eighth (1.03 per cent); the Russians, ninth (0.75 per cent); and the Negroes, last (0.28 per cent). The ethnic affiliations of 0.56 per cent were not determined.

Of all property ownership 56.21 per cent was by natives; 24.05 per cent, by the Irish; 5.20 per cent, by the French Canadians; 3.79 per cent, by the Jews; 2.39 per cent, by the Greeks; 2.33 per cent, by the Poles; 1.98 per cent, by the Italians; 1.84 per cent, by the Armenians; 1.01 per cent, by the Russians; and 0.60 per cent, by the Negroes. The ethnic affiliations of 0.60 per cent of these ownerships were not accounted for.

7. The Poles were tenth (13.58 per cent); the Negroes, ninth (14.29 per cent); and the Russians, eighth (22.86 per cent). The Jews led all others in the percentage of their ownerships which were of property other than their

286   The Social Life of a Modern Community

Most of the ethnic groups which tended to be lowest in the economic and class hierarchy were home owners and not holders of other property; but the two groups which were socially highest, the natives and Irish, fell in between the highest and lowest ranking groups for both types of ownership. The Jews, who were first in ownership of property other than their homes, were last for the possession of property in homes exclusively.

homes; 53.03 per cent of all their ownerships were of this kind. The Greeks were next (43.37 per cent); the Italians, third (36.23 per cent); the Armenians, fourth (31.25 per cent); the natives, fifth (30.37 per cent); the French Canadians, sixth (29.83 per cent); and the Irish, seventh (28.91 per cent).

XV
HOW THE SIX CLASSES SPENT THEIR MONEY

1. *The Several Categories of Expense*

WHEN an individual in Yankee City spent money for articles which could be purchased, he was acting in accordance with his system of values and thereby satisfying certain of his desires. The desires of all those who spent money for the things they wanted were basically physical, but the values which dominated the expression of their wants were social. All men and women in Yankee City as physical organisms needed food and shelter, but the values which dictated their choice of a house or of food for a meal were socially determined and also expressed the demands, needs, and limitations of their social personalities in a status system.

When a man in the lower-upper class rented a house he paid for physical shelter for his family, but he also paid for the "right kind" of house in the "right" neighborhood which would bring the approval of his friends and his social superiors. In other words, he rented a house which he believed would correspond with and reflect his family's way of life. When his wife gave a dinner party, she bought food that would meet the values of the dinner ritual; and when she dressed that evening, she, her family, and her friends wore clothes proper to the ritual. Many people in classes below the two upper ones earned more money, but the things they purchased were part of a different system of values and were used differently. The average income, however, was greater in the upper classes and consequently they had fewer economic limitations on their social choices; greater economic freedom did not necessarily mean greater social freedom in their selection of the "things they wanted." The etiquette and social rules of the higher classes were more rigid and more restricted; choice in action was much more than in the lower classes.

All this reduces to the fact that the budget of an individual or family is a symbol system, or a set of collective representations, that expresses the social values of a person's membership in a group life. The following section of this chapter will analyze the expenditures of the people of Yankee City to determine what are the class values in expenditure of money. The comparative proportion of the budgets of the members of each class for twenty-six kinds of items will be presented. There will be no attempt in this book to interpret this behavior as symbolic—that will be done in a later volume in this series. A brief examination of the selection and rejection of different items by the six classes will demonstrate the necessity of this kind of interpretation.

The field study of the budgetary behavior of the classes in Yankee City was done with a forty-page schedule which was used in most cases while a person was interviewed about his expenditures. The total income, twenty-six items of expense, and all the separate expenditures under each item were listed. In this chapter the total income will be treated briefly and we shall confine ourselves almost entirely to an analysis of what was spent on the several types of expenditure. The problem to which we address ourselves is essentially "social" rather than "economic." [1]

The budgets collected were selected from a cross section —1,094 individuals represented—of each class. Twenty-one were from the upper-upper class, 28 from the lower-upper class, 319 from the upper-middle class, 397 from the lower-middle class, 209 from the upper-lower class, and 120 from the lower-lower class. The average income of each social class was larger than that of the class beneath it, but the range of income of each class overlapped the range of one or more of the classes below and above. The lower range of the upper-upper class overlapped the highest end of the range of the lower-lower class.

Let us now define what is meant by each of the twenty-six items of expense. Under rent and shelter, the ordinary rental expenses were included; when a man owned the house in which he lived, the taxes on his house and lot, the interest on mortgages, insurance, water rates, and the upkeep on the physical plant were treated as part of his expenditures for shelter.

1. The percentages of the totals are for total expenditures and not for total income.

All money spent for food at home or at restaurants was classified under the heading of food. Clothes included money spent for ready-made clothes, for the material and making of men's and women's wearing apparel, and for cleaning, pressing, and general upkeep.

Fuel, light, ice, telephone, telegraph, laundry, and household help expenses were listed under the general heading of house operation.

Money spent on furniture of all kinds, including radio and musical instruments, was included under house equipment. If these articles were bought by installment, only payments made during the year of the budget were included.

Automobile expenses included general upkeep, fines, taxes, and insurance, and that part of the purchase price which was expended for the year of the budget study.

Amusements covered expenditures in theaters, motion pictures, dances, and admission to other entertainments.

A separate item of expense was made for money expended on associations, clubs, and churches (hereafter referred to simply as associations). The expenses listed here were dues and donations, but no moneys spent for charity.

Charitable contributions did not include gifts but such items as community and personal philanthropies to the poor and the needy. Gifts were defined as birthday and holiday presents and those given to friends during such crises as sickness and childbirth. A gift essentially is a symbol given to another who is sufficiently co-ordinate with the giver to return a similar one, while charity and philanthropy are moneys spent on those who cannot return it. Charities subordinate the receiver and superordinate the giver; presents co-ordinate a relationship in the Yankee City system of class.

Education was divided into formal and informal categories. The former included all money spent on school tuition, textbooks, music and art lessons, and correspondence courses. Informal education consisted of money spent on home reading, magazines, newspapers, library dues, and book subscriptions and purchases.

Legal expenses were fees paid to lawyers and money spent in the courts.

Medical and health expenditures were for doctors, dentists,

oculists, nurses, hospitals, and medicine; and mortuary expenses were for undertakers and cemeteries.

Money spent on personal appearance included payments to barber and beauty shops and for toothpaste and similar items.

Professional and craft equipments were such things as carpenters' tools, X-ray machines, and other tools and instruments used by artisans and professional people.

All money spent on photography, including the expense of amateur photography and of professional services, was classed under this general heading. Sporting and athletic equipment was given a separate listing.

State and federal income taxes, poll taxes, and all other taxes, except those on the house and automobile, were treated under one general heading.

The other items were postage, tobacco and stationery, moving, travel for pleasure (including vacation expenses), and travel for business. There was a miscellaneous heading which included all expenses which the informant could not otherwise classify.

2. *General Income and General Expense of the Six Classes*

THE highest average income for each individual was in the lower-upper class. Each person averaged $2,652.61 and the average income for each family was $6,189.42 in that class. The individuals in the upper-upper class received the next highest income. Each person averaged $2,133.61, and each family, $6,400.83. Because the size of the family was smaller in the upper-upper class than in the lower-upper class, the income per family was smaller, but the income per person in the latter was larger than that in the upper-upper class. The income of the upper-middle class averaged $832.75 per person or $2,887.48 for each family. The incomes of the two upper classes were approximately the same, but that of the upper-middle was considerably smaller than the two upper classes. However, it was much larger than the income of the lower-middle class. The income of the lower-middle class for each person was $449.33 per year and $1,621.69 for a family. The income of the upper-lower class was considerably lower than that of the lower-middle. Each upper-lower person averaged $279.28 per year, and each family, $1,216.02 a year. The lower-lower class received the smallest average income of all classes. Each person in that class averaged $154.47, and each family, $882.71.

The average expense per year for each person in the lower-upper class was higher than in any other. The total expenses of each person in this class averaged $2,279.62. The average expense of the upper-upper class was second: each person in this class spent an average of $2,004.44. The average expense per family was highest in the upper-upper class. Each family spent $6,013.32. Each family in the lower-upper class spent an average of $5,319.12 per year.

Each person in the upper-middle class spent an average of $697.95. Each family spent an average each year of $2,420.07. In the lower-middle class, each person spent an average of $444.24, and each family spent $1,603.29. The members of the upper-lower class spent $284.29 per person, and the families of the upper-lower class averaged $1,237.84 for their total expenses for a year. In the lower-lower class, each person had an average expense of $164.46 a year, and each family spent, on the average, $939.79 a year. All classes except the lower two had a higher income than their total expenses, but the members of each of the lower classes were spending more than they were making. It must be remembered that this budget study was made in 1933, which was one of the "worst years" of the 1930–35 economic depression.

The highest total expense of any family in the upper-upper class was $18,000, and the lowest was $1,485. The highest total expense of any family in the lower-lower class was $2,725, and the lowest, $340. The highest expense in the lowest class was almost twice that of the lowest expense in the highest class. The expense figures are given rather than the total income figures because at the time of the study the expenses in the several classes were often larger than the income. The total expense, therefore, brings the lowest figures of the lower classes up higher than the total income figures do.

The range of expenditures in the lower-upper class was from $12,185 to $851; in the upper-middle class, from $7,800 to $353; in the lower-middle class, from $3,400 to $468; and in the upper-lower class, from $4,425 to $345.

In order that the reader may have the figures for the range

of income in each of the classes, we shall present them here. We feel, however, that the total expense figures are of greater significance, inasmuch as they describe what the people got by their spending in Yankee City. The range of income in the upper-upper class was from $20,000 to $1,105; in the lower-upper, from $1,800 to $810; in the upper-middle, from $8,300 to $400; in the lower-middle, from $4,300 to $245; in the upper-lower, from $5,000 to $210; and in the lower-lower class, from $2,800 to $305.

3. What They Spent Their Money For

ALL items of expense are arranged in rank order in Table 24. The table is arranged with the twenty-six items of expense at the top; the rank order for all budgets regardless of class is designated by the term "general"; and the six classes are found below it.

The five categories of expenditure which lead all others for the average amount of money spent yearly by the people of Yankee City are, in the order named, food, house operation, rent, automobiles, and clothing. Each of these five categories is more than 8 per cent and less than 27 per cent of the total amount spent.

The next seven items of largest expense listed in the table are taxes, formal education, medical care, house equipment, gifts, charity, and associations. All of these items are over 1 per cent and below 4 per cent. The next two items are above 1 per cent and below 2 per cent; they are informal education and travel for vacation purposes. The last categories of expense are 1 per cent or below. They are listed in the order of their size: personal appearance, amusement, travel for business purposes, tobacco, postage and stamps, legal expenses, sporting equipment, professional and technical equipment, mortuary expenses, photographic equipment, and furniture moving.

Food ranks first for the four lowest classes; rent, second; house operations, third; and clothing is fourth for the middle and lower classes. On the other hand, house operation is first for the two upper classes, reflecting the great value placed by them on the house. While food is second in the expenditures of the upper-upper class, it is third for the lower-upper stratum. The automobile ranks second for the lower-upper class, indicating

How the Six Classes Spent Their Money

TABLE 24

The Comparative Rank Order of the Proportion of the Budget of Each Class Which Was Spent for Each Item

	General	UU	LU	UM	LM	UL	LL
Moving	26	24	23	26	25	22	18
Photography	25	22	24	24	24	25	19
Mortuary	24	0	0	21	20	16	0
Professional Equipment	23	25	0	23	19	13	0
Sporting Equipment	22	23	21	25	23	24	0
Legal	21	21	20	22	0	23	0
Postage	20	20	17	21	21	21	17
Tobacco	19	19	18	14	15	10	8
Business-Travel	18	15	19	17	17	20	0
Amusements	17	18	15	15	13	16	14
Personal Appearance	16	16	16	16	12	15	10
Informal Education	15	17	13	13	14	7	12
Unclassified	14	10	22	19	22	0	0
Vacation-Travel	13	14	12	11	9	19	0
Associations	12	12	8	12	16	9	13
Charity	11	11	11	7	11	12	11
Gifts	10	9	10	9	8	11	6
House Equipment	9	13	7	8	7	8	7
Medical	8	8	9	6	6	5	5
Formal Education	7	6	14	10	10	14	16
Taxes	6	5	6	18	18	18	15
Clothing	5	3	5	4	4	4	4
Automobile	4	7	2	5	5	6	9
Rent and Shelter	3	4	4	2	2	2	2
House Operation	2	1	1	3	3	3	3
Food	1	2	3	1	1	1	1

the high selective value placed on conspicuous display by this class. A glance at Table 24 shows that the middle classes, giving the automobile fifth place, are nearest to the lower-upper class, but they place food, rent, house operation, and clothing before the car in their scale of expenditures. The upper-lower class expends a greater proportion of its budget on the same items as well as medical expenses than on the automobile. The upper-upper people spend a greater proportion of their money on taxes and formal education than on the automobile. The lower-lower class ranks the automobile as ninth out of the eighteen categories on which it spends money. It is noteworthy that whereas all other classes had few or no categories missing from their lists, almost one third were missing from the lower-lower budget.

The problem among the lower classes of paying the doctor bill ranks on equal terms with that of paying the tax collector among the two upper classes. Medical expense ranked fifth for the two lower classes and sixth for the two middle ones and eighth and ninth for the upper-upper and lower-upper classes; on the other hand, taxes ranked fifth and sixth for the upper-upper and lower-upper classes.

A close scrutiny of Table 24 gives the reader a ready comparison of the rank of each expenditure in each class. It does not inform him of the percentage of each class's budget which is spent on all items. Table 25 supplies this information, while Table 26 tells the average amount in dollars and cents that the people in the six classes spent on the twenty-six categories.

The proportion of the expense money spent for food was higher in the lower-lower class than in any other. The proportion of the money spent for food by each class decreased as the rank of the class increased, but the amount of money spent in each case was more than for the class below (see Table 25). The lower-lower class spent $74.69 per person a year for its food, or $426.86 each year for the average family (see Table 26). This represented 45.42 per cent of its total budget. The upper-lower class spent $105.21 for each person, or $458.11 for the average family. This was 37.01 per cent of its total budget (see Table 25).

The lower-middle class spent $139.21, or $502.38 for the average family. This was 31.35 per cent of its total expense

TABLE 25

Per Cent of the Budget of Each Class Spent on Each Item

Item	UU	LU	UM	LM	UL	LL
Moving	4-5 0.05	2 0.07	3 0.06	4-5 0.05	1 0.08	6 0.04
Photography	2 0.08	4 0.06	1 0.13	3 0.07	5 0.05	6 0.03
Mortuary	—	—	2 0.29	3 0.26	1 0.67	—
Professional Equipment	4 0.01	—	3 0.13	2 0.26	1 1.09	—
Sporting Equipment	4 0.07	1 0.16	2-3 0.09	2-3 0.09	5 0.06	—
Legal	3 0.12	1 0.26	2 0.22	—	4 0.06	—
Postage	3-4 0.22	1 0.57	2 0.29	3-4 0.22	5 0.18	6 0.08
Tobacco	6 0.27	5 0.56	3 1.06	4 1.05	2 1.57	1 1.75
Business-Travel	1 1.34	4 0.41	2 0.64	3 0.47	5 0.27	—
Amusements	4-5 0.67	3 0.89	2 1.00	1 1.15	4-5 0.67	6 0.46
Personal Appearance	2 1.02	6 0.81	3-4 0.99	1 1.16	3-4 0.99	5 0.93
Informal Education	5 0.72	2 1.32	3 1.10	4 1.06	1 2.44	6 0.50
Unclassified	1 3.71	4 0.12	2 0.54	3 0.13	—	—
Vacation-Travel	4 1.57	1 2.25	3 1.64	2 1.83	5 0.32	6 —
Associations	2 1.86	1 3.34	4 1.14	5 1.03	3 1.69	6 0.48
Charity	1 3.61	3 2.36	2 3.22	4 1.43	5 1.40	6 0.54
Gifts	1 3.73	4 2.46	3 2.59	5 1.86	6 1.42	2 2.60
House Equipment	6 1.81	1 4.43	2 3.04	5 2.02	3 2.13	4 2.10
Medical	1 5.21	6 2.98	4 3.83	3 3.96	5 3.32	2 4.94
Formal Education	1 9.79	5 0.91	2 2.51	3 1.66	4 1.06	6 0.14
Taxes	1 9.83	2 5.09	3 0.62	6 0.28	5 0.32	4 0.39
Clothing	1 11.25	6 8.53	2 10.09	3 9.88	4 9.00	5 8.60
Automobile	4 6.04	1 17.19	2 8.58	3 8.21	5 2.88	6 1.25
Rent and Shelter	6 10.38	5 12.73	4 16.67	3 17.31	2 20.25	1 20.76
House Operation	3 14.87	1 18.86	2 15.41	4 13.21	5 11.07	6 8.99
Food	6 11.77	5 13.64	4 24.12	3 31.35	2 37.01	1 45.42

TABLE 26
Amount Spent by Each Class on Each Category

	Food	House Operation	Rent and Shelter	Automobile	Clothing	Taxes	Formal Education	Medical	House Equipment	Gifts	Charity	Associations	Vacation-Travel	Unclassified	Informal Education	Personal Appearance	Amusements	Business-Travel	Tobacco	Postage	Legal	Sporting Equipment	Professional Equipment	Mortuary	Photography	Moving
UU Individual	236.09	298.34	208.15	121.06	225.59	197.01	196.18	104.41	36.28	74.76	72.27	37.30	31.43	3.71	14.49	20.35	13.38	26.82	5.36	4.35	2.38	1.37	0.24	—	1.57	0.95
UU Family	708.30	895.06	624.47	363.17	676.75	591.03	588.54	313.22	108.82	224.27	216.82	111.90	94.29	—	43.48	61.04	40.13	80.48	16.07	13.05	7.14	4.10	0.71	—	4.71	2.86
LU Individual	311.22	430.13	290.09	391.91	194.54	116.07	20.75	67.84	100.99	56.10	53.71	76.18	51.26	0.12	29.98	18.57	20.27	9.33	12.68	12.92	5.89	3.57	—	—	1.39	1.54
LU Family	726.21	1,003.63	676.87	914.46	453.91	270.84	48.42	158.30	233.65	130.90	125.83	177.75	119.60	—	69.95	43.33	47.30	21.77	29.58	30.18	13.75	8.33	—	—	3.25	3.58
UM Individual	168.40	107.54	116.36	59.89	70.59	4.31	17.50	26.77	21.19	18.11	22.45	7.93	11.43	0.54	7.66	6.92	7.01	4.49	7.41	2.01	1.55	0.64	0.90	2.04	0.89	0.42
UM Family	583.92	372.90	403.48	207.66	244.10	14.93	60.67	92.81	73.46	62.80	77.85	27.49	39.64	—	26.55	23.98	24.80	15.57	25.68	6.98	5.37	2.23	3.12	7.08	3.25	1.45
LM Individual	139.21	58.68	76.88	36.45	43.91	1.22	7.36	17.61	8.97	8.27	6.35	4.60	8.14	0.13	4.71	5.18	5.12	2.09	4.68	0.99	—	0.42	1.14	1.13	0.33	0.23
LM Family	502.88	211.77	277.46	131.57	158.46	4.42	26.58	63.56	32.36	29.84	22.92	16.59	23.39	—	16.99	18.68	18.48	7.55	16.88	3.59	—	1.50	4.13	4.09	1.19	0.85
UL Individual	105.21	31.46	57.54	8.18	25.58	0.90	3.01	9.45	6.04	4.04	3.98	4.81	0.92	—	6.95	2.83	1.90	0.77	4.47	0.50	0.18	0.16	3.11	1.91	0.15	0.24
UL Family	458.11	136.98	250.53	35.62	111.40	3.94	13.08	41.13	26.32	17.58	17.33	20.95	4.01	—	30.24	12.31	8.28	3.35	19.45	2.17	0.79	0.69	13.54	8.33	1.19	1.04
LL Individual	74.69	14.79	34.15	2.06	14.14	0.64	0.22	8.13	3.46	4.28	0.89	0.79	—	—	0.82	1.53	0.75	—	2.87	0.13	—	—	—	—	0.13	0.07
LL Family	426.86	84.51	195.14	11.76	80.79	3.67	1.27	46.47	19.74	24.48	5.09	4.50	—	—	4.68	8.74	4.23	—	16.40	0.74	—	—	—	—	0.29	0.38

for a year. Each upper-middle-class person spent an average of $168.40 a year for food, or a family spent $583.92. This was 24.12 per cent of all their expenses. Each lower-upper-class person spent $311.22, and each lower-upper-class family spent $726.21 a year for its food. This represented 13.64 per cent of their total expenses. The average member of the upper-upper class spent $236.09 a year for his food, and each family spent an average of $708.30 a year for food.

The lower-lower class spent a higher proportion of its money for rent and shelter than any other class. Again, the position of a class was in direct relation to the proportion of its budget spent for rent. The lower the class, the higher the proportion, and the higher the class, the lower the proportion. The lower-lower class used 20.76 per cent of all the money spent for a year on rent and shelter. The upper-lower class spent 20.25 per cent, and the lower-middle class, 17.31 per cent. The upper-middle class spent 16.67 per cent of its budget for rent; the lower-upper, 12.73 per cent; and the upper-upper spent 10.38 per cent. The two lower classes spent approximately twice as much as the upper-upper, and the two middle classes spent slightly over one-and-one-half times as much as the upper-upper class.

The average rent of the lower-lower-class family was $195.14 a year, or $34.15 for each person. The average rent of the upper-lower class was $250.53, or $57.54 per person. The average rent of the lower-middle-class family was $277.46, or $76.88 for each person. The rent for the upper-middle class was $403.48 for each family, or $116.36 for each person. The average rental for the lower-upper class was $676.87 for each family, or $290.09 per person. The average rental for each upper-upper family was $624.47, or $208.15 for each person. Although the percentage of the expenses is smaller, the amount of money spent for rent, except in the upper-upper class, tends to increase as the rank of the class increases.

The upper-upper class spent a larger percentage of its income on clothes than any other class: 11.25 per cent of its expenses were for clothing. The average person spent $225.59, and the average family in the upper-upper class, $676.75. The upper-middle class spent the next highest proportion of its budget for clothing: 10.09 per cent of its total expenses were for clothing. This amounted to $70.39 for the average person and $244.10 for the average family for the year's expenditure on clothing.

The lower-middle class ranked third for the proportion of its budget spent on clothing: 9.88 per cent of its total expenses were for clothing. The average individual spent $43.91, and the average family spent $158.46. The upper-lower class ranked fourth for the proportion of its budget spent on clothing: 9 per cent of its expenses for a year were for clothing. Each person in that class averaged $25.58 a year for clothing expense, and each family, $111.40. The lower-upper class ranked fifth: 8.53 per cent of the total expenses of each member of that class were for clothing. This represented $194.54 for each individual, or $453.91 for each family. The lower-lower class ranked last for the percentage of its income spent on clothing. Only 8.60 per cent of its expenses were for clothing. The average lower-lower-class person spent $14.14 a year for clothing, while the average family spent $80.79.

The expenditures for food, shelter, and clothing comprised three fourths of the lower-lower-class budget, two thirds of the upper-lower-class budget, approximately three fifths of the lower-middle-class budget, one half of the upper-middle-class budget, and about one third each of the budgets of the two upper classes. For these three items of expense, the lower-lower class used 74.78 per cent of its total yearly expense; the upper-lower class, 66.26 per cent; the lower-middle, 58.54 per cent; the upper-middle, 50.88 per cent; the lower-upper, 34.90 per cent; and the upper-upper, 33.40 per cent. Whereas the lower-lower class had only one fourth of its small income left to spend for the other things this society offers for money, and the upper-lower class one third of its budget, the two upper classes had two thirds of their money left to spend for the other things that money will buy in our society.

The upper-upper class spent a higher percentage of its money on clothing, taxes, formal education, doctors, gifts, charity, and on traveling for business purposes than did any other class. On the other hand, it spent a smaller proportion of its money on food, rent, house equipment, and tobacco than the other five classes. As Tables 20 and 21 indicate, these people also spent a relatively small amount on amusements, informal education, and moving.

The lower-upper class presents a very different picture. They spent more money than any other on automobiles, on providing new equipment for the house and for operating it, than any other social group. They spent a larger percentage of their budget on traveling for pleasure and on their clubs and formal associations than all other classes. They were ahead of the others for legal advice, in their correspondence, and on sporting equipment. They, too, were forced to spend a high proportion of their money on taxes. But unlike the class above them they tended to spend their money on moving and informal education.

They spent less of their money on doctors and personal appearance than all the classes and were next to last on formal education and for such necessities as clothing and rent.

Since the lower-lower class is at the other end of the class order it is enlightening to compare their expenditure order with that of the two upper groups. The lower-lower people led the others for the proportion of their budget spent on food, rent, and tobacco. (There seems clear evidence here that people will eliminate other items from their expenses to spend it on tobacco.) The lower-lower class was sixth and last for most expenditures. These included clothing, automobiles, house operation, charity, formal and informal education, associations, traveling for business or pleasure, amusements, sporting equipment, photography, and moving.

The upper-middle class tends to rank second for a large number of categories and resembles the lower-upper class for the proportion of its money spent on items which are not necessities and the lower-middle for those which are necessities.

The lower-middle class ranks third for a fairly large number of expenditures.

In the budget study one sees the upper-upper class a settled, somewhat sober-minded people spending their money not for automobiles and other items of conspicuous expenditure but on charity, taxes, and traveling for business purposes. The lower-upper class, with money to express its preferences, goes in for conspicuous display, as indicated by expenditures on houses, automobiles, travel for pleasure, and for sports.

The upper-lower class in contrast with the lowest one clearly indicates that their values accent social mobility as much as their pocketbooks will allow. For example, they outranked all others for the proportion of their budget spent on informal education and on moving (the lower-upper class was second). Yet they show the pinch of circumstances by ranking second only to the lower-lower people for the money they spent on food and shelter. The lower-lower people ordinarily spend their money on the sheer necessities but the upper-lower extend themselves to add a few activities to their lives "to improve their lot."

XVI

THE FORMAL AND INFORMAL ASSOCIATIONS OF YANKEE CITY

1. The Members of the Associations

THE associational structure of Yankee City extends to virtually every part of the society—to individuals of both sexes and all ages, to native and ethnic groups, and to all other structures such as the family, the school, the church, and the economic and political organizations. Most associations are themselves interconnected. These affiliations with other groups are so extensive that the individual need only be a member of one of the many associations to be brought more or less intimately into contact with members of these organizations which crosscut the entire community. The association thus acts as one of the foremost mechanisms of integration in Yankee City society.

In the chapters describing the methods used in this research, the formal association is defined as a mechanism which helps place the members of a society in a class hierarchy. It is a type of grouping highly favored in our society, and arranges individuals in an organization which characteristically includes some and excludes others.

The association differs from kinship institutions in that it is a voluntary grouping rather than one into which the individual is born. The behavior of its members, which it helps to regulate, may include almost any kind of activity occurring in the entire society. Again, the association differs primarily from economic structures because ultimate control ordinarily rests with all of the members; decisions on the entrance and exclusion of members are ultimately made by the whole organization rather than by a superordinate group, such as management in the economic structure. Both associations and economic structures have ordinary members and officers. Economic organizations such as the bank, the factory, and the store are divided into two internal groups: that of the owner-manager where final control is located and that of the workers who are subordinate and make no ultimate decisions. When discussions are carried on between workers and management, the workers are frequently represented through workers' associations or labor unions which are separately organized for such purposes. Matters of policy and procedure which ultimately concern the existence of the organization are decided by the managerial group, while the employees have only the smallest part in the control of the internal and external relations of the organization. The labor union only diminishes the absolute position of the owner-managers.

We first analyzed our associational material to determine how the association functioned in the community and developed our first hypothesis on the behavior of this institution. We held the view that one of its basic functions was to integrate the larger inner structures of the society to the whole community. Such larger structures as the church and economic organizations create antagonisms for their members when they attempt to integrate their behavior to the total community. As an adjunct to such structures, the association helps to resolve these antagonisms; at the same time it may also organize the antagonisms of the members of these structures against the larger community.

All churches and many economic organizations, as well as the school and political structures of Yankee City, surround themselves with associations which act as implements in organizing and resolving their antagonisms toward the larger community. Such associations play a subordinate role to the structure to which they are affiliated. For instance, the Yankee City Second Church has surrounded itself with some twenty associations whose behavior consists largely of secular activities that cannot be included in the sacred programs to which the church restricts its behavior, thus partially isolating itself. One of these connected associations is the Second Church Men's Club. This group has virtually no connection with the sacred ritual of the Church but helps to integrate the Church with the larger society; and, through the participation of its members in the club's activities, the Church is directly related to the larger community itself. At meetings of the Men's Club, a speaker, chosen from the community regardless of his religious affiliation, talks on some topic of current interest, and a discussion by members and their invited guests follows. At occasional meetings the members of the Second Church Ladies' Aid Society prepare and serve supper to the Men's Club and take part in the recreational program that follows. The activities of such associations are almost unlimited in their variation.

We first made a careful analysis of 357 associations in terms of the 6,874 individuals of Yankee City who composed their 12,876 memberships.

Small[1] associations were in the preponderance, and over one fourth, 28.29 per cent (101), had ten or less members and over a half, 54.34 per cent (194), had twenty or less. There were in all 12,876 members of the 357 associations. Of the total, 2,021 members (15.70 per cent) belonged to 194 (54.34 per cent) associations whose memberships were 20 or less; and 5,260 to 131 (36.69 per cent) associations whose memberships ranged between 21 and 80. The remaining 8.96 per cent (32) of the associations had memberships ranging from 81 to 312; and to them belonged 43.44 per cent (5,595) of all members we are considering in the Yankee City associational structure.

Thus, somewhat more than two fifths of the members belonged to large associations comprising less than one tenth of the associations, while numerous small and medium-sized groups account for the balance of the members.

Each association was analyzed by class, age, sex, and ethnic and religious affiliation.

The distinction made here between an individual and a member is that an individual is a socio-organic unit while a member is a purely social unit. An individual is counted only once in the population but many times in terms of memberships in organizations like the family, the clique, and the association. One individual, for example, may be a member of six associations while another may belong to only three: the total number of individuals is two; the total number of members, nine.

Individuals of all ages and both sexes are found in the associational structure of Yankee City; memberships of these associations, however, we classified by age and sex. Three age classifications were made: (1) a subadult group of those twenty

1. We shall refer to those associations which have 20 members or less as small associations; those with 21 to 80 members as of medium size; and those with 81 to 312 members as large.

years of age or younger, (2) an adult group of those over twenty years of age, and (3) a group including both subadults and adults. Behavior patterns of the groups were markedly different for each of these classifications.

Most frequently the association is a structure composed only of adults. A variety of subadult associations exists, but these are usually organized and directed by adults who are members of related groups. An adult member of the Y. W. C. A., for instance, may assume a supervisory position in such subadult associations as the Blue Birds, the Always Ready Club, or the Tri-Hi. Adult sponsorship frequently enrolls the first members, introduces rules of organizations, and later directs the activity of the group.

Subadult associations are frequently short-lived. Often when most of the members of such a group have exceeded certain loosely defined age limits, the association automatically passes out of existence to be replaced by a new one with a different name and membership. Short life, moreover, is not conducive to large membership; so subadult associations frequently do not expand much beyond their original membership.

In most subadult associations of mixed sex, a rigid sexual dichotomy is maintained in order to supervise moral behavior. There is no such segregation, however, in groups of very young children who are usually treated more like females. They are customarily supervised by women who play a role similar to that of mother in the family.

Subadult associations which range upward in age toward the twenty-year limit are more likely to be associations of mixed sex. Apparently this is due to the desires of the members themselves rather than to the wishes of the sponsors. Consequently, conflict frequently results between the interests of the sponsors and members, and many of the older subadult groups are held together only by the efforts of adult sponsors or directors. For example, one girls' club at the Y. W. C. A. has members between the ages of fifteen and eighteen. The director, a young woman of thirty, commented on this problem as follows: "I can't seem to find any programs that interest the girls. They should be learning to do things such as block printing and leather work, and I have tried to interest them. All they want to do on meeting nights is to get away from the Y. W. as early as they can and meet their boy friends who wait outside for them. I guess that their families won't let them out on week nights except for club meetings."

Adult associations of one sex hold many joint meetings with adult associations of the other sex and frequently collaborate in programs.

Male adult associations are most numerous.

Association structure resembles family structure. The male adult association may be likened to the father and husband, the female adult association to the wife and mother, and sub-adult associations to the sons and daughters. Joint meetings serve to illustrate this point. For example, the men of the American Legion hold a parade on Memorial Day to commemorate the death of members of the community who fought and died in past wars. The women of the American Legion Auxiliary prepare and serve lunch. Two troops of the Boy Scouts, sponsored by the Legion, parade with the men and assist them in the ceremonial activities of the day.

Associations are found among Yankees and all ethnic groups: Armenian, French Canadian, Greek, Irish, Italian, Jewish, Negro, Polish, and Russian. In certain instances the members are all Yankees or are drawn entirely from a single ethnic group; in other associational combinations there are representatives of all ethnic groups.

Those associations whose membership is taken from one ethnic group concern themselves principally with the maintenance of the solidarity of the group; they keep alive the members' interest in the homeland, and help to adjust their relations to the Yankee City community which is new to them. These "closed" associations are of predominantly immigrant membership, since newcomers unaccustomed to the ways of the community protect themselves and their folkways by joining associations comprising members of their own culture. The closed ethnic association thus supplies them with a focal point of organization and gives them the necessary feelings of strength and security.

Subsequent generations of ethnics tend to join associations which are not closed to all but one ethnic group. This has proved to be an effective device for moving more quickly into the social life of the total community. Native members are in the majority in most associations (other than the closed variety); and the ethnic is thus brought into contact with other members, persons who will help him integrate himself to the behavior of the larger community.

Most people of Yankee City either attend, or claim an affiliation with, one of the fifteen different churches; some profess no religious connection. These fifteen churches are of four different general religious faiths: Roman Catholic (two); Greek Orthodox (one); Jewish (one); and Protestant (eleven). Many of the 357 associations are directly connected with one of these fifteen churches, and their members in most cases are of the same religion.[2]

The religious faiths of the members of the Yankee City associational system faithfully reflect ethnic affiliation and cultural heritage. Most Protestants are Yankees; and most Catholics, Jews, and Orthodox Greeks are ethnics. Negroes and Armenians in Yankee City are the two non-native groups whose members are usually Protestant.

There are also associations open to members of but one religious faith. These associations, however, take on an added significance since, as adjuncts of the church, they carry its influence into the community.

While the church structure restricts behavior to the sacred rituals of its dogma, the associations connected with it may take part in the profane activities of the community at large. Such associations include in their behavior patterns almost every kind of activity indulged in by the entire associational structure. They bowl, play basketball, baseball, and other athletic games; present plays, shows, and specialty acts; hold sales and suppers; and take part in many other activities outside the realm of the sacred.

Usually, but not always, such associations are closed religious groups. Occasionally associations affiliated with some specific church are used as proselytizing mechanisms of this church. This is done by receiving members of other churches and religions, who sometimes become affiliated with the church itself or at least come indirectly under its influence. Certain Boy Scout troops sponsored by the various churches are examples of this practice.

2. The term church refers to the separate religious organizations in the community; each of the churches was classified in one of four religious faiths.

Associations whose members are from more than one religion ordinarily help integrate the members of two or more ethnic groups. In such associations there is a minimum of religious influence and usually little influence from any particular sect. A few associations, however, do have their own religious rites which are designed to be nonsectarian. In this they compete with the church, and because of this competition certain churches refuse to recognize them.

Those associations whose members are entirely from a single religion are ordinarily small in size. As the number of religions represented in the membership of associations increases from two to three and from three to four, the size of the associations changes from medium to large. A marked exception to this rule occurs in those associations whose membership is wholly of the Catholic faith; there large associations are found.

Both Protestants and Catholics are in a far greater number of associations than are people of the Greek Orthodox and Jewish faiths.

Finally, through analysis by class representation of membership, the 357 associations were typed on the basis of the degree to which their membership extended or failed to extend through the six classes. This investigation of the class composition of membership defined nineteen different class types which were combinations of the six classes. These types are:

Type 1: associations whose members are from the upper-upper class only;

Type 2: associations whose members are from the upper-upper and lower-upper classes only;

Type 3: associations whose members are from the upper-upper, lower-upper, and upper-middle classes only;

Type 4: associations whose members are from the upper-upper, lower-upper, upper-middle, and lower-middle classes only;

Type 5: associations whose members are from the upper-upper, lower-upper, upper-middle, lower-middle, and upper-lower classes and no other;

Type 6: associations whose membership extends through all six classes from the upper-upper through the lower-lower class;

Type 7: associations whose members are from the lower-upper and upper-middle classes only;

Type 8: associations with a membership from the lower-upper, upper-middle, and lower-middle classes only;

Type 9: associations which have members from the lower-upper, upper-middle, lower-middle, and upper-lower classes and no other;

Type 10: associations whose members come from all classes from the lower-upper through the lower-lower;

Type 11: associations with members from the upper-middle and lower-middle classes only;

Type 12: associations whose members are of the upper-middle, lower-middle, and upper-lower classes and no other;

Type 13: associations with members extending from the upper-middle through all classes to the lower-lower class;

Type 14: associations with lower-middle-class members only;

Type 15: associations with members from the lower-middle and upper-lower classes and no other;

Type 16: associations whose members are from the lower-middle, upper-lower, and lower-lower classes;

Type 17: associations with members from the upper-lower class only;

Type 18: associations whose members are from the upper-lower and lower-lower classes and no other;

Type 19: associations with members from the lower-lower class only.

In every one of the nineteen class types, it will be seen that members are drawn either from a single class or from a combination of two or more of the six classes in the hierarchy. In no case is there a skip of a single class in any of the combinations. If every possible class combination were present, there would be twenty-one associational class types; however, there are two places in which none of the 357 associations is represented—one with members wholly from the lower-upper class and the other with members entirely from the upper-middle class.

2. *The Structure of the Associational System*

THE majority of the associations in the Yankee City community are either formally connected to others in the association structure or to other structures such as the family, economic organizations, schools, churches, and political structures. These connections are sometimes established in the association's constitution or by-laws, or through the joint work of committees whose membership is drawn from several associations. Through such formal connections, the influence of a single association may reach to other associations and to every other structure of the community. For example, 238 associations are connected with the Y. M. C. A. Connected to these and once removed from the Y. M. C. A. are twenty-five associations, economic organizations, schools, and churches; connected with these are 231 associations twice removed from the Y. M. C. A., and so on until the most distant connections are nine times removed. A total of 650 direct and indirect connections of the Y. M. C. A. relate this association to other associations, economic organizations, schools, churches, and to the political structure. Many other associations present this identical pattern inasmuch as they are a part of the 650 Y. M. C. A. connections, and any one could be similarly used as a focus.

Two different kinds of structural types are found in the association structure of Yankee City. These are the simple or single associations and the complex or multiple or integrative. Chart XXVIII illustrates the elaboration of both types.

The simple or single associations are separate entities (see [1] on Chart XXVIII) and have no formal [3] affiliations with other associations or other structures.

Single associations fall into four generally recognizable subtypes. The first are those associations which are organized around total community interests and crises: hospital associations, charitable societies, and groups which aim to improve the parks and the appearance of the community. The second are certain secret societies which, although not formally affiliated with any other local groups, are usually units of national organizations. In the third category are the closed ethnic associations. A large number of the latter are directly connected with Americanization programs and with benefit and burial functions. The fourth are free-lance associations formed primarily for recreational (athletic) purposes. The birth and mor-

---

3. The members of these associations, however, may be members of other associations.

tality rate of these athletic groups is very high as they are loosely organized with a small hierarchy of officers and lacking written rules. Organized on a geographical basis, most of their members live in the lowlands of Riverbrook where much of the ethnic and lower-class population is concentrated. With few exceptions their members were born in this country; and most of them are from the younger age grades. Occasionally these

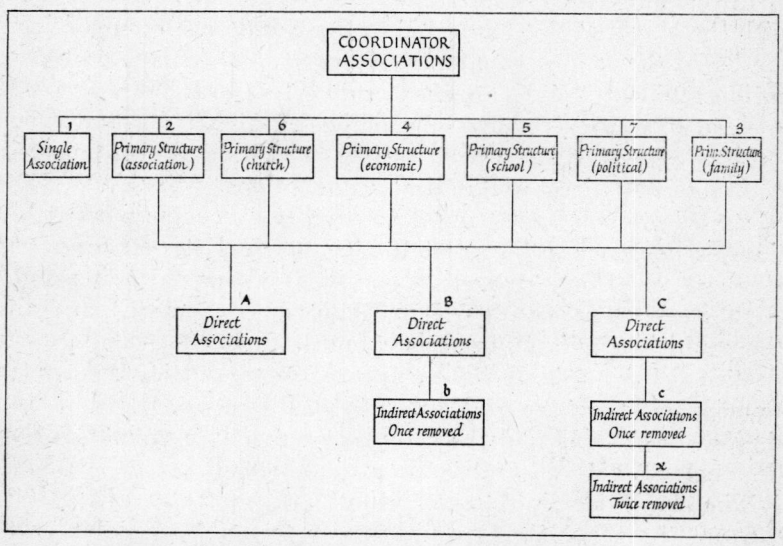

```
                        COORDINATOR
                        ASSOCIATIONS
    ┌──────┬──────┬──────┼──────┬──────┬──────┐
    1      2      6      4      5      7      3
  Single Primary Primary Primary Primary Primary Prim.Structure
Association Structure Structure Structure Structure Structure (family)
         (association) (church) (economic) (school) (political)
                          │             │             │
                          A             B             C
                        Direct        Direct        Direct
                      Associations  Associations  Associations
                                        │             │
                                        b             c
                                   Indirect Associations  Indirect Associations
                                   Once removed          Once removed
                                                              │
                                                              x
                                                         Indirect Associations
                                                         Twice removed
```

XXVIII. *Structural Types of Associations*

associations affiliate with other associations or other structures and become satellites.

Complex (or multiple or integrative) associations fall into three subgroups according to their structural relationships with each other and with other structures. The first two subgroups always occur together, forming what we have called an associated group, and include, (1) primary (parent or dominant) associations or other structures; and (2) satellite (secondary or subordinate) associations. The third is the coordinate (linked) type of association.

The primary association (church, factory, etc.) is the focal point around which satellite associations are clustered. These affiliated satellites are in most cases made up of members who are also members of the dominant association or structure. Frequently committees from the membership of the primary group are appointed to guide and co-operate in programs of activity of the satellites. It is the primary association (or other structure) which rests at the top of the associated group hierarchy and ultimately controls the behavior and policies of the secondary associations. The smallest number of secondary associations connected to a single primary association or other structure of Yankee City is one; the greatest number is 238.

Chart XXVIII shows that in addition to primary associations other primary structures of the family, economic, school, church, and political organizations may hold the dominant position in the associated group. Secondary associations may be (1) immediately connected to parent associations or other structures as in the case of the direct satellite, or (2) indirectly affiliated through other associations. Indirect satellite associations are of two varieties: *(a)* once-removed, i.e., immediately subordinate to those of the direct kind and connected to the primary structure through them; and *(b)* twice-removed, i.e., satellites which are in turn inferior to other indirect, once-removed associations and are affiliated to the parent group through both indirect, once-removed satellites and direct, secondary associations.

Thus, as is shown in Chart XXVIII, there are three kinds of associated groups, each of which forms an associational hierarchy with a dominant association or other structure at the top wherein ultimate control is lodged. These associated groups are (1) the simple associated group which is composed of a dominant association or other structure and its direct satellites (A) in the chart; (2) the once-extended associated group with a dominant association or other structure to which are connected one or more direct satellites (B) which in turn are connected to one or more once-removed secondary associations (b) in descending order; and (3) the twice-extended associated group composed of a dominant association or other structure to which are connected one or more direct satellites (C) which in turn are superior to one or more once-removed secondary associations (c) which are again superior to one or more twice-removed satellites (x).

Associated groups are frequently subdivided into several

separate groups of satellites, all of which are clustered about the same primary association or other structure. Several of the three kinds of associated groups—the simple, the once-extended, and the twice-extended—may be organized around the same dominant association, in which case they become subassociated groups within the same general associated group.

If an associated group contains any combinations of simple, once-extended, and twice-extended associated groups, it becomes a subassociated group.[4]

Dominant associations tend to have a much wider range of activity than do their secondary associations, and in most instances these satellites confine their activities to a narrow range. Many of them are organized around a single athletic game, such as baseball, basketball, or bowling. This is probably due to an interest in these sports on the part of only certain members of the larger parent groups.

The third complex (or integrative) variety of association is the co-ordinate or link type (see top of Chart XXVIII). Such associations are neither superordinate nor subordinate to any other association or structure. Their membership is composed of delegates from two or more associations or other structures, and their purpose is the co-ordination of interests common to these groups. In Yankee City, co-ordinate associations link together structures of the same order as well as structures of different orders. The groups thus co-ordinated are as follows: (1) associations, (2) families, (3) economic organizations, (4) churches, (5) schools, (6) associations and churches, (7) associations, churches, and schools, (8) schools and families, and (9) all structures combined. Associations and other structures so linked may be of the single variety with no affiliation or frequently may hold the place of primary associations or other structures as well as satellites.

The Masonic Temple Association, for example, is organized to care for the clubhouse or temple in which the five Masonic groups of Yankee City hold their meetings. Its membership

---

4. A satellite association may be affiliated with two separate dominant structures of the same or of different types. For example, the secondary association, Harry's Haberdashers, is subordinate to the primary association, the City Bowling League, and to the economic organization, Harry's Hollywood Shop.

comprises several members of the Royal Arch Masons, the Knights Templar, St. John's Lodge, St. Mark's Lodge, and the Eastern Star. This administrative group is not connected with any of these five associations either as a parent or a secondary association but links them by serving their mutual interests in their meeting place.

Likewise, the clergymen of eleven Yankee City Protestant churches have organized into an association called the "Federation of Religious Workers." Its purpose is to promote unity of action among the churches and to devise means for bringing nonchurchgoers into regular church attendance. Their program includes an annual outdoor sunrise service attended by the clergy and members of the congregations of the eleven churches, exchange of pulpits by the pastors, and promotion of an annual Go-to-Church Sunday. At bimonthly business meetings questions pertaining to church affairs are discussed, speeches heard, and food served by the women of one of the churches.

The Federation of Religious Workers, as well as other associations which we have defined as units that link other associations or other structures together, acts as an adjunct to the several groups which it connects. The initiative in organizing it and other such associations came from the several separate groups themselves.

Thus it may be said that the single associations are independent of one another in their formal organization and behavior, but are linked together through associations which act to co-ordinate certain of their interests.

Secondary associations were classified according to the origin of their members into two types: first, with members entirely from the groups interlocked, and, second, with members in part or entirely from outside of the primary structure.

Secondary associations whose membership completely interlocks with part of that of their parent associations were subdivided into two varieties according to their organization. One of these subtypes is an associated group which is commonly called a league. In the league, two or more small associations form a group for the purpose of competing with each other in some of the following athletic games: baseball, basketball, volleyball, bowling, gymnastics, and miniature golf. The combined membership of all of the secondary associations of this kind forms the whole membership of their superordinate association. The memberships of the satellites of the same associate group, however, do not overlap. The organization of a league may be said to come from the bottom up, as two or more subordinate associations must be formed before the dominant association is brought into existence at all. In all instances the dominant structure must be an association and not one of the other structures.

In the leagues, the superordinate association acts somewhat as a co-ordinator inasmuch as its entire membership is gained from other associations. It is, however, in close connection with these groups. It arranges their game schedules and holds occasional meetings which all members are expected to attend. Such meetings are customarily of a recreational nature, and occasional suppers and banquets are held when speeches are heard.

This kind of satellite is perhaps the most impermanent of all; its ephemeral life is probably due to the nature of its athletic behavior patterns, its simple hierarchy of officers which usually includes only a captain and a manager, and its meager rules of organization which are seldom given the more permanent written form. While such associations have a less permanent type of organization than do other satellites, these secondary associations are much more tightly organized than the clique. Unlike the clique, they meet regularly at designated places and govern themselves with a prescribed set of rules.

The second type of secondary associations whose membership completely interlocks with part of that of the dominant groups may be subordinate to primary associations or to other structures. The associated groups in which these secondary associations exist are organized from the top down because the membership of their satellites is derived from the dominant structure. This is the exact reverse of the league where the satellites must first be organized before the dominant association can exist. In further contrast, this second type of satellite association with derivative membership may have a membership which in part overlaps that of other satellites of the same associated group.

Satellites whose membership is selected from that of their superordinate groups are connected with associations, families, economic organizations, schools, churches, and the political structure. They alone occur in every possible kind of connection with their dominant associations or other structures. They are the only secondary associations to be represented in every possible place in simple, once-extended, and twice-extended groups, and occur in subassociated groups.

Such secondary associations fall into three distinct patterns as defined by the behavior in which they take part. The first are those satellite associations which play athletic games to the almost complete exclusion of any other activity. The second are similar to the first, but they concentrate their attention on talent display and on the study and discussion of the arts and literature. The third comprise those satellites whose behavior covers a wide variety of activity of all kinds. Frequently their activities play an important role in the everyday life of the community.

Satellites whose membership is derived from that of their dominant associations (or other structures) are more tightly organized than are those whose combined membership forms that of the superordinate association and creates the league. They tend to have an extensive hierarchy of officers, written rules, and a more highly systemized plan of organization. Such secondary associations are as a rule of longer life than the leagues.

An example of the satellite whose membership is derived from that of its primary association is the Forty and Eight. All of its members are also members of the Yankee City American Legion. The Forty and Eight has occasional meetings called "wrecks" which are mostly of a recreational nature; its members carry on drives for members for the parent body and interest themselves in child-welfare work. The Forty and Eight extends the behavior patterns of the American Legion and attracts a select group of members from the dominant body who are desirous of intensifying their activity as Legion members.

There are also satellites whose membership rolls do not coincide with those of the primary associations or other structures with which they are affiliated. When the dominant structure is an association, the members of these secondary associations are usually taken from the immediate and extended families of the members of the dominant groups but differ from them in that they are of the opposite sex or of another age grade. Such satellites may be composed of the female kin of the members of the parent association or of subadult blood relatives of this primary group's members. These kinship qualifications are not always necessary, but they form the underlying pattern.

Most satellites whose membership is drawn from outside the superordinate associations carry on a wide range of activity at their meetings. Both parents and their satellites are formally organized with an extensive hierarchy of officers and written rules of conduct.

One remaining type of secondary association, classified according to the derivation of its membership, is that in which only a part of the members interlock with those of the primary structure. They are subordinate to the dominant structures which include churches, economic organizations, and the political structure. Satellites of this type have direct connection with primary structures only and function as proselytizing devices for them. In every instance the nuclear members belong also to the dominant structure and interlock the two. Outsiders are added in some cases to increase the prestige in the community of the entire associated group and in others to augment the membership of the secondary association to enable it to function with a large membership in more varied activities.

As with the satellites whose membership is entirely extraneous to that of their dominant structure, associations of this type may have more members than the parent structure.

Examples of secondary associations of this type which were subordinate to churches were eight Boy Scout troops, each of which was affiliated with a church of the Protestant faith. These satellites had subadult males drawn from the members of the several dominant churches as the nucleus of their membership. A great effort was made, however, to bring in boys who belonged to other church organizations and frequently of other religious affiliations.

The Second Church of Yankee City dominated a Boy Scout troop which drew a large proportion of its members from other churches and religions. The church membership was predominantly Yankee, but the Boy Scout troop was commonly known as the "League of Nations" because of the great number and variety of ethnics among its members. The minister of the church took a great interest in the group and frequently addressed it. Upon several occasions he emphatically stated that the Scouts was an organization for all boys regardless of race or creed and that it was a great institution for the creation of good will. However, the boys who belonged to other churches were brought directly under the influence of the church which dominated the satellite Boy Scout troop to which they belonged.

Secondary associations with membership drawn partly from the rolls of parent economic organizations and partly from the rest of the community consist almost entirely of satellites whose behavior is centered in a specific athletic game. They compete with other associations whose behavior is similar to their own and attract spectators from the community at large. The attention which these games draw is in some measure reflected upon the dominant economic organization. Approximately one fourth of the economic structures which had satellite connections brought in members from outside of, as well as from within, their own organizations. Those that did so were without exception small organizations which depended upon retail trade for their existence. Such parent groups did not have a sufficiently large membership of their own to form satellite associations whose members competed in athletic games, and it was considered important that the parent group should be identified with satellites which had athletic prestige.

The one association which is subordinate to the library (a part of the political structure of Yankee City) is a group organized for the study and appreciation of music. It is in no way a proselytizing or advertising device as are the satellites of this type which are affiliated with dominant churches and economic organizations. Its membership is both subadult and adult, and of both sexes. It is sponsored and directed by several prominent women of Yankee City.

Before beginning our structural analysis, we first made a statistical analysis of the associations of Yankee City: twelve types of associations were used and correlations according to class and sex of members were made. In this analysis, persons who belonged to one or more associations were included according to association types in which they held memberships. If we knew that the individual belonged to three associations, all of different types, his membership was entered under each of these three. If, however, he belonged to three associations of the same type, he was listed only once under the type in which he held three associational memberships. In other words, what was counted was neither the number of persons nor the number of memberships but the number of persons according to the association types in which they held one or more memberships.

The twelve types are (1) fraternal with auxiliary; (2) fraternal without auxiliary; (3) sororal with auxiliary; (4) sororal without auxiliary; (5) semiauxiliary; (6) social male; (7) social female; (8) social mixed; (9) charity; (10) economic structure; (11) occupational structure; and (12) age-grade transition.

The first type, Fraternal with Auxiliary, comprises associations of male members which are organized principally to carry on ritualistic programs for the initiation of new members and the advancement of certain members in their official hierarchy. Symbolic objects are abundantly used at their meetings, and members wear uniforms and special regalia. Their groups are commonly referred to as secret societies and as patriotic societies. Affiliated with them are other associations often referred to as auxiliaries. These auxiliaries are either their counterparts with female membership, or associations with subadult membership which the fraternal groups instruct in activities similar to their own.

Fraternal associations without auxiliary are fraternal groups which have no association connections with female or subadult counterparts.

The Sororal with Auxiliary type is a female association organized, as are the male fraternal groups, for ritualistic activity. Subadult associations connected with them are instructed in ritualistic behavior similar to their own. Semi-auxiliaries are of the variety commonly called secret societies with both male and female members.

The Social Male type, as well as the Female and Mixed types, includes associations whose behavior is recreational; and it comprises such activity as card playing, and athletic and sedentary games.

Associations of the Charity variety gather funds, clothing, food, etc., and distribute them among the needy families of the community.

The Economic type of association is organized around purely economic matters and includes such associations as the Yankee City Mutual Fire Insurance Association, which insures dwelling houses against fire.

The Occupational variety of association is organized around types of occupation and includes labor unions.

Associations of the Age-Grade Transition type are composed largely of subadult members, and are sponsored and directed by adult members of the society. They are of several age ranges, roughly including members from four to seven, from eight to twelve, from thirteen to sixteen, and from seventeen to twenty years of age respectively. Adult sponsors impose upon these associations programs of activity devised to orientate their behavior to the adult society of the community.

The upper-upper class had a significantly high number of persons in three types of organizations: social-female; social-mixed; and charity organizations. In the fraternal and sororal organizations, as well as those of the age-grading and semiauxiliary type, the upper-upper class was significantly low.

The lower-upper class was significantly high in male, female, mixed social organizations, charity and economic organizations. It was significantly low in fraternal, sororal with auxiliary, semiauxiliary, and in the age-grading organizations.

The upper-middle class had a significantly high number of persons in organizations of the social-female type, in the charity organizations, the economic structure, and occupational organizations. It was significantly low in fraternal orders with auxiliaries and sororal orders without auxiliaries, in semiauxiliaries, in the mixed social type, and in the age-grading organizations.

A significantly high number of the lower-middle class were in fraternal organizations, in the semiauxiliaries; a significantly low number in sororal organizations without auxiliaries, in the mixed social organizations, in social organizations devoted to females, and in charity organizations.

A significantly high number of upper-lower members were

in fraternal organizations with auxiliaries, in sororal organizations with or without auxiliaries, in semiauxiliaries, and in age-grading associations. A significantly low number belonged to fraternal organizations without auxiliaries. In the male social groups, in the female social groups, in the charity organizations, and in the economic organizations, a significantly low number of the upper-lower class were found.

The lower-lower members were significantly high for fraternal orders without auxiliaries, for sororal orders with auxiliaries, and for age-grading groups; and significantly low for female social groups, for charity groups, and for economic structure groups.

This analysis of associations by structure and kind of activity proved useful for our earlier analysis of the class structure, but the two criteria needed to be separated. This we did by making a separate study of each of these aspects of the associations. A behavior analysis of 219 of the associations and a record of the incidence of all the activities of each were made. The results of this particular study are given in the volume on symbol systems.

We were ultimately able to list a total of 899 associations in Yankee City. Most of them were ephemeral and lasted only for a short period of time; many of them which existed when the study began were dead before the end of the study. The 357 groups studied included the great majority of the permanent associations of the community. Although not all associations were examined for the names of their members, they were analyzed for structural type to determine how they fitted into the larger social system of Yankee City. Of the grand total, 151 were single or simple associations and were independent of any formal connections with other associations or other structures such as a church or factory; 41 were parent or dominant associations to which satellite associations were attached; 676 were satellites; and 31 were co-ordinates of other associations.

As we have said, there were three different kinds of associated groups. The simple associated group included the primary association or other structures and its direct satellites. The American Legion was an example of this type of associated group of primary association and its direct satellites; the Forty and Eight, the Rifle Club, the American Legion Auxiliary, the

American Legion Juniors' Baseball Club, and Boy Scout troops were connected with it.

In each case, these satellites of the American Legion were dependent upon it, although they had their own set of rules and by-laws and their own hierarchy of officers which controlled their immediate policies.

The once-extended group, or second type of associated group, consists of a primary association or other structure with one direct satellite and once-removed satellites. An example of an associated group of the once-extended variety was the Greek-American Progressive Association (a primary association) with a direct satellite of the Greek-American Progressive Association Juniors and a once-removed indirect satellite, the Dillboy Juniors Bowling Club. The Greek-American Progressive Association was composed almost entirely of Greek immigrants and organized largely for the purpose of Americanization and the discussion of topics of interest to Greeks. The G. A. P. A. Juniors was a closed Greek association of mostly first-generation subadults, who participated in total community affairs to a greater extent than did their parents. Their activity was largely recreational. They were sponsored by members of the parent association and were encouraged to take part in community-wide programs. The Dillboy Juniors Bowling Club was a satellite of the G. A. P. A. Juniors and, through them, an indirect satellite of the G. A. P. A.

The twice-extended group or third type of associated group is a primary association or other structure which has one immediate direct satellite linked to a once-removed satellite which has one or more twice-removed secondary organizations. For example, the Immaculate Conception Catholic Church was the parent structure to the Catholic Boys' Club directly connected with it; the latter had a once-removed indirect satellite of the Immaculate Conception Church which was the C. B. C. Basketball League. This last organization was composed of six associations which were its satellites and were indirect satellites of the Immaculate Conception Church.

In many cases combinations of different associated groups were found to cluster around the same primary association or other structure. The Y. M. C. A. is a very good illustration of how one primary association may have a series of associated groups of all kinds. All told, it had 238 satellite connections which were composed of indirect and indirect-secondary associations of both once- and twice-removed varieties. The Y. M. C. A. was organized by adults for the subadult males of the community; it supplied a clubhouse with facilities for games and rooms for business meetings. One subassociated group consisted of direct satellites, such as a Boy Scout troop, the Stamp Club, and the Friendly Indians.

The second of the seventeen subassociated groups of the Y. M. C. A. typified the once-extended variety of connected as-

TABLE 27

The Structural Types of Associations

	Direct		Once-Extended			Twice-Extended			
	P	S	P	S^1	S^2	P	S^1	S^2	S^3
Association	39	203	6	22	145	2	10	19	93
Church	18	130	2	5	6	1	1	7	42
Economic	35	49	1	1	2	—	—	—	—
School	3	45	2	10	46	—	—	—	—
Political	1	12	0	0	0	—	—	—	—
Family	1	1	0	0	0	—	—	—	—
Totals	97	440	11	38	199	3	11	26	135

sociations. It was called the Y Basketball League and had four groups subordinate to it, called the Boys' Club, the Collegians, the Freshmen Independents, and the Record Breakers.

Numerically, the primary association and its satellites composed almost three fifths of all the associations, and they were the outstanding structures around which the various associated groups formed. Thus it may be seen that the association is the most effective medium for reaching through the society by its connections with other associations and with other structures.

There were ninety-seven associated groups (see Table 27). Each was headed by a primary structure, around which a group of satellites were clustered. Thirty-nine of the parent or primary structures were associations; eighteen groups were subordinate to churches; thirty-five parent associations were economic organizations; three were schools; the political organization headed one group; and the family was a primary structure for one associated group.

The reader should use Tables 27 and 28 while studying this material. Table 27 (The Structural Types of Associations) lists the six types of social structure in the left-hand column. The three types of interconnections are placed at the top of the table: they are direct, once-extended, and twice-extended. Below these terms in the next horizontal column, parent or primary is referred to by the letter *P* and satellite by *S*.

In Table 28 (Membership Types of Satellites) the six structural types are listed in the left-hand column and the four types of satellites at the top of the table. The definition of each type is given in the next few paragraphs.

TABLE 28

Membership Types of Satellites

	Type I	Type II	Type III	Type IV	Totals
Association	346	121	25	—	492
Church	42	137	4	8	191
Economic	2	39	2	9	52
School	46	52	3	—	101
Political	—	11	—	1	12
Family	—	1	—	—	1
Totals	436	361	34	18	849

There were 97 primary structures which were superordinate directly to 440 satellites (see Table 27). Eleven primary structures in the once-extended groups were dominant over 237 satellites. And 3 parent structures were primary to 172 satellites. By definition, 440 direct satellites had no subordinate associations attached to them; the 11 parent structures of the once-extended associated groups had 38 satellites which were

324 *The Social Life of a Modern Community*

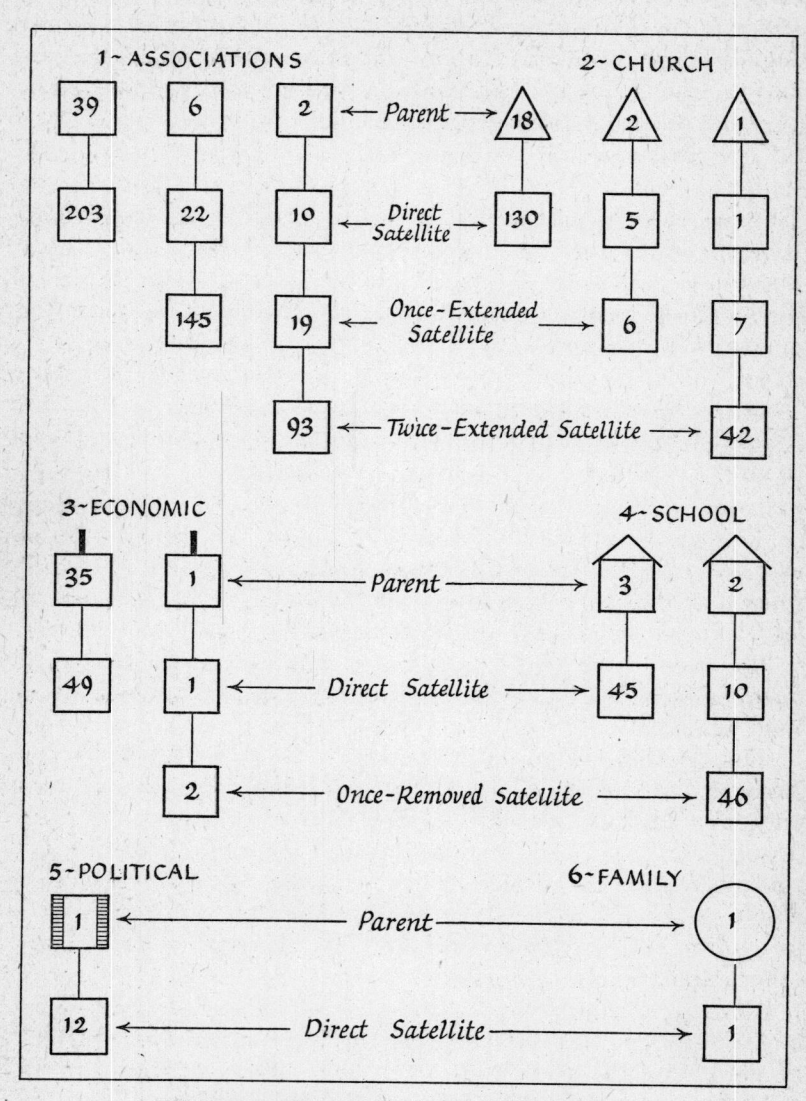

XXIX. *The Associational Structure*

directly connected to them; and the satellite associations had 199 subordinate associations attached to them. The 3 primary structures in the twice-extended associated groups had 11 satellites immediately connected to them; the 11 immediate satellites were superordinate to 26 additional ones; and the latter, in their turn, had 135 satellite associations which were subordinate to them.

Chart XXIX represents the integration of the associations into the social organization of Yankee City. The six types of structure are listed and the several forms of parent and satellite associations are charted for each type of institution. The number of parent and satellite is found in the appropriate rectangle. This chart should be used with Table 27.

Thirty-nine of the primary structures of the direct type of parent and satellite groups were associations (see Chart XXIX). They had 203 satellites connected to them. Eighteen primary structures were churches; they were superordinate to 130 associations. Thirty-five economic structures had 49 associations interlocked with them; 3 schools had 45 associations related to them; the political structure had 12 associations; and 1 family had 1 satellite association.

The membership of co-ordinates was composed of certain members selected from the associations and structures which they linked.

The Masonic Temple Association, the Veteran Fireman's Association, and the Community Center linked groups of associations. The Community Center, like the Masonic Temple Association, supplied and maintained housing facilities and equipment for use of the groups it linked. The Veteran Fireman's Association linked two associations whose interest was in running their hand-operated fire engines, bowling, and other recreational activities.

All churches joined by the three co-ordinates were Protestant. The Young People's Interdenominational Council was composed of young people from these churches. Their purpose was to co-ordinate the programs of activity, both religious and profane, carried on by the Protestant churches of the community. The second co-ordinate was the Bethel Society, organized to extend charity to sailors and their widows. It was financed largely by contributions collected from the members of Protestant churches. The members of the associations were representatives of the churches in question. The third, the Federation of Religious Workers, has already been described.

Fourteen associations co-ordinated various economic organizations. Their membership included seven employer-manager groups and seven different groups of employees. They composed such organizations as the trade associations on the one hand and labor unions on the other. Five of them combined members involved with all varieties of different economic organizations, while nine combined members whose occupations tended to be the same. For the most part, their activities were closely related to the economic organization itself; however, in two instances a wide variety of activity of a recreational nature was included.

The Rotary Club is an example of those owner-manager, co-ordinator associations which link members of various kinds of economic organizations; and the Hairdressers' Association is an example of those which link economic organizations within a specific occupation.

The Rotary Club had members from many of the retail, wholesale, and manufacturing groups, as well as members from each of the professions. Its membership, for example, included the managers from hardware, clothing, and department stores; one from a wholesale coal company; an oil distributor; the owner and manager from a shoe manufacturing enterprise and a foundry; a doctor; a lawyer; and a clergyman.

The behavior of the owner-manager associations is varied. Some have only business meetings; others have weekly luncheon meetings at which a speaker is present. These groups attempt to bring new industries to the community as well as to improve and protect the existing trade and manufacturing conditions. Others are active only in athletic programs.

The Hairdressers' Association included the owner-managers of local hairdressing and beauty parlors. The membership of this and similar groups was restricted to the owner-managers of economic organizations which were confined to a specific business.

Employees associations, like the owner-manager groups, were of two orders: those which included workers in all kinds of occupations and those whose members were employed in occupations within one economic activity.

Associations which linked employee members from all kinds of occupations confined their activity largely to athletic games. They co-ordinated the interests of members of the economic organizations whose employees composed their memberships.

An example of link associations whose members are limited to one economic activity is the shoe workers organizations. There were three organizations of shoe workers, and they were all labor unions. These unions co-ordinated the workers of the several different shoe factories. Another workers' co-ordinate association is the Yankee City Musicians Association. It, too, may be called a labor union; it bound the local orchestra organizations together in its common membership of orchestra employees. Such associations were formed principally for the protection and advancement of the workers' interests in relation to their jobs.

Although the behavior of these co-ordinator associations was not in every instance related to matters directly involving the operations of the economic organizations which they linked together, all of them restricted their membership to a certain defined personnel in the economic structure.

One association co-ordinated the public schools of Yankee City. This was the Teachers' Association and, as the name implies, its membership was composed of schoolteachers. It closely resembled a labor union in several respects for salaries, work procedures, and similar topics were discussed at its business meetings. A minimum of recreational activity was connected with it.

There was one association which linked families together. Its membership was restricted to those families which were descended from the persons who first settled Yankee City in the early 1600's. Its principal activity lay in preserving the symbols of ancestry, such as old houses in the community.

Four associations linked associations and churches together. They were made up of members of the churches of the Protestant faith, and in three instances the Y. M. C. A. was linked to them. One of these associations, the Scout Masters, also included the American Legion. This co-ordinate had a membership of adult sponsors or directors of the Boy Scout troops. Each of these troops was a satellite of one or another of eight different churches of the Protestant faith, of the Y. M. C. A., or of the American Legion. The representatives of these ten structures co-ordinate churches, the American Legion, and the Y. M. C. A.

The second co-ordinator association of this kind linked eleven churches and the Y. M. C. A. It was the Interchurch Basketball League, and members of the Protestant churches and of the Y. M. C. A. competed. Each team bore the name of one of the churches or of the Y. M. C. A. The other two associations which linked associations and churches were the Church Baseball League and the Church Bowling League. The first of these two linked six churches of the Protestant faith, the Greek-Orthodox Church, and the Y. M. C. A.; the second co-ordinated six different Protestant churches and the Y. M. C. A.

Two associations linked associations, churches and schools. They were the Campfire Advisory Committee[5] and the Campfire Guardians Association. Both had as their members the adult sponsors of the Campfire groups. Each of these Campfire groups is a satellite of a church of Protestant faith and of a school, or of the Y. W. C. A. As representative members of these four structures, the members of the Campfire Advisory Committee and of the Campfire Guardians Association co-ordinated them.

Two Parent-Teachers Associations in Yankee City covered two sections of the community. They co-ordinated both schools and families and their membership was composed of the school-teachers and parents of children in the city schools. The members met to discuss their common interests in the orientation of the child in the community.

The last association of the co-ordinate type was the Citizens Aid Committee; it linked associations, families, schools, churches, and the political structure. This group was organized during the economic emergency in the early days of the depression when the unemployment situation in Yankee City threatened to rend the whole social and economic fabric of the society. At that time the members of all these structures appointed individuals to the membership of the Citizens Aid

5. Although the Campfire Advisory Committee was called a committee, it was in every sense of our definition an association in its own right. It was not a part of another association. Furthermore, it was neither superordinate nor subordinate to any other associations or other structure.

Committee. This association made plans for furnishing work to the unemployed by encouraging people who were financially able to furnish work to the needy.

Membership status in both the simple and the co-ordinate associations thus was clearly defined. Members of a simple association did not connect it with other groups, while those of the co-ordinates were recruited from the groups they linked. Associations and other structures of the primary type were always formally affiliated with one or more satellite associations (as defined in their constitutions or by-laws), but such affiliations were not always organized by interlocking memberships.

The membership of a secondary association may (1) be wholly derived from the superordinate structure with which it affiliates, but in no case does it include the entire membership; or (2) have members who are entirely different from those of the parent organization; or (3) have a membership of which part interlocks with that of the primary association and part does not.

3. The Associations to Which the Members of Each Class Belonged

As THE class rank increases, the proportion of its members who belong to associations also increases; and as the position of a class decreases the percentage of those who belong to associations decreases. Forty-one per cent of the total Yankee City population are members of one or more associations. In the upper-upper class, 72 per cent of the people are members of associations; 71 per cent of the lower-upper, 64 of the upper-middle, 49 of the lower-middle, 39 of the upper-lower, and 22 per cent of the lower-lower are associational members. Hence there is a constant decrease in memberships from the upper-upper to lower-lower stratum.

Of all persons belonging to associations, those from the upper-upper class account for 2.55 per cent; the lower-upper, 2.72 per cent; the upper-middle, 16.01 per cent; the lower-middle, 33.63 per cent; the upper-lower, 31.41 per cent; and the lower-lower class, 13.68 per cent.[6]

6. It will be remembered that in Yankee City members of the upper-upper class compose 1.44 per cent of the population; the lower-upper, 1.56 per cent; the upper-middle, 10.22 per cent; the lower-middle, 28.12 per cent; the upper-

Persons in the lower-middle and upper-lower classes are the most numerous, each with about the same number of members of associations; together they compose about two thirds of all individuals in the association structure.

The upper and middle classes are represented in greater numbers than would be expected; the upper-lower class has fewer members; but the most marked drop appears in the lower-lower class. It seems that the association is a far less important structure to lower-lower-class persons than to those of other classes.

If we consider each class separately, we find that of the 357 associations, upper-upper-class members are in 22.96 per cent (82) of them; lower-uppers in 34.72 per cent (124); upper-middles in 72.26 per cent (258); lower-middles in 89.08 per cent (318); upper-lowers in 77.60 per cent (277); and lower-lower members are found in 59.12 per cent (211) of the associations.

Small associations of twenty members or less exceeded in number those of larger membership. Small associations constituted the greatest proportion of associations composed of members from the upper-middle, lower-middle, upper-lower, and lower-lower classes; medium associations were the most frequent among those where the upper-middle, lower-middle, and upper-lower classes were represented; and large associations, where members of the lower-upper, upper-middle, and lower-middle classes were present.

Small associations ordinarily had members from three classes, but a fourth class was often represented also. All one-class associations were small. Most associations of medium size, with from twenty-one to eighty members, had members from four classes; but some had members from three or five classes. Associations of more than eighty members most frequently had members from three, four, and five classes.

Thus it appears that as the associations increase in size, the opportunity increases for the members of the lower classes to move upward in the class hierarchy, inasmuch as in the large groups they are in contact with more individuals of the other

lower, 32.60 per cent; and the lower-lower class, 25.22 per cent. (Persons of unknown class represent 0.84 per cent.)

classes. In like manner, the large association furnishes a device by which members from the upper brackets of the class system may subordinate and control those inferior to them.

Of all classes, the two middle ones have the greatest representation in the medium and large associations. However, the association as a means of gaining status in the community is most popular with persons from the upper-middle and the lower-middle classes. Probably the members of these classes are the most desirous of upward social mobility.

Small associations more frequently have members from one

XXX. *Class and Number of Associations*

and two classes than do those of large and medium size. Their members are most often from the three lower classes.

An examination of Table 29 and Chart XXX shows that less than one third of the upper-upper-class persons who are associational members belong to but one association. This proportion increases as we descend the class hierarchy, and in the lower-lower class reaches its maximum with about three quarters of the individuals of this class. Conversely, a greater proportion of persons of the upper-upper class (7.43 per cent) belongs to ten or more associations than of any of the inferior classes. The amount becomes progressively less as we approach

TABLE 29

The Number of Associations to Which the Members of Each Class Belonged

	UU		LU		UM		LM		UL		LL		Total
1 Association	1.44	32.56	1.57	33.15	10.66	38.24	33.22	56.74	35.06	64.15	18.05	73.85	3,950
	57		62		421		1,312		1,385		713		57.47
2 Associations	2.08	18.29	2.40	19.79	17.09	23.89	34.77	23.14	33.33	23.76	10.33	16.91	1,539
	32		37		263		535		513		159		22.39
3 Associations	2.98	11.43	2.53	9.09	25.48	15.53	38.31	11.12	24.59	7.64	6.11	4.36	671
	20		17		171		257		165		41		9.76
4 Associations	4.91	9.14	6.44	11.23	29.45	8.72	35.58	5.02	18.71	2.83	4.91	1.70	326
	16		21		96		116		61		16		4.74
5 Associations	8.91	7.43	8.22	6.42	40.41	5.36	26.71	1.69	13.01	0.88	2.74	0.43	146
	13		12		59		39		19		4		2.12
6 Associations	7.55	4.57	9.44	5.35	39.62	3.81	31.13	1.43	8.49	0.42	3.77	0.43	106
	8		10		42		33		9		4		1.54

TABLE 29 (Continued)

	UU		LU		UM		LM		UL		LL		Total
7 Associations	12.50	2.86	20.00	4.28	27.50	1.00	32.50	0.56	7.50	0.14	—		40 0.58
	5		8		11		13		3				
8 Associations	12.12	2.29	18.18	3.21	48.49	1.45	9.09	0.13	6.06	0.09	6.06	0.21	33 0.48
	4		6		16		3		2		2		
9 Associations	24.14	4.00	24.14	3.74	37.93	1.00	10.34	0.13	—		3.45 0.11		29 0.42
	7		7		11		3				1		
10+ Associations	38.24	7.43	20.59	3.74	32.35	1.00	2.94	0.04	5.88	0.09	—		34 0.50
	13		7		11		1		2				
Total	2.55		2.72		16.01		33.63		31.41		13.68		6,874
	175		187		1,101		2,312		2,159		940		

the lower-lower class where there is none at all. Furthermore, when persons of the upper-upper class belong to a large number of associations the proportion of individuals from other classes in these associations increases, but this pattern tends to shift further down in the class system until it exactly reverses itself in the lower-lower class. Over one third of all persons with memberships in the associational structure are from the lower-middle and less than one third from the upper-lower classes. Those from the three largest classes—lower-middle, upper-lower, and upper-middle—compose 81.05 per cent of the total.

More members of the upper-lower class belong to but one association than the members of any other class; and as the rank of the class increases the number of individuals belonging to only one diminishes in each succeeding class. For members who belong to two, to three, and to four associations, the lower-middle class ranks first. The number of such members grows consecutively smaller in each class as we approach either end of the class structure. The upper-middle class exceeds all others for persons belonging to five, six, eight, and nine associations; and, as we ascend or descend in the class hierarchy, the number of individuals in each class becomes successively smaller. The largest number of persons with seven associational memberships is in the lower-middle class. There are more persons of the upper-upper class who belonged to ten or more associations than in any other class. There is none in the lower-lower class.

Of all classes, persons of the upper-upper and lower-upper who hold associational memberships tend to belong to the greatest number of groups, particularly to nine, ten, or more. However, of those who belong to six or less, the representation in these two classes is small. These two classes are more active in the associational structure within the limits of their size than are any others. The smallness of their numbers permits persons of the upper classes to make an effort as a group to exert control over the society through this medium. Although the members of these two classes often do not hold offices in the controlling hierarchies of the various groups, they nevertheless effectively exercise certain pressures upon those who do.

4. How the Men of the Six Classes Belonged to Associations

THERE are 3,648 males (53.07 per cent) and 3,226 females (46.93 per cent) who belonged to associations.[7]

In each of the six classes, males who were members of one association ranked first (see Chart XXXI); those who were members of two ranked second; of three, ranked third; and of four, ranked fourth. However, the proportion of males in each

XXXI. *Number of Men in Each Class Who Belonged to One or More Associations*

class who belonged to one association increases as we descend the class scale from the upper-upper class to the lower-lower. The representation in each class is almost equal for those who belonged to two associations. It is higher in the upper and middle classes than in the lower for those with three and with four memberships. It is also higher in the three upper classes than in the three lower for five and six memberships, and larger for seven, eight, nine, and ten or more in the two upper classes than in the four inferior classes.

7. Of the 3,648 males, 2,100 (57.56 per cent) belonged to but one association; 820 (22.48 per cent) belonged to two; 336 (9.21 per cent) to three; 182 (4.99 per cent) to four; 61 (1.67 per cent) to five; 67 (1.84 per cent) to six; 20 (0.55 per cent) to seven; 22 (0.60 per cent) to eight; 21 (0.58 per cent) to nine; and 19 (0.52 per cent) belonged to ten or more associations.

5. How the Women of the Six Classes Belonged to Associations

THE number of women who belonged to but one association ranked first; as the number of memberships in associations increases, the percentage of women holding memberships decreases. There is but one exception in the regularity of this rank order: females who belonged to ten or more associations ranked eighth while those who belonged to eight ranked ninth and those who belonged to nine ranked tenth.[8]

XXXII. *Number of Women in Each Class Who Belonged to One or More Associations*

Females who belonged to one, two, three, and seven associations were most frequent in the lower-middle class. Those who belonged to four, five, and six predominated in the upper-middle; those women with eight memberships in associations were most liberally represented in both upper-upper and upper-middle classes; and those with nine, in both upper-upper and lower-upper classes. Females with ten or more asso-

---

8. Of the 3,226 females who were members of associations, 1,850 (57.36 per cent) were members of one association; 719 (22.29 per cent) were members of two; 335 (10.38 per cent) were members of three; 144 (4.46 per cent) were members of four; 85 (2.63 per cent) were members of five; 39 (1.21 per cent) were members of six; 20 (0.62 per cent) were members of seven; 11 (0.34 per cent) belonged to eight associations; 8 (0.25 per cent) to nine; and 15 (0.46 per cent) were members of ten or more associations.

ciational memberships were in the greatest number in the upper-upper class.

Women were most frequent members of associations in the three superior classes while the men led in the three inferior classes.

Let us compare the relative frequency of male and female membership in the associations in each of the six classes. In the upper-upper class, 58.86 per cent of the individuals who were members of associations were women, and 41.14 per cent were men. Half (50.27 per cent) of the individuals who were members of associations in the lower-upper class were women, and half were men (49.73 per cent). In the upper-middle class, the women formed 53.22 per cent of the individuals in associations, and men formed 46.78 per cent.

In all three of the higher classes, there were more women in associations than men. In all three of the lower classes there were more men than women.

Over 46 per cent (46.84 per cent) of the lower-middle individuals in associations were women, and 53.16 per cent were men; in the upper-lower class 45.43 per cent were women, and 54.57 per cent were men; and in the lower-lower class, 40.32 per cent were women, and 59.68 per cent were men.

The women in the three top classes demonstrate their superior class status by organizing their abundant leisure, while the women of the three inferior classes must hold a job, work at home, or both. Furthermore, the women's associations in which the upper classes participate contribute greatly to the control exercised by the higher classes over the inferior ones. A wife who is attempting to climb socially by means of the Woman's Club or the Garden Club will subordinate herself to the women over her to gain social status; and she will attempt to influence her husband to express the proper sentiments in his relations with these women's husbands to prevent any interference with her social ambitions. This behavior was frequently observed.

A few well-placed women at the top who belong to an interlocking set of associations exercise great power in a community like Yankee City.

The males of the three top classes are frequent associational members; but while the males in the three bottom classes make an effort to participate in the activities of the community, the women are expected to keep more closely to the home and stay within the family structure.

6. The Ethnic, Religious, Sex, and Age Composition of the Associations

THE social characteristics of members of associations studied included: class, age, sex, religion, and ethnic affiliation. We will analyze the associational membership by using these elements as criteria.

An examination of the 357 associations according to sex and age shows that 40 per cent (143) had all male members; 31 per cent (110) entirely female; and 29 per cent (104) had both male and female members (see Table 30).

TABLE 30

Sex and Age Composition of Associations

	Both Sexes	Male	Female	Totals
All Ages	22.11 71.87 23	1.40 6.25 2	6.36 21.88 7	8.96 32
Subadult	24.04 25.00 25	23.08 33.00 33	38.18 42.00 42	28.01 100
Adult	53.85 24.89 56	75.52 48.00 108	55.46 27.11 61	63.03 225
Totals	29.13 104	40.06 143	30.81 110	357

There is a strong tendency for associations with subadult membership to be small and for those with membership of all ages to be medium-sized. The associations with exclusively male and those with exclusively female membership show a slight tendency to be of small size; associations which are of both sexes tend to be large or medium in size.

Of the 12,876 members, 33.90 per cent (4,365) belonged to associations of male membership; 25 per cent (3,219) to those of female membership; and 41.10 per cent (5,292) to associations whose members were males and females.

According to the ethnic composition, the 357 associations fall into twenty different types. Eight types are composed of members from one ethnic group exclusively and are either entirely Yankee or confined to members of a single ethnic group. The remaining twelve types have a membership consisting of two or more groups which may be made up of natives and ethnics or entirely of two or more ethnic groups.

More than a third of the associations with only native members are connected with one or more of the local Protestant churches (all of which were predominantly Yankee in membership). The remaining native associations include seven of the so-called secret societies, such as certain lodges of the Masons and the Odd Fellows. These secret societies and several other formal groups, such as the Langdon Club and the Daughters of the American Revolution, are partly closed Yankee associations; they may purposely bar all ethnics from their rolls by common consent even though no formal recognition is given to such restrictions in their charters. In many instances, though by no means all, the entire community is well aware of these membership restrictions and considerable antagonism is aroused among socially ambitious ethnics. The Yankees have the advantage of prestige gained by having been the earliest arrivals in Yankee City and are the most prominent of all groups in the upper bracket of the class structure.

Twenty-three of the fifty-four entirely native associations have some members from the upper-upper class; fifteen have members from below the upper-middle class. Although members of all six classes are found in some of these groups, a large proportion of the members are from the top strata of the class hierarchy.

The Langdon Club has more than one hundred male members from the three upper classes, and is a focal point of ethnic antagonism to exclusively native associations. Mr. Goffrey, an upper-middle person who is first-generation Irish and a local politician of some prominence, said to an interviewer of

Yankee extraction while passing the Langdon Clubhouse: "Don't you belong to the Langdon Club? You're not a Catholic! All the best people you know! such as Joe Horn and Alfred Lincoln—they like to hit the bottle pretty well! Nothing but the best!" Mr. Goffrey preferred to think of his religion as a barrier to his entrance into the club. There were, however, no ethnic members; and the fact that he was not a native would seem sufficient to prevent his becoming a member. Of twenty-five associations whose members were from one or all of the upper-upper, lower-upper, or upper-middle classes, fifteen were of native membership only. Probably ethnic antagonism is in part directed toward native associations as symbols of the class superiority of the Yankees in the community.

The closed ethnic associations usually have somewhat different purposes from associations of exclusively native membership. While certain native groupings operate largely to protect the Yankees from ethnic invasion, their security in the community is not threatened as is that of the immigrant groups whose knowledge of the mores and customs of Yankee City is confused by the influence of those of their native lands. These people cannot adjust themselves immediately to the community which is new to them, and they seek security by the formation of closed ethnic associations. Succeeding generations who grow up in and adjust to the community are much less dependent upon such associations.[9]

Many associations which were once open only to Irish or French-Canadian members have broadened their membership through religious affiliation and now include Catholics from the native and from other ethnic groups. One of the two Catholic churches in Yankee City was established by the Irish, the other by the French Canadians, and persons of other groups who are members of them also tend toward association with the Irish or the French Canadians. Thus while the Ancient Order of Hibernians remains a closed Irish group, the Knights of Columbus, although still largely Irish, has a sprinkling of native, French, Italian, and Polish members.

Those associations whose members are all Yankee or who are from a single ethnic group tend to have a smaller member-

9. The ethnic associations are fully treated in the volume on ethnic minorities.

Associations of Yankee City 341

ship.[10] The closed Irish and French-Canadian associations do not follow this pattern but possess memberships of medium size.

Twelve of the fifty-eight associations whose members are Irish and native are satellites of the church structure; eleven of these are of the Protestant faith, one Catholic. These twelve associations are used in part by the churches which are their parent structure as proselytizing devices. Native and Irish intermarriage has been partially responsible for the mixed membership of these groups.

There is another representative group of associations which is independent and not an adjunct to the churches. The Homeopathic Hospital Association is composed of Irish and Yankee members. It is a group organized to aid and assist one of the two local hospitals. It is a community-wide organization operated for the benefit of all the inhabitants. The natives and Irish, the two largest groups of the community, have taken it upon themselves to support this hospital. The members of this group were from the upper-middle, lower-middle, and upper-lower classes.

Associations with native and Jewish members and no others include only adult groups. All of them have members of the upper-upper class. The Y. M. C. A. auxiliary, one example, in-

10. Associations with both native and Irish members accounted for 16.25 per cent (58) of the total number of associations and had 9.35 per cent (1,204) of all members; those associations with native and French-Canadian members, for 2.24 per cent (8), and for 0.96 per cent (124) of the members; native and Jewish associations, for 0.84 per cent (3), and for 0.71 per cent (91) of the members; native, Irish, and French-Canadian associations, for 14.01 per cent (50), and for 13.98 per cent (1,801) of the members; native, Irish, French-Canadian, and Jewish associations, for 3.08 per cent (11), and for 4.47 per cent (575) of the members; native, Irish, and Jewish associations, for 3.36 per cent (12), and for 5.72 per cent (737) of the members; native, Irish, French-Canadian, Italian, and Polish associations, for 17.09 per cent (61), and for 33.54 per cent (4,320) of the members; and native, Armenian, Irish, and French-Canadian associations, for 5.60 per cent (20), and for 5.78 per cent (744) of the members. Associations with Irish and French-Canadian members accounted for 0.84 per cent (3) of the total number of associations and for 0.58 per cent (75) of the entire associational membership.

Those associations with Irish and other ethnics but no natives composed 1.12 per cent (4) of all associations and 0.70 per cent (90) of the members; those with Jewish and other ethnics but no natives, 0.28 per cent (1), and 0.12 per cent (16) of the members. Associations with natives in combination with other ethnic groups not listed in the above enumeration numbered 11.76 per cent (42) of the total associations and had 12.40 per cent (1,596) of all association membership.

cludes women of the various Protestant churches who carry out programs to aid the Y. M. C. A. They may donate money or prepare meals for meetings of the Y. M. C. A. and its satellite associations. Other associations of native and Jewish members are wholly Protestant; intermarriage of the two groups and identification of some of the Jews with the natives partly explain this situation.

The Health Center is an association organized by members of the three upper classes who make donations of money and campaign for further donations from other members of the community. The money is spent on medical care of the poor, most of whom are in subordinate classes.

Associations whose members were Yankees and French Canadians included two which were independent of connections with other associations or structures and six which were satellites. Four of the latter had churches of the Protestant faith as their parent organizations. The other two were satellites of other associations and had a membership which was Catholic and Protestant. Five of the associations were adult in membership, two were subadult, and one had both adult and subadult members. As with the native and Irish associations, the church appears to have made use of the secondary association to proselytize. Of all eight of these associations, six had only Protestant members. When the French Canadians are members of associations in combination with Yankees only, there is a strong tendency for them to leave the Catholic for the Protestant faith.

Some of the fifty associations with native, Irish, and French-Canadian members had only Protestant members; others, only Catholic; while still others had combinations of both. Outstanding are church satellites: fifteen of the fifty associations were in this category; fourteen were satellites of churches of the Protestant faith; while one was a satellite of a Catholic church. Again, proselytizing, particularly on the part of the Protestant churches, is practiced.

The Men's Club of the Second Church, a satellite of this order, is affiliated to this Protestant church. It holds meetings at the church building, where its members also worship.

Associations with native, Irish, and Jewish members included a large proportion of the three upper classes. Of the twelve associations with this ethnic membership composition, six had members from these classes, and two were made up of members who ranged from the upper-upper through the lower-middle class. The remaining four came from the lower part of the class structure, below the upper-middle class. Three of these four were the only associations of this group which had a subadult membership. There was but one association of the twelve whose members were of all ages; those with adult membership accounted for eight.

A typical association with Yankee, Irish, and Jewish members is the Yankee City Hospital Society. Its members are adult males and females from the upper-upper, lower-upper, and upper-middle classes. This is the larger and wealthier of two hospital groups found in Yankee City. In this situation the members of an association take over the responsibility of caring for the people in the community in times of crises. Thus they consolidate their own position at the top of the class hierarchy and subordinate the lower classes who are dependent upon them.

The Irish belonged to a far greater number of associations in combination with the natives than did the Jews, but the Jews were in more associations whose members were from the upper half of the class structure. When both the Irish and Jews are in associations with natives, a significantly large number of these groups have members who are in the upper-upper and lower-upper classes.

Of the eleven associations whose members were Yankees, Irish, French Canadians, and Jews, seven had members from the upper-middle class or classes below, and four had upper-upper-class members. The Rotary Club is one of those found in this group. Its members are chosen as a representative cross section of Yankee City business life. It includes only persons in or above the lower-middle class and excludes businessmen who deal primarily with people of their own ethnic group.

There were twenty associations with members who were natives, Armenians, Irish, and French Canadians. Of these, eight were adult, five were subadult, and seven were both adult and subadult in membership. The church was outstandingly the primary structure of the secondary associations in this group, and eleven of these associations were satellites of various Protestant churches. The Ladies Aid Society of the Second Church of Yankee City offers a typical example. Armenians came to Yankee City during the period of the massacres in their homeland. The funds to effect this migration were raised by the Protestant churches and their satellite associations. Once these immigrants arrived in the community, they were aided in adjusting to the society by those groups and in many cases became affiliated with them as members.

Sixty-one associations had natives, Irish, French Canadians, Italians, and Poles. This was the largest group of associations according to ethnic type, and it included members of all the six classes. There were associations in this type whose membership was male, female, and both male and female in combination, as well as adult, subadult, and both adult and subadult. All structural types were also represented, including independent associations, co-ordinates, and parents and satellites of the associational, economic, church, and school structures. The Kiwanis Club, the Elks, and many of the Boy Scout troops were in this group of associations.

Only three associations were limited to Irish and French-Canadian members. None had members above the upper-middle class, and all included lower-lower people. Two were of subadult; one had both adult and subadult members; and all three had both males and females. These associations were benefit groups organized for insurance and burial purposes. They financed themselves by holding public or semipublic card parties, dances, and other entertainments. Saint Jeans Society (Juniors) was typical of these associations. It was predominantly French-Canadian and was identified with this group. Irish members, for the most part, were members of this association because of intermarriage with the French Canadians.

Four associations which had no natives but had Irish and combinations of ethnic members are not mentioned above. These had male members from the lower-middle, upper-lower, and lower-lower classes; two of them were adult associations, two were subadult groups. The Catholic Boys Club (Baseball), an example of this type, was a satellite of one of the Catholic churches. It was subordinate to the Catholic Boys Club, a satellite of the church. Its activity centered around the playing of baseball with other similar groups.

There was but one association whose members were Jewish and other ethnic but not Yankee. Its members were adult males from the upper-middle, lower-middle, and upper-lower classes. This was one of two lodges of the Knights of Pythias in Yankee City and was almost entirely Jewish in membership. The Jews had taken over this lodge from a group which at one time had been predominantly Yankee. With the influx of Jewish members, the natives withdrew to form another separate lodge which came to include Irish and French-Canadian members as well. It seems significant that in the lower part of the class structure the Jews superimposed their ways upon an association (which the natives did not accept), while in the associations whose membership was from the three upper classes, the Jews who belonged took over the Yankee pattern even to the point of giving up their religion.

There were forty-two associations whose membership was native in combination with ethnics other than those previously described. They included the many associations which lacked any ethnic restrictions. The Greeks and Negroes, however, were conspicuously absent in most of them. All but one had members from the lower classes, and that one had only lower-middle membership. Only eight had members from the two upper classes and, with one exception, they included members from all inferior classes through the lower-lower. The exception was one group with lower-upper, upper-middle, and upper-lower members. These associations had all sex and age combinations in their membership; they also represented every structural type. Fully one third of these associations were organized around the playing of some athletic game as their central activity. Only seven were church satellites, and six of these were secondary associations of one of the Catholic churches. The American Legion and its auxiliary are examples of associations which have members from the Yankees and all, or almost all, ethnic groups. Their membership is restricted to those persons who participated in the World War crisis of 1917-18 or whose kin were in it.

All upper-class associations were predominantly native, but some had a few Irish members. Associations whose members were from the three upper classes formed a significantly large proportion of those whose members were natives and Jews and of those whose members were natives, Irish, and Jews; but, of the fifty-eight groups with native and Irish members, only one belonged to this combination of classes. It appears that the Jews were using the associational structure more effectively than others as a means of contact with the top of the class

TABLE 31

Religious Faith and Associations

Religion	Number of Associations	Percentage
Protestant	124	34.74
Catholic	38	10.64
Jewish	9	2.52
Greek Orthodox	4	1.12
Protestant-Catholic	118	33.06
Protestant-Jewish	1	0.28
Catholic-Jewish	2	0.56
Protestant-Catholic-Jewish	35	9.80
Protestant-Catholic-Jewish-Greek	19	5.32
Protestant-Greek	1	0.28
Catholic-Greek	1	0.28
Protestant-Catholic-Greek	4	1.12
Protestant-Jewish-Greek	1	0.28
Totals	357	

system. It is significant, however, that the Jews who participated in these upper and upper-middle-class associations were no longer orthodox in their religion, while the Irish in these and similar groups remained Catholics.

The 357 associations in Yankee City fell into thirteen religious types according to whether their members were affiliated with one of the four religions or with a combination of them.

Somewhat more than one third of the 357 associations were

Protestant, and almost one half had members who belonged to but one of the four religions (see Table 31). More than one fifth of all members belonged to wholly Protestant groups, and almost two fifths to associations whose members were of but a single religion. Associations whose members were Protestant and Catholic accounted for almost one third of the total number of associations and had almost one quarter of all associational members. Close to one tenth of the associations had Protestant, Catholic, and Jewish members and included almost one sixth of the entire associational membership. One twentieth of the 357 associations had members who were Protestant, Catholic, Jewish, and Greek Orthodox and had almost one fifth of all members. Associations whose members were of other religious combinations were few in number and in membership.

More than one third of the 357 associations had members exclusively of the Protestant faith. Almost half of the Protestant associations were satellites of the various Protestant churches of Yankee City. Members of these associations were of all classes and of every class type, the only exception being the type in which only upper-lower members occur. In this Protestant group were seventeen of the twenty-five associations whose membership was composed of upper-upper, or of upper-upper and lower-upper, or of upper-upper, lower-upper, and upper-middle-class people. Furthermore, this group included over one half of all associations whose memberships had one or more upper-upper or lower-upper-class members. All ages and both sexes are represented. All structural types are in this group.

Of the thirty-eight associations whose members were Catholic, fifteen were satellites of the two Catholic churches. None of these associations had upper-upper-class members, and there were only three in which lower-upper members were present. The largest number had members from the middle and lower classes.

The nine associations whose members were of the Jewish religion were made up of combinations of members of the upper-middle, lower-middle, and upper-lower classes.

The four associations whose members were of the Greek Orthodox religion had a predominance of lower-class members with an occasional upper-middle and lower-middle person.

The second largest group were those associations whose members were both Protestant and Catholic. Like those of exclusively Protestant members, persons of all classes and all class types were represented.

Two groups were Catholic and Jewish in membership. One was male adult in membership; the other, female subadult. Both were predominantly lower class in membership but had middle-class members as well. Members of the Jewish ethnic group who are not Jewish in religion are often in associations in combination with both Protestants and Catholics, but those of the Jewish religion infrequently are with Catholics.

There were thirty-five associations whose members were Protestants, Catholics, and Jews. Of these, over half included members of the upper-upper or the lower-upper classes. They comprised five of the twenty-five associations whose members were all upper-upper, or upper-upper with lower-upper members, or upper-upper, lower-upper, and upper-middle-class people. They were evenly divided between adults and subadults, and only two had both adults and subadults in their membership. There were male, female, and both male and female memberships.

The Yankee City Woman's Club and the Yankee City Country Club had Protestants, Catholics, and Jews in their membership and were composed of members from the higher classes. In earlier times, both had only native members. An informant remarked of the Woman's Club that "they brought the Irish in only because they needed their money."

The Rotary Club, the Chamber of Commerce, several Boy Scout troops, and six secondary associations of the school structure were among associations of this ethnic composition.

With the exception of those associations whose membership was entirely Protestant this group had the highest number of associations with upper-class members.

There were nineteen associations whose members were Protestant, Catholic, Jewish, and Greek Orthodox. Nine of them included either upper-upper or lower-upper members, but all of them had members who were from the lower-middle class or below. Eleven had members all of whom were from the lower-middle class or below.

The Veterans of Foreign Wars, the Shoemakers Association,

and the Loyal Order of Moose were typical associations of this group.

The Employed Boys of the Y. M. C. A. was the only association with Catholic and Greek Orthodox members.

The four associations whose members were Protestant, Catholic, and Greek Orthodox were predominantly middle and lower class. One of them included members from the lower-upper class.

The Odd Fellows was the one association whose members were Protestant, Jewish, and Greek Orthodox.

7. *The Class Membership of the Associations of Yankee City*

THE 357 associations comprised members who belonged to from one to six different classes. The nineteen different combinations of classes in the associations of Yankee City were listed at the beginning of this chapter. Those associations with members from three or four different classes accounted for the majority, or almost two thirds, of the associations and over three fifths of all members.[11] About one tenth of all associations had members from two classes, and another one tenth had members from five different classes. The associations composed of two classes accounted for only 6.07 per cent of the associational members, and those of five had about one sixth. The associations of two classes were very small, while those of five classes were of all sizes.

The associations whose members were from six classes were few in number, and those of one class, still fewer. There is a tendency for those with six classes to be large associations, and those with one to be small.

In most cases, the ranking of the associations in the various types corresponds closely to that for the number of memberships. There were, however, certain marked differences, such

---

11. Those who belonged to 1 class were in 9 associations (2.52 per cent) and comprised 55 (0.43 per cent) of the 12,876 members of the associational structure. Those who belonged to 2 classes were in 46 associations (12.89 per cent) and had 783 (6.08 per cent) of all members. Those who belonged to 3 classes had 119 (33.33 per cent) of the associations and 3,750 (29.12 per cent) of the members. Those belonging to 4 classes had 124 (34.74 per cent) with 4,446 (34.53 per cent); to 5 classes, 38 (10.64 per cent) with 2,124 (16.50 per cent); and those who belonged to all six classes accounted for 21 (5.88 per cent) of the associations and had 1,718 (13.34 per cent) of the total members of the associational structure.

as in Type 6 where the associations ranked sixth and the members second; this indicates that associations whose members included all classes from the lower-upper down through the lower-lower tended to be larger in size. Associations ranked eleventh, and the members, seventh, in Class Type 8. This means that associations whose members were from the lower-upper, upper-middle, and lower-middle classes tended to be large and of medium size. Associations in Class Type 12 ranked third, and the members, ninth; members from the upper-middle, lower-middle, and upper-lower classes belonged to smaller associations.

The evidence from male and female membership in associations points to the women's acting more exclusively than the men. There is only one upper-upper association, a woman's group. There are more women in associations that include only the two upper classes and the upper-middle class; on the other hand, the membership in those associations which extend from the two upper classes into the lower strata of the society are more favored by men. A glance at Table 32 shows this to be true; Class Types 4, 5, and 6 for the upper-upper class, 8, 9, and 10 for the lower-upper, 13 for the upper-middle, and 16 for the lower-middle are examples of high male membership in such associations.

Associations in which both sexes are members also tend to be more "democratic" and extend through several classes.

When the upper classes belong to exclusive clubs they do not join those with both men and women, but those with only men or only women. All of the hundred-odd people who belonged to associations which included only the two upper classes were in groups which included only males or only females (see Table 32). On the other hand, over half of the associations in Class Type 3 (upper-upper to upper-middle) included men and women.

8. *The Informal Association or Clique*

THE informal association is a group not organized on the basis of a formal set of rules which explicitly control the behavior of its members as do the rules of the formal association. Such rules define the methods of entrance and exit and state the obligations and privileges of the members during their membership. In general they formally relate (1) the members to each other and (2) their group to the larger society. By establishing these two forms of relationship they determine the internal and external formal structure of the association. The informal association has no formally stated rules but the members of the group are controlled by informal rules which regulate the behavior of the members of the group. On the basis of custom, certain things are done or not done with other intimate associates in the clique.

The informal association has no explicit entrance and exit rules or membership lists; its members are informally known to each other. The formal association has a name by which its members and others refer to it; the clique has no formal name but depends upon colloquial expressions for its names. The members of a clique refer to themselves as "our gang," "our crowd," "the bunch I go around with," and similar terms; they refer to members of other cliques as the "Jones crowd," or "Hill Street crowd," or the "Low Street gang."

Despite the apparent fluidity of its structure, the clique has a powerful control over individual behavior. An adolescent member of a boys' or girls' clique will sometimes defy his or her family to maintain the respect of clique mates, should the interests of the two groups run counter to each other; or a mature man or woman may renounce a family of lower status and class to satisfy the claims of his higher status clique.

The clique is one of the structures most favored by social climbers. Once in an association in which there were members of higher classes, a socially ambitious woman often found it possible to gain the "friendship" of certain people of prominence who would sponsor her entrance into their more intimate cliques. Constant identification with clique members of a higher class and possession of the "right" behavior symbols almost guarantee upward mobility. On the other hand, the complete exclusion of a person from the cliques of a class contributes to his downward mobility.

The cliques of Yankee City were divided among those in which all the members were male, all female, or both male and female. The cliques were also age graded in the same manner as the formal associations: some of them were of young people and children, and others were of the old and mature; but a few

TABLE 32
Membership in Associations by Sex in Each Class Type

		Male		Female		Male and Female		Totals
UU	C1	—	0.12	100.00 4		—		4
UU + LU	C2	38.78 38	0.87	61.22 60	1.86	—		98
UU − UM	C3	17.03 201	4.60	31.19 368	11.44	51.78 611	11.55	1,180
UU − LM	C4	42.43 580	13.30	25.60 350	10.87	31.97 437	8.26	1,367
UU − UL	C5	16.92 89	2.04	30.80 162	5.03	52.28 275	5.20	526
UU − LL	C6	35.74 614	14.07	19.21 330	10.25	45.05 774	14.63	1,718
LU + UM	C7	100.00 4	0.09	—		—		4
LU − LM	C8	45.67 290	6.64	6.77 43	1.34	47.56 302	5.71	635
LU − UL	C9	26.01 58	1.33	13.00 29	0.90	60.99 136	2.57	223
LU − LL	C10	26.41 422	9.67	17.83 285	8.85	55.76 891	16.83	1,598
UM + LM	C11	30.73 110	2.52	25.70 92	2.86	43.57 156	2.95	358

TABLE 32 (Continued)

		Male		Female		Male and Female		Totals
UM – UL	C12	2.59	22.03 / 113	4.10	25.73 / 132	5.06	52.24 / 268	513
UM – LL	C13	28.46	43.48 / 1,242	27.68	31.20 / 891	13.65	25.32 / 723	2,856
LM	C14	0.11	17.24 / 5	0.75	82.76 / 24		—	29
LM + UL	C15	1.40	28.64 / 61	4.04	61.03 / 130	0.42	10.33 / 22	213
LM – LL	C16	10.97	33.68 / 479	9.32	21.10 / 300	12.15	45.22 / 643	1,422
UL	C17	0.11	100.00 / 5		—		—	5
UL – LL	C18	1.12	44.54 / 49	0.47	13.64 / 15	0.87	41.82 / 46	110
LL	C19	0.11	29.41 / 5	0.12	23.53 / 4	0.15	47.06 / 8	17
Totals		100.00	33.90 / 4,365	100.00	25.00 / 3,219	100.00	41.10 / 5,292	12,876

had members who were young, mature, and old. Some of the cliques were entirely Yankee, others had members from only one ethnic group, and still others were of mixed ethnicity.

Clique members listed in our study of Yankee City amounted to 22,063. There were 757 upper-upper-class members; 897 lower-upper-class members; 2,744 upper-middle-class members; 7,041 lower-middle-class members; 7,333 upper-lower-class members; and 3,291 lower-lower-class members.

Clique participation tended to be in one or two classes (see

354   *The Social Life of a Modern Community*

Chart **XXXIII**). The upper-upper class led all others for the proportion of its clique members who were in one-class groups (37 per cent). It was followed by the lower-lower class; however, a slightly higher percentage (39 per cent) were in cliques with lower-upper members. The other upper-upper clique com-

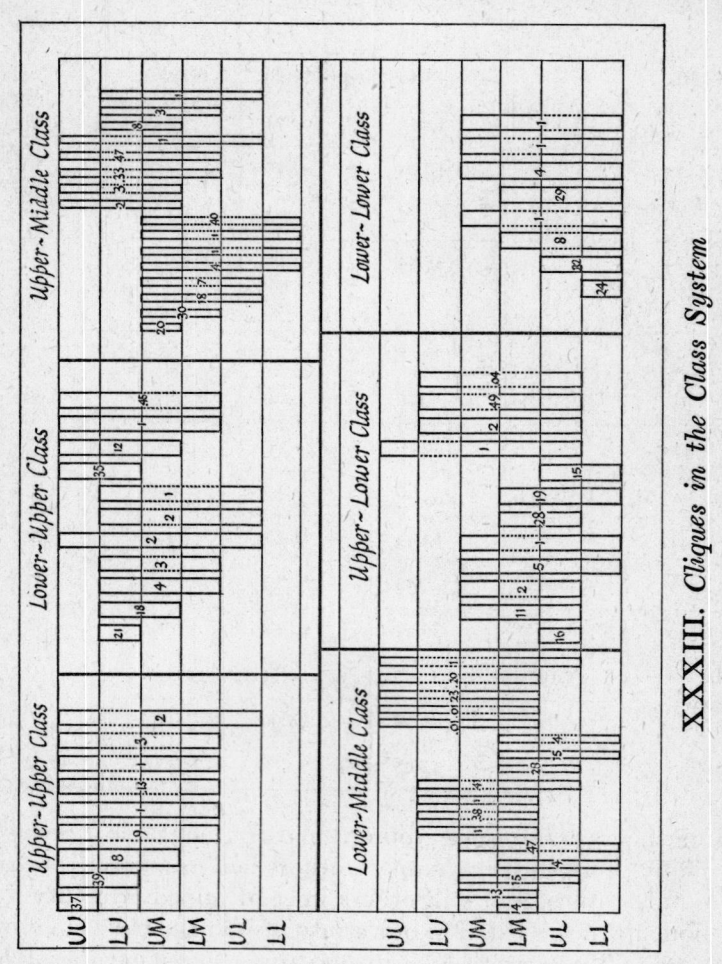

XXXIII. *Cliques in the Class System*

binations were far fewer and, with two exceptions, unimportant. Chart **XXXIII** shows how the total population of Yankee City was organized in cliques. The small rectangles show the class spread of the members and the numbers in each give the percentages of the clique members from various classes. The lower-upper class tended to participate more with the upper-upper class (36 per cent) than with the upper-middle (18 per cent). All the other classes participated downward more than they did upward in cliques.

Clique membership ordinarily held an individual in his own class or permitted relations with a class above or below. There was relatively little membership in cliques between members of two classes when one or more intermediate strata were missing. Cliques, however, do allow upward mobile people to form intimate associations with people above them and thereby improve their chances of climbing.

XVII

THE CHURCH AND SCHOOL IN YANKEE CITY

1. The Church in the Class System

THIRTEEN churches of four different faiths cared for the religious needs of the Yankee City community. The majority were of the Protestant faith and comprised eleven congregations; two churches were Catholic, one Greek Orthodox, and one Jewish. The Greek Orthodox and the Jewish religions were not included in this statistical study because our material was incomplete at the time of the church analysis.

The first Catholic church was formed by the Irish immigrants to Yankee City in the middle of the nineteenth century, and is now the largest single church in the community. Commonly referred to as the Irish Catholic church, it was attended by other ethnics of the Catholic faith including most Italians, a very few French Canadians, and a few Poles. Socially ambitious members of these ethnic groups attended it rather than the other Catholic church.

The second Catholic church was founded by the French Canadians who came from the province of Quebec as early as 1880. Many of these people still spoke French and lived in the Riverbrook and Uptown sections of Yankee City, the area of the largest concentration of ethnics in the community.

The First Church of Yankee City was the oldest Protestant organization in the community. Located in Oldtown (the earliest settled section of Yankee City), many of its members were families descended from first settlers who had attended for several generations. It was one of three Congregationalist churches. This denomination was first to establish itself in the community.

Old South Church, located in Uptown, was Presbyterian. This church was notable because certain upper-upper-class families supported it financially and paid for repairs and upkeep of the building. The building has considerable importance in community symbolism because it is old and is related to the ancestors and ancestral objects. It also drew members from the lower-class Yankees as well as ethnics who were concentrated in the Uptown and Riverbrook sections of Yankee City in which this church was located.

Central Church, the newest of the three Congregational churches, had the most modern building and equipment of any church in Yankee City.

The Homeville Church was the third and last organization of the Congregational denomination and was located in the solidly middle-class residential section of Homeville. It was built and endowed by a wealthy upper-class family who formerly resided in this section.

The Methodist Church was the only one in the Riverbrook section of the town, and it drew its congregation mostly from the lower classes of this section. Its membership included a large proportion of Yankee Riverbrookers and a few individuals from various ethnic groups which resided in its vicinity. The class position of this church was closer to the bottom of the class hierarchy than that of any other Protestant church.

The Baptist Church was one of the more recent Protestant churches; it had few upper-class members. It had dropped in membership, probably because some people in the community placed a low status evaluation upon membership in this church.

St. Paul's Church, the only Episcopal church in Yankee City, was composed of more upper-upper and lower-upper-class members than any other church of the community. Great emphasis was placed by this group upon the preservation of symbols of antiquity. This was most apparent when their old wooden church building, erected in the early years of Yankee City's establishment, burned down. In its reconstruction, the plan of the destroyed wooden building was faithfully followed except that it was made of stone. Certain ornaments saved from the original building have been preserved as relics and placed on exhibit in the new church building in receptacles which guard them from destruction. The importance of ancestry may be seen in this behavior in that the upper class dominated St. Paul's Church and related itself to the past history of the Yankee City community and placed itself above the other churches which existed there.

The Unitarian Church was the only one which could offer

competition in any way to St. Paul's Episcopal Church. It was housed in one of the most beautiful buildings of the community, designed by Bulfinch, the architect for many other noteworthy buildings in early New England. Although the Unitarian Church boasted a rather large membership, few people attended its regular Sunday services. It was, however, very well endowed, and many upper-class members of Yankee City held themselves responsible for preserving it as an ancestral object.

The Christian Science Church was the most recently established of all churches in Yankee City. Although it had a small membership, mostly from the upper-middle and lower-middle classes, it was gaining rather than losing in class position.

The two churches with the largest proportion of upper-class individuals in their congregations have devised a method of limiting the number of persons from the lower parts of the class hierarchy. St. Paul's Church had a branch in Newtown called Christ's Chapel which functioned as a mission and was composed of many persons from the upper-lower and lower-lower classes. The Unitarian Church also had a mission unit called St. Peter's Chapel which was located in the Riverbrook section and was also composed of many people from the lower classes.

All churches save the Christian Science have had a large number of satellite associations connected with them. These organizations offered all kinds of secular activity to the church members and helped to bring more people into church affairs. While the churches restricted themselves to sacred rituals at their meetings, they were enabled, through these satellite associations, to enter other activities. Such satellite associations not only held existing members to these various churches, but also acted as proselytizing agencies in attracting new members from other churches. The nine Protestant churches had many more of these organizations than those of the Catholic faith although satellites of Catholic churches had larger memberships.

Our statistics show that about 53 per cent of the 10,866 Yankee City church attendants were women.[1]

1. Christ's Chapel, which was connected with St. Paul's Church, and St. Peter's Chapel, connected with the Unitarian Church, are included in these fifteen churches. The Greek Orthodox and Jewish churches have not been included in the above statistical analysis. Christ's Chapel and St. Peter's Chapel were included in the St. Paul's and Unitarian totals.

The Catholic and Methodist churches are predominantly lower class, the latter the lower-lower class only. The First, Central, and Homeville churches are favored by the middle classes. St. Paul's and the Unitarian churches are favored by the upper and middle classes and avoided by the lower ones. The Christian Science Church is favored by the upper-middle class.

Upper-upper-class persons who attend the various churches in Yankee City are significantly predominant in St. Paul's Episcopal Church and the Unitarian Church. They are significantly absent in the two Catholic churches, the Central Church, and the Homeville Congregational Church. Lower-upper-class persons attend St. Paul's, the Unitarian, and the Central churches in significantly high numbers and are significantly low in the Immaculate Conception and St. Aloysius Catholic churches (see Table 33).

Upper-middle-class persons have a significantly high attendance at the First Church, the Central, Homeville, Baptist, Unitarian, and Christian Science churches. Upper-middle-class individuals are significantly low in attendance at the two Catholic churches and at one Protestant church, the Methodist. Lower-middle-class persons have a significantly high membership in St. Paul's, First Church, and the Central and Homeville churches but a significantly low attendance at the two Catholic churches.

Upper-lower-class individuals attend the two Catholic churches in significantly high numbers, but are significantly low in attendance at all Protestant churches with the exception of the Methodist. Lower-lower-class individuals are significantly high in attendance at the two Catholic churches and the four Protestant churches including the Old South, Homeville, Methodist, and Baptist churches. Lower-lower-class individuals have a significantly low attendance at St. Paul's, the Unitarian, Central, and First churches.

2. The Schools of Yankee City

THE Yankee City High School is located in the approximate center of population in the Business District. It draws its students from three elementary schools located in the Middletown section, the Business District, and the Homeville area. In addi-

TABLE 33
Class Composition of Church Membership

H — Significantly High
L — Significantly Low
— — Non-Significant
0 — Not Present

	Immaculate Conception 1	St. Aloysius 2	First Church 3	Old South 4	Central 5	Belleville 6	Methodist 7	Baptist 8	St. Paul 9	Unitarian 10	Christian Scientist 11
UU	L	L	—	—	L	L	0	0	H	—	0
LU	L	L	—	—	H	—	—	—	H	H	—
UM	L	L	H	—	H	H	L	H	—	H	H
LM	L	L	H	—	H	H	—	—	H	—	—
UL	H	H	L	L	L	L	—	L	L	L	L
LL	H	H	L	H	L	H	H	H	L	L	—

tion to these city grammar schools, there are two parochial schools, financed and operated by the Catholic churches of the community. There are no parochial high schools in Yankee City and boys and girls who attend the parochial grammar schools pass on to the city high school for advanced education. The latter draws its students from all segments of the society and from all sections of Yankee City.

Few subadult persons from the two upper classes attend the local high school. Most of them go to private schools in Boston or to boarding school for a period covering at least the last two years of the high school course.

The elementary school in the Middletown area is composed mostly of lower-class Yankee and ethnic students from the Riverbrook, Middletown, Downtown, and Uptown sections of the city. It is in these sections that the most recently arrived ethnic groups are concentrated, together with many of the lower-class Yankees. A grammar school located in the Business District has a cross section of subadults of different social types in Yankee City, with Yankees of all classes and persons from all ethnic groups. An elementary school located in Homeville is largely attended by middle-class Yankees and Irish who come from Middletown, Centerville, Newtown, and Hill Street.

The parochial school, operated by the Immaculate Conception Church, is predominantly Irish, while the school operated by the St. Aloysius Church is attended almost entirely by French Canadians.

The Yankee City High School offers four courses in its program of study. They are the Latin, scientific, commercial, and general courses. The Latin course concentrated on such subjects as languages, history, and mathematics. Over two thirds of the upper-middle-class youth take this course, and upper-upper and lower-upper-class girls usually make it their choice. This course is not designed to train students for business careers but to give them a cultural background preparatory for college. More girls than boys are enrolled in this course.

The scientific course offers special technical preparation for college work and includes a maximum of mathematics, physics, and chemistry, with secondary subjects such as languages and English.

A wealthy upper-class resident of the community some generations ago left a sizable amount of money, the interest from which was to be spent in payment of college tuition and other expenses for Protestant students of Yankee City. The Wright Fund, as it is called, was designated entirely for scientific study and, therefore, applied to male rather than female students. Boys of all classes take this course, with upper-upper and lower-upper students in the majority. Boys from the three upper classes usually prepare themselves for and attend the Massachusetts Institute of Technology, Harvard, and Yale, while boys of the three lower classes more often go to Northwestern Y. M. C. A. College where the study programs are scheduled to allow them to alternate work and school attendance at intermittent periods.

The Wright Fund seems to be one of the many devices for subordinating people in the lower classes, particularly ethnic groups, and consolidating the control of the upper-class Yankee City persons.

The commercial course includes such subjects as typing, shorthand, bookkeeping, business arithmetic, and allied studies which teach skills suitable to business and office work. The commercial course is aimed to equip students to enter the economy of the society immediately upon completion. Most of the people taking the commercial course are girls who are training for secretarial and other jobs; but such courses are frequently taken in preparation for a year or two years' work at a business college.

The general course is a catchall for those students who attend the Yankee City High School but do not intend to prepare for college and have no particular objective in mind for earning a living.

In the Latin and commercial courses female students predominated, while all students in the scientific course and the larger proportion of those who took the general course were males. Of the 599 students, 290 (48.41 per cent) were male and 309 (51.59 per cent) were female.

The Yankee City High School was attended by students from all ethnic groups.[2] Yankee students composed somewhat

2. Of the 599 students, 263 (43.91 per cent) were native, and 336 (56.09 per cent) were ethnic. In the total enrollment, 181 (30.22 per cent) were Irish;

over two fifths of all who attended, and ethnic students had somewhat under three fifths. Native students had a significantly high representation in the scientific course, while ethnics were significantly low in number.

Of all ethnic groups, the Russians were significantly high and the Irish students were significantly low in representation in the scientific course. The French-Canadian and Jewish students were almost evenly represented. Italians were high in the commercial course and low in the scientific and general courses. The Armenian students were high in the Latin and commercial courses; Greeks were low in the general course.

The Polish students had a low representation in the Latin and scientific courses but were high in the commercial course. The Russians had no members in the Latin course and were heavily represented in the scientific and commercial courses.

The numbers of Italian, Armenian, Russian, and Negro students, however, were too small to be of any significance.

Most of the ethnic groups were affiliated with the Catholic Church and were not eligible for participation in the advantages of the Wright Fund and, therefore, could not be expected to rank high in the scientific course. Natives, however, ranked very high in this course because of the advantage of this fund.

Of all Yankee City High School students, none was found in the upper-upper class; 4 (0.67 per cent) were in the lower-upper class; 57 (9.52 per cent) belonged to the upper-middle; 217 (36.23 per cent) to the lower-middle; 245 (40.91 per cent) to the upper-lower; and 76 (12.69 per cent) belonged to the lower-lower class.

The commercial course attracted almost two fifths of the students, and the Latin course slightly over one fifth of all students.

With the exception of the lower-upper-class students, the percentage of each class who took the Latin course declines with lower position in the class hierarchy. Only four lower-upper students in all were represented, and one of the four took

---

49 (8.18 per cent) were French Canadian; 31 (5.18 per cent) were Jewish; 8 (1.34 per cent) were Italian; 3 (0.50 per cent) were Armenian; 22 (3.67 per cent) Greek; 29 (4.84 per cent) Polish; 7 (1.17 per cent) Russian; and 6 (1 per cent) were Negro.

the Latin course. Chart XXXIV shows that more than two thirds of the upper-middle-class students were in this course. Except for students of the lower-upper class, those of the lower-middle class had the highest proportion of persons who attended the scientific course, and upper-middle-class students were next in number. A larger proportion of persons from the middle classes than from the lower classes took the scientific course. Persons in the lower-upper class, however, were greatly

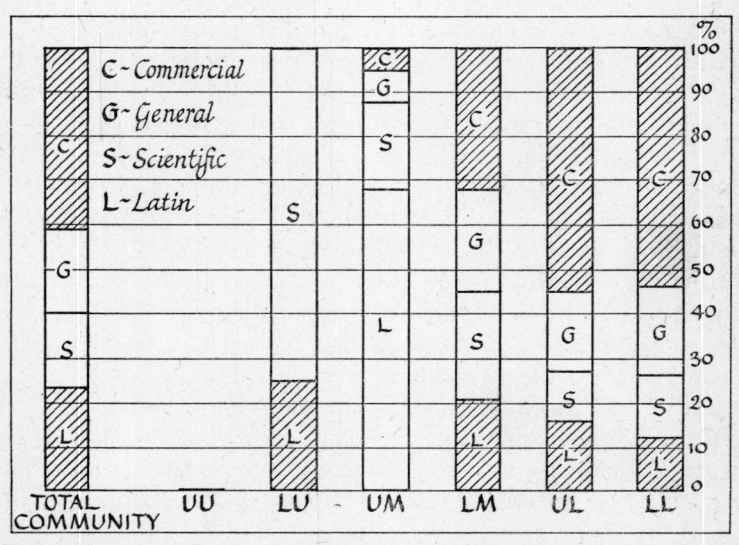

XXXIV. *The Courses Selected by High School Students from the Six Classes*

in the majority and had three fourths of their number within this group. More than half of the lower-class persons who attended the Yankee City High School took the commercial course, and about one third of the lower-middle-class students were in this course. Upper-middle-class students were not significantly represented in the commercial course, and students of the two upper classes did not appear.

Only students from the two middle and the two lower classes were enrolled in the general course, and those of the upper-middle class had a significantly small representation. Students of the upper part of the class hierarchy attended the Latin and scientific courses more frequently than those of the lower classes, while conversely those of the lower classes more frequently attended the commercial and general courses than did students of superior classes.

XVIII
THE POLITICAL STRUCTURE IN THE CLASS SYSTEM

1. *Voters and Officeholders*

THE political structure of Yankee City was composed of a group of officers and a group of voters. The officers were elected by the voters or appointed by other officers who had been elected by the voters. Voters were distinguished from nonvoters: the latter were people below twenty-one years of age, citizens who did not have the residence requirements, people of foreign birth who were not citizens, and residents who had failed to register or fulfill other technical requirements.

Although the voters among the three lower classes far outnumbered those in the three higher, they had a disproportionately small percentage of officers in the political hierarchy. In other words, the upper classes held a greater proportion of the higher offices than their numbers in the voting and general population would by mere chance allow them. Indeed, as the importance of the political offices increased, the proportion of upper-class officeholders increased. Class is therefore an important factor in Yankee City politics.

The political structure is ordinarily the only one which is thought of as being coterminous with the totality of the community, as distinguished from the segmentary character of other structures, such as the family, associations, and economic organizations. The functions of government in our own society are numerous; the most important ones are listed below. They are: (1) Administration of the legal sanctions, incorporated in civil and criminal codes, of the whole society. This is generally called law enforcement. (2) Protection of the community against certain crises to which its members are exposed. Such crises include fire, disease, and poverty. These functions are implied in the phrase "public safety." (3) Provision of certain monopoly services, or public works, such as water and streets and highways. (4) Absorption of the members of the community into the traditions and techniques of the society by the use of such institutions as schools and libraries. (5) Provision and organization of recreational facilities through playgrounds and parks. (6) Local supervision of the economic structure through licensing and inspection. And (7) perpetuation and support of its own organization through elections and appointments and by taxes and bond issues.

The political structure of Yankee City helps to articulate the various internal institutions to each other through their common relation to this political structure. The governmental structure is a hierarchy of offices through which the political functions are exercised. At the top of the structure are the mayor and city council. The council has eleven elected members: six representing their respective wards, and five, the city at large. Most of the final powers of control are assigned to the council. Those concerning appropriations and the budget, appointments to office, control over the various departments and over the various boards are all lodged with the city council. The council is not a salaried group and does not give full time to its office. It is an instrument of supervision and direction which represents the community directly and has control over the whole political structure. Besides the mayor and the school board, its members are the only elected officers in the hierarchy. It has its own internal organization. It elects a president who presides as chairman at the meetings and apportions the councilors among the five standing committees which consider specific kinds of business before the council finally passes on them. These committees are public safety (fire and police departments), public service (street and highway department), licenses and recreation, general government (finances), and soldiers' relief.

The council as a whole supervises directly the work of the different departments which have specific functions to perform. In times of political crises the council may conduct public hearings in order to sound out general community opinion on the issue involved.

In addition to the departments there are the boards, which are intermediate supervisory offices whose members are appointed with the approval of the council. The members of these boards are also nonsalaried, although they employ full-time clerks and agents to carry out their business. These boards have the power of final decision within the limits defined by their special function, but the ultimate authority rests with the council. The council has such authority because it allocates the annual funds to each board, each board has to make an annual report to the council, and all appointments of each board have to be approved by the council. The boards are (1) the water board, (2) welfare board, (3) board of registrars, (4) board of health, (5) commons commission, and (6) library board.

The school board, which is elected, has final authority in appointing the personnel for the schools. The school board prepares its own budgets but its funds must be approved by the city council. The mayor is the chairman ex officio of the school board and is the intermediary between it and the city council.

The final control of the city council lies in its powers to create such departments and boards as are necessary to serve the community. During the field work for this study, the council created a department of public works combining functions which were hitherto unco-ordinated among different departments. The mayor stands in relation to the city council somewhat as the corporation president does to his board of directors, inasmuch as the city council represents the community as the board of directors does the stockholders, and like the board of directors, the city council holds the purse and the power of policy making and of supervision.

The mayor, an elected, salaried officer, gives full time to the office. His relations to the city council are well symbolized by the ritual performed at all meetings of the council when he is in attendance. The president of the council, while in the chair, appoints a committee of two to escort the mayor into the chamber. There he is given a place at the foot of the table with the president of the council at the head and the other councilors seated along the sides. The language used by the council and the mayor is also significant to show the relation of each to the other. Thus the mayor "proposes to the city council," or he may "recommend to the city council"; we also hear "on plea of the mayor, the city council considered" and "the mayor hopes the council will not oppose." On the other hand, the council in making its decisions "orders" or "instructs" the mayor as to its will. The mayor makes recommendations to the council which the latter may either accept or reject. He is expected to bring before the council all business which belongs within the functions of the political structure. The mayor has direct and defined relations with all the administrative boards and departments since he is the liaison officer between these and the city council. As the chairman ex officio of most of the boards, he presides at their meetings. He ordinarily appears before the council as a representative of the boards. By reason of his central position in the political structure, which both serves and is identified with the community, he obtains a central position in the life of the community. This is expressed especially in times of crisis when certain actions beyond the strict functions of the political structure are necessary to organize the community. The activities of the mayor who was in office during the World War, and the behavior of the mayor during the early years of the depression, were examples of the mayor functioning as the leader of the community in behavior which was in large part not politically defined.

One more group of offices in the political structure remains to be considered. These are the auxiliaries of the executive function of the mayor, and consist of the following: (1) city clerk; (2) city auditor; (3) city solicitor; and (4) treasurer and collector. These offices are all appointive and full-time; they have specialized functions in the political structure as a whole. The officers who fill them are underfunctionaries who keep the political structure running and help provide continuity to the city government.

Let us now examine the structure in terms of the kinds of people in the community who are voters and those who control and operate the political hierarchy.

The voters in the Yankee City political organization were unequally distributed throughout the several classes. The lower-middle class and the upper-lower class possessed about an equal number of voting citizens. (See column at the left of Chart XXXV.) There were 2,161 (34.34 per cent) voters in the lower-middle class, and 2,151 (34.19 per cent) in the upper-lower class. The lower-lower class had the next largest percentage of voters (14.49 per cent), but far fewer in number (912) than its percentage of the total population. Although the upper-middle class had approximately 10 per cent of the population of Yankee City, it possessed 14.11 per cent (888) of the voters. The lower-upper class had the fifth largest percentage of voters, 1.61 per cent (101); and the upper-upper class had the smallest percentage of voters, 1.26 per cent (79).

In order to clarify our analysis of the political hierarchy, we must distinguish three classes of office in the political structure: (1) offices of high control where there are final authority

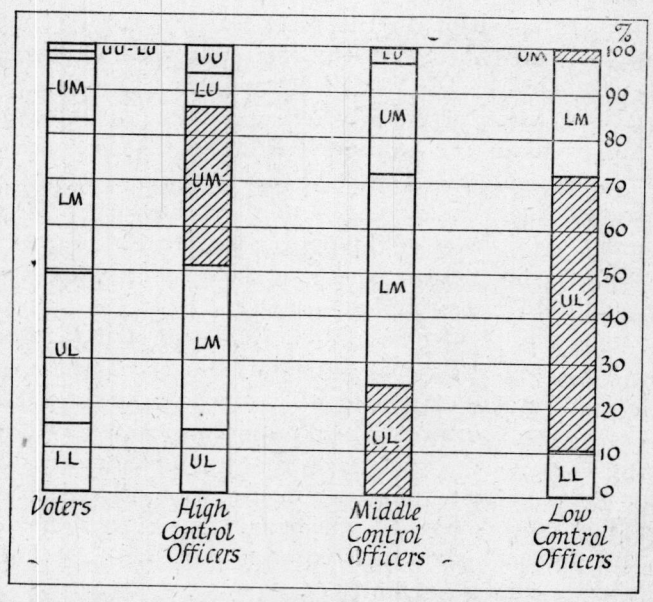

XXXV. *The Class Composition of the Officeholders and Voters*

and broad supervision, i.e., the city council, the mayor, and the several boards; (2) offices of mediate control, where authority and supervision are limited, i.e., auxiliary executive offices, heads of departments, and agents of the several boards; and (3) administrative subordinates who are the employees of the various departments.

Let us examine the relation of the six classes to these various types of offices. There were 136 persons who held office in the city government during the years 1930-31. They were distributed among the three major classes as follows: upper, 6 per cent; middle, 53.60 per cent; lower, 40.40 per cent. There were 2.30 per cent of the offices held by upper-upper people; 3.70 per cent by lower-upper people; 19.10 per cent by upper-middle individuals; 34.50 per cent by lower-middle-class people; 35.30 per cent by upper-lower people; and 5.10 per cent by lower-lower individuals. The upper class held twice as many political posts in the city as its proportion of the total population. The upper-middle class occupied about twice as many offices as its proportion in the community; the lower-middle class and the upper-lower classes, somewhat more than their proportion of the total population; while the lower-lower class had about one fourth as many offices as its proportion of the general population.

The disproportions of the several classes in the political hierarchy become more apparent when the three types of control—high, middle, and low—are examined. In the high control group, the class proportions were as follows: 14.30 per cent from the two upper classes; 71.40 per cent came from the two middle classes; and 14.30 per cent from the two lower classes. The upper-upper class held 6.10 per cent of these offices; the lower-upper 8.20 per cent; the upper-middle 34.70 per cent; the lower-middle 36.70 per cent; the upper-lower 14.30 per cent; and there were no lower-lower people in these positions. Over 85 per cent of the high control offices were in the upper and middle classes (see Chart XXXV).

In the mediate control group, the class percentages were as follows: The two upper classes had 3.20 per cent of the offices; the middle classes had 71.80 per cent; and the lower classes 25 per cent. There were no upper-upper-class people in these positions. Twenty-five per cent of these positions were occupied by upper-middle-class people; 46.80 per cent by lower-middle people; 25 per cent by upper-lower people; and there were no lower-lower-class people in the offices of mediate control. In the mediate control group, the middle class maintains the same high proportions as in the high control group, the upper-class representation falls off sharply, and there is corresponding gain in the upper-lower class.

In the lowest and subordinate group of officers, the class proportions continue to shift. The two upper classes were not represented; the two middle classes held 27.30 per cent of the offices; and the two lower classes, 72.70 per cent. Only 1.80 per cent of the officers in this lowest political stratum were upper middle; 25.50 per cent were lower middle; 61.80 per cent were upper lower; and 10.90 per cent were lower lower. Most of the firemen and policemen belong in this category.

In summary it can be said that the upper classes, together with the upper-middle class, dominate the high control offices. They have a proportion of these offices far out of keeping with their representation in the general population. The mediate control offices tend to be upper-middle and lower-middle class, while the subordinate offices tend to belong in the order named to the upper-lower, lower-middle, and lower-lower classes.

The positions of sixteen members of the city council in office during 1930 and 1931 were examined to determine their place in the class system. Of these, 6.40 per cent were lower upper; 18.70 per cent were upper middle; 43.70 per cent, lower middle; and 31.20 per cent, upper lower. There were no upper-upper or lower-lower persons in the council.

The personnel of the school board was also examined for the class status of its several members. Because of the high importance of the educational structure in American society, the class position of the members of this board is of obvious importance. One member of the board was upper-upper, one lower-upper, five upper-middle, and one lower-middle. No members of the two low classes served on the school board. It is perhaps significant that the two unsuccessful candidates in the election in which these members took office were both of the lower-middle class. The library board, which had a high symbolic function in the community, was, unlike the school board, an appointive group. But it, too, shows just as strikingly the disproportionate representation of the several classes. There was one upper-upper person on the board, two lower-upper, six upper-middle, and one lower-middle person. The single representative of the lower-middle class was the priest of the Greek church. He was placed there deliberately because of his position as the head of one of the ethnic churches in order that the "foreign interest" might be represented on the library board.

Sixty-one of the 136 persons in the political service of the city were native, and 75 were ethnic. Of the ethnics, 65 were

Irish, 5 French, 1 Jewish, and 1 Greek. The Armenians, Italians, Poles, Russians, and Negroes had no representatives. The Irish had a higher proportion of members in the city's political organization than did the natives. Although the Irish outnumbered the natives in the city service, the natives had twice as many representatives in the high control group of offices as the Irish, about the same number in the mediate group, and about half as many in the administrative subordinate group of offices. One of the members of the library board was Jewish, and another was Greek. French Canadians were largely in the subordinate groups.

2. Crime (Arrests) and Class

Class and ethnic factors are very important in determining liability to, and protection from, arrest by the local police in Yankee City. The person most likely to be arrested in Yankee City is a Polish lower-lower-class male around thirty years of age. If the Pole were in a higher class he would be less liable to arrest. The person least likely to be arrested is an upper-class or upper-middle-class female Yankee below twenty years of age. As we have said earlier, our interview records show that a man's position in a higher class helped protect him from police interference, while a less powerful position in a lower class made him more vulnerable to police action. It may be argued that the members of the lower classes are more inclined to break the rules of the community, but the interviews demonstrated that the same acts committed in the higher and lower classes resulted in fewer arrests for those who were better placed socially. An upper-class position protects a person from many undesirable experiences in Yankee City, one of them being haled before a judge and acquiring a police record.

From an analysis of the arrests over seven years, we found that the males had the highest percentage of those arrested: 89.06 per cent were males and 10.94 per cent were females. The median age for first arrest for males was 29.50 years; and that for females was 31.70 years.[1]

---

[1]. Over 20 per cent (20.26 per cent) of the males were first arrested before they were eighteen years of age and 22.08 per cent of the females were arrested before they were eighteen years old; 9.25 per cent of the males were first arrested between the years of eighteen and twenty and 2.60 per cent of

The highest percentage of the population of any area that had been arrested came from Middletown and Uptown. Downtown and Riverbrook ranked third and fourth. Newtown, Homeville, and Hill Street were significantly low.[2] In other words, the areas in which the higher classes live tend to have fewer arrests, and those sections where the lower classes reside have higher crime records.

The ethnic groups, as Table 34 shows, form a larger percentage of those arrested by the police of Yankee City than do the Yankees: 60 per cent of all those arrested are ethnics, and 40 per cent are natives. It will be remembered that the Yankees comprise 54 per cent, and the combined ethnics 46 per cent, of the population of Yankee City. It is clear that the members of the ethnic groups are more liable to arrest than are the Yankees.[3]

The newer ethnic groups and the Negroes, both tending to be lower class, are the ones who are most liable to arrest. This is true for all groups except the Armenians who have the lowest percentage of arrested individuals. The full explanation for the low rate of arrests for the Armenians cannot be given; they were, however, slightly higher in class than most other ethnic groups and were a closely organized community. Furthermore, they were better related than the others to the larger Yankee community through their affiliation with Protestant churches.[4]

the females; 21.53 per cent of the males were arrested between the ages of twenty-one and twenty-nine years, and 18.18 per cent of the females; 24.24 per cent of the males were arrested at the age level of thirty to thirty-nine years, and 36.36 per cent of the females were first arrested at this time. This last is the only age level in which the proportion of females arrested is higher than the proportion of males. Approximately 25 per cent (24.72 per cent) of the arrested males were forty years and over; and 20.78 per cent of the females were arrested at that age.

2. Across the River (1.30 per cent) and Oldtown (0.60 per cent) were also low, but our figures are incomplete for the arrested in those areas, since part of those who were arrested were taken to other courts.

3. The ethnic affiliation of 0.99 per cent of those arrested was unknown.

4. There was a higher percentage of the Polish population arrested than any other ethnic group: 13 per cent of the members of this group had been arrested. The Russians were second: 12.77 per cent had their names on the police records. The police had arrested 9.51 per cent of the Italians. The Negroes ranked fourth for the percentage of their population which had been arrested: 8.75 per cent. There were 6.31 per cent of the Greeks, 5.32 per cent of the French Canadians, and 4.79 per cent of the Jews who had been arrested; 3.91 per cent of the Irish, 3.07 per cent of the Yankees, and 2.85 per cent of the Armenians.

TABLE 34
Crime and Ethnic Group

	Presence		Absence		Total	
Native	39.12	3.07 / 277	54.45	96.93 / 8,753	53.80	9,030
Total Ethnic	59.89	5.55 / 424	44.92	94.45 / 7,222	45.55	7,646
Irish	21.76	3.91 / 154	23.57	96.09 / 3,789	23.49	3,943
French	11.02	5.32 / 78	8.63	94.68 / 1,388	8.73	1,466
Jewish	2.68	4.79 / 19	2.35	95.21 / 378	2.37	397
Italian	3.81	9.51 / 27	1.60	90.49 / 257	1.69	284
Armenian	0.99	2.85 / 7	1.49	97.15 / 239	1.47	246
Greek	3.67	6.31 / 26	2.40	93.69 / 386	2.45	412
Polish	12.43	13.00 / 88	3.66	87.00 / 589	4.03	677
Russian	2.54	12.77 / 18	0.77	87.23 / 123	0.84	141
Negro	0.99	8.75 / 7	0.45	91.25 / 73	0.48	80
Unknown	0.99	6.42 / 7	0.63	93.58 / 102	0.65	109
Total		4.22 / 708		95.78 / 16,077		16,785

The two upper classes accounted for less than three fourths of 1 per cent of those arrested; the two middle classes, for about 10 per cent; and the two lower classes, for approximately

90 per cent of the crime in Yankee City[5] (see Table 35).

All of the causes for arrest in the three upper classes were petty ones. Some of them were for driving and parking offenses. One of them developed from a quarrel over a dog, and there were other minor offenses. The crimes in the lower class

TABLE 35

Class and Crime

	Presence	Absence	Total
UU	.43 1.24 3	1.50 98.76 239	1.45 242
LU	.28 0.76 2	1.63 99.24 260	1.57 262
UM	1.84 0.76 13	10.68 99.24 1,702	10.30 1,715
LM	7.80 1.17 55	29.27 98.83 4,665	28.36 4,720
UL	24.96 3.22 176	33.22 96.78 5,295	32.88 5,471
LL	64.69 10.77 456	23.70 89.23 3,778	25.44 4,234
Total	4.24 705	95.76 15,939	16,644

ranged from the most serious, such as rape and theft, to the least serious, such as drunkenness and improper driving of automobiles.

Eleven per cent of the lower-lower class and 3 per cent of

[5] Approximately 65 per cent (64.69 per cent) of all those arrested were in the lower-lower class; 24.96 per cent were in the upper-lower class; 7.80 per cent were in the lower-middle class; 1.84 per cent were in the upper-middle; 0.43 per cent in the upper-upper; and 0.28 per cent in the lower-upper class.

the upper-lower class had records of arrest. One per cent of the lower-middle class had their names on the police records and less than 1 per cent of the lower-upper and the upper-middle were recorded. Only two of the lower-upper class had their names on the police records. Three of the upper-upper class had been arrested by the police. All five of these cases were minor violations. Thirteen of the upper-middle class had been arrested. Each of these cases was for a minor infraction of the law.

Sixty-three per cent of all the arrests of the lower-lower class were ethnic, and 37 per cent were native. In the upper-lower class, 63 per cent were ethnic and 37 per cent were native. In the lower-middle class, 49 per cent were ethnic and 51 per cent were native. In the upper-middle class, 15 per cent were ethnic and 85 per cent were native.

Since the ethnic population of the lowest class was only 56.57 per cent of the stratum, it holds that being an ethnic in that class (many of them foreign-born) contributed to a man's chance of arrest; this chance became less in the upper-lower class and disappeared in the lower-middle class. The Yankees in this class had a higher rate of arrest, but in the upper-middle class the ethnics again were more liable to arrest. The discrepancy in the lower-middle class is more than likely accounted for by the extreme emphasis placed on being "respectable" and Yankee by the ethnics in that class.

XIX

READING AND OTHER SYMBOLIC BEHAVIOR OF THE SIX CLASSES

1. *The Reading Habits of the Six Classes*

THE symbolic behavior which this chapter describes includes the selection of books from the local library, subscriptions to magazines and newspapers, attendance at the local motion picture theater, and the preference for doctors and undertakers.

The books which people read were analyzed under eleven headings. They were: social techniques, science and knowledge, biography, children's books and fantasy, farce and humor, adventure, mystery and detective, man's struggle against fate, courtship and the family, class and mobility, and "God and Country."

Social techniques were the books which accented the proper forms of social behavior and included etiquette books and other similar volumes which emphasized how to live according to the proper standards. Such books as *What Every Young Girl Should Know*, the books of Emily Post, and *How to Become Successful* were classed under this heading. Fundamentally, such books in our society serve the same function as the oral teaching of tribal ritual in the nonliterate societies. Books of science and knowledge accented technological subjects and their ideologies. They included such books as De Kruif's *Microbe Hunters* and Eddington's *Our Expanding Universe*.

Biographical books are the equivalent in our society of the culture hero stories in primitive society, and celebrate deeds of virtue or those which are condemned by the group. The biographies of Lincoln, Roosevelt, and the founders of the republic were so classified.

The next four categories included books which are generally called "light fiction" and give the readers vicarious release from the social controls around them. Children's books included fairy stories, books of fantasy, and such books as Grimm's and

Andersen's fairy tales. Adventure stories were concerned with escape themes. *Anthony Adverse* and similar picaresque novels were in this group. The stories of Conan Doyle, Sax Rohmer, Agatha Christie, and similar writers were classed as detective stories. Farce and humor stories made fun of the "serious things of life." The works of Stephen Leacock, Mark Twain, Don Marquis, and George Bernard Shaw were in this category.

The next four categories of books were fictional but of the nonrealistic type. They portrayed the conflict of the individual with his society and tended to tighten rather than release social control over the individual who read them.

The first of these included books in which the individual in a series of crises fights against "fate." The novels of Willa Cather, Knut Hamsun, most of the Russian novelists, and of the modern American writers such as Dos Passos, Steinbeck, and Wolfe were in this category. The courtship and family books included those on the "eternal triangle," "family honor," and "love is so beautiful" themes, and portrayed the problems surrounding sex control and the maintenance of the family's members in the community and their relations among themselves. The works of Galsworthy and Ellen Glasgow illustrate this type of work.

The class and mobility themes concerned the individual's attempt to adjust to the standards of his own class and to move into a higher class. They tell such tales as Irwin's *North Shore*, where a poor boy faces the question of marrying a rich girl without love or a poor girl with love, or they describe how strong men disregard the ritual of class and despite their refusal to reform, achieve social mobility.

The God and Country category included such books as the historical novel and similar tales of historical interest when the hero's life crises are designed by the author to fit into the crises of his country, thereby usually benefiting the nation. The works of Sabatini, Walter Scott, and Kenneth Roberts are examples of this type.

The reading habits of the people were highly influenced by class values; they read certain books, magazines, and newspapers in varying percentages according to their place in the class hierarchy. The members of the several classes also liked books of certain types and showed small interest in others. The books most read in the community were those in which the theme of courtship and the family was predominant. Detective stories and adventure stories were second and third in popularity. The theme of man's struggle against fate was a comparatively popular theme in the books read; such books ranked fourth in popularity. Stories which played up class and mobility were among the more preferred books and ranked fifth. All other books were below these in the reader's interests. Books in which scientific subjects dominated were least popular of all. Preferences of the ethnic groups and of the Yankees were very similar.

The members of the upper-upper class evinced more than an average interest in books which were concerned with science and with biography and history; they were also interested more than the average in detective stories, farce and humor, and books in which the predominant interest was patriotism and warfare. The lower-upper class had an above-average reading preference for books in which the dominant interest was man's struggle against fate. They were also interested in books where warfare was the predominant theme, and in books of biography and history. The upper-middle-class readers had an above-average interest in books on social techniques, courtship and the family, and warfare. The lower-middle class showed a strong preference for books on courtship and the family. The upper-lower class were interested in children's books and those of farce and humor, while the lower-lower had an interest above the average in children's books, adventure and detective stories, farce and humor, and man's struggle against fate.

The ten most popular magazines in Yankee City were *Needlecraft, Pictorial Review, McCall's, Cosmopolitan, Better Homes and Gardens, National Geographic, Delineator, Ladies' Home Journal, Woman's Home Companion,* and the *Saturday Evening Post.*

Class has a decided effect upon magazine reading in Yankee City. Lower-class readers definitely prefer certain magazines, and upper-class readers show a high preference for others. Ordinarily, when upper-class readers prefer a particular magazine, lower-class readers avoid it, and when lower-lower-class readers prefer a particular magazine, upper-class readers avoid it. The evidence of class preference is even stronger when the distribution of the subscriptions of most of the magazines through all the classes is examined, since if a magazine ranks high in the upper-upper class, its rank drops in the lower-upper and in the two middle classes, and is at the bottom of the ranking in the two lower classes. On the other hand, if a magazine such as the *Cosmopolitan* or the *Delineator* is highly favored by the lower-lower class, its rank is slightly lower in the upper-lower class, still lower in the lower-middle, and continues to decrease as it goes through the upper-middle class into the upper-upper class. Although there is a very high correlation between class position and magazine preference, this correlation is not absolute. The tendency is sufficiently high, however, to make it significant.

The upper-middle subscribed to a larger variety of magazines than any other class. Fifty-nine magazine titles were listed for them. The lower-middle class was second with fifty-five, and the lower-upper third with forty-five. The upper-upper and upper-lower classes ranked fourth and fifth for the variety of magazines, with forty-one titles each; and the lower-lower subscribed to but twenty-nine magazines.

The selection of the daily newspapers by Yankee City people also showed a definite class bias. Many newspapers little read by the upper classes were preferred by the lower ones, while the lower classes did not subscribe to those papers which the upper classes selected. The journals read included one local paper and seven papers from Boston. The Boston papers were the *Transcript*, the *Herald*, the *Traveler*, the *Globe*, the *Post*, the *American*, and the *Record*.

Hence the conclusion that the people of Yankee City showed a strong class influence in most of their reading, but their newspaper and magazine reading showed more class interests than their book reading.

2. Evidence of the Influence of Class and Ethnic Affiliation on the Reading of Books

Books on courtship and the family, detective and adventure stories comprise more than half of the books read. They ranked in the order named.[1] The books taken most infrequently from

1. Twenty-one per cent emphasized themes of courtship and the family. The second most popular type of book was the detective story: 18.35 per cent of

the library are biography and history, farce and humor, and scientific books.

The largest percentage of the users of the library were women. Sixty per cent of the library users were women, as compared with 51 per cent of females in the general population.

The upper-upper class had the smallest percentage of its members using the library. Part of this failure to use the library is due to their having their own libraries and buying current books which are advertised or reviewed in the periodicals they read. The upper-middle class is the only one which was significantly high for the use of the library.

The family and courtship, detective stories, adventure stories, man's struggle against fate, and class and social-climbing books were the types of stories preferred by all age levels. The first four subjects were preferred more by all ages than that of class and social climbing except by people who were above thirty-nine and below fifty and those who were below fourteen years of age. These two ages preferred social-climbing stories in addition to the other four interests.[2]

The ethnic preferences correspond fairly closely to those of the Yankees. Both the natives and ethnics preferred books on courtship and the family more than any other type.[3] Their

all books read from the library were of this type. Books of adventure followed the detective story: 16.32 per cent of all books read were of this kind. The theme of man's struggle against fate ranked fourth (12.69 per cent); books whose interest was focused around class and mobility were fifth (11.14 per cent). Books which emphasized patriotic endeavors, such as war and national crises, were sixth (6.93 per cent). Children's stories and fantasies were seventh (4.39 per cent); and books in which the interest was the correct use of social techniques and ways of behavior were eighth (4.33 per cent). Biography and history (2.51 per cent), farce and humor (1.92 per cent), and scientific books (0.34 per cent) were read the least. The books on courtship and the family, and detective and adventure stories, composed more than half of the books tabulated.

2. Persons who were above thirty and below forty years of age led all others (15.72 per cent) in the number of books read; those who were above thirty-nine and under fifty were second (14.05 per cent). Persons who were over seventeen and under twenty-one years were third (13.41 per cent); and those over sixty were fourth (12.13 per cent). Those who were above fourteen and below eighteen were fifth (11.55 per cent). Readers who were above twenty and under twenty-five were sixth (11.45 per cent). Persons who were above fifty and below sixty were seventh (11.07 per cent); those above twenty-four and below thirty were eighth (9.59 per cent); and those below fourteen were ninth (1.03 per cent). These percentages are of the users of the general library and not of the children's room.

3. The percentages have all been analyzed but only summaries will be given.

next choice was detective stories, which in turn was followed by adventure stories. Both the ethnics and the Yankees showed their next greatest interest in stories of man's fight against fate; in social climbing stories, fifth; and in warfare stories, next. The Yankees preferred books on social techniques next, but the ethnics generally chose children's stories before books on social techniques. Children's stories ranked eighth for the

XXXVI. *The Types of Library Books Selected by the Six Classes*

Yankees. Biographical and historical subjects, those of farce and humor, and scientific ones had the least reader interest for both the Yankees and the ethnics.

The natives read more books in each type than did the combined ethnics, and the Irish read more than any other ethnic group. The larger number of books read in both cases seems primarily due to the larger proportion of these two ethnic groups in the general population of Yankee City (see Table 36 and Chart XXXVI).

TABLE 36
Book Reading of the Six Classes

Class	1 Social Techniques	2 Science	3 Biography and History	4 Children Fantasy	5 Adventure	6 Detective	7 Farce and Humor	8 Courtship and Family	9 Class and Mobility	10 Nation Fight	11 Fate	Total
UU	4.55 / 1.42	4.55 / 18.18	6.82 / 3.70	2.27 / 0.70	9.09 / 0.76	22.73 / 1.69	2.27 / 1.61	18.18 / 1.18	9.09 / 1.11	9.09 / 1.79	11.36 / 1.22	1.36
LU	3.23 / 1.42		6.45 / 4.94	1.61 / 0.70	11.29 / 1.33	16.13 / 1.69		20.97 / 1.91	9.68 / 1.67	11.29 / 3.12	19.35 / 2.93	1.92
UM	5.80 / 20.00	0.83 / 36.36	5.38 / 32.10	2.90 / 9.86	14.91 / 13.66	16.15 / 13.15	1.66 / 12.90	22.98 / 16.35	10.14 / 13.61	8.90 / 19.20	10.35 / 12.20	14.95
LM	4.65 / 35.00	0.47 / 45.45	2.47 / 32.10	3.32 / 24.65	16.13 / 32.26	18.02 / 32.03	1.52 / 25.81	22.30 / 34.61	10.72 / 31.39	7.50 / 35.27	12.81 / 32.92	32.62
UL	4.30 / 29.30		1.68 / 19.75	4.93 / 33.10	16.04 / 29.03	18.45 / 29.68	2.31 / 33.49	21.48 / 30.19	11.95 / 31.66	6.29 / 26.78	12.47 / 29.02	29.53
LL	2.90 / 12.86		0.97 / 7.41	7.10 / 30.99	19.35 / 22.77	20.33 / 21.25	2.42 / 24.19	16.45 / 15.02	11.13 / 19.17	5.00 / 13.84	14.35 / 21.71	19.19
Unknown					7.14 / 0.19	21.44 / 0.51		35.71 / 0.74	35.71 / 1.39			0.43
Total	4.33	0.34	2.51	4.39	16.32	18.35	1.92	21.08	11.14	6.93	12.69	

Let us now examine the preferences of the six classes for the eleven different types of books. We shall begin with the most generally popular and proceed to the least. The upper-middle and lower-middle classes showed a preference for books on courtship and the family which was slightly above the average; the upper-lower and lower-upper classes approximated the average; while the upper-upper and lower-upper were somewhat below the average.

The upper-upper and lower-lower classes read a larger percentage of detective stories than the readers of any other class; 22.73 per cent of all the books read by the upper-upper class and 20.33 per cent of those read by the lower-lower class belonged to this category. The upper-lower and the lower-middle classes approximated the average for the general population. There is an obvious likeness in the preferences of the upper-upper and lower-lower classes for detective stories; there is also a likeness between the upper-lower and lower-middle classes and between the upper-middle and lower-upper classes.

The lower-lower class is the only one which read adventure stories above the average for the general population: 19.35 per cent of all the books read by the lower-lower class were of this type. The lower-middle and upper-lower classes read about the same amount of adventure stories as the general population. The upper-middle, lower-upper, and upper-upper classes read a smaller number of them. In general, it can be said that the percentage of adventure stories read decreases as we ascend the class hierarchy.

The lower-upper class read more books which expressed the general theme of man's struggle against fate than did the members of any other class, whereas of the books read by the general population, 12.69 per cent were of this kind, 19.35 per cent of the books read by the lower-upper class, and 11.36 per cent of the upper-upper.

The two upper classes were the only ones substantially below the average for books read which were focused on the general theme of class and social climbing. All the others approached the average for the whole group. The three upper classes read books focused on the theme of warfare and the nation more than any other class. The upper-lower and lower-middle classes approximated the average. The lower-lower class read fewer of such books than any of the other five classes; only 5 per cent of the books read by them emphasized this theme. Except for the fact that the lower-upper ranks first for all classes, the percentage decreases regularly for books which emphasize the theme of warfare and the nation as the rank of the class decreases.

The lower-lower class read a larger percentage of books of fantasy, some of which were designed for children, than any of the other classes; 7.10 per cent of all the books read by the lower-lower class were of this type. The upper-lower and lower-middle classes approximated the average. The upper-middle, upper-upper, and lower-upper read a smaller percentage of books which belonged to this category than the three lower classes. The percentage of this kind of books read decreases as we ascend the class hierarchy.

The upper-middle class is the only one which read more than the average percentage of books which stress the theme of social techniques; 5.80 per cent of the books read by them were of this kind. The lower-middle, upper-upper, and upper-lower classes approached the average. The lower-upper and lower-lower classes were below the average. The three upper classes read a higher percentage of books of biography and history than the three lower ones. The percentage of books read in this category steadily declines as the rank of the class decreases.

The upper-upper class read far more scientific books than any other class: 4.55 per cent of the books read by them were of this type, whereas only 0.83 per cent of the upper-middle books, 0.47 per cent of the lower-middle, and none of the lower-upper and the two lower classes were concerned with scientific themes.

3. *Evidence of the Influence of Class on Magazine Reading*

The magazine reading of Yankee City was studied by examining the subscription lists and newsstand purchases of the several magazines. The subscriptions and purchases were analyzed first to determine which magazines were most and least popular in the community, and the magazines were then ranked accordingly for general popularity. The class preferences were next examined. The total number of sales for each class was computed, and the percentage of the total of each class which each magazine's sales represented was analyzed, and the rank order of each magazine in each class determined. Thus we knew how the different magazines compared in popularity among the six classes, and it quickly became apparent that there was a strong class bias in magazine reading.

The upper-upper class subscribed to or bought 4.84 per cent of the magazines in Yankee City; the lower-upper class, 5.71 per cent; the upper-middle, 28.01 per cent; the lower-middle, 35.79 per cent; the upper-lower, 18.39 per cent; and the lower-lower, 7.26 per cent. The percentage of magazines subscribed to out of the total number purchased by each class was approximately the same throughout the structure.[4] The upper class was somewhat lower in percentage of subscriptions than the middle or lower class. The upper-middle class ranked higher in the percentage of its members who subscribed to magazines than any other class, the upper-lower was next, and the lower-lower was third. The lower-middle class ranked fourth; the lower-upper class, fifth; and the upper-upper was last in the percentage of its members who subscribed to magazines.

Each subscriber of the lower-upper class subscribed to more magazines than those of the other five classes; they averaged 2.09 magazines per subscriber. The upper-upper class was next with 1.87 magazines per subscriber. The upper-middle class was third with 1.63 magazines per subscriber. The lower-middle was fourth (1.45); the lower-lower was fifth (1.38); and the upper-lower was last with 1.28 magazines for each subscriber.

As the rank of the class decreases the percentage of magazine subscribers decreases. The number of magazines subscribed to by each subscriber also tends to decrease as we descend in the class hierarchy.

4. We cannot give the exact number or exact percentage of the total population which purchased magazines because the subscription lists were obtained as confidential data. We will in all cases give the percentage of purchasers but not the numbers. Hereafter when we refer to subscribers and readers of magazines and newspapers, we refer to purchasers of all kinds.
The figures for all types of sales of newspapers and magazines have been combined. Figures include sales from newsstands outside the community as well as within it. Furthermore, Yankee City as determined by this research includes certain areas not ordinarily considered part of the community and excludes others which are ordinarily included.

TABLE 37
Magazine Preferences of the Six Classes

UU

1	National Geographic
2	Saturday Evening Post
3	Sports Afield
4-5-6	Ladies' Home Journal
4-5-6	Reader's Digest
4-5-6	Atlantic Monthly
7-8	Pictorial Review
7-8	Time
9-10	Literary Digest
9-10	Harper's
1	Delineator
2-3	American Boy
2-3	Financial World
4-13	Cosmopolitan
4-13	Country Gentleman
4-13	Open Road for Boys
4-13	Hunting and Fishing
4-13	House Beautiful
4-13	Popular Science
4-13	Harper's Bazaar
4-13	Vanity Fair
4-13	New Yorker
4-13	Life

(All others less than 1 per cent)

LU

1	National Geographic
2	Saturday Evening Post
3	Time
4	Reader's Digest
5	Ladies' Home Journal
6-8	Better Homes and Gardens
6-8	Literary Digest
6-8	American Home
9	Cosmopolitan
10-11	Harper's
10-11	Vogue
1-3	Country Gentleman
1-3	House Beautiful
1-3	Judge
4-8	American
4-8	Sports Afield
4-8	Atlantic Monthly
4-8	Asia
4-8	New Yorker
9-16	Pictorial Review
9-16	McCall's
9-16	Delineator
9-16	Woman's Home Companion
9-16	Red Book
9-16	Parents' Magazine
9-16	Popular Science
9-16	Financial World

(All others below 1 per cent)

UM

1	National Geographic
2	Better Homes and Gardens
3	McCall's
4	Ladies' Home Journal
5	Saturday Evening Post
6	Literary Digest
7-8	Woman's Home Companion
7-8	American
9	Pictorial Review
10	Cosmopolitan
1-2	Country Gentleman
1-2	Reader's Digest
3	Needlecraft
4	Delineator
5-6	Woman's World
5-6	Collier's
7	Parents' Magazine
8-11	Red Book
8-11	Time
8-11	American Home
8-11	House Beautiful
1	Atlantic Monthly
2	Sports Afield
3	Open Road for Boys
4-5	Review of Reviews
4-5	Harper's
6-8	American Boy
6-8	Popular Science
6-8	Liberty
9-11	Hunting and Fishing
9-11	Judge
9-11	New Outlook

(All others below 0.60 per cent)

Reading and Symbolic Behavior of the Six Classes 389

TABLE 37 (Continued)

LM

1	Needlecraft
2	McCall's
3	Better Homes and Gardens
4	Pictorial Review
5	Cosmopolitan
6	Ladies' Home Journal
7	Delineator
8	National Geographic
9	Woman's Home Companion
10	Literary Digest
1	American
2	Country Gentleman
3	Saturday Evening Post
4	Woman's World
5	Red Book
6	Open Road for Boys
7	Hunting and Fishing
8	Collier's
9	Parents' Magazine
10	Sports Afield
1	American Home
2	Etude
3–4	Review of Reviews
3–4	Boys' Life
5	American Boy
6	National Sportsman
7–9	Reader's Digest
7–9	Time
7–9	Popular Science
10–11	House Beautiful
10–11	True Story

(All others below 0.39 per cent)

UL

1	Needlecraft
2	Pictorial Review
3	Cosmopolitan
4	McCall's
5	Delineator
6	Woman's Home Companion
7	Better Homes and Gardens
8	Woman's World
9	Country Gentleman
10–11	Red Book
10–11	Open Road for Boys
1	Hunting and Fishing
2–3	American
2–3	Parents' Magazine
4–5	Ladies' Home Journal
4–5	Collier's
6–7	National Geographic
6–7	Literary Digest
8	Saturday Evening Post
9	American Boy
10	Sports Afield
1	National Sportsman
2–4	Review of Reviews
2–4	Popular Science
2–4	True Story
5	Judge
6–11	Time
6–11	American Home
6–11	Boys' Life
6–11	Liberty
6–11	St. Nicholas
6–11	True Romances

(All others below 0.37 per cent)

LL

1–2	Needlecraft
1–2	Cosmopolitan
3	Delineator
4	Pictorial Review
5	Red Book
6	Woman's Home Companion
7	Better Homes and Gardens
8	McCall's
9	Collier's
10–11	Open Road for Boys
10–11	Parents' Magazine
1–2	American
1–2	Boys' Life
3–6	Country Gentleman
3–6	Woman's World
3–6	National Sportsman
3–6	True Story
7–10	Ladies' Home Journal
7–10	Sports Afield
7–10	Outdoor Life
7–10	Hunting and Fishing

(All others below 0.94 per cent)

TABLE 38

The Distribution of the Purchasers of Each Magazine in the Six Classes; the Per cent of the Purchasers in Each Class by Magazine; and the Per cent of the Total by Magazine

	UU		LU		UM		LM		UL		LL		Total
1. Needlecraft	0.44	0.77	0.44	0.64	11.95	3.24	42.92	9.42	31.86	13.36	12.39	13.21	7.79
2. Pictorial Review	2.83	4.66	0.94	1.27	19.34	4.92	32.55	6.70	33.02	12.99	11.32	11.32	7.31
3. McCall's	0.52	0.77	1.04	1.27	30.05	6.97	44.56	8.35	18.65	6.68	5.18	4.72	6.66
4. Cosmopolitan	1.05	1.55	2.62	3.18	19.37	4.44	35.08	6.50	27.23	9.65	14.66	13.21	6.59
5. Better Homes and Gardens	0.56	0.77	3.89	4.46	32.78	7.09	42.22	7.38	14.44	4.82	6.11	5.19	6.21
6. National Geographic	10.49	13.19	9.88	10.19	42.59	8.29	30.25	4.76	6.79	2.03			5.59
7. Delineator	2.74	3.10	1.37	1.27	17.12	3.00	38.36	5.44	23.29	6.31	17.12	11.79	5.03
8. Ladies' Home Journal	4.96	5.44	5.67	5.10	37.59	6.37	41.84	5.73	8.51	2.23	1.42	0.94	4.86

...ng and Symbolic Behavior of the Six Classes — 391

TABLE 36 (Continued)

	UU	LU	UM	LM				
9. Woman's Home Companion	0.76 / 0.77	1.53 / 1.27	32.06 / 5.04	35.11 / 4.47	2.23 / 5.01	3.77 / —	— / —	1.90 / —
10. Saturday Evening Post	10.57 / 10.09	11.38 / 8.92	40.65 / 6.00	30.08 / 3.59	2.96 / 1.48	2.88 / —	— / —	2.03 / —
11. Literary Digest	4.35 / 3.88	6.09 / 4.46	39.13 / 5.40	40.00 / 4.47	2.96 / 2.03	7.08 / 2.36	4.76 / 3.62	2.48 / 3.45
12. American	0.95 / 0.77	2.86 / 1.91	40.00 / 5.04	39.05 / 3.98	4.08 / 2.41	1.42 / 1.42	3.00 / —	2.66 / —
13. Country Gentleman	2.00 / 1.55	4.00 / 2.55	32.00 / 3.84	39.00 / 3.79	28.57 / 3.71	1.42 / —	3.90 / —	3.45 / —
14. Woman's World	1.30 / 0.77	— / 1.27	23.38 / 2.16	42.86 / 3.20	20.00 / —	— / —	— / —	— / —
15. Red Book	3.39 / 1.55	2.78 / 1.27	16.67 / 1.44	37.50 / 2.62	22.22 / 2.96	— / —	20.83 / —	3.62 / —
16. Open Road for Boys	— / —	1.69 / 0.64	15.25 / 1.80	42.37 / 2.43	27.12 / 2.96	7.08 / —	10.17 / —	2.48 / —
17. Collier's	1.82 / 0.77	— / —	32.73 / 2.16	29.09 / 1.55	21.82 / 2.23	3.77 / —	14.55 / —	1.90 / —

TABLE 38 (Continued)

	UU	LU	UM	LM	UL	LL	Total
18. *Parents' Magazine*	13.46 / 5.44	3.77 / 1.27	32.08 / 2.04	28.30 / 2.41	24.53 / 2.83	11.32	1.83
19. *Reader's Digest*	4.35 / 1.55	19.23 / 6.37	55.77 / 3.48	9.62 / 0.49	0 / 0.47	1.92	1.79
20. *Hunting and Fishing*	19.51 / 6.20	2.17 / 0.64	10.87 / 0.60	47.83 / 2.14	30.43 / 2.60	4.35	1.59
21. *Sports Afield*	16.22 / 4.66	7.32 / 1.91	24.39 / 1.20	29.27 / 1.17	14.63 / 1.11	4.88	1.41
22. *Time*	3.03 / 0.77	32.43 / 7.64	32.43 / 1.44	13.51 / 0.49	5.41 / 0.37	0 / 0.94	1.28
23. *American Home*	12.50 / 2.33	21.21 / 4.46	36.36 / 1.44	33.33 / 1.07	6.06 / 0.37	0 / 0.94	1.14
24. *American Boy*	29.17 / 5.44	0 / —	25.00 / 0.72	33.33 / 0.78	29.17 / 1.30		
25. *Atlantic Monthly*	8.70 / 1.55	12.50 / 1.91	45.83 / 1.32	8.33 / 0.19	4.17 / 0.19	0 / 0.47	
26. *House Beautiful*		17.39 / 2.35	52.17 / 1.44	17.39 / 0.39	0.19		

Reading and Symbolic Behavior of the Six Classes

	UU	LU	UM	LM	UL	LL	Total
27. Review of Reviews	0	4.35	34.78	39.13	17.39	4.35	0.79
28. Boys' Life	5.00	0	15.00	45.00	10.00	25.00	0.69
29. Harper's	26.32	26.32	42.11	5.26	0	0	0.66
30. Popular Science	10.53	10.53	31.58	26.32	21.05	0	0.66
31. National Sportsman	5.88	5.88	5.88	35.29	29.41	17.65	0.59
32. Judge	7.14	28.57	35.71	0	21.43	7.14	0.48
33. Étude	0	0	15.38	76.92	7.69	0	0.45
34. True Story	0	0	15.38	30.77	30.77	23.08	0.45
35. Financial World	27.27	18.18	27.27	27.27	0	0	0.38

TABLE 38 (Continued)

	UU	LU	UM	LM	UL	LL	Total
36. Vogue		45.45 / 3.18	27.27 / 0.36	18.18 / 0.19	9.09 / 0.19	0	0.38
37. Liberty	12.50 / 0.77		60.00 / 0.72	10.00 / 0.10	20.00 / 0.37	10.00 / 0.47	0.34
38. College Humor	28.57 / 1.55	12.50 / 0.64	25.00 / 0.24	37.50 / 0.28		12.50 / 0.47	0.28
39. Harper's Bazaar	/ 0.77	/ 0.64	42.86 / 0.36	14.29 / 0.10			0.24
40. Outdoor Life	14.29 / 1.55	14.29 / 0.64	14.29 / 0.12	28.57 / 0.19	14.29 / 0.19	28.57 / 0.94	0.24
41. St. Nicholas	28.57 / 1.55		14.29 / 0.12	42.86 / 0.28	14.29 / 0.19		0.24
42. Vanity Fair		50.00 / 1.91	42.86 / 0.36	14.29 / 0.10	28.57 / 0.37		0.24
43. Asia	33.33 / 1.55		16.67 / 0.12	33.33 / 0.19			0.21
44. New Yorker		50.00 / 1.91	16.67 / 0.12				0.21

TABLE 38 (Continued)

	UU	LU	UM	LM	UL	LL	Total
45. Field and Stream	20.00 0.77	20.00 0.64	40.00 0.24		20.00 0.19		0.17
46. Life (old)	40.00 1.55	20.00 0.64	20.00 0.12	20.00 0.10			0.17
47. New Outlook			100.0 0.60				0.17
48. Current History	25.00 0.77	25.00 0.64	25.00 0.12	25.00 0.10			0.14
49. Fortune	25.00 0.77	25.00 0.64	25.00 0.12	25.00 0.10			0.14
50. Junior Home Magazine			100.0 0.48				0.14
51. Physical Culture			25.00 0.12	50.00 0.19			0.14
52. Nautilus			33.33 0.12	33.33 0.10	33.33 0.19	25.00 0.47	0.10
53. Power Boating				66.67 0.19	33.33 0.19		0.10

TABLE 38 (Continued)

	UU	LU	UM	LM	UL	LL	Total
54. Scribner's		33.33	33.33	33.33			0.10
55. True Romances	50.00			33.33	66.67		0.10
56. Commonweal		50.00		50.00			0.07
57. Forbes		50.00	50.00	50.00			0.07
58. Forum		50.00	50.00				0.07
59. Golden Book	50.00		50.00				0.07
60. Golfer and Sportsman			50.00	50.00			0.07
61. Nation			100.0				0.07
62. Arts and Decoration							0.08

TABLE 38 (Continued)

	UU	LU	UM	LM	UL	LL	Total
63. Hunter-Trader-Trapper		0.64 100.0					0.03
64. Motor Boating				0.10 100.0			0.03
65. Radio Digest		0.64 100.0		0.10 100.0			0.03
66. Stage			0.12 100.0				0.03
67. Writer							0.03

4. The Magazine Preferences of the Six Classes

When the ten most popular magazines of the upper-upper class are examined to see how they rank in the preferences of the five classes below the upper-upper, there is for most of them a clear demonstration of a diminution of interest; when the ten most popular magazines of the lower-lower class are examined to determine how the five higher classes purchase them, there is a steady decline in reader interest as the class position increases from the lowest to the highest. Table 37 presents the magazine preferences of each class.

A summary of how each class made its choices for most of the magazines now follows. It should be read in conjunction with Table 38.

Four kinds of information on magazine buying are to be found in this table. The magazines are listed at the left of the page. The rank order for all Yankee City is placed by each magazine. The extreme right-hand column gives the percentage of magazines bought in Yankee City which was enjoyed by that particular magazine. For example, *Needlecraft* ranks first with a percentage of the total purchases of 7.79 while *Pictorial Review* with 7.31 per cent is second.

The vertical percentages in each of the class columns give the proportion of that class's purchases which each magazine had. It tells, for example, that while the *Pictorial Review* had 4.66 per cent of the upper-upper subscriptions and purchases, *Needlecraft*, which led all magazines for the whole community, was little favored (0.77 per cent) by that class. Furthermore, it shows that the two lower classes were far above the 7.79 per cent average for all classes and the two upper ones far below it. All magazines were examined from this point of view to enable a clear comparison of magazine choices among the six classes to be made.

The horizontal figures give a class analysis of all the buyers of each magazine; they treat each magazine's subscriptions as a unit. For example, of all the purchasers of *Needlecraft* 42.92 per cent were lower-middle, 31.86 per cent were upper-lower, and 12.39 per cent were lower-lower. The lower-middle class ranks first for the highest percentage of those who buy *Needle-*

craft and is above the two lower classes who outrank it in preference shown for this magazine (see vertical figures).

A larger percentage of the two lower classes read *Needlecraft* than did any other class (see vertical figures in column of each class, Table 38); and the lower-middle members read it more than the average. The upper-middle class approximated the average for the whole society and the two upper classes were far below the average for the group.

The two lower classes read the *Pictorial Review* more frequently than all others and were the only ones who read it above the average; while the lower-middle, upper-middle, and upper-upper-class subscribers approximated the average, and the lower-upper were well below it.

The upper-middle, lower-middle, and upper-lower classes were above the average for subscriptions to *McCall's;* the lower-lower approximated the average, while the two lower classes were well below the average for the whole group.

Cosmopolitan was most favored by the two lower classes, particularly the lower-lower, and only these two classes were above the average of subscribers to this magazine. The lower-middle preferred this magazine in about the same proportion as the general population. The three upper classes, particularly the upper-upper, tended to avoid it.

The two middle classes showed a decided preference for *Better Homes and Gardens;* and the upper-upper class refused to read it, while the three other classes approximated, but were below the average for, the whole group.

The *National Geographic* was favored by the three upper classes and in particular by the two upper ones. The lower-middle class approached the average for the total group; the upper-lower was well below the average; and the lower-lower did not read it at all.

The *Delineator* was favored by the two lower classes: twice as many of the lower-lower subscribers preferred this magazine as did the average subscribers in the general population. The lower-middle-class subscribers were slightly above but approximated the average for the total group, while the three upper classes were well below. The *Ladies' Home Journal* was preferred by the two middle and upper classes and was not favored by the two lower classes (well below the average).

The *Woman's Home Companion* was most favored by the lower-lower class, but the upper-middle and upper-lower classes also read it more than the average reader in the population. The lower-middle class approximated the average, while the two upper classes were far below.

The *Saturday Evening Post* was read more by the three upper classes than by any others, the upper-upper class having particularly frequent subscribers to it; the lower-middle class approximated the average; while the two lower classes seemed to avoid it.

The *Literary Digest* was read most by the two middle classes; the lower-upper class was also above the average; the upper-upper approached the average, while the two lower classes were well below it.

The *American* was favored only by the two middle classes. The two lower classes approximated the average; while the two upper classes were much below it.

The *Country Gentleman* was preferred by subscribers from the upper-middle, lower-middle, and upper-lower classes. The two upper classes and the lower-lower class were below the average of readers.

Woman's World was favored by the upper-lower and lower-middle classes; the upper-middle and lower-lower classes approached the average; while the upper-upper-class subscribers were much below the average for the total number of subscribers in Yankee City. There were no lower-upper-class subscribers.

Red Book was preferred by the three lower classes, particularly by the lower-lower whose readers read it about three times more than the general population. The upper-middle and lower-upper approximated the average but were below it, while the upper-upper did not read it at all. There is a continuous diminution of the percentage of readers from the lower-lower class through all classes to the upper-upper for subscribers to this magazine.

The *Open Road for Boys* was favored by the three lower classes; the three upper classes were below the average. *Collier's* was subscribed to more than the general average by the lower and middle classes and not by the two upper classes. The two lower classes preferred it the most, and the upper-upper classes, the least. There were no lower-upper-class subscribers.

Parents' Magazine was subscribed to above the average for the general population by the two lower classes and the upper-middle. The lower-middle and lower-upper were well below the average, and the upper-upper did not read it at all.

The *Reader's Digest* was read by the three upper classes. It was particularly favored by the lower-upper, who subscribed to it about four times as frequently as the general population. The lower-middle and lower-lower classes read it much below the average, and the upper-lower did not read it at all.

Hunting and Fishing magazine was preferred by the upper-lower and lower-middle classes; the upper-upper subscribers approximated the average for the entire group, while the other three classes were much below the average.

Sports Afield was much preferred by the upper-upper class; the lower-upper class was slightly above the average; and the other four classes were far below. The two lower classes subscribed to it the least of all classes.

Time Magazine was read above the average by the two upper classes; the lower-upper subscribed to it over five times more than the general population. The upper-middle class was below but approximated the average; the lower-middle and upper-lower were well below; while the lower-lower did not read it at all.

The *American Home* was preferred by the upper-middle and lower-upper classes but not by the upper-upper; the lower-middle approached the average for the general group; while the upper-upper and upper-lower were well below the average; and the lower-lower did not subscribe to it.

The *American Boy* was preferred by the upper-upper and upper-lower classes. The two middle classes subscribed to it in an average way, while the lower-lower and lower-upper did not read it. The boys' magazines frequently show a distribution in which classes not in sequence are found to favor the magazine.

The *Atlantic Monthly* was highly favored by the upper-upper class. Six times more subscribers of that class read it than did the average for the total population. The lower-upper and upper-middle read it well above the average; the lower-middle and upper-lower were below; and the lower-lower did not read it at all. The distribution of subscribers to the *Atlantic Monthly* runs in sequence through the classes from a very high preference in the upper uppers to none in the lower lowers.

House Beautiful was preferred by the three upper classes, in particular by the lower-upper; the lower-middle and upper-lower read it below the average; and the lower-lower did not read it at all. With the strong emphasis that the lower-upper class places on having "houses that are perfect" their very strong preference for this magazine is easily understood.

Review of Reviews was read above the average for the two middle classes; the lower-upper and upper-lower classes approximated the average, while the lower-lower was below it, and the upper-upper did not read it at all.

Boys' Life was most preferred by the lower-lower class; it was also subscribed to above the average by the lower-middle and upper-upper; read below the average by the upper-middle and upper-lower; and not read at all by the lower-upper.

Harper's was strongly preferred (over five times above the average for the general population) by the two upper classes. The upper-middle class approximated the average but was slightly above it; the lower-middle class was well below it; and the two lower classes did not read this magazine at all.

Popular Science was most preferred by the two upper classes; the upper-lower and upper-middle approximated but were slightly above the average for the general population; the lower-middle was below; and the lower-lower class did not read the magazine.

National Sportsman was read the most by the two lower classes; the two upper classes and the lower-middle approximated the average; while the upper-middle class was well below the average.

Judge was highly favored by the lower-upper class; read above the average by the upper-upper, upper-middle, and upper-lower classes; below the average by the lower-lower; and was not read by the lower-middle class.

Étude was read by the lower-middle class more frequently than the average for the general group. The upper-middle and upper-lower classes read it next most frequently, and the two upper classes and the lower-lower did not subscribe to it.

True Story was most favored by the lower-lower class; and

next, by the upper-lower class. The lower-middle and upper-middle were below the average, while the two upper classes did not subscribe to it. The lower the class of the reader, the more frequently he prefers *True Story*.

Liberty was highly favored by the upper-middle class. The two lower classes read it slightly above the average; the lower-middle, well below the average; and the two upper classes did not subscribe to it.

College Humor was favored by the two upper classes and the lower-lower; the two middle classes approached the average; and the upper-lower did not read it.

Harper's Bazaar was highly favored by the upper-upper class; the upper-middle class was slightly above the average; the upper-lower and lower-middle, below it; and the lower-upper and lower-lower did not subscribe to it.

The *New Yorker* was much preferred by the two upper classes; the upper-middle was below the average; and the three lower classes did not subscribe to it.

Field and Stream was highly preferred by the two upper classes; the upper-middle and upper-lower approximated but were above the average; while the lower-middle and lower-lower did not subscribe to this magazine.

Fortune was read by the two upper classes more than the average for the general population. The upper-middle and lower-middle classes were below the average and the two lower classes did not read it.

The *Nation* was read by the two middle classes and no others.

By this examination of the reader's preference for magazines which had more than a scattering of subscribers, it is clear that no magazine is read or preferred exclusively by the upper-upper class. The *Atlantic Monthly*, however, approaches this position.

The upper-upper and lower-upper classes, however, did show a preference above all others for certain popular magazines. They were *Sports Afield, Financial World*, the *New Yorker, Current History*, and *Fortune*.

Judge, Vogue, and *Asia* were most preferred by the lower-upper class.

The three higher classes demonstrated a decided preference

for the *National Geographic*, the *Saturday Evening Post*, *Reader's Digest*, *Time*, *Atlantic Monthly*, *House Beautiful*, *Harper's*, *Vanity Fair*, and *Field and Stream*.

The upper-upper and upper-middle classes preferred *Harper's Bazaar*.

The lower-upper and upper-middle classes preferred the *American Home*.

The lower-upper, upper-middle, and lower-middle classes preferred the *Literary Digest*.

The two upper classes and the two middle classes showed a preference for the *Ladies' Home Journal*.

The upper-middle class preferred the *Junior Home Magazine*.

The upper-middle and lower-middle classes had a high percentage of readers of *Better Homes and Gardens*, the *American*, and *Review of Reviews*.

The lower-middle class was the only one which showed a high preference for *Étude*.

The upper-middle, lower-middle, and upper-lower classes favored *McCall's* and the *Country Gentleman*.

The two middle classes and the two lower classes preferred the *Woman's Home Companion* and *Collier's*.

The two middle classes and the lower-lower preferred *Physical Culture*.

The upper-middle and the two lower classes preferred *Parents' Magazine* and *Liberty*.

The upper-middle, lower-middle, and upper-lower classes preferred *Woman's World*. The lower-middle and upper-lower classes preferred *Hunting and Fishing*.

The three lower classes favored *Needlecraft*, the *Delineator*, *Red Book*, and the *Open Road for Boys*.

The two lower classes were the only ones which showed a high preference for *Pictorial Review*, *Cosmopolitan*, and *True Story*.

5. *The Class of the Purchasers of Each of the Magazines*

The above analysis has given us an exact picture of the preferences of the six classes for the various magazines which are subscribed to in Yankee City, but it has not told us what percentage of the purchasers of each magazine belongs to a particular class.

Reading and Symbolic Behavior of the Six Classes 405

For example, the former analysis might tell us that the upper class preferred a particular magazine above all others and that 5 per cent of all their subscriptions were to this magazine, and that the lower-middle class showed average preference for it and only 1 per cent of their readers subscribed to it. However, since the lower-middle class is far larger than the upper-upper the number of purchasers of the magazine in question from

XXXVII. *Class Composition of a Magazine's Readers*

this class might be greater than the number of those from the upper-upper class. The horizontal figures in Table 38 give the exact percentage of the purchases of each magazine which were made by each class. Chart XXXVII represents these same percentages. The magazines are arranged in groups of ten in the order of their preference for all Yankee City. This chart is given because it allows rapid inspection of the class composition of purchasers of each magazine and a quick comparison among them.

6. Evidence of the Influence of Class and Ethnic Affiliation on Newspaper Reading

Class and ethnic influences are quite apparent in the choice of newspapers in Yankee City.

The natives favored the Boston *Herald*, the Boston *Traveler*, and the Boston *Transcript* in significantly high percentages, and they avoided the Boston *American* and the Boston *Record* in significant numbers (see Table 39). The French purchased the *American* and the *Record* in significantly high numbers and did not read the local newspaper and the *Herald* in significant numbers. The Poles also favored the *American* and the *Record* in significantly high numbers and did not read the Boston *Post*, Boston *Globe*, *Herald*, and *Traveler* in significant numbers. The Irish purchased and subscribed in significant numbers to the local newspaper, the *American*, the *Post*, and the *Globe;* and they avoided reading the *Herald*, *Transcript*, *Traveler*, and the *Record* in significant numbers. The Greeks preferred the *American* and *Record* in significant numbers and avoided the local newspaper, the *Post*, and the *Traveler* in significant numbers.

The Armenians avoided the *Herald* in significant numbers. The Italians favored the *American* in significant numbers. They failed to read the local newspaper and the *Herald* in significant numbers.

The Jews preferred the *Traveler*, the *Transcript*, and the *Record* in significant numbers. They avoided the local newspaper in significant numbers. The Jews and the Yankees were the only two groups who favored the *Transcript* in significant numbers. The Irish and the Yankees were the only two groups who avoided the *Record* in significant numbers.

On the other hand, the French, Poles, Greeks, and Jews were the only people who favored the *Record* in significant numbers. The natives were the only people who favored the *Herald* in significant numbers, while five groups—the French, Poles,

TABLE 39
Newspaper Reading of the Ethnic Groups

	1 Local Paper	2 Boston American	3 Boston Post	4 Boston Globe	5 Boston Herald	6 Boston Traveler	7 Boston Transcript	8 Boston Record
Native	—	L	—	—	H	H	H	L
Irish	H	H	H	H	L	L	L	L
French	L	H	—	—	L	—	—	H
Jewish	L	—	—	—	—	H	H	H
Italian	L	H	—	—	L	—	—	—
Armenian	—	—	—	—	L	—	—	—
Greek	L	H	L	L	—	L	—	H
Polish	—	H	L	L	L	L	—	H
Russian	—	—	—	—	—	—	—	—
Negro	—	—	—	—	—	—	—	—

H — Significantly High
L — Significantly Low
— — Non-Significant
0 — Not Present

Irish, Armenians, and Italians—significantly avoided reading this newspaper.

Chart XXXVIII represents the percentage of each newspaper's subscribers who belonged to the various ethnic groups. The Yankees were heavy purchasers (well above their proportion of the population) of the Boston *Transcript, Herald,* and *Traveler* and well below on the *Record* and *American.* The Irish were large subscribers to the *Post* and *Globe.*

XXXVIII. *Newspaper Purchases of the Ethnic Groups*

The upper-lower class comprised a larger percentage of the newspaper subscribers in Yankee City than any other place (33.41 per cent).[5] The lower-middle class ranked second (31.49 per cent); the upper-middle class, third (14.60 per cent); the lower-lower class, fourth (14.59 per cent); the lower-upper, fifth (2.80 per cent); and the upper-upper, sixth (2.39 per cent).

The three upper classes tended to have a larger proportion of newspaper subscribers than they did of the population of Yankee City (see Table 40 and Chart XXXIX). The lower-

5. It is impossible to give the percentage of the population which subscribed to newspapers because it would divulge the amount of subscriptions each newspaper had in this community. When the newspapers were kind enough to give their subscription list they were promised that the names and numbers of their subscribers would be kept confidential. The terms subscriber, reader, and purchaser are used interchangeably and refer to total purchasers.

TABLE 40
Newspaper Readers in the Six Classes

Class	1 Local Paper	2 Boston American	3 Boston Post	4 Boston Globe	5 Boston Herald	6 Boston Traveler	7 Boston Transcript	8 Boston Record	Total
UU	41.10	1.84	3.68	0.00	37.43	7.98	7.36	0.61	2.39
LU	40.83	1.05	1.05	10.99	28.80	15.71	1.57	0.00	2.80
UM	45.89	2.81	10.44	11.65	18.57	6.93	2.51	1.20	14.60
LM	54.01	9.12	14.39	9.45	5.26	4.93	0.28	2.56	31.49
UL	54.99	15.18	14.22	7.81	1.18	2.85	0.04	3.73	33.41
LL	50.85	25.23	8.84	5.13	1.41	0.40	0.00	8.14	14.59
Unknown	48.97	14.29	16.33	20.41	0.00	0.00	0.00	0.00	0.72
Total	51.97	12.21	12.33	8.49	6.67	4.21	0.69	3.43	

Class	1	2	3	4	5	6	7	8
UU	1.89	0.36	0.71	0.00	13.40	4.53	25.53	.043
LU	2.20	0.24	0.24	3.63	12.09	10.45	6.38	0.00
UM	12.89	3.36	12.37	20.03	12.66	24.04	53.19	5.13
LM	32.72	23.53	36.74	35.06	40.66	36.94	12.77	23.50
UL	35.35	41.54	38.53	30.74	24.84	22.65	2.13	36.32
LL	14.27	30.13	10.46	8.81	5.93	1.39	0.00	34.62
Unknown	0.68	0.84	0.95	1.73	3.08	0.00	0.00	0.00

lower class had a smaller proportion of newspaper subscribers than it did of the total population of the community. All classes read the local newspaper more than any other: 41.10 per cent of the upper-upper class who subscribed to newspapers took the local newspaper; 40.83 per cent of the lower-upper class subscribed to it; 45.89 per cent of the upper-middle class; 54.01 per cent of the lower-middle class; 54.99 per cent of the upper-lower class; and 50.85 per cent of the lower-lower class.

XXXIX. *The Newspaper Purchases by Members of the Six Classes*

The lower-middle class was significantly high in the number of its subscribers to the local newspaper. The three lower classes tended to read this newspaper more than the three upper classes.

The Boston *Herald* was read more than any other Boston paper by the three upper classes: 37.43 per cent of the newspaper subscribers of the upper-upper class read this newspaper; 28.80 per cent of the lower-upper class; 18.57 per cent of the upper-middle class; 5.26 per cent of the lower-middle class; 1.18 per cent of the upper-lower class; and 1.41 per cent of the lower-lower class. As the rank of a class decreases the percentage of its subscribers to the Boston *Herald* also tends to decrease.

The Boston *American* tends to be a lower-class paper. The two lower classes had a significantly high number of buyers of this paper; the middle and upper classes had a significantly low number of them. The lower-lower class read the *American* more than any other class: 25.23 per cent of the subscribers in this class took the *American;* 15.18 per cent of the upper-lower class subscribed to it; 9.12 per cent of the lower-middle class; 2.81 per cent of the upper-middle; 1.84 per cent of the upper-upper; and 1.05 per cent of the lower-upper.

The Boston *Post* tends to be middle and lower class. A significantly high number of the upper-lower and lower-middle classes read it, and a significantly low number of the upper-upper and lower-upper classes read it. More readers of newspapers from the lower-middle class subscribed to the *Post* than did the newspaper readers of any other class: 14.39 per cent of the newspaper readers of the lower-middle class preferred the *Post;* 14.22 per cent of the upper-lower read it; 10.44 per cent of the newspaper readers of the upper-middle class purchased it; 8.84 per cent of the lower-lower; 3.68 per cent of the upper-upper; and 1.05 per cent of the lower-upper.

About 8.50 per cent of the Yankee City newspaper readers purchased the Boston *Globe*. None of them was upper-upper; 11.65 per cent of the upper-middle class read the *Globe;* 10.99 per cent of the lower-upper; 9.45 per cent of the lower-middle class; 7.81 per cent of the upper-lower; and 5.13 per cent of the lower-lower. The *Globe* tends to be a middle-class paper. There is a significantly low number of upper-upper purchasers and a significantly low number of lower-class purchasers.

Slightly over 4 per cent of the Yankee City newspaper readers bought the Boston *Traveler*. Of the lower-upper class, 15.71 per cent bought this paper; of the upper-upper, 7.98 per cent; of the upper-middle, 6.93 per cent; of the lower-middle, 4.93 per cent; of the upper-lower, 2.85 per cent; and of the lower-lower, less than half of 1 per cent.

The *Traveler* is a paper favored by the three upper classes. It showed a significantly high number of lower-upper and upper-middle-class readers and a significantly low number of readers from the two lower classes.

Less than 1 per cent of the Yankee City newspaper readers took the Boston *Transcript:* 7.36 per cent of the upper-upper class did; 2.51 per cent of the upper-middle; 1.57 per cent of the lower-upper; 0.28 per cent of the lower-middle; and 0.04 per cent of the upper-lower. The *Transcript* is primarily a paper favored by the three upper classes of Yankee City. The upper-upper and upper-middle classes had a significantly high number of *Transcript* readers, and the lower-middle and upper-lower classes, a significantly low number, while no one in the lower-lower class read this paper.

The Boston *Record* was read by 3.43 per cent of the Yankee City newspaper readers: 8.14 per cent of the lower-lower class read this newspaper; 3.73 per cent of the upper-lower; 2.56 per cent of the lower-middle; 1.20 per cent of the upper-middle; 0.61 per cent of the upper-upper; and none of the lower-upper. The *Record* is definitely a lower-class paper. The lower-lower class had a significantly high number of readers of this newspaper, and the two middle classes had a significantly low number of readers.

7. The Motion Picture in Yankee City

ONLY one moving picture theater was in operation in Yankee City at the time of our field work, and it was owned by one of the large national chains with central offices in New York City. The manager, a resident of Yankee City, was extremely active in the associations and other institutions of the community. When interviewed, he stated that since the theater had been taken over by the chain, it had been necessary to give out more free passes to local people. It seems probable that this was necessary because of the impersonal relationship between the absentee owners and the Yankee City community. It was only through the co-operation of the local manager and one of the officers of the company at its New York office that we were able to make an effective study of motion-picture attendance at the Yankee City moving picture theater. Their box-office records and other reports were made accessible to us, and we were allowed to make a check of the patrons during two different periods, one of two weeks during the spring of 1935 and the other of ten days in the first part of October of the same year. The management, furthermore, donated the services of an usher who was acquainted with a large part of the Yankee City population.

Programs were changed three times a week, on Sunday,

Wednesday, and Friday. The Sunday, Monday, and Tuesday shows were of a preferred type and were chosen by the management because they were expected to be well-accepted by the audience. It is possible that Sunday censorship laws and a strong consciousness of the Sabbath in Yankee City influenced the management to select the best exhibits for this day. Furthermore, large audiences at the Sunday performances made a good showing at the start of the week. Wednesday and Thursday exhibits were considered perhaps the least important in the eyes of the management. An appeal was made to a female audience and most frequently pictures shown were of the light fictional type of romance. Wednesday and Thursday audiences averaged the smallest of the week. The Friday and Saturday shows included pictures of the action type which were designed to sustain excitement in the audience; Western and mystery stories were the type usually presented.

Attendance figures showed increases and decreases on both yearly and weekly cycles. Each week, Saturday and Sunday had the highest attendance of Yankee City moving picture patrons. This was largely because these two days are regarded as holidays for both adults and subadults, and on Saturday people from surrounding towns came to Yankee City to do their shopping and to attend the movies.

There was a considerable drop in the number of patrons on Mondays, Wednesdays, and Fridays, while on Tuesdays and Thursdays there was the smallest attendance of all days of the week. A larger audience came on Wednesdays and Fridays because on these days changes in program occurred. The audience on Mondays was about as large as Wednesday and Friday audiences.

During the year more people attended the movies in the fall season, after Labor Day, and the peak of attendance for all times was reached during October. Attendance, though still large, fell off during the winter months of December, January, and February, and the Christmas and Lenten seasons cut into it deeply. In the spring months of March, April, and May there was a marked decline in the number of admissions, and April 1 marked an abrupt falling off of interest in motion-picture shows. The summer season of June, July, and August was lowest, when most people of Yankee City were more interested in outdoor activities than in attending motion-picture shows. Well-publicized pictures of a superior quality drew a large crowd in any season of the year, and several record attendances were established even during the summer months.

In order to discover what people attended the motion-picture shows in Yankee City, an observer who was an upper-lower Irish member and an interviewer who was a lower-upper native member of the Yankee City community listed the patrons as they entered the theater through the lobby and recorded the names of those who attended during the two different periods, which in all totaled twenty-five days.

The lower-upper-class interviewer knew most of the members of the three upper classes, while the upper-lower member of the theater staff was acquainted with a large part of the members of the three lower classes of the Yankee City society. Because the management of the theater insisted that all figures be confidential we shall give only percentages of those people who attended.

Of those who went to the movies 39.84 per cent attended about once a month; 24.76 per cent twice a month; 25.88 per cent once a week; 9.10 per cent twice a week; and 0.42 per cent three times a week or every show.

The average attendance of movie patrons during these twenty-five days was 2.31 times. Upper-upper-class people averaged 2 times; the lower-upper class, 1.92 times; the upper-middle, 1.95 times; the lower-middle-class people, 2.30 times; upper-lower class, 2.43 times; and lower-lower persons came on an average of 2.65 times.

Upper-upper, lower-upper, and upper-middle-class persons attended less frequently than the average for all persons. Lower-middle-class persons attended about the average number of times; while upper-lower and lower-lower patrons attended more frequently than would be expected. Although upper-upper-class persons attended more frequently than did those of the lower-upper and upper-middle class, patrons of the movies in each class inferior to the lower-upper attended more and more often.

Male patrons attended 2.42 times; female, 2.22 times. Although males show a slightly greater tendency to attend movies than do females, this difference is hardly great enough to be of much significance.

People in the age range of eight to sixteen years had an average attendance of 2.18 times; those between seventeen and twenty-five years of age averaged 2.63 times; those of twenty-six to thirty-four years had an average attendance of 2.20 times; those of thirty-five to fifty-four years of age an average attendance of 2.09 times; those of fifty-five years of age and over an average attendance of 1.95 times; and those of unknown age attended, on an average, 1.90 times. Thus, the average attendance of the group between the ages of seventeen and twenty-five years ranked first; between twenty-six and thirty-four years of age, second; between eight and sixteen years of age, third; between thirty-five and fifty-four years of age, fourth; and fifty-five years and over, fifth.

Almost all of the people between seventeen and twenty-five years of age attended the movies at least once every two weeks. As the theater usher commented, even those people who were queer and kept to themselves all of the time, who were seventeen to twenty-five years of age, came to the movies. They came in groups of boys and girls, and they met after the show and then went out to a dance or to some other place. Theater attendance falls off after the age of twenty-six, as these people compose the younger married group who tend to organize their interests more around the family.

The ethnic groups averaged 2.43 movie attendances in twenty-five days, a higher average than that of the Yankees (2.18). Armenians had an average attendance of 3.60 times during the twenty-five days, French 2.35 times, Greeks 2.56 times, Irish 2.38 times, Italians 2.33 times, Jews 2.38 times, Negroes 6 times, Polish 2.93 times, Russians 3 times, and the Yankees 2.18 times.

Although the Negroes ranked first, the small size of their patronage makes this ranking of little significance. Armenians ranked second; Russians, third; Poles, fourth; Greeks, fifth; Irish and Jews, sixth and seventh; French, eighth; Italians, ninth; and natives, tenth. The Irish, French Canadians, and Italians are the oldest of the ethnic groups and show a tendency to follow the natives in the infrequency of their motion-picture attendance. The Armenians, Russians, and Poles are among the most recent arrivals in the Yankee City society and attend with greater than expected frequency. The Greeks, who are also among the most recent arrivals, however, attend with relative infrequency.

Catholic patrons attended the movies on an average of 2.31 times during the twenty-five-day period; Protestant patrons, 2.12 times; patrons of the Greek Orthodox religion, 1.40 times; and of the Jewish religion, 2.33 times. Patrons who professed no religion averaged 2.42 motion-picture attendances. That part of the audience which professed no religion ranked first in frequency of attendance; those who were of the Jewish religion were second; those of the Catholic, third; those of the Protestant were fourth; those of the Greek Orthodox religion ranked fifth.

Upper-upper-class persons accounted for 2.12 per cent of the movie patrons but formed only 1.45 per cent of the Yankee City population. Lower-upper-class persons had 3.44 per cent of the movie patronage but only 1.57 per cent of the population. Upper-middle-class persons composed 14.87 per cent of the movie patrons with 10.30 per cent of the population. Lower-middle-class persons had 34.38 per cent of the movie patrons and 28.36 per cent of the population. Upper-lower-class persons composed 32.86 per cent of the movie patrons and 32.88 per cent of the population. And lower-lower-class persons accounted for only 12.33 per cent of the persons of all classes who go to the movies but had 25.44 per cent of the population.

Thus a larger proportion of movie patrons than expected comes from the upper-upper, lower-upper, upper-middle, and lower-middle classes, and about the expected number come from the upper-lower class, and a much smaller than expected number come from the lower-lower class.

We have seen how many moving-picture patrons of the Yankee City community attended the moving-picture shows according to their social characteristics, and how they compared in class with its total population. We shall now examine the total attendance of the motion-picture theater during the twenty-five-day period according to the social characteristics of the persons attending.

Upper-upper-class paid admissions accounted for 1.83 per

cent of the total attendance (not individuals, but the total times the individuals went to the movies); lower-upper, for 2.90 per cent; upper-middle, for 12.53 per cent; lower-middle, for 34.16 per cent; upper-lower, for 34.47 per cent; and lower-lower paid admissions composed 14.11 per cent of the total attendance. Persons of the upper-lower class ranked first in attendance; those of the lower-middle class, second; those of the lower-lower, third; those of the upper-middle, fourth; of the lower-upper, fifth; and persons of the upper-upper, sixth.

With the exception of the lower-lower class, attendance decreases as the status of the class increases. Lower-lower-class members were significantly low in attendance.

Persons from the ages of eight to sixteen years composed 5.49 per cent of the movie attendance; those of seventeen to twenty-five years of age, 46.63 per cent; those of twenty-six to thirty-four years, 13.13 per cent; those of thirty-five to fifty-four years of age, 24.03 per cent; and those of fifty-five years and over, 9.03 per cent; and of unknown age, 1.69 per cent.

The attendance of persons between the ages of seventeen and twenty-five was significantly large and ranked first; between the ages of thirty-five and fifty-four, second; between twenty-six and thirty-four years of age ranked third; fifty-five years and above ranked fourth; and the attendance of persons from eight to sixteen years of age ranked fifth; and those of unknown age, sixth and last. Persons between the ages of eight and sixteen were significantly small in admittances. School programs prohibited them from coming in very great numbers on days other than Saturday or Sunday.

Male patrons composed 52.14 per cent of the attendance, and female patrons had 47.86 per cent. There was no significant difference in the male and female figures although a few more males than females attended the Yankee City motion-picture theater during our twenty-five-day sampling.

The Yankees composed 43.29 per cent of all motion-picture attendance of the community; the Armenians, 1.23 per cent; the French, 6.45 per cent; Greeks, 0.94 per cent; Irish, 37.57 per cent; Italians, 2.45 per cent; Jews, 3.98 per cent; Negroes, 0.14 per cent; Poles, 3.68 per cent; and Russians, 0.27 per cent.

The Yankees ranked first in attendance; the Irish, second;

French, third; Jews, fourth; Poles, fifth; Italians, sixth; Armenians, seventh; Greeks, eighth; Russians, ninth; and Negroes, tenth. The natives and Irish accounted for over four fifths of the moving-picture attendance; other ethnic groups were small in number but for the most part attended more frequently.

If we examine the movie attendance according to the religion of the patrons, we find that 24.97 per cent were Catholic; 22.73 per cent were of the Protestant faith; 0.16 per cent, of the Greek Orthodox religion; 3.36 per cent, of the Jewish religion; and 48.78 per cent professed no religion.

Almost one half were nonreligionists and ranked first; Catholics ranked second; Protestants, third; those of the Jewish religion, fourth; and those of the Greek Orthodox faith ranked fifth. Although there were more Protestants in the Yankee City community, the Catholic attendance at the motion pictures was higher. Patrons of the Jewish and Greek Orthodox religions were significantly smaller in number.

Members of the two upper classes who attended movies fell largely in the higher age grades, with over one half of the upper-upper-class and almost three fourths of the lower-upper-class patrons in ages between thirty-five and fifty-four and fifty-five and above. Almost two thirds of the upper-middle-class patrons were in age groups which ranged from seventeen to twenty-five years and from thirty-five to fifty-four years; and over two thirds of the lower-middle-class attendance fell in the same age groupings. Almost three fifths of the upper-lower-class patrons were of the one age group between seventeen and twenty-five years, and somewhat over three fifths of the lower-lower-class attendance was in the same age range.

Patrons of the upper-upper class were predominantly female; those of the lower-upper, upper-middle, lower-middle, and upper-lower classes were fairly evenly divided between male and female patrons; and those of the lower-lower class had more than double the number of male than female admissions. Thus, the females of the upper-upper class attended the motion picture much more frequently than males, indicating, possibly, that they had more leisure time.

Both male and female moving picture patrons attended in approximately the same proportion in all age grades, with female patrons somewhat in excess of male patrons for the eight- to sixteen-year group and the thirty-five- to fifty-four-age range.

8. Influences on the Selection of Doctors and Undertakers

Of the fifteen doctors in general practice in Yankee City when we made our study, four belonged to the upper-upper class, three to the lower-upper, and eight to the upper-middle, below which there was none. Our data reveal that the physician-patient relationship tends, within certain limitations, to favor class lines, so that the following generalization can be made: the higher the rank of the patient, the higher the rank of the doctor he patronizes; or, the higher the rank of the doctor, the higher the rank of the patient he treats. A generalization of this same order can be made for a variety of relationship situations which provide services of one kind or another. As examples we may mention only a few: dentists, undertakers, lawyers, architects, and ministers. This situation is modified considerably, of course, by such factors as ethnicity, skill, specialization, and limitation of choice, most of which are also determinants of class position. Obviously, a lower-lower-class patient cannot patronize a lower-lower-class physician when there are no representatives of the medical profession in the lower-lower class; nor can an upper-upper-class person be buried by an upper-upper-class undertaker when there are no undertakers in the upper-upper class. What we are interested in pointing out here is that the professional services rendered in Yankee City tend to conform with the class hierarchy; we are not interested in pointing out the variables which affect that conformity.

The lower-upper class preferred upper-upper doctors more than any other class. The upper-middle was second; lower-middle, third; upper-lower, fourth; and the lower-lower preferred them least of all. The lower-upper class preferred lower-upper-class doctors more than any other class; the upper-middle class preferred them next; the lower-middle ranked third; the upper-lower, fourth; and the lower-lower, fifth.

The lower-lower class preferred upper-middle-class doctors more than all others; the upper-lower class preferred them next; the lower-middle class ranked third; the upper-middle, fourth; and the lower-upper, fifth. The preference for middle-class doctors is the exact reverse of the preference by the members of the several classes for the doctors of the two upper classes.

The six undertakers range in social class from upper-lower to upper-middle. Two of them were in the upper-middle class, two in the lower-middle, one in the upper-lower class, and there was one undertaker whose class was undetermined. Three of the undertakers were Yankee Protestants and three were Irish Catholics.

The class factor is definitely present in the preference expressed by the family of the deceased for undertakers, but it is not so important as in the preference for doctors. The upper-lower class tended to favor lower-middle-class and upper-lower-class undertakers more than any other class, and the lower-lower-class favored them next. The three upper classes favored the upper-middle-class undertakers more than any others, lower-middle class next, and the two lower classes were buried by upper-middle-class morticians in smaller percentages than any other class.

The Catholic ethnics definitely favored Catholic undertakers whether or not the undertaker was of the same ethnic group as they. On the other hand, the other ethnic groups tended to prefer Protestant and Yankee undertakers, although most of them belonged to other faiths than those of the undertakers. The religious factor seems to be of greater importance than the class factor preferences for undertakers.

The three undertakers most preferred by the ethnics were Catholic. The Protestant and Yankee undertaker who received most of the business of Yankee City (43 per cent) obtained but 13 per cent of the ethnic burials. Of the funerals conducted by the ethnic undertakers who had the highest percentage of them, 90 per cent were ethnic, and only 10 per cent were Yankee burials.

The next most popular ethnic undertaker had 80 per cent ethnic burials and 21 per cent native burials. The burials of the third ethnic undertaker were 86 per cent ethnic and 14 per cent Yankee. The most preferred Yankee undertaker's burials were 88 per cent Yankee and 12 per cent ethnic. The burials of the second most preferred Protestant and Yankee undertaker were 93 per cent Yankee and only 7 per cent ethnic. The burials of the third Yankee Protestant undertaker were 78 per cent Yankee and 22 per cent ethnic.

Of the total number of Yankee burials, 88.13 per cent went to Yankee and Protestant undertakers; 8.47 per cent went to local Catholic and ethnic undertakers; and 3.39 per cent, to outsiders.

Of the Irish burials, 89.39 per cent went to Irish Catholic undertakers, 8.34 per cent went to Yankee Protestant undertakers, and 2.27 per cent to outside undertakers.

The French burials were largely conducted by Catholic undertakers: 76.92 per cent of their burials went to Catholic undertakers; only 19.23 per cent, to local Protestant; and 3.85 per cent, to outsiders.

All of the Jewish burials went to Protestant undertakers. Of the Italian, 83.33 per cent went to Catholic undertakers, and 16.67 per cent, to Protestant.

All of the Polish burials conducted by Yankee City undertakers went to Catholic morticians. Eighty per cent of the Armenian burials were conducted by Protestants, and only 20 per cent of them, by Catholic undertakers. Half of the Greek burials were Protestant, and half were Catholic.

All of the upper-upper funerals were conducted by the upper-middle-class undertakers. All of the lower-upper burials went to upper-middle-class undertakers. Seventy-five per cent of the upper-middle-class funerals went to the upper-middle-class undertakers. Of the lower-middle-class funerals, 73.48 per cent were conducted by upper-middle-class morticians. Upper-middle-class undertakers conducted 43.03 per cent of the upper-lower-class burials.

XX

THE SOCIAL CHARACTERISTICS OF THE PEOPLE OF THE TWO UPPER CLASSES

1. *The Upper-Upper Class*

AN upper-upper person in Yankee City belongs to a class having a much larger number of women than men and a larger percentage of females (over 60 per cent) than any other class in the community. In this respect it differs markedly from the lower-lower class, which has the smallest percentage of women, and is most like the upper-middle class, which also has an excess of females. The preponderance of females in the upper-upper class is statistically significant.[1]

The upper-upper class has the smallest percentage of children and the largest proportion of people over sixty years of age. In both respects it stands in strongest contrast to the lower-lower class, containing about 11 per cent of persons under twenty-one, as against 28 per cent, and over 39 per cent of persons sixty years of age or older, as against fewer than 11 per cent. The upper-upper most closely resembles the lower-upper and upper-middle classes in numbers of old people, the upper-middle in percentage of children. The excess of older people in the upper-upper population is accounted for in part by the large number of unmarried females who are the sisters and maiden aunts of other members of the group, in part by the number of "ladies" who have lived on in the old family houses after their parents' death and after their brothers and sons have gone elsewhere to marry and rear their families.

All members of the upper-upper class are Yankees, none belonging to any ethnic group in the community. The lower-upper class, which contains less than 5 per cent with an ethnic background, all of them Irish whose families have been in

---

[1]. The measurement used to test significances in this volume is that of mean-square contingency. All percentages were figures for two points beyond the decimal. This was done not because such detail is ordinarily necessary for most social data, but to insure statistical accuracy.

America for several generations, approximates the upper-upper class most closely in this. By contrast, 57 per cent of the lower-lower and 61 per cent of the upper-lower classes belong to ethnic minorities, with large concentrations of Irish, Poles, Russians, Greeks, French Canadians, Italians, Jews, Armenians, and Negroes. Upper-upper individuals rarely associate with persons of other ethnic stocks. Lower-class Yankees try hard not to do so and sometimes join associations having "racial" prejudices; physically, however, they are continually in the company of people with traditions which differ from their own.

Upper-upper individuals marry later than those of any other class.[2] Their median age at marriage is almost twenty-eight years (27.90), which is closest to that of the lower-upper class (26.60 years) and furthest from that of the lower-lower class (23.20 years). Very few of the upper-upper marry before reaching twenty-one (3.70 per cent), whereas over thirty-five per cent of the lower-lower do; none of the lower-upper class in our survey was married before twenty-one years of age. Over half of the upper-upper class married during the ages from twenty-one to twenty-nine years, while about one third married between thirty and thirty-nine. This class has a larger percentage of single people than any other, and a smaller percentage of married members; about 40 per cent are single, while in all other classes the range is from 31 to 33 per cent. It has a larger number of widowed individuals than any other class, being most similar to the lower-upper in this respect and least like the lower-lower.

From the viewpoint of occupation, upper-upper-class people cluster overwhelmingly in professional and proprietary positions, over 83 per cent being thus employed. They are most like the lower-upper class in this respect and least like the lower-lower, less than 1 per cent of whom are gainfully occupied in these occupations. Upper-upper people are listed in only one other occupational classification: that of clerks and kindred workers (16.67 per cent). Hence they are the least differentiated occupationally, although the lower-upper class follows

---

2. Cf. pp. 94ff. for a full description of marriage in Yankee City. Each characteristic which is summarized in this general description of the six classes is fully described in earlier chapters of this book.

them in this. The upper-upper class has no gainfully occupied people who are classified as skilled, semiskilled, or unskilled workers, as against 85 per cent of the lower-lower class so designated. No wholesale or retail dealers are members of the topmost class. The lower-upper class likewise lacks any who are listed as "workers." The members of the upper-upper class are but slightly represented in the principal industries of the town—shoe and silverware manufacturing—with only 5 per cent in the former and none in the latter, whereas 40 per cent of the lower-lower class are employed in the shoe industry alone.

The topmost class has the highest percentage of employable individuals who have never worked, being most like the lower-upper in this respect and least like the lower-middle. When the unemployment census was taken, the community was suffering from the 1930-35 business depression. But the upper class was most favorably placed, since 90 per cent of its employables had jobs, while only 27.57 per cent of the lower-lower were fully employed. No members of either of the two upper classes were on relief, although some of them were penniless. All other classes had a greater or lesser number on relief, topped by the lower-lower among whom one out of three had his name on the relief rolls.

The upper-upper families are inferior only to the lower-upper in the percentage who own their own homes, being least like the lower-lower class. The median value of their homes is less than that for the lower-upper class but more than that for any other, the median for the lower-lower class being lowest of all. The median value of all real estate owned in Yankee City is higher than in any other class ($5,833); it is most like the lower-upper ($5,600) and least like the lower-lower class ($1,606).[3] Few upper-upper people pay rent. All who do, pay by the month instead of the week, and all fall in the higher rent classification.[4] Again this class is most like the lower-upper, least like the lower-lower.

3. These evaluations are from the assessor's records. They do not represent, as near as we could determine, the actual market value of the properties.

4. Our interviews had suggested that people who paid rent by the month tended to be higher class while those who paid by the week tended to be lower class. The statistics bore out this influence.

A larger percentage of upper-upper members (67 per cent) live in large houses and smaller percentage in medium- and small-sized houses than of any other class. The size of the house is important if for no other reason than the fact that it was so considered in Yankee City. Eighty per cent of the upper-upper houses were found in good condition, 19 per cent in medium or ordinary condition, and less than 1 per cent in poor condition. Once again, the two upper classes are most alike. By contrast, 71 per cent of the houses occupied by the lower-lower class were in bad condition, and only 3 per cent in good condition.[5] Fifty-six per cent of the upper-upper class have large and good houses, 10 per cent have large ones in medium condition, and less than 1 per cent have large houses in bad condition. In all these respects the upper-upper class is most like the lower-upper and least like the lower-lower. It is, moreover, the only class which does not occupy small houses in bad condition, none of its members living in medium-sized and small houses in bad condition or in business dwellings. On the basis of the mean square contingency, both the upper-upper and lower-upper classes are significantly high for houses which are large and good, large and medium, and medium-sized and in good condition. The lower-lower class, on the other hand, is the only class significantly high for houses of all sizes in bad condition and for dwellings built primarily for business purposes. As regards the ecological areas, the upper-upper and lower-upper classes are concentrated in significantly high numbers in the Hill Street, Oldtown, and Newtown areas, and they are significantly low elsewhere, with the exception of Centerville. The two classes differ only in the fact that no one in the lower-upper class is found in the Newtown area. In living areas the upper-upper is least like the two lower classes.

Up to this point in this brief descriptive summary of the upper-upper class, we have concerned ourselves largely with observable characteristics of its members and have not attempted to describe their participation in social institutions of the community. Let us now look at the kinds of voluntary associations to which they belong. Both men and women of the upper-upper class have a significantly high membership in

5. Business dwellings comprise the remainder of this total.

what are ordinarily called social clubs. They also have a significantly high percentage of associations organized for charity, and are significantly low in membership in fraternal organizations (lodges and secret societies), or in associations which are age graded.[6] The upper-upper class, moreover, does not stress membership in associations having auxiliaries. In its associations it is most like the lower-upper class and least like the lower-lower class, the latter being significantly high for male and female fraternities, for auxiliaries, and for age-graded associations, and significantly low for female associations organized for sociable and charitable purposes.

The upper-upper class is also different from the other classes in religious affiliations. Its members favor the Unitarian and Episcopal churches in significantly high numbers. Moreover, they neither attend the Catholic churches nor favor other Protestant sects. In these respects the upper-upper is most like the lower-upper class and least like the lower-lower class, which is significantly high in membership in the two Catholic, the Methodist, Baptist, and Presbyterian churches and significantly low in membership in the Unitarian and Episcopal churches.

Members of the upper-upper and lower-upper classes give their children a different formal and informal education. No children of the former attended the local high school at the time of our census, and, as far as we could determine, but few had attended this institution previously. Moreover, only four lower-upper-class children were enrolled in the high school. Most of the children of the two upper classes are sent to private preparatory schools, where they not only prepare for college but also acquire the etiquette and attributes of their group. Because the two upper classes were so sparsely represented in the local school, it is impossible to show how the higher classes select their courses of study, but we know that the subjects chosen are the conventional ones which colleges and universities demand as entrance requirements.

Formal education of adolescents does not always take place in school, since some are employed before they reach twenty-one. There is obviously a relationship between the kind of high school course chosen by the children and the age at which they

6. For definitions of the various types of associations, see the earlier chapter on associations.

intend to go to work. If one knew nothing about the American class system, he might suppose that since only a few members of the two upper classes attended the local high schools they would be found in the town's economic life. However, in a study of subadult employment, we found no upper-uppers represented and but eight lower-uppers, as contrasted with a large percentage of lower-lower adolescents who worked.

Yankee City has one large and well-stocked library. A smaller percentage of the upper-upper than of any other class uses this institution. In this respect it is most like the lower-lower and least like the upper-middle. From interviews we learned that the upper-upper buy their books and belong to discussion clubs where they get the "latest and most current books," while the lower-lower class's failure to use the library is due to the fact that they read less. Of the upper-upper members who use the library, over 85 per cent are adults and slightly over 14 per cent children, whereas of the lower-lower users, over 50 per cent are children.

The frequency with which members of a class are arrested and get their names on the police blotter is a fair index both of the kind of authority exercised by political organization over each class and of the kind of behavior in each class which is sufficiently disapproved by the whole community to warrant the more drastic sanctions of police action. Of the total arrests in the city, the upper-upper class accounts for but one half of 1 per cent, while the lower-lower accounts for 65 per cent. As regards the figures within the class itself, only a little over 1 per cent have been arrested, a slightly larger percentage than the classes just below it, while 11 per cent of the lower-lower class have had their names placed on the police records. Moreover, none of the upper-upper and lower-upper-class arrests is below twenty-one years of age, while 30 per cent of the lower-lower-class arrests are juveniles. This great disparity is not to be accounted for by the fact that "criminal behavior" is proportionately higher among lower-class juveniles or that there are more ethnic members whose children have been imperfectly adapted to Yankee City life. It must be understood as a product of the amount of protection from outside interference the parents can give the members of their families. Our interviews together with police records demonstrate that the lower-lower adolescent boys are guilty of crimes against property, and that some girls are caught in sexual delinquencies. But these same interviews likewise demonstrate that boys and girls in the higher classes as frequently commit the same acts but do not get on the police records. They are not arrested because social pressure prevents the police from taking action when they make threats to do so or forces them to overlook the behavior at their own volition, or, more important, because the social controls of the class system operate in such a way as to hide successfully all such activities from the authorities.

The security of younger members of upper-upper-class families from outside interference is further demonstrated by the fact that all charitable associations, in which the upper classes are represented in large numbers, serve to subordinate the lower classes and interfere with their ordinary family life. An organization such as the Society for the Prevention of Cruelty to Children, for example, is ostensibly free from class bias; yet all of the cases with which it dealt came from below the two upper classes, and most of them, from below the three uppermost classes. In brief, the social power of the upper classes highly protects their families, while the subordinate position of the lower classes leaves their families more vulnerable to the sanctions of the rest of the community.

The upper-upper is most like the lower-upper and least like the lower-lower class in the type of books its members read. Seven per cent of the upper-upper members read books classified as biography and history. The upper-upper also read more books on science than any other class. They and the lower-upper likewise read fewer, while the lower-lower read more, children's books than the other classes. The members of the upper-upper class also read a smaller, and the lower-lower a larger, percentage of adventure stories, than any other class. The upper-upper people read a larger percentage of detective stories than did the members of any other class, but in this respect they are most like the lower-lower and least like the lower-upper and upper-middle classes. They are also most like the lower-lower and least like the upper-middle in the percentage of the reading which falls under the general heading of family and courtship.

For books which accent social climbing, the upper-upper class ranks last, the upper-lower first, in the percentage of its reading members. For those which emphasize patriotism and warlike activities, the upper-upper class is below the lower-upper, which leads all others, and it is least like the lower-lower. The upper-upper is most like the upper-middle class for the percentage of readers of books which emphasize the theme of man's fight against fate, and most like the two middle and least like the lower-upper and lower-lower classes in the interest it shows in reading books about social techniques such as manners. Generally speaking, the upper-upper-class readers show a special interest in detective stories, courtship and the family, and man's fight against fate, and less interest in farce and humor, children's stories, social techniques, and scientific books. But it is not significantly high or low in its preference for any category of book.

The upper-upper (28.51 per cent) is most like the lower-upper and least like the lower-lower class (3.64 per cent) in the number of its magazine subscribers, in the number of magazines per subscriber (1.87 per cent for the upper-upper class), and in preferences and avoidances in the magazines its members read, these being in most cases almost exactly opposite those of the lower-lower class.

The newspapers read in Yankee City include a local and several Boston dailies. The upper-upper class subscribes in significantly high numbers to the Boston *Herald* and the Boston *Transcript*. The *Herald* is a paper which has a reputation for a good financial section, for a very conservative editorial policy in state and national politics, and in general for a semi-conservative treatment of the news. It recognizes sex and crime in its news but does not "overemphasize them," people say, "as do the Hearst papers." The *Transcript* is more like an English newspaper than any other paper in the United States. It is one of the few papers in this country which still carries advertisements on its front page after the manner of the London papers. It carries a weekly page of genealogies, columns on intellectual and expensive hobbies, and contains a very conservative, scholarly editorial page. The *Transcript* has become a New England symbol of better reading as a newspaper, as has the *Atlantic Monthly* as a magazine. This gives it favor among the higher classes as a symbol to grace the library table or to be quoted in dinner-table conversation.

The upper-upper people subscribe in significantly low numbers to the Boston *American,* the Boston *Post,* and the Boston *Globe*. The Boston *American* is a typical Hearst paper which depends on sex and crime for its headlines and news stories and has a policy of playing up "entertaining" syndicated columns and comic strips. The *Post* is a liberal democratic paper and, by general reputation, tends to favor the Irish in public life. It relies on its sport section in large part for its popularity. It also goes in heavily for banner headlines. The *Globe* is a semi-conservative paper which emphasizes suburban and small-community news. Its policies are more liberal than either the *Herald* or *Transcript*.

The upper-upper class is most like the lower-upper and least like the two lower classes in its newspaper reading.

2. *The Lower-Upper Class*

THE lower-upper has already been compared in part with the upper-upper class, but its own special characteristics will now be summarized. The sex ratio of the lower-upper class is slightly over 50 per cent female, 49 per cent male. In this respect, it is most like the lower-middle and least like the upper-upper and lower-lower classes.

In age distribution, the lower-upper class has approximately the same percentage of subadults as the upper-middle class and also approximates the age ranges from twenty-one to thirty-nine, and sixty years or more. It has a somewhat higher percentage of people aged forty to fifty-nine years. The lower-upper is least like the lower-lower class in the percentage of subadults and of those from twenty-one to thirty-nine, and it differs most from the lower-lower class in the age group over sixty.

The lower-upper is most like the upper-upper and least like the lower-lower in the birthplaces of its members. Half of the lower-upper were born in Yankee City and less than 1 per cent outside the United States. The other members of the class were born in contiguous areas (12.39 per cent), in the rest of New

England (13.27 per cent), or in the remainder of the United States (23.02 per cent).

As regards ethnic composition, 95.42 per cent of the lower-upper class are Yankee and but 4.58 per cent ethnic, all of whom are Irish. In this respect it is most like the upper-upper class, the members of which are all Yankee, and least like the lower-lower, which contains representatives of all ethnic groups.

Sixty per cent of the lower-upper class are married or widowed. In marital status, the lower-upper members are most like the upper-middle but vary little from all other classes except the upper-upper, which is decidedly different. The lower-upper tend to marry late; only the upper-upper members marry later. The median age for marriage in the lower-upper class is 26.60 years. In this respect it is most like the upper-middle and least like the lower-lower class. The percentage of those who marry under twenty-one years in the lower-upper class is most like that of the upper-upper, but for all other age ranges it is also most like that of the upper-middle.

The relative age of the spouse is approximately the same for all classes. Seventy-four per cent of the lower-upper men marry women younger than themselves, 10 per cent have wives of the same age, and 6 per cent wives older than they are.

Eighty-six per cent of the occupations of the lower-upper class are professional or proprietary. There are only two other classifications in which lower-upper members are found: (1) wholesale and retail dealers and (2) clerks and kindred workers. Each of these two types of occupation comprises 7 per cent of those who are or have been gainfully employed in this class. The lower-upper is most like the upper-upper and least like the lower-lower in its occupational distribution.

The industries in which the members of the lower-upper class participate are chiefly shoe and silverware manufacturing—similar to those of the upper-upper and, to a certain extent, to those of the upper-middle—and least like those of the lower-lower. Ninety-four per cent of the employables of the lower-upper class are fully employed, none has a part-time job, and 6 per cent are unemployed (most of these latter not seeking employment). The lower-upper is most like the upper-upper and least like the lower-lower in these respects.

The lower-upper class has a higher percentage of home owners (24.05 per cent) than any other class. In this regard it also most closely approximates the upper-upper and is least like the lower-lower class.

The median value of all real estate of the lower-upper class is $5,600. This figure is topped only by that of the upper-upper class and is far above that of the lowest class, which it is least like. All rentals of the lower-upper, like those of the upper-upper class, are paid monthly, while those of the lower-lower class are paid weekly. The median rental for the lower-upper could not be computed exactly because of too few cases, but it seemed to fall between $60 and $50 per month, being least like the median monthly rental of the lower-lower class ($16.23).

The majority of the lower-upper class live in large houses, a high percentage in medium-sized houses, and a small number in small houses. Seventy per cent of the cases live in houses which are in good condition, about 30 per cent in houses ordinarily well cared for, and but a small percentage in houses in bad repair. There are no houses occupied by members of the lower-upper class which are large or medium in size and in bad repair, and less than 1 per cent are small and in poor repair. None of the lower-upper class lives in dwellings built primarily for business purposes. The lower-upper occupy houses which are significantly high in respect to size and condition (large and good, large and medium, and medium and good). The two upper classes are most alike both as to size and condition of the house and least like the lower-lower class.

As regards ecological distribution, members of the lower-upper class are concentrated in significantly high numbers in areas where the upper-upper persons are also significantly high. The areas with the highest lower-upper concentrations are Hill Street and Oldtown. All other areas are significantly low except Centerville.

The lower-upper members participate in significantly high numbers in "social clubs" which are for men only, for women only, and for both sexes. They are also found in associations organized for charity and in social-economic associations such as the Rotary Club. The lower-upper members, however, are not found in men's or women's fraternal organizations, organizations with auxiliaries, or those which are formally age graded. In all these respects they closely resemble the upper-upper class and are least like the lower-lower class.

The lower-upper are members of the same churches as the upper-upper people and they are not members of those churches in which the lower classes are represented in significantly high numbers.

Only about one fourth of 1 per cent of all the arrests in Yankee City are from the lower-upper class, and but 0.76 per cent of the class membership has been arrested. Interviews attest the same kind of "delinquent" behavior for the children of this class as that for which the lower-class children are classified as delinquent, but like the upper-upper-class children, they are protected from the police and do not appear on their records.

The lower-upper children, like those of the class above them and unlike those of other classes, tend to avoid the local high school and to attend private preparatory schools. There were only four lower-upper children in the local high school, all of whom subscribed to either the science or Latin curriculum in preparation for college. Moreover, very few of the lower-upper children worked, and these were distributed in a variety of economic activities.

Slightly over 18 per cent of the lower-upper, which is a little more than the upper-upper class and slightly less than the upper-middle, utilize the library. Over 70 per cent of these are adults. In age of library users the lower-upper is most like the lower-middle and least like the lower-lower class.

The following is the order of popularity (by theme) of books which are read by members of the lower-upper class: (1) courtship and family, (2) man's fight against fate, (3) detective, (4) adventure, (5) patriotism in war and national crises. They are least interested in science and farce and humor and rank highest of all classes in interest shown in the general category of man's fight against fate. In reading habits the lower-upper differs from all other classes, but is not significantly high or low for any category of book.

The lower-upper class contains the second highest percentage of magazine subscribers, being topped only by the upper-middle. Although slightly higher than the upper-upper class in this respect, the lower-upper is most like it and least like the lower-lower class. In selection of magazines it is also like the upper-upper class. In newspaper reading as well, the lower-upper is like the upper-upper class. Its members read the Boston *Herald* and the Boston *Traveler* (the afternoon counterpart of the morning *Herald*), in significantly high numbers and are significantly low in their reading of the Hearst Boston *American* and the liberal Boston *Post*. Also, they do not read the local paper in significantly high numbers.

XXI

THE SOCIAL CHARACTERISTICS OF THE PEOPLE OF THE TWO MIDDLE CLASSES

1. *The Upper-Middle Class*

THE upper-middle class most resembles the upper-upper in sex ratio, since slightly over 55 per cent of its representatives are female, and least resembles the lower-lower which contains a disproportionate number of men. About 40 per cent of the upper-middle class are below fifty years of age, in which respect this class is most like the lower-upper and least like the upper-upper and lower-lower. For the proportion of young and old people it most closely approximates the lower-upper class, then the upper-upper class, and is least like the lower-lower class.

Eighty-three per cent of the upper-middle are Yankee by birth and tradition, being most like the lower-upper and least like the upper-lower class. This class is also most like the lower-upper class (next like the lower-middle) in the composition of its ethnic population, most of which is Irish, less than 1 per cent of the class membership being from any other ethnic group. About 6 per cent of the Irish, 3 per cent of the Jews, 2 per cent of the Greeks, 1 per cent of the Armenians, and less than 1 per cent of all other ethnic groups in Yankee City belong to the upper-middle class. It contains no Russians, Poles, or Negroes. The total membership of the upper-middle class comprises 10 per cent of the total population of the city.

Over 94 per cent of the upper-middle class were born in the United States. They are most like the lower-upper and lower-middle classes for the percentage of native-born and least like the two lower classes. Approximately 58 per cent were born in Yankee City, the same percentage as the lower-middle class, this being least like that of the lower-lower class. About 13 per cent were born in the region near Yankee City, about 26 per cent in the rest of New England, and only 6 per cent in the rest of the United States. They are most like the lower-middle and least like the two upper classes in the amount of population born in the rest of the New England States.

Almost four times as many members of the upper-upper as members of the upper-middle class were born outside of Yankee City in the rest of the United States. A good part of this difference can be accounted for by the fact that many of those listed as "old family" in the study of Yankee City have been elsewhere and have frequently returned with spouses and children born outside of Yankee City. It is also true that a person who has married into an upper family has a better chance of being classed in that stratum if he was born a sufficient distance away from Yankee City to be unplaceable in class except by marriage and by judgments of present behavior. A New Englander is likely to be identifiable and, if he is not of the "proper" class, less likely to be chosen as a spouse by a member of that class.

The median age for marriage in the upper-middle class is 26.10 years. This figure is slightly lower than that of the lower-upper and somewhat higher than that of the lower-middle class and least resembles that of the lower-lower class. The upper-middle is most like the lower-middle class in the percentage of those who marry before the age of twenty-one. About 50 per cent of the members of this class are married, 21 per cent are single, and 10 per cent are widowed. With the exception of the upper-upper class, it is like all other classes in the percentage of those who were single and married. The comparative age of husbands and wives resembled that of the other five classes.

The occupations of the upper-middle class are, in many respects, most like those of the lower-upper and in others, like those of the lower-middle and least like those of the lower-lower class. The upper-middle is like the higher classes in the percentage of members who are in professions or are proprietors. More of their number are wholesale and retail dealers (the great majority of retail dealers are middle-class) than in the lower-upper and upper-upper classes, and fewer are clerks than in the lower-middle class. A small percentage of skilled and semiskilled workers appear for the first time in the upper-middle class, but it contains no unskilled workers.

Eighty per cent of the upper-middle class were fully employed, which is smaller than the lower-upper class and higher than the lower-middle class. For this characteristic the upper-middle is least like the lower-lower class. Less than 1 per cent of the upper-middle class were on relief at the very worst point in the 1930-35 depression.

The upper-middle is most like the upper-upper and least like the lower-lower class in percentage of home owners. The median value of upper-middle-class homes is less than that of the lower-upper class. The median value of all property, including houses, owned by this class is most like that of the lower-middle class. The upper-middle has a higher percentage than the lower-upper class of owners of property worth less than $1,000; whereas, when compared with the lower-middle class, less than half its members belong to this category of ownership. However, it most resembles these two classes in this respect and is least like the lower-lower class.

Over 86 per cent of the upper-middle-class renters pay by the month; the rest, by the week. It is most like the two upper classes in this respect and next like the lower-middle class. The median rental for the upper-middle class is $29.75 a month, while that for the nearest class to it, the lower-middle, is $20.80.

Sixty per cent of the upper-middle-class houses are medium in size, 23 per cent are small, 16 per cent are large, and 1 per cent were built primarily for business purposes. The upper-middle class, having the highest percentage of its members living in medium-sized houses, most resembles the lower-middle (50 per cent) and the lower-upper (43 per cent). Both of the two upper classes have relatively more large houses; and the three lower classes, relatively more small houses.

Fifty per cent of the houses of the upper-middle class are in good repair, 45 per cent in medium, and 5 per cent in bad condition. It has twice the percentage of houses in good repair as the lower-middle class and 30 per cent less than the lower-upper and upper-upper classes. It has about the same per cent of houses in medium repair and about one sixth the percentage in poor repair as the lower-middle class.

The upper-middle-class members live in significantly high numbers in houses which are medium in size and in ordinary repair and large or medium in size and in good repair. They resemble the lower-middle class for houses which are medium-sized and in good or ordinary repair, and the lower-upper and upper-upper classes for the large houses which are in good or ordinary repair and medium-sized houses which are in good repair. This class is the only one of the upper three which has members living in business buildings. Like the upper classes it has a significantly high participation in female social clubs and a significantly low participation in male and female fraternities, auxiliaries, and female age-graded associations. Like the lower-upper class it is significantly high for charitable and economic associations but unlike this class, significantly low in participation in mixed social clubs.

The upper-middle class favors the Unitarian Church, but it also belongs in significant percentages to the Baptist, Christian Science, and the Congregational Churches. It avoids in significant numbers the Catholic and Methodist churches.

This class accounts for but 2 per cent of all the arrests in Yankee City. Its members are socially powerful enough to prevent their arrests for many crimes such as drunkenness which would ordinarily cause arrest in the lower classes. Less than 1 per cent of the members of the class have been arrested. In this respect they are exactly the same as the lower-upper class.

Approximately 87 per cent of the upper-middle children in the high school were enrolled in the Latin and scientific courses. The upper-middle most resembles the lower-upper class in the type of education its children choose in the high school, but it is most like the lower-middle in the way it educates them, since most of them go to the public school and but very few attend private preparatory schools. It is like the two upper classes in the small number of its children who work. Our records show but seventeen cases.

About 22 per cent—the highest of all classes—of the upper-middle class use the library; this class is followed by the lower-middle, which is followed by the lower-upper. Over 83 per cent of the users of the library in the upper-middle class are adults. This class is only exceeded by the upper-upper class in the percentage of adults and is followed by the lower-upper and lower-middle classes respectively.

The upper-middle class read more books on courtship and the family than any other type of book. Detective stories are second and adventure stories third. Books which emphasize the theme of class and social climbing and those which discuss the theme of man against fate rank fourth and fifth. The upper-middle-class users of the library are least interested in books which emphasize science and farce and humor.

The upper-middle class has a higher percentage of magazine subscribers than any other class. It is closely followed by the lower-upper class. Its reading habits in magazines are most like the two upper classes.

The upper-middle class subscribes in significantly high numbers to the *Herald*, the *Traveler*, the *Transcript*, and the *Globe*. It subscribes in significantly low numbers to the local paper and to the Boston *American*. It is like the lower-upper class in its preference for the *Herald* and the *Traveler* and for its avoidance of the *American* and the local paper. It resembles the upper-upper class in its liking for the *Herald* and *Transcript* and also in its failure to read the *American*. The upper-middle readers show a high preference for the *Globe*, for which the upper-upper evince a significant avoidance. It is like the lower-middle class in its avoidance of the Hearst paper; but the lower-middle class has a high preference for the local paper and refuses to read the *Herald* and *Transcript*.

2. *The Lower-Middle Class*

THE sex ratio of the lower-middle class shows a slight excess of females; it is most similar to the distribution of the sexes in the upper-lower class. About 50 per cent of its members are below forty years of age. It is most like the lower-upper and upper-middle classes in the percentage of its subadults; it has about the same percentage of people in the age range of twenty-one to thirty-one and is very similar to the upper-middle and upper-lower classes.

Sixty-seven per cent of the lower-middle class are Yankee. It is most like the upper-middle class in the number of Yankees in its population and least like the upper-lower and lower-lower classes. The great majority of ethnics in the lower-middle class are Irish, 4 per cent are French Canadian, and 3.50 per cent Jewish. All the other ethnic members have a representation of less than 1 per cent in the lower-middle class. Over 86 per cent of the lower-middle class were born in the United States. In this respect it is most like the upper-middle class and least like the two lower classes. Sixty per cent were born in or near Yankee City. It is similar to the upper-middle class for the per cent of its population born in the community. It also has a distribution of people born in the rest of New England and people born outside of New England but in the United States similar to that of the upper-middle class. It has over double the amount of foreign-born that the upper-middle has, but about half as many as the upper-lower class.

The median age at marriage for the lower-middle-class members is 25.10 years. This figure falls midway between that of the upper-middle and the upper-lower classes. In the lower-middle class, the professional and proprietary groups are no longer first in occupational affiliation as in the three upper classes. This category of occupation ranks fourth and contains approximately 14 per cent of those employed or employable. Clerks exceed all others in the percentage of occupations in the lower-middle class, semiskilled workers are second, and skilled workers, third. They are followed by wholesale and retail dealers and unskilled workers. The lower-middle class is the highest of the six classes for the per cent of skilled workers; such workers are present in significantly high numbers. The lower-middle class is most like the upper-middle for the number of clerks: about three fifths of the clerks in Yankee City are lower-middle. Most of the wholesale and retail dealers are in the two middle classes. The percentages of skilled and semiskilled workers in the lower-middle class are most like the upper-lower class.

Slightly over 62 per cent of the workers in the lower-middle class are fully employed, and about 15 per cent are unemployed. This class has about twice as many unemployed as the upper-middle and less than one fifth as many as the upper-lower class. It is the first of the four upper classes which has a sizable amount of the relief population: about 4 per cent, as compared with about 1 per cent of the upper-middle, none of the two upper classes, and over 10 per cent of the upper-lower class.

About 17 per cent of the lower-middle class own their own homes, in this respect being most like the upper-lower class and then the upper-middle class. They are most like the upper-lower class in value of their homes. The median value of all their real estate is $2,477, being, in this respect, most like the upper-middle and upper-lower classes. The upper-middle class owns more and the upper-lower, less.

The lower-middle class pays rent by the month, and its median rental is $20.80. It is the only one of the three lower classes which is significantly high for rent paid by the month. Its median rental is most like that of the upper-lower class and falls in between the median rentals of the upper-middle and upper-lower classes.

Fifty per cent of the lower-middle class live in medium-sized houses, 42 per cent in small houses, and only 7 per cent in large houses. In all but house size it falls between the upper-middle and upper-lower classes, but it is most like the upper-lower for all characteristics. Slightly under 50 per cent of its houses are in ordinary condition, about 25 per cent in good repair, and the same per cent in bad repair. The percentage of its houses in good and bad repair falls between the upper-middle and upper-lower classes. There is a slightly higher percentage of those in ordinary repair in the lower-middle class than in the upper-middle class. The lower-middle-class dwellers live in significantly high numbers in houses which are medium in size and in ordinary repair, small in size and in good repair, and small in size and medium in repair. They are most like the upper-middle class in preferring medium-sized houses but unlike it because they do not have large houses in significantly high numbers. In other respects they are most like the upper-lower class in the types of houses in which they live.

The lower-middle-class houses are located in significantly high numbers in Homeville, Newtown, and Oldtown. This preference for Newtown is shared only with the upper-upper class, but their choice of Oldtown is shared with all three upper classes. They avoid Riverbrook, which is significantly high for the two lower classes, Downtown and Middletown, which are significantly high for the lower-lower class and significantly low for the upper classes. They also avoid the Business Area, which is significantly high for the upper-lower class and low for all the upper classes.

The members of the lower-middle class favor men's fraternal organizations and the semiauxiliary type of association. But they are represented in significantly low numbers in social clubs for women, for both sexes, and in associations organized for charity. They are like the two lower classes for their small membership in charitable organizations and unlike the three upper classes where membership in such associations is high. They are like the lower classes in the avoidance of social clubs and unlike the upper classes where a preference for them is strong. They are unlike the upper-middle class in their preference for fraternal and semiauxiliary organizations. In general, the lower-middle class is more like the lower than the upper classes in the types of associations it joins and does not join. The churches which this class favors are the Congregational and Episcopal. It avoids the two Catholic churches in significantly high numbers. It is like the two upper classes in its preference for the Episcopal church and avoidance of the Catholic church.

Eight per cent of all those who were arrested in Yankee City were in the lower-middle class. This comprises 1.17 per cent of the whole membership of the lower-middle class. The lower-middle class is more like the three upper classes than the two lower classes in its rate of arrests. Like the upper-middle class, over three times as many juveniles were arrested than adults.

Less than one half of the lower-middle-class children favor the Latin and scientific courses in the high school. This is the first of the four upper classes where the preference changes from a type of course which prepares for college to one which is designed for immediate use. The lower-middle class falls between the upper-middle, where 87 per cent of the children take Latin and scientific courses, and the upper-lower, where only 27 per cent are enrolled in such courses.

There were 183 subadults in the lower-middle class who had jobs. A high percentage of them were in the chain or locally owned stores and a low percentage in shoe manufacturing.

The lower-middle class ranks next to the upper-middle in the per cent of library users. About 69 per cent of its library users are adult; it is most like the lower-upper and upper-middle in this respect and least like the upper-upper and lower-upper classes. Those in the class who read books show a preference for themes of courtship and the family, detective and adventure stories, and are least interested in scientific books, farce and humor, and biography and history. This class drops far below the upper-middle in percentage of magazine subscribers, but has a little over double the per cent of the upper-lower class. It is outranked by the three upper classes and outranks the two lower ones.

The lower-middle class is the only one in Yankee City which reads the local newspaper in significantly high numbers. Its members also prefer the Boston *Post* but avoid the *American*, the *Herald*, the *Transcript*, and the *Record*. The *American* and the *Record* are avoided because they sometimes are spoken of as "too low," while the *Herald* and *Transcript* are not read by many because they are believed to be "too dull and uninteresting." The *Post* is read partly because it is liberal and "supports the underdog" and partly because it is believed to favor the Irish. The lower-middle is unlike the upper-middle in its preference for the *Post* and avoidance of the *Herald* and the *Transcript*.

XXII

THE SOCIAL CHARACTERISTICS OF THE PEOPLE OF THE TWO LOWER CLASSES

1. *The Upper-Lower Class*

FIFTY-TWO per cent of the upper-lower class are female, 48 per cent male. It is most like the lower-middle class and least like the lower-lower class. It falls between the lower-middle and lower-lower classes in percentage of its various age groups.

The upper-lower class has the smallest percentage of Yankees of all six classes (38 per cent) and is followed by the lower-lower class with 43 per cent. About one half of the Irish and Armenians, between 40 and 50 per cent of the Jews, French Canadians, and Italians, about one third of the Greeks, one fourth of the Russians, and one tenth of the Poles are in this class.

Seventy per cent of its membership were born in the United States. The upper-lower class falls exactly between the lower-middle and lower-lower classes. About one half of the members were born in or near Yankee City. This compares with 60 per cent of the lower-middle and 45 per cent of the lower-lower.

The upper-lower class has next to the lowest median age for marriage. Only the lower-lower class has a lower one. Their age for marriage falls between the lower-middle and lower-lower classes. Twenty-one per cent of their marriages occur before the individuals are twenty-one years old, being exceeded in this respect only by the lower-lower class. Although their age preference for spouses is in general similar to that of other classes, the upper-lower men lead all others in having wives older than they (20.14 per cent).

The principal industries in which they are employed are shoe manufacturing, retail stores, transportation, and building trades. This class has a significantly high number of workers in shoe factories and a significantly low number in silverware factories. Over 21 per cent of the upper-lower class had no jobs. Only the lower-lower class has a larger percentage of its population unemployed. In all categories of employment, the upper-lower class falls between the lower-middle and lower-lower classes but is nearer the lower-lower group.

The upper-lower class is most like the lower-lower class in percentage of home owners and next resembles the lower-middle class. It also falls in between these two classes for the median value of its homes, and is most like the lower-lower class in the median value of all real estate owned.

Fifty-two per cent of all houses where upper-lower-class members reside are small dwellings, 41 per cent are medium size, 4 per cent are large, and slightly under 3 per cent are business structures. The several house sizes compare closely with those of the lower-lower and lower-middle classes but in general they most resemble those of the lower-lower class.

Forty-two per cent of the houses in which the upper-lower members live are in poor condition, the same percentage in medium condition, and but 13 per cent in good condition.[1] They live in four times as many good houses, about twice as many ordinary houses and three fifths as many poor houses, as the lower-lower class. The upper-lower class lives in significantly high numbers in small houses in medium condition. It has double the number of small houses in bad repair as the lower-middle class and slightly less than one half as many as the lower-lower class. The upper-lower class has a significantly high percentage of its members living in the Business Area, Centerville, Littletown, and Riverbrook, and a significantly low number living in Hill Street, Middletown, Oldtown, and Across the River. It shares living areas with the lower-lower in Riverbrook, but it is concentrated in Centerville where the lower-lower class is significantly low. Moreover, it is low in Middletown where the lower-lower class has a high concentration of population. It is like the lower-lower class in its avoidance of Hill Street and Oldtown, areas of the upper classes.

The upper-lower class participates in significantly high percentages in male fraternities with auxiliaries, in female fraternities with and without auxiliaries, in semiauxiliary organizations, and in associations which emphasize formal age grading. They are not found in male and female social groups,

1. It will be noted that the other 3 per cent are business houses.

charitable associations, and economic associations. The upper-lower resembles the lower-lower and lower-middle classes in participation in associations.

The upper-lower class is pre-eminently the Roman Catholic class of Yankee City. It is significantly high for membership in both Catholic churches and for no others in the community, and it is significantly low for all Protestant churches, except the Methodist. It is most like the lower-lower class insofar as the two classes are the only ones which have such a high percentage of Catholics, but it is different from the lower-lower since the latter is also significantly high for several Protestant churches. In general, this means that a large number of the members of the various ethnic groups were sufficiently mobile to get into a higher class than the Protestant Yankees in the lower-lower class. The upper-lower class is least like the two upper classes in its church affiliations.

About one fourth of all the arrested people of Yankee City are in the upper-lower class. In this respect it is exceeded only by the lower-lower class. Over 3 per cent of the members of the upper-lower class have been arrested. This class resembles the one below it in its relations with the police of the city. Approximately 23 per cent of those arrested were below the age of twenty-one, but it has a smaller percentage of juvenile offenders than either the lower-middle or lower-lower classes.

Some 18 per cent of the library users come from the upper-lower class, slightly over half of whom are adults. Only the lower-lower class has a smaller percentage of adults using the library. The books which upper-lower persons read most are those of courtship and the family, detective stories, adventure stories, man's fight against fate, and social-climbing stories. The books they read least are science, farce and humor, and biography and history.

All classes, except the lower-lower, exceed the upper-lower class in the percentage of magazine subscribers. However, each subscriber takes fewer magazines than those in the lower-lower class. In type of magazines read the upper-lower class is most like the lower-lower and least like the two upper classes.

The upper-lower-class members are significantly high readers of the Boston *American* and the Boston *Post*. They avoid reading the *Herald*, the *Transcript*, and the *Traveler*. They are like the lower-lower class in their preference for the *American* and like the lower-middle in their preference for the *Post*. The upper-lower class is like the lower-lower in its refusal to read the *Herald* and *Traveler* and like the lower-middle in its avoidance of the *Herald* and *Transcript*.

2. The Lower-Lower Class

THE sex ratio of the lower-lower class is not like that of any other in Yankee City. It is the only class in which men are more numerous than women (52.83 per cent males). It is the exact opposite of the upper-upper class. The lower-lower class has the highest percentage of children in its population of all classes. It also has the smallest percentage of people over sixty years of age. It is most like the two other lower classes in this respect and least like the upper three. The lower-lower class is most like the upper-lower for its large number of people with ethnic affiliations. All the Negroes, about nine tenths of the Poles, seven tenths of the Russians, more than half of the Greeks, slightly less than one half of the French Canadians, and Italians are in the lower-lower class. But only one third of the Armenians, one tenth of the Irish, and one fourteenth of the Jews are in this class.

Approximately 70 per cent of the lower-lower class were born in the United States, in which respect it is most like the upper-lower and least like the upper-upper class. Forty-five per cent of the lower-lower class were born in or near Yankee City. It is most like the upper-lower class for the region of birth of its members.

The members of the lower-lower class marry earlier than those of any other class. They are most like the upper-lower and least like the upper-upper class for age at marriage. Over 35 per cent of lower-lower marriages were under twenty-one years of age. Although in general the lower-lower class is like all other classes for the age differences between spouses, the men of this class show a greater preference for women younger than themselves, and a smaller percentage married older women than any other class. A slightly larger per cent of this class was married than of any other class.

Most of those who work for a living are in semiskilled occupations. This class has a higher percentage of the semiskilled and of the unskilled than any other class. There is a larger percentage of skilled people in the upper-middle, lower-middle, and upper-lower classes than in this one. In its choice of occupations, the lower-lower class is most like the upper-lower class. Members of the lower-lower class are employed in significantly high numbers in the shoe and hat factories and in transport. Two thirds of all clammers are in the lower-lower class. This class contains a significantly low percentage of workers in retail and business enterprises and in the silverware factory.

The lower-lower class has the largest percentage of unemployed of all six classes. A greater percentage of this class than of any other class has only part-time employment. About one out of every three people in this class is on relief, and the lower-lower class contains over 65 per cent of the total relief population of Yankee City.

Less than 6 per cent of the members of the lower-lower class own their own homes. They diverge from all other classes in this respect but are nearest the upper-lower class. The value of their homes is also less than that of all other classes, in which respect they are most like the upper-lower and least like the lower-upper class. The members of the lower-lower class own less property than those of any other class and are most like those of the upper-lower class in the value of property owned. The lower-lower class pays the smallest rentals in Yankee City, and it is the only class which is significantly low for paying rent by the month.

The lower-lower class has a larger percentage of small houses and a smaller percentage of large houses than any other class. Only the upper-upper class is below it in the occupancy of medium-sized houses. The lower-lower class occupies a larger percentage of bad houses and a smaller percentage of good houses than any other class. In general, the lower-lower class most resembles the upper-lower in condition of house. The lower-lower class lives in significantly high numbers in business buildings, in small houses in bad repair, in medium-sized houses in bad repair, and in large houses in poor condition. The houses in which the lower-lower class reside are located in significantly high numbers in Middletown, Downtown, Riverbrook, and Uptown, and in significantly low numbers in Hill Street, Centerville, Homeville, Newtown, and Oldtown. The lower-lower class

Social Characteristics of the Two Lower Classes 449

is most like the upper-lower in dwelling areas and least like the upper-upper.

The members of the lower-lower class form a high percentage of those who join male fraternities of the nonauxiliary type. They also join female fraternities with auxiliaries and age-graded associations. They avoid, or are prevented from joining, female social clubs, charitable and economic associations. Their associational behavior is most like that of the upper-lower class and least like that of the two upper classes.

The police arrest the members of the lower-lower class more frequently than any others in the community. As we said earlier, 65 per cent of those arrested in Yankee City are from this class, and approximately 11 per cent of its members have been arrested. By way of comparison, about one out of every three people in the lower-lower class, three out of a hundred in the upper-lower class, one out of a hundred in the upper-upper and lower-middle classes, and still less in the lower-upper and upper-middle classes have been arrested. About one fourth of those arrested in the lower-lower class are below eighteen years of age, and about 33 per cent are below twenty-one. The lower-lower class has not sufficient power to protect its young from the police.

The members of the lower-lower class are affiliated in significantly high numbers with the Presbyterian, Methodist, and Baptist churches, one of the Congregational churches, and the two Catholic churches. They avoid the Episcopal, Unitarian, and two Congregational churches located in middle- and upper-class areas.

Approximately three fourths of the high school children of the lower-lower class are enrolled in commercial and general courses, and of these, 54 per cent are in commercial courses. Only 12 per cent are enrolled in the Latin and 14 per cent in the scientific courses. A larger percentage of the lower-lower children work, and more of them go to work before sixteen than do those of any other class. They are in this respect most like the upper-lower class.

A smaller percentage of the library users come from the lower-lower class than from any others; of these, a smaller per cent are adults than those of any other class. The lower-lower class contains a significantly high percentage of readers of children's books and a significantly low percentage of readers of biography and history and courtship and the family. They show least interest in scientific books, biography and history, and farce and humor.

Slightly less than 4 per cent of the lower-lower-class members subscribe to magazines. This is the lowest figure for any class. In magazine reading habits, the lower-lower is most like the upper-lower class. As we said earlier, they show a preference for Hearst's Boston *American* and for the tabloid *Record;* and they avoid reading the *Herald, Traveler,* and *Globe.* They are similar to the upper-lower class in their newspaper reading and least like the two upper classes.

INDEX

Adaptations, and individual variation, 23
"Adjustment," 2, 26
Adult, membership in associations, 122–123, 304; membership in class, 205–206, 224
Africa, age-grade divisions, 35; associations, 113
Age-grading institutions, Africa, 35; and class membership, 89; cliques, 111; functions, 29; New Guinean, 35. *See* Age groupings
Age groupings, with sex groupings, 30–31; in simple societies, 35; social age, 31–32; as social structure, 28–29. *See* Sex groupings; *Rites de passage*
Age statistics, of arrests, 373; of classes, 224, 226; of ethnics, 218–219; of motion-picture attendance, 415, 417–419
Aggression. *See* Social relations
Agricultural societies, 25; political organization, 35
American Legion, activities, 305; function, 120; membership by class, 118; sponsors of Boy Scouts, 122, 305, 327; and structural types, 328. *See* Patriotic societies
Analysis. *See* Methodology
"Anomia." *See* Durkheim
Antagonisms, community to structures, 114; resolved by associations, 302; structural members to community, 114. *See* Associations
Anthropology, theory, 9–10, 36. *See* Social anthropology; Ethnology
Antiques. *See* Property
Apes. *See* Social relations
Armenians, arrests, 374–375; association membership, 341, 344; birthplace, 221; church affiliation, 216; in class, 224–225; in ecological areas, 232–233, 236–237; education, 363; employment, 270–277; in government, 373; history, 216; and house types, 245–250; in industry, 257–259; marital status, 253; motion-picture attendance, 415, 417–418; newspaper preference, 406–408; occupation, 216; ownership of real estate, 281–282, 284–285; population statistics, 78, 214; on relief, 278. *See* Ethnics

Armistice day, ritual, 120–121. *See* Patriotic societies
Arrests, and class, 373, 376–377; by ecological area, 374; ethnic factors, 374–375, 377; sex factors, 373–374
Assimilation, of ethnics, 214–217
Associations, activities, 304–305, 314–316, 325; analysis, 301; and church, 306, 358; by class, 88–89, 123–125, 307–308, 329; and class hierarchy, 114; class types, 307–308, 350, 352–353; ethnic membership, 305, 339–345; functions, 112, 114–116, 301–302, 305; and government organization, 34; interconnecting associations, 126; membership by religion, 307, 346–349; membership by sex, age, 122, 335–338; and mobility, 115; organization, 32, 113; ritual, 112; satellites, 122, 322, 358; size of membership, 303, 330–331; as social ranking, 83, 87; as social structure, 28, 112; and structure, 302, 322; as subunities, 32; types and class, 89, 118, 120, 122. *See* Clique
Australia, Murngin kinship, 35; social organization, 3, 25
Auxiliaries, activities, 305; and class membership, 89, 118, 177; organization, 119

Babbitt, 132–134
Baptist church, 79, 357; class, 357, 359
Behavior, social, asocial (suicide), 26; class, 99; of ethnics, 222; "low," 84; "right," 83, 351; social code, 2. *See* Class
Beliefs. *See* Religion
Biologic group, continuity, 17; and distribution, 202–207; functions of social group, 18, 20; and technical system, 24. *See* Life cycle
Biology, method, 3, 15
Birth, ceremony, 29; rates, 206
Birthplace, and class, 210; as classification, 211; statistics, 207–210, 220
Boston, relation to Yankee City, 77, 133
Boy Scouts, activities, 305; as satellite associations, 122; sponsored by churches, 306, 316–317
Bridgman, P. W., 11, 36

Budget, by class, 290-300; schedule, 288-290; as symbol system, 287
Burgess, Dr. Ernest W., 4, 58

Canadians and assimilation, 213. See Ethnics
Caste, and class, 82, 90; and family, 92; hierarchy (India, Natchez), 35; and marriage, 93; Negro, 217; as social structure, 28; as subordinating and superordinating, 34
Catholic, attitude toward, 170, 180-181; church, 79, 306; class, 143, 355-357, 359; French Canadians, 79; history, 356; Irish, 79, 214, 356; Italians, 356; Poles, 356; symbol system, 28
Cemetery, 155; and class, 155-156. See Graveyard
Census data, 39, 78, 211. See Methodology
Chamber of Commerce, "solid people," 143
Charitable organizations, functions, 107; as upper class, 118
Chicago, factory study, 4; social study, 4
Christian Science Church, 358
Church, as age and sex groupings, 31; associations, 122, 306; attendance by sex, 358; function regarding supernatural, 33, 120; hierarchy, 33; patriotic organizations, 120, 122; philanthropy, 179; in simpler societies, 33; as social structure, 28, 302; symbolism, 357; types in Yankee City, 79, 306, 356-357. See Protestant; Catholic; Secret societies
Civilization, rise and fall, 16. See Culture
Clamming, clam flats, 178. See Industry
Class, age distribution, 224, 226; and association, 112, 124, 319-320; behavior, 83, 100; biologic characteristics of each, 202-204; and birthplace, 210; and birth rate, 226; budgets, 290-300; definition, 82; discovery, 81; distinctions, 91, 161; distribution of property, 251; of doctors and patients, 419; in ecological areas, 234; and education, 261-262; hierarchy, 84, 94, 112, 114; house and neighborhood, 287; and house types, 244-246; hypothesis, 82; interconnections through associations, 125; maintained by family, 252; maintenance of position, 94; marital status, 255; membership of cliques, 353-355; membership of churches, 355-359; of motion-picture attendance, 414, 416-418; ownership of real estate, 282-283; ranking, 83, 87; rank order, 84, 90; range of ethnics, 223-224; of relief recipients, 279; sanctions and values, 92; as social structure, 28; as subordinating and superordinating, 34; symbols, 204; terminology, 84-86, 89, 91; values in expenditure, 288; of voters and officeholders, 369-372; and wealth, 83; of workers in industry, 259-261. See Social status; Social ranking
Class types, of associations, 123-125, 131, 350, 352-353
Clique, and class membership, 90, 124, 193, 353-355; definition and functions, 110, 350, 355; discovery, 110; as informal association, 32; membership by sex and age, 351, 353; and mobility, 193-195, 351; and social ranking, 83; as social structure, 28, 110; types, 111
Clubs, social, activities, 145, 152, 162; and class membership, 89, 143, 153, 177, 193; discussion, 148; and social ranking, 83, 87-88
Cohesion. See Interaction
Collaboration, human, 2. See Social code
College. See Education
Committee of Industrial Physiology, 1
Community, autonomy, 17; definition, 16; purpose, 16-17
Community studies, 4
Companies, as social structure, 28
Complexity, of social relations, 16
Conceptual framework. See Methodology
Confucius, 8
Congregational church, 79, 356; class, 357, 359
Control, social, 23
Crime. See Arrests
Criteria, 5. See Methodology
Culture, definition, 9. See Civilization

Data Book, 235, 253
Death, ceremony, 29
Delinquency rate, and class, 182
Democratic. See Goods and labor
Dickson, William J., 49
Disintegration, social, and individual variance, 23
Doctors, class, 419; class of patients, 419. See Occupation
Dominance. See Social relations

Durkheim, Émile, 10; on suicide and "anomia," 26
Duties, distribution by class, 82; as social control, 22

Ecological areas, and arrests, 374; class distribution, 234–238; criteria, 227; ethnic distribution, 232–234; house type distribution, 244; rentals, 230; sex statistics, 229
Economic activities, 77; groupings, 112–113; logic, 3; occupation, 78; structure, 35, 302; terms for status, 81
Economic institutions, function, 32; in primitive society, 32; as social structure, 28; types of, 28, 32
Education, college, 162, 188; courses and class, 361–362; courses and ethnic groups, 362–363; for mobility, 119; social ranking, 83. *See* School
Employment, by class, 278–279; by ethnics, 270–277; by industry, 265
Endogamy, upper class, 101–102
English, assimilation, 213; ethnics, 220. *See* Ethnics
Episcopal church, 79, 357; class, 357, 359; membership, 152; symbols, 357
Ethnics, age composition, 218; arrests, 373–375, 377; association membership, 339–345; attitude toward, 211; birthplace, 220–221; class distribution, 205–207; as criterion for community, 38–39; definition, 211, 220; distribution by ecological area, 232–238; distribution by house types, 246–250; distribution in industry, 257–259; employment, 270–277; generations, 213; in government, 372–373; history, 213–214; marital status, 253–254; motion picture attendance, 415, 417–418; native interaction, 213; ownership of real estate, 281–282, 284–285; population statistics, 78, 214; reading habits, 381–382, 406–408; and relief, 278–279; sex, 205, 217; school attendance, 362–363; social organization, 211; types of employment, 79; unemployment, 267–269, 271–277
Ethnology. *See* Anthropology
Euphoria, in crises, 120. *See* Integration

Factories, criterion for community study, 39; and larger community, 4; management, 176; as social structure, 28; technique of study, 54. *See* Henderson; Mayo
Factory workers, in economic occupation, 77; social behavior, 1, 4; in social context, 4. *See* Henderson; Mayo; Social relations
Family, and class membership, 90, 92, 124, 183; and class system, 252; descent, 94, 97; of ethnics, 217; function, 29; histories, 93–97; relationship, 13–14, 104; and social ranking, 83; as social structure, 28; solidarity and class, 119; vertical extension, 93, 99; wife's status, 118
Farming. *See* Industry
Fraternities, 79; and class membership, 89; and social ranking, 83
French Canadians, arrests, 374–375; association membership, 340–344; birthplace, 221; church attendance, 356; in class, 224; in ecological areas, 232–233, 236–237; education, 363; employment, 270–277; in government, 373; history, 215; and house types, 245–258; in industry, 257–259; marital status, 253; motion-picture attendance, 415, 417–418; newspaper, 406–408; ownership of real estate, 281–282, 284–285; population statistics, 78, 214; priests and nuns, 79; on relief, 278. *See* Ethnics
French Huguenots, 213
Freudian theories, 2
Furniture, 142; attitude toward, 162; lower class, 185–186. *See* Property; Houses

Genealogies, and class, 87, 137
Geographic, location and social space, 84; terms for class, 84. *See* Residential areas
Ginsberg, M., 25, 34
Girl Scouts, membership, 150
Goods, distribution of, as social control, 24. *See* Property
Government, and class, 369–372; divisions and offices, 79; and ethnics, 372–373; functions, 366–367; organization, 367–369; relation of officers to community, 34; in simple and complex societies. *See* Political organization
Graveyards, attitude toward 139. *See* Cemetery
Greek Orthodox church, 79, 306; Armenians in, 216

Greeks and arrests, 374–375; association membership, 341, 345; birthplace, 221; church, 79; in class, 224; delinquency, 182; in ecological areas, 232–233, 236–237; education, 363; employment, 270–277; in government, 373; history, 216; and house types, 245–251; in industry, 257–259; motion-picture attendance, 415, 417–418; newspaper preference, 406–408; occupation, 217; ownership of real estate, 281–282, 284–285; on relief, 278; vital statistics, 78, 214. *See* Ethnics

Harvard Graduate School of Business Administration, 43. *See* Committee on Industrial Physiology
Heirlooms. *See* Property
Henderson, Dr. L. J., 1
Hierarchy, social, caste, 34; in church, 33; class, 34, 84, 88; of cliques, 112; and geographic space, 84; in government control, 34; in population, 204
"Hill Streeter," attitude toward, 175; and club and association membership, 87–89; as ecological area, 227–229; as geographic term for class, 89, 91. *See* Upper class
History, of ethnics, 213; of upper-upper families, 94; of Yankee City, 78, 99
Hobbies, and clubs, 88
Hobhouse, L. T., 25, 34
"Homeville," as ecological area, 227–229; and club membership, 89; as geographic term for class, 85, 91. *See* Middle class
Homosexuality, 84; and class, 184
Household ritual, 105–106; in relations among family members, 106; as training, 107
Houses, assessed value, 240; distribution through population, 239–240; distribution through classes, 244–245, 283; distribution of type by ecological area, 241–243; history, 137; lineages, 107; lower-class, 180, 185–186, 188–189; rentals, 240; ritual treatment of, 108; and social mobility, 108, 141; types, 154, 239; use of, 105–107. *See* Residential areas
Hunger, satisfaction of, 25
Hunting and gathering societies, political organization, 34; technical systems, 25
Hypotheses. *See* Methodology

Ideologies, of supernatural world, 22
Immigration. *See* Ethnics
Incest, 84; and class, 184
Income, and social ranking, 83
Individual, social, and society, 12; variance of, 23
Individuality, in social structure, 15, 23. *See* Social personality
Inductive method, 15. *See* Scientific method
Industrial centers, 2, 4; social relations, 26
Industrial Research Department of Harvard, 1–2. *See* Mayo
Industry, as criterion for selection of community, 39; degree of employment and unemployment, 264–267; distribution of ethnics in each, 257–259; percentage of workers in each, 256; in Yankee City, 79
Insanity. *See* Individual, social
Insurance orders, and class membership, 89, 118
Integration, and associations, 116, 301, 307, 325; in complex societies, 15; as criterion in community selection, 38; in simple societies, 35; for social unity, 35
Integrative structure, 35; class, 81; economic, 35, 81
Interaction, dyadic, 13; between individuals, 12–13, 21, 24, 203; native-ethnic, 213; triadic, 13, 196. *See* Reciprocal relations; Social organization
Interview, for ethnic definition, 211; psychoanalytic, 49; as social relation, 47; techniques, 44–46, 48, 50–55, 59. *See* Methodology
Ireland, social system, 28
Irish, arrests, 374–375; association membership, 340–346; class, 218, 223–224; delinquency, 182; distribution in ecological area, 232–233, 235–237; early immigrants, 79, 214; education, 363; employment, 270–277; in government, 373; and house types, 245–250; in industry, 257–259; marital status, 253–254; motion-picture attendance, 415, 417–418; newspaper preference, 406–408; North Irish and assimilation, 213, 220; ownership of real estate, 281–282, 284–285; population statistics, 78, 214; priests and nuns, 79; on relief, 278–279. *See* Ethnics
Italians, arrests, 374–375; association membership, 340–341; in class, 224; in

Index

ecological areas, 232–233, 236–237; employment, 270–277; education, 363; in government, 373; history, 216; and house types, 245–251; in industry, 257–259; in Irish churches, 214, 356; marital status, 253; motion-picture attendance, 415, 417–418; newspaper preference, 406–408; population statistics, 78, 214; on relief, 278. See Ethnics

Janet, 2
Jews, arrests, 374–375; assimilation, 215; association membership, 341–343, 346; birthplace, 221; in class, 224; early settlement, 213, 215; in ecological areas, 232–233, 236–237; education, 363; employment, 270–277; in government, 373; and house types, 244–250; in industry, 257–259; marital status, 253; motion-picture attendance, 415, 417–418; newspaper preference, 406–408; occupation, 215; ownership of real estate, 281–282, 284–285; population statistics, 78, 214; on relief, 278; synagogue, 79, 306. See Ethnics

Kinship, 15; distant, 101; in simple societies, 35; terminology and class, 100
Kiwanis, 79

Law, 10. See Arrests
Lewis, Sinclair, *Babbitt*, 132
Life cycle, 20
Lineage, bilateral, 100; definition, 99; of houses, 107; and property, 107
Lodges, 79, 114, 143; class, 143–144; membership by class, 169
Logics, absolute, 22–23, 25–26; social and secular, 22. See Sanctions
Lower class, 86; in American Legion, 120; delinquency, 182; family organization, 119; naming principle in associations, 117–118; women's position, 119. See Lower-lower class; Upper-lower class
Lower-lower class, 87; age composition, 226; arrests, 373, 376–377; association membership, 123–125, 307–308, 319–320; biologic characteristics, 204–206; budget expenditures, 290–300; churches, 357–360; clique membership, 90, 352–354; degree of employment, 278–279; in ecological area, 234–238; education, 363–364; ethnic composition, 225; family membership, 90; house types, 244–246; in industry, 259–261; marriage age, 255; motion-picture attendance, 414, 416–418; newspaper and magazine reading, 179; occupation, 261–262; ownership of real estate, 282–283; personal examples, 143, 155, 170, 174, 177–179, 183–184, 187, 190; preference for professional people by class, 419–421; professional people, 419–420; reading habits, 380–412; and relief, 279; size, 88; summary of characteristics, 444–450; voters and officeholders, 369–372. See Class types; Lower class; Upper-lower class

Lower-middle class, 87; arrests, 376–377; association membership, 89, 123–125, 307–308; biologic characteristics, 204–206; budget expenditures, 290–300; churches, 357–360; clique membership, 90, 319–320, 330–337, 352–354; degree of employment, 278–279; as ecological areas, 234–238; education, 363–364; ethnic composition, 224–225; family membership, 90; house types, 244–246; in industry, 260–261; marriage age, 255; motion-picture attendance, 414, 416–418; occupation, 261–262; ownership of real estate, 282–283; personal examples, 143, 151, 155, 171, 173, 188; preference for professional people by class, 419–421; professional people, 419–420; reading habits, 380–412; and relief, 279; size, 88; summary of characteristics, 433–443; voters and officeholders, 369–372. See Class types; Middle class; Upper-middle class

Lower-upper class, 87; arrests, 376–377; association membership, 123–125, 307–308; behavior examples, 104; biologic characteristics, 204–206; budget expenditures, 290–300; clique membership, 90, 102, 352–354; churches, 357–360; in ecological area, 234–238; education, 363–364; employment, 278–279; ethnic composition, 224–225; and family membership, 90, 102; hostile environment, 104; house types, 244–246; imitation of upper-upper, 109; in industry, 259–261; marriage age, 255; motion-picture attendance, 414, 416–418; movement to upper-upper, 98; "new family," 93, 102–103; and occupation, 261–262; ownership of real estate, 282–283; personal examples,

129–132, 144, 146–148, 151–152, 158, 169, 176, 319–320, 330–337; preference for professional people by class, 419–421; professional people, 419–420; reading habits, 142, 176, 380–412; and relief, 279; size, 88; subordinated by upper-upper, 109; summary of characteristics, 422–434; unstable families, 103; voters and officeholders, 369–372. *See* Class types; Upper class; Upper-upper class

Lowie, Professor Robert H., 3

"Maladjustment," 2, 26
Management, and workers, 1. *See* Henderson; Mayo
Manufacturing. *See* Industry
Marital status, by class, 255; of ethnics, 253–254; statistics, 252–253
Marriage, ceremony, 29; and class, 82, 92–94, 102–190; median age by sex, 254; native-ethnic, 212; Negro, 268
Masons, 33. *See* Church
Maturity, ceremony, 29
Mayo, Dr. Elton, 1, 4. *See* Western Electric Study
Mayor, 79; clubs, 114. *See* Government
Melanesia, associations, 113
Memorial Day, ritual, 120–121. *See* Patriotic societies
Methodist church, 79, 357; and class, 357, 359
Methodology, 14, 41; analysis, 37, 69, 72, 83, 86, 111, 114–116, 121–122, 199, 202–203, 212–213, 301–308; assessor's records, 42; associations, 43, 81, 121–122, 303–307, 314; books, magazines, newspapers, 65, 378–381; budget schedules, 288; case histories, biographies, etc., 59; census data, 39; churches, 43; class study, 94, 202 (*see* Class); clique study, 111; community selection, 4–5, 38–39; comparisons of, 6; conceptual framework, 6, 8, 14; co-operation of community, 39–40, 42; dwellings, 239; ethnic study, 42, 211; factory, 43; field techniques, 38–39 (*see* Interview); genealogies, 60–61; geography, 76–77, 227; hypotheses, 10–11, 29, 36, 81, 82, 112, 114, 116, 302; maps, handbooks, directories, histories, 40, 44, 60–65, 214; membership lists, 62; motion-picture study, 412; personal records, 66; personality cards, 71–72, 203; physical index, 40, 76; politics, 43; questionnaire and schedule, 55–58; school study, 42; social structure, 90; staff, 42; synthesis, 37, 90; theory, 35–36, 114, 119, 121–122; vital statistics, 77, 202–207. *See* Criteria

Middle class, "Homeville," 86; naming principle in associations, 117; women's position, 119. *See* Upper-middle class; Lower-middle class

Mobility. *See* Social mobility
Monkeys. *See* Social relations
Motion picture, attendance by age, 415, 417–419; attendance by class, 414, 416–418; attendance by ethnic group, 415, 417–418; attendance by religion, 416, 418; attendance by sex, 418–419; type, 412–413

Myth. *See* Primitive society

Naming principle, in association membership, 117; and talent, 118
Natives, age composition, 220; arrests, 373–375, 377; birthplace, 220; class, 223–225; degree of employment, 270–277; dominance in social structures, 214; in ecological areas, 234–238; as ethnic classification, 211; ethnic interaction, 213; in government, 372–373; and house types, 246–250; in industry, 257–259; marital status, 253; membership in associations, 305, 339–345; motion-picture attendance, 415, 417–418; newspaper preference, 406–408; ownership of real estate, 281–282, 284–285; on relief, 278–279; population, 214; school attendance, 362–363. *See* Yankee

Nature, and technology, 21–22
Negroes, arrests, 374–375; association membership, 345; birthplace, 221; as caste, 217, 268; in class, 224; in ecological areas, 232–233, 237; education, 363; employment, 270–277; in government, 373; history and occupation, 217; and house types, 247–250; in industry, 257–259; marital status, 253–254; motion-picture attendance, 415, 417–418; newspaper preference, 406–408; ownership of real estate, 281–282, 284–285; population statistics, 78, 214; on relief, 278. *See* Ethnics

New England, and community selection,

Index

39; community types, 5; relation with New York, 135
"New Family," as class criterion, 86–87, 93; examples, 141, 196; Irish, 137. *See* Genealogy
New Guinea, age grading, 35
Newspapers, Boston *American*, 406–412; Boston *Globe*, 406–412; Boston *Herald*, 134, 142, 176, 406–412; Boston *Post*, 406–412; Boston *Record*, 179, 406–412; Boston *Transcript*, 142, 406–412; Boston *Traveler*, 406–412; local paper, 406–412. *See* Reading habits
New York, relation to Yankee City, 77, 133, 135

Obligations, distribution by class, 82; as social control, 22
Occupation, business and industry and status, 83; of ethnics, 215–217; professions and status, 82, 419–420; skilled and semiskilled workers, 78, 203–204; and social status, 81, 98, 203, 261–262. *See* Economic; Workers
"Old Family," as class criterion, 86–87, 93, 100, 160–161; and history of Yankee City, 138; influence, 139. *See* Genealogy
Opposition. *See* Interaction
Organism, definition, 13
Orientation, social, as family function, 29; as school function, 34

Park, Dr. Robert E., 4, 58
Parochial school. *See* School
Pastoral societies, 25
Patriotic societies, activities, 168; class membership, 118, 143; for community integration, 116, 120; ritual, 118, 120–121, 170; symbolism, 120, 170
Patronymic, 93, 100–101
Philanthropic associations, as upper class, 118
Pitt-Rivers, G. H., 16
Poles, arrests, 373–375; association membership, 340–341, 344; birthplace, 221; church attendance, 356; in class, 224; delinquency, 182; in ecological areas, 232–233, 236–237; education, 363; employment, 270–277; in government, 373; history, 217; and house types, 245–250; in industry, 257–259; marital status, 253; motion-picture attendance, 415, 417–418; newspaper preference, 406–408; ownership of real estate, 281–282, 284–285; personal examples, 188; on relief, 278; vital statistics, 78, 214. *See* Ethnics
Police, 79; arrests, 373. *See* Government
Political organization (government), as social structure, 28, 302, 366
Political parties, as association, 34
Presbyterian church, 79, 356, 359
Primitive society, 25; church in South East Africa, 33; communities, 16; methods of study of, 4; mythology as adaptation, 9; social behavior, 15; and social personality, 27. *See* Simple societies; Australia
Privileges, distribution by class, 82; as social control, 22
Property, antiques and heirlooms, 107–109, 162; attitude toward, 107; control by economic organization, 32; distribution by class, 251; ethnics and class type, 286; inheritance, 107, 162; real estate ownership by age, 280–281. *See* Goods
Protestant, ascendancy in Ireland, 28; churches, 79, 306, 356
Psychology, as method, 1–2
Puberty, ceremony, 29
Public school. *See* School

Quantitative relationship. *See* Methodology

Radcliffe-Brown, A. R., 3
Rank order, 199. *See* Methodology
Reading habits, categories of books, 378–380; by class, 380–405, 406–412; by ethnics, 406–408; of magazines, 142, 380, 386–406; of newspapers, 142, 176, 381, 406–412
Real estate. *See* Property
Reciprocal relations, between individuals, 12. *See* Interaction
Relief, by class, 279; and ecological areas, 234; by ethnics, 278–279; and lower class, 179; statistics, 78
Religion, 10; ideology, 23; as social adjustment, 21. *See* Social organization, Sacred relations
Rentals, by ecological area, 230–231; by house type, 240
Research, 6. *See* Biology; Psychology; Social Anthropology; Social Science; Methodology

Residence, as class criterion, 87
Residential area, and business district, 79; Homeville, 152–154; "right kind," 287. *See* Ecological areas
Rights, distribution by class, 82; as social control, 22
Rites de passage, 53; definition, 29
Ritual, American Legion, 305; of associations, 307; relations with supernatural, 22; and social value, 24; of technical behavior, 24; total community, 120
"Riverbrook," church attendance, 356–357; as ecological area, 227–229; examples, 180–181; as geographic term for class, 84–85; as low class, 86, 91, 189–190; and union organizations, 143. *See* Lower class
Roethlisberger, F. J., 49
Rotary, 79; "solid people," 143
Russians, arrests, 374–375; association membership, 345; birthplace, 221; church, 79; in class, 224; in ecological areas, 232–233, 236–237; education, 363; employment, 270–277; in government, 373; history and occupation, 217; and house types, 247–250; in industry, 257–259; marital status, 253–254; motion-picture attendance, 415, 417–418; newspaper preference, 406–408; ownership of real estate, 281–282, 284–285; population statistics, 78. 214; on relief, 278. *See* Ethnics

Sacred relations, and ritual, 22. *See* Religion
Sanctions, and class, 92; political, 34; religious, 21–23; social, 22, 197; of social logics, 22
School, as age-grading institution, 34; attendance by class, 361–365; attendance by ethnic groups, 362–363; board, 79, 372; elementary, 361; function, 34; high, 359, 361; for mobility, 199; parochial, 215, 217, 361; as social structure, 302; superintendent organizations, 114; types, 79, 162; types of courses, 361. *See* Government
Scientific law, as adaptation, 9
Scientific method, 10–11; definition, 9; inductive, 10
Scotch, 220; assimilation of, 213. *See* Ethnics
Secret societies, 79; and class membership, 89; and government control, 34

Sex groupings, with age groupings, 30–31 in associations, 119; of cliques, 111; in simple societies, 35; as social status, 30; as social structure, 28. *See* Age groupings
Sex statistics, of arrests, 373; of association membership, 335–338; of ecological areas, 229; of ethnics, 217
Sexual behavior, socialized, 29
Sexual solidarities, in lower classes, 119; ritual relations, 119
Shipping. *See* Industry
"Side Streeter," as geographic term for class, 85, 91; as high status, 86
Simmel, George, 12–13
Simple societies, kinship and age-sex divisions, 34. *See* Primitive societies
Skills, as social acts, 24
Social anthropology, as method, 1–4, 9, 14–15, 45; objectives, 11; theory, 10, 36, 113. *See* Anthropology
Social behavior, in group interaction, 21; socially communicable, 21
Social change. *See* Social evolution
Social climbing. *See* Social mobility
Social differentiation, 31; among classes, 91
Social distance, mechanisms, 92; of upper class, 92, 100. *See* Social proximity
Social evolution, 15; and "progress," 26
Social interaction. *See* Interaction
Socialization, as family function, 29
Social mobility, through associations, 115–116, 131; behavior for, 91, 351; through class, 82; through cliques, 351; through economic success, 267; through education, 119, 300; of ethnics, 222–223; through expenditure, 300; through houses, 108; of Irish, 218; and lineage, 87, 99; lower-lower to lower-middle, 190; lower-upper to upper-upper, 98; to lower-upper, 103; of outsiders, 162, 197; through time, 223; upper-lower to lower-middle, 188
Social organization, 10; of apes and monkeys, 19; for biologic functions, 18; disfunctional, 4; and nature, 25; for placing members, 24; and social structure, 29, 325; and symbol systems, 23–24; and technology, 17, 21–22, 24–26. *See* Religion
Social personality, effect of mobility, 223; and expenditure, 287; of lower-class women, 118; in simple and complex societies, 27; in social space, 26

Index

Social proximity, and kinship terminology, 100. *See* Social distance
Social ranking, and birthplace, 209–210; criteria, 83; method, 90; and occupation, 82; and servants, 106
Social relations, dominance and aggression among animals, 18–19; dominance of family, 98; of workers, 3. *See* Interaction
Social sciences, methods, 5, 8, 10. *See* Methodology; Scientific method
Social stability, maintaining, 31
Social status, and associations, 131; of churches, 357; demands of, 197; and occupation, 81–82; and security, 197; and wealth, 82. *See* Status system
Social structure, 16; and associations, 302, 310–312; complexity; 15; definition, 14; types, 28
Social system, analysis, 203; maintaining, 31
Society, definition, 12–13
Society for Prevention of Cruelty to Children, and lower class, 179, 181; membership, 148, 152
South, community study, 5
Spykman, Nicholas J., 12
Staff, research, 42. *See* Methodology
State, the, as age- and sex-graded, 31
Statistics, of population, 77–78. *See* Sex statistics; Age statistics; Methodology
Status system, acquiring status, 31; class and caste, 34; cliques, 110, 112; and expenditure, 287; *rites de passage*, 29
Stores, as social structures, 28
Stratification, of associations, 31; of population, 204
Subadults, in associations, 122–123, 304; in class, 205–206, 224; in schools, 361–364
Subordination, in age and sex groupings, 30–31; among apes and monkeys, 19; in church, 33; and class, 85, 196; of lower-upper by upper-upper, 109; among men, 20; in primitive institutions, 34; of workers to management, 302
Suicide. *See* Durkheim
Superordination, 20; and age and sex groupings, 30–31; among associations, 323; in church hierarchy, 33; among cliques, 112; in primitive institutions, 34; of upper-upper to lower-upper class, 103–104

Symbol systems, abstraction of, 23; and budget, 287; of classes, 127; and houses, 251; patriotic, 120; and ritual objects, 107; and social organization, 22
Synthesis. *See* Methodology

Technology, 10; as adaptation, 17, 19, 20, 22, 24; and economic organization, 32; skills, 24–25. *See* Social organization
"Total personality," 4
Tradition, social, 4
Traits. *See* Methodology
Truant officer, and lower class, 179–181, 191

Unemployment, by class, 278–279; by ethnics, 267–269; statistics, 78, 262–264. *See* Economic occupation
Unions, labor, 143, 174–175, 179, 302
Unitarian church, 79, 357–358; and class, 358
Unity of group, 29; in cliques, 111; and sacred ideologies, 23
Upper class, 85; behavior, 99; naming principle in associations, 117; and social distance, 92; women's associations, 118; women's position, 119. *See* "Hill Streeter"; Upper-upper class; Lower-upper class
Upper-lower class, 87; arrests, 376–377; association membership, 123–125, 307–308, 319–320, 330–337; biologic characteristics, 204–206; budget expenditures, 290–300; churches, 357–360; clique membership, 90; in ecological areas, 234–238; education, 363–364; ethnic composition, 224–225; family membership, 90; house types, 244–246; in industry, 259–261; marriage age, 255; motion-picture attendance, 414, 416–418; occupation, 261–262; ownership of real estate, 282–283; personal examples, 140, 171, 173, 185, 188, 193–194; preference for professional people by class, 419–421; professional people, 419–420; reading habits, 380–412; and relief, 279; size, 88; summary of characteristics, 444–450. *See* Class types; Lower class; Lower-lower class
Upper-middle class, 87; age composition, 226; arrests, 373, 376–377; and association membership, 89, 123–125, 307–308, 319–320, 330–337; attitude toward upper class, 107; biologic character-

istics, 204–206; budget expenditures, 290–300; churches, 357–360; clique membership, 90, 352–354; in ecological areas, 234–238; education, 363–364; employment, 278–279; ethnic composition, 224–225; family membership, 90; house types, 244–246; in industry, 260–261; marriage age, 255; motion-picture attendance, 414, 416–418; and occupation, 261–262; ownership of real estate, 282–283; personal examples, 131–132, 143, 152, 172; preference for professional people by class, 419–421; professional people, 419–420; reading habits, 380–412; and relief, 279; size, 88; voters and officeholders, 369–372; summary of characteristics, 435–443. *See* Class types; Middle class; Lower-middle class

Upper-upper class, 87; arrests, 373, 376–377; association membership, 123–125, 307–308; 319–320, 330–337; biologic characteristics, 204; budget expenditures, 290–300; churches, 356–360; clique membership, 90, 352–354; control, 199; in ecological areas, 234–238; education, 363–364; employment, 278–279; ethnic composition, 223–225; examples, 94–97; and family membership, 90; house types, 244–246; in industry, 259–261; lineage, 100; marriage age, 255; motion-picture attendance, 414, 416–418; movement from lower-upper, 99; occupation, 261–262; "old family," 93; ownership of real estate, 282–283; personal examples, 128–141, 143–146, 151–152, 158, 160, 171–172, 177; preference for professional people by class, 419–421; professional people, 419–420; reading habits, 380–412; and relief, 279; ritual objects, 107–109; size, 88; summary of characteristics, 422–434; values and attitudes, 196; voters and officeholders, 369–372. *See* Class types; Upper class; Lower-upper class

Value system, and budget, 288; and expenditures, 287; as social expression, 287
Veterans' organizations. *See* Patriotic organizations, and philanthropy, 179
Voters. *See* Government

Wealth, and social status, 82–83, 98–99
Welfare, city, 181. *See* Relief
Western Electric study, 4. *See* Mayo; Chicago; Factory workers
Wheeler, G. C., 25, 34
Workers, and class distribution, 259–261; ethnic distribution, 257–259; percentage in each industry, 256; sex distribution, 256–257. *See* Occupation

Yankees, 211; population statistics, 78. *See* Ethnics; Natives
Yerkes, R. M. and A. W., 19–20
Y.M.C.A., age- and sex-graded, 31; as associational type, 321, 327; function, 114; membership, 152; as structure, 309, 327
Y.W.C.A., function, 114, 151; membership, 148, 152, 304

Zuckerman, S., 18–19